THE COLLECTED WORKS OF JEREMY BENTHAM

General Editor

J. R. Dinwiddy

Correspondence

Volume 5

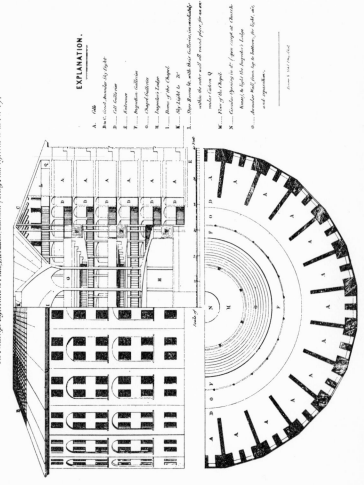

The original plan, as illustrated in *Panopticon, or the Inspection House* (1791)

The
CORRESPONDENCE
of
JEREMY BENTHAM

Volume 5
January 1794 to December 1797

edited by
ALEXANDER TAYLOR MILNE

THE ATHLONE PRESS
1981

First published 1981 by
THE ATHLONE PRESS LTD
at 90–91 Great Russell Street, London WC1B 3PY

Distributor in U.S.A. and Canada
Humanities Press Inc
New Jersey

© University College London 1981

British Library Cataloguing in Publication Data
Bentham, Jeremy
The correspondence of Jeremy Bentham.—(The
collected works of Jeremy Bentham).
Vol. 5: January 1794 to December 1797
1. Philosophers—England—Correspondence
2. Bentham, Jeremy
I. Milne, Alexander Taylor
192   B1574.B3

ISBN 0 485 13205 2

Printed in Great Britain by
WESTERN PRINTING SERVICES LTD
BRISTOL

CONTENTS

The editor's Preface and Introduction
to Volumes 4 and 5 of *The Correspondence*
appear in Volume 4

LIST OF LETTERS IN VOLUME 5

LIST OF LETTERS IN VOLUME 5

xiii

MISSING LETTERS OF JEREMY BENTHAM
REFERRED TO IN THE CORRESPONDENCE

January 1794 to December 1797

	1794	*Letter*
To – Pollard	14 January	941
To Lady Baring	*c.* 20 February	949
To Samuel Romilly	[?] early March	951
To Charles Abbot	14 April	957
To Sir Charles Bunbury	*c.* 16 June	977
To William Pitt and	*c.* 20 June	980
Henry Dundas		
To Sir John Hort	*c.* 2 August	985
To Sir John Sinclair	early September	995
To Samuel Romilly	late September	1006
To Charles Long	early October	1008
To Arthur Young	early October	1013
To John Peake	*c.* 7 October	1011
To James Trail	mid-October	1017
To Samuel Bentham	25 October	1018 and n. 2
To James Trail	25 October [?]	1018 and n. 4
	1795	
To Lady Ashburton	*c.* 24 March	1047
To Samuel Bentham	*c.* 30 March	1050 and n. 1
To Samuel Bentham	September	1082 and n. 1
To Sir John Freeman Mitford	18 October	1086 and n. 1
To Baron St Helens	November	1090
To Count Rumford	early December	1091
To Baron St Helens	*c.* 22 December	1092
To Baron St Helens	26 December	1093
	1796	
To Samuel Bentham	23 February	1110
To the Marquis of Lansdowne	*c.* 3 April	1120 and n. 2
To Sir Charles Bunbury	*c.* 18 April	1123 and n. 2
To Thomas Powys	early May	1130 and n. 1
To Baron St Helens	[?] late May	1138 and n. 2
To the Marquis of Lansdowne	early July	1147
To Caroline Fox	early July	1148 and n. 4
To Count Rumford	early July	1150
To Baron St Helens	early September	1177 and n. 2
To Samuel Bentham	9 September	1178 and n. 3
To 'The Cat'	October	1196 and n. 8

MISSING LETTERS

	1796	*Letter*
To Jonathan White	22 October	1197 and n. 2
To William Wilberforce	c. 6 November	1203
To William Skinner	c. 22 November	1238 and n. 8
To Richard Horwood	c. 23 November	1238
To George Rose	24 November	1219
To Samuel Bentham	c. 27 November	1226
To William Bentham	c. 2 December	1229 and n. 2
To Andrew Lindigren	c. 8 December	1235
To Charles Abbot	c. 24 December	1249
To Patrick Colquhoun	c. 30 December	1253 and n. 2
	1797	
To William Robertson	c. 9 February	1263
To Arthur Young	c. 20 March	1269
To Arthur Young	c. 1 April	1275 and n. 1
To Samuel Romilly	c. 30 April	1277 and n. 1
To Samuel Romilly	c. 18 May	1280
To Arthur Young	c. 8 September	1289 and n. 1
To [?] Martha Young	c. 15 October	1292
To Arthur Young	October	1295
To Arthur Young	late October	1297
To John Rackman	3 November	1298 and n. 1
To Arthur Young	c. 3 December	1301 and n. 1
To Sir Frederick Morton Eden	c. 12 December	1302

xvi

KEY TO SYMBOLS AND ABBREVIATIONS

SYMBOLS

/ In / Interlineations or alternative versions included in drafts. Crossed-out words have not usually been indicated.

| | Space left in Ms.

[to] No such word in Ms.; it has been supplied by the editor according to sense.

⟨ so ⟩ Conjectural restoration of mutilated word.

⟨ ... ⟩ Word torn away or hidden in binding of Mss.

[?] Reading doubtful.

[...?] Word proved illegible.

Editorial comments in the text are printed in italics within square brackets.

ABBREVIATIONS

Apart from standard abbreviations, the following should be noted:

B.L. I, II . . . etc.: refer to the main series of Bentham papers in the British Library, Additional Mss. 33537–64, the volumes of which are numbered from I to XXVIII. Thus B.L. V and B.L. VI, the volumes in the collection most frequently cited in these years, refer to Add. Mss. 33541 and 33542.

U.C.: refers to the Bentham papers in the Library of University College London. Roman numerals refer to the boxes in which the papers are placed, Arabic to the leaves within each box.

Bowring: refers to *The Works of Jeremy Bentham*, published under the superintendence of . . . John Bowring (11 vols.), Edinburgh, 1838–43. Volumes x and xi contain Bowring's Memoirs of Bentham and selections from his correspondence.

NOTE

Apart from sources cited in the notes, the following standard works have been in frequent use and have not usually been cited:

Dictionary of National Biography

Joseph Foster, ed., *Alumni Oxonienses* . . . *1715–1886*, 4 v., 1887–8

John and John Archibald Venn, comps., *Alumni Cantabrigienses*. Pt. I (to 1751), 4 v., 1922–7. Pt. II (1752–1900), 6 v., 1940–54

KEY TO SYMBOLS AND ABBREVIATIONS

G. F. R. Barker and A. H. Stenning, eds., *The record of Old Westminsters*, 2 v., 1928

Sir Lewis Namier and John Brooke, *The History of Parliament. The House of Commons, 1754–90*, 3 v., 1964

J. C. Sainty and J. M. Collinge, comps., *Office-holders in modern Britain*: v. I, *Treasury officials, 1660–1870* (1972); v. II, *Officials of the Secretaries of State, 1660–1782* (1973); v. III, *Officials of the Board of Trade, 1660–1870* (1974); v. IV, *Admiralty officials, 1660–1870* (1975); v. V, *Home Office officials, 1782–1870* (1975); v. VI, *Colonial Office officials* [1794–1870], (1976); v. VII, *Navy Board officials, 1660–1832* (1978); v. VIII, *Foreign Office officials, 1782–1870* (1979).

J. F. Michaud, ed. *Biographie universelle, ancienne et moderne*, 52 v., 1811–28

Jules Balteau and others, eds.; *Dictionnaire de biographie française*, v. 1— , 1929– . In progress.

Correspondence
January 1794 to
December 1797

937

TO SAMUEL BENTHAM

5 January 1794 (Aet 45)

Hendon Jan: 5 – 1794

Who would have thought of Sylvester Douglas's governing Ireland![2] The papers talk of his setting out so soon as Wednesday. He might catch ⟨Mice?⟩ and I should suppose would not be ill disposed to do so. Pity he had not seen Panopticon Model etc. There can hardly now be time for it. When Panopticon is set up here, he can surely make no difficulty of setting it up there. Go to Wilson and consult him about it, and whether any thing is to be done now—though probably Douglas will be coming to England on a Furlough before we should want any thing to be done about Panopticon in Ireland. Douglas can surely have no time to eat victuals at Q.S.P. If he would I would come to town on purpose.

As to Law[3] I cannot afford to come to London on purpose. It is possible I might be ready to come by that day, but I hardly expect it.

You were certainly in high luck at Knowle.[4]

937. [1] B.L. V: 479–80. Autograph. No docket. Addressed: 'To / Colonel Bentham / Queen's Square Place / Westminster.'
Evidently a reply to a missing letter from Samuel.
[2] Sylvester Douglas, Baron Glenbervie (1743–1823), who had known the Benthams since the mid-seventies (see *Correspondence*, ii passim, especially 124 n. 2). He succeeded Lord Hobart as Chief Secretary of the lord lieutenant of Ireland in January 1794, but was himself succeeded by Viscount Milton in January 1795. He entered the British House of Commons in that year, became a lord of the Treasury, 1797–1800, and was raised to the Irish peerage in 1800.
[3] Thomas Law.
[4] The seat of the Sackville family at Sevenoaks, Kent.

938

TO SAMUEL BENTHAM

7 January 1794 (Aet 45)

Hendon Jany 7 1794

I think it probable I shall be with you by Saturday but the one first mentioned will poison the pleasure from the ride. I wish you had had him all to yourself as you proposed.

Collins[2] I should have liked much to dine with. But I can't afford to come to town on purpose.

But make him promise to come again soon when I am in town.

939

TO SAMUEL BENTHAM

9 January 1794 (Aet 45)

Hendon Friday Jan. 9th. 1794

I was a Goose for saying what I did about C.[2] It was not worth writing, much less sending about. My antipathies are not so strong as that comes to. His being there would not keep me from thence by any means: but the fact is I can not afford to come. I hope I shall by Monday, so as to meet Mr Chauvet[3] at Mr Browne's. But if the day is not fixed I could be surer of Tuesday.

As to Mr Poole,[4] it is impossible for me to give him any account from hence. Panopticon Bill is now to me what Specification was to you: though thank Heaven not quite so bad.

938. [1] B.L. V: 481. Autograph. No signature. Addressed: 'To / Colonel Bentham / Queens Square Place / Westminster.'
Evidently a reply to a missing letter from Samuel.
[2] Probably William or his son, Edward Collins, who visited them later (see letters 1088–9) and assisted both brothers in their various schemes.
939. [1] King's College, Cambridge. Bentham Ms 73/1. Autograph, unsigned. No docket. Addressed: 'Colonel Bentham / Queen's Square Place / Westminster.'
[2] An allusion to the first paragraph of his letter of 7 January (938), to which Samuel had evidently replied. Clearly 'C' does not refer to either Collins or Chauvet.
[3] David Chauvet. See *Correspondence*, iv, 387 n. 3.
[4] Perhaps Josiah. See Poole *Correspondence*, iii, 96 n. 11.

940

To Samuel Bentham

14 January 1794 (Aet 45)

Panopt

Hendon Jan: 14 1794.

Steam Engine if underground so much the better, and the smoke condensed makes Tar, which is what they call burning the smoke, though it is only condensing and collecting it. See this recommended in Trans. of Soc.y of Arts Vol. 9th for 1790 or thereabouts.[2] This paper contains useful information. I do not recollect our meeting with it. If we have not got that Volume you may as well send for it (in my name to Payne's).

Burning the smoke could not be performed I suppose without a red hot iron tube, which would soon wear away and be very expensive.

Impregn.

In 30 years experience timbers for under-water work have been preserved unimpaired and unworm-eaten by soaking in Oil. An American at Boston has '*sollicited*' of the United States a Patent for it. New Ann. Register for 1791. Occurrences p. 32. Said to be communicated from Jefferson to an eminent House in the City.[3] (It was Vaughan's, I remember his shewing us the letter.)

940. [1] B.L. V: 482. Autograph. No docket. Addressed: 'To / Colonel Bentham.'

[2] The reference is to an article in the *Transactions of the Society for the Encouragement of Arts, Manufactures and Commerce*, vol. ix. Most of this was reprinted under the title: 'Process of converting the SMOKE of STEAM-ENGINES, etc. into Tar', in the *New Annual Register* for 1791, *Philosophical Papers*, pp. 125–6.

[3] The passage in the *New Annual Register* for 1791, *Principal Occurrences*, p. 32, reads: 'Mr. Jefferson, the late American minister at the court of France, has communicated to an eminent house in the city a discovery, which, if sanctioned by experience, will be of the utmost importance. A person near Boston, who was a ship-builder, has solicited a patent from the United States for a mode of preserving shiptimber from being worm-eaten. During the thirty years he has been a bridge-builder, he has always soaked such timbers as were to be under water in oil, and has found this method to preserve them ever since he was in that employment.'

Bentham's recollection is that the communication was made to the business house of William Vaughan, Benjamin's brother (see *Correspondence*, iv, 426, letter 898, n. 2).

3

941

TO ARCHBISHOP MARKHAM AND EARL SPENCER

14 January 1794 (Aet 45)

Q.S.P. Jan. 14. 1794.

Mr Bentham presents his respectful Complts. to the Archbp of York /Compliments to Lord Spencer/ and takes the liberty of requesting the return, as soon as consists with his Lordship's /Grace's/ convenience of such of the Papers he was troubled with some time ago relative to the Panopticon business: those excepted which were mentioned as meant for his Lordship's /Grace's/ acceptance. Those wanted are

1. A printed copy of two Reports of the /a Committee of/ the House of Commons: the last of the year 1784. Sent as believed to Ld Spencer only

2. A Ms. Copy of the last of those two Reports. Sent as believed to the Archbp of York only.

3. A copy of a Memorial relative to the intended disposition of the purchase-money of the Estate at Battersea Rise specifying the leases according to the valuation made of it by a Jury in Sept. 1782. Sent first to Lord Spencer and by him perhaps at the request of Mr B. to the Archb of York.

4. A small drawing of the intended Panopticon Building according to the plan and proportions once intended. Sent to Lord Spencer: and perhaps by his Lordship to the Archbishop of York.

941. [1] B.L. V: 483. Autograph draft of two separate letters. Docketed: '1794 Jan 14 / J. B. Hendon / to / Archbp of York / and / Lord Spencer Brouillon / Dated Q.S.P. / Copies sent from Hendon / by penny post as above under cover to Pollard.'
The covering note to Bentham's servant, Pollard, is missing.

942

FROM DAVID GRAY

15 January 1794

Dresden Jany 15th 1794

Dear Sirs,

I hope you will not impute my long silence either to indolence or forgetfulness. Neither I assure you is the case. The truth is that in this melancholy War of opinion when the passions of Individuals enter so much into all political reasonings I thought it imprudent for one even in my humble Diplomatique station to hazard any observations which might appear unfavourable to the conduct of Government in the measures adopted in the present most arduous and interesting contest which the history of Mankind can produce. It is somewhat singular that in two Countries whose Politics are at present so very opposite the same terms should be made use of, tho' in a sense very different in regard to Aristocracy and Democracy. *Moderantisme* in England as well as in France leads persons to become *suspecte*. If I were not most perfectly convinced of your discretion in not making any improper use of the few observations I may happen to make I should even now hesitate to write, for the Idea of doing anything inconsistent with propriety with regard to my employ hurts me very much. Indeed the present Crisis appears so very alarming that every person more or less may be permitted to deliver his Sentiments. No events in the course of last year's campaign, even the most favourable, could be reckoned so decisive as to supersede the necessity of another. To carry on this the concurrence of the Court of Berlin happens to be absolutely necessary. Notwithstanding His Prussian Majesty's aversion, in common with other Sovereigns, to Frenchmen and principles, he seems nevertheless fully aware of the advantage of his present situation and very prudently for himself appears desirous to relinquish the very honorable, tho very expensive, cause of Kings, and to substitute

---

942. [1] B.L. V: 484–9. Autograph. Docketed: '1794 Jan 15 / Gray Dresden to J.B. Q.S.P. / Reced at Hendon Feb. 9.'

Addressed: 'To Jeremy Bentham Esqr / Queen's Square Place / Westminster.' Postmark mostly illegible. The whole of this letter, with a few inaccuracies, is printed in Bowring, x, 297–300.

David Gray was at this time *chargé d'affaires* at Dresden. He had been appointed secretary of the British legation there in 1791 and continued in that office until 1806, acting as *chargé* on several other occasions; he also acted in that capacity at Berlin in 1795.

in its place the more lucrative Idea of commercial hostility—
Hence arises the expedition of Lord Malmesbury and Mr de
Lehrbach to Berlin[2] to prevail with his said Majesty by golden
arguments to give this year at least the same number of troops as
he afforded last year gratis according to Treaty with Austria. The
unfortunate turn which the War has lately taken, the loss of Toulon
and the total defeat, I might almost say annihilation, of Wurmser's
army on the Rhine and the consequences that may yet result from
these misfortunes will undoubtedly suspend for the present all
negociations at the Court of Berlin.[3] When to these successes we
add the deplorable state of the Royalists in Britanny, the increase
in value of the French Assignats and the energy which the Convention has now assumed, by making as they have well said
terror the order of the day, I think everybody must be convinced
that in regard to another Campaign the resources of the French
are increased while those of the Coalized Powers are diminished.
It is the peculiar misfortune of this War that if it is difficult to go on,
it is no less so to go back, and the present hostilities must terminate
if not in the extinction at least in extreme humiliation to either of
the parties concerned. It is at this awful moment much to be
regretted that the possibility of misfortune has hardly been supposed which might have been some check to the too free indulgence of the passions and the reciprocal abuse which has resulted
therefrom—God forbid that I should ever attempt to extenuate
the criminality of the numberless horrors daily committed in France,
that I should hesitate to say that murder is murder or that robbery
is robbery, to defend confiscation when to be rich is to be criminal,
or to panegerize the activity of the Guillotine. But I know there
are some people who are somewhat uncertain whether these horrors
are to be attributed to an original malignity in the French character,
or to be considered as an effect of some cause not yet ascertained.
The principle, of the right of one nation to interpose in the internal
affairs of another is of a most dangerous nature. It was formally

---

[2] In autumn 1793 Lord Malmesbury was sent on a special mission to Berlin to
enlist Prussia's help against France. Count Lehrbach, Austria's representative at
Berlin, warned him that Prussia might side with France, but Malmesbury, after an
interview with King Frederick William on 25 December 1793, advised the British
government to give Prussia a subsidy for a French campaign (*Cambridge History of
British Foreign Policy, 1783–1815*, 3 vols., 1922, i, 243–5).

[3] The Austrian general, Count Dagobert Siegmund von Wurmser (1724–97),
attacked the French lines at Weissenburg, 13 October 1793, but was forced to retreat
across the Rhine in December. Wurmser defeated a French army in 1795 and captured
Mannheim, but he was defeated by Napoleon in Italy, 1796–7.

announced by the Emperor Leopold's circular letter from Padua,[4] repeated by the declaration of Pilnitz[5] and proclaimed aloud by the Manifestos of the Duke of Brunswick.[6] Similar pretensions on the part of the French with regard to the Low Countries and Holland have been considered by everybody with becoming disapprobation. Whoev⟨er⟩ wishes to investigate the real origin of this melancholy War ought particularly to consider in their chronological order the different facts and measures which have been adopted, and which imply the assertion of the above right—Without presuming to say what is really the truth one may readily allow that hostilities are virtually commenced by a *Coup de plume* equally as by a *coup de canon*—It would be happy for Mankind if the dignity of Courts would permit them like Individuals to retract an error and acknowledge honestly a mistake. When Leopold received Mr de Noailles[7] as French Ambassador after the acceptation of the new Constitution by the King, he only acquiesced in the arrangement, but did not renounce the principle he had previously asserted. If this War is singular in its origin the views in continuing it appear no less extraordinary. There is a negative unanimity indeed agreed on by all parties viz. that the present Individuals who govern France ought to be set aside, but what particular arrangement is then to follow, the Legislative Armies of the coali⟨zed⟩ Powers have not yet explicitly exhibited. One declaration approves of the late Constitution, while another proposes a different form of limited Monarchy, only however to take place after a provisional restitution of Despotism. The late reestablishment of the old feudal forms and police in Alsace, Condé, Valenciennes etc. seem highly impolitic, as if no act of common sense had passed any of the three Assemblys and when every body allows that the first carried some dignity

---

[4] The Padua Circular, issued by the Emperor Leopold II on 6 July 1791, called on European powers to demand the liberation of Louis XVI of France, after the failure of the flight to Varennes, and to affirm their refusal to recognise any French constitution not freely accepted by the King. The response of Britain was non-committal (*New Cambridge Modern History*, viii, 693–4).

[5] The Declaration of Pillnitz, issued by the Emperor of Austria and the King of Prussia on 27 August 1791, invited European powers to join in assisting Louis XVI to establish a French monarchy compatible with the rights of kings and the welfare of subjects. No immediate action resulted, but French fears of armed intervention increased (*New Cambridge Modern History*, viii, 695–6).

[6] The Manifesto issued by the Duke of Brunswick on 26 July 1792 stated that the allies were marching on France not for the sake of conquest but to restore the position of the monarch, for whose personal safety they held the National Assembly and the National Guard responsible, on pain of death.

[7] Emmanuel Marie Louis, Marquis de Noailles (1743–1822), French ambassador to Austria, 1783–92.

7

along with it. In short there is in every public Paper on this subject a degree of contradiction which is unaccountable. In one sentence a right to internal interference is solemnly renounced, while at the same time a following paragraph issues a *Congé d'elire* in favour of Monarchy. But whatever may have been the origin or the object of the present atrocious hostilitys, the manner of conducting the present war is out of the common way. The libertys taken in respect to foreign Neutral nations are great beyond example. Indeed Foreigners are not a little surprised at the arbitrary conduct of of some of the Agents of a free Government at Foreign Courts, for independence is but an empty title as soon as any power presumes to pass its opinions for the criterion of truth in regard to the intercourse of one Country with another. Of this there are many examples, from the proposal of erecting something like a Dutch tribunal to condemn French Regicides, to the effrontery at Florence and the *cacade* at Genoa inclusive. I question whether at some future period when facts remain and passions will be evaporated, it will not be thought that even for the sake of a good cause we should not have kept such very bad company. Posterity may think it somewhat extraordinary for England the first Government in point of liberty in Europe to coalize with the bigotted Spaniard, the ignorant Austrian, the barbarous Russian, together with the military mechanism of Prussia, in support of Social order and legitimate government, and that too, at the very time when the two last Powers commit an act agt an innocent and independent nation which in point of arrogance and depravity cannot be equalled in History. I mean the scandalous partition of Poland, an act equally hostile to Social order and Legitimate Government. If the daily enormities committed in France tend to excite disgust in respect to popular governments, the iniquitous conduct of Russia and Prussia with regard to Poland reconcile again Men's minds to Democracy. The political fiction of considering France as a garrison in order to starve it and the counterpart of the tale in converting Toulon into a Country for the purpose of legalising supplies not permitted by the custom of Nations to the Towns in a state of siege are circumstances which further distinguish the manner of carrying on the present War. The Idea of *Starvation* in regard to an extensive Country may be accompanied with such frightful consequences as to shock the common feelings of Humanity. The necessities of a Garrison starved into capitulation may be immediately supplied by the Besiegers— but in a Country starved into submission Millions must perish before the circulation of provisions can effectively be re-established. In

8

every point of view as a Wellwisher to my country I am frightened
at this War, as I think the danger resulting from it to us increases
in the ratio of its duration. I am afraid that our Ministers have been
hitherto much deceived by false intelligence and many of our Public
Agents have been rather too time serving in accomodating their
reports to Ministerial volition. In this Country I can assure you
peace is much desired if it could be procured on any kind of decent
terms. The 5,000 Men which the Elector[8] gives as his Contingent
cost exactly as much as his whole Army of 30,000 Men on the Peace
establishment and by all Accounts the resources of Austria are
completely exhausted. The only resource remaining is *confiscation*
not of private property indeed but of some independent German
states protected by the laws of the Empire, and poor Poland
likewise furnishes a further fund. You will hardly believe than
another act of the infamous Tragedy is likely again to take place.
Both the King of Poland and Siewers[9] have fallen lately under the
Empress's displeasure, the latter being recalled. A new Diet is
talked of to compleat the suicide and the name of Poland may soon
cease to exist. Prussia still covets another Palatinate or two. The
Empress of *All* the Russias has pretension on Galicia as formerly
bearing *that* name and the Emperor perhaps in spite of himself may
be obliged in his present state of humiliation to accept some of the
spoils of that unfortunate Country in exchange—It is somewhat
singular that notwithstanding the present coalition, the national
jealousy between Austria and Prussia exists perhaps more than
ever. I was at Vienna when the news came of the taking the lines of
Weissemburg by Wurmser. As this plan had always been opposed
by the Duke of Brunswick the unexpected success elated the
Austrians extremely and even led them I thought at the time to
make many unguarded and impolitic observations not very honorable either to Prussian tactics or Prussian sincerity—The retreat
of Wurmser has afforded the Prussians their revenge and indeed
the retreat of that army was accompanied with such circumstances
the 26 and 28th of last month as appears by a letter of Gen Kalck-
reuths[10] which I have read as will remain a lasting reproach to the

8 Frederick Augustus (1750–1827), called the Just, Elector of Saxony, 1768–1806,
and King of Saxony, 1806–27. He fought against France 1792–1806, but after the
defeat of Jena was made nominal ruler of the new duchy of Warsaw.
9 Count Yakov Efimovich Sivers (1731–1808), Russian statesman of German origin;
he was ambassador to Poland and shared in negotiating its partition; although
recalled in 1794 he held subsequent government posts. He is sometimes called by his
German name, Jakob Johann Sievers.
10 Count Friedrich Adolf von Kalckreuth (1737–1818), Prussian general and statesman. He commanded an army in Brunswick's invasion of France and served under

Austrian arms. In short the soldiers wd fight no longer and in running away not only pillaged the peasants but their own Officers. The retreat of the Duke of Brunswick is variously talked of. By some it is said that he has conceived too formidable an Idea of the French arms to undertake any enterprize of consequence agt them and what perhaps may appear ridiculous he is not exempted from a *soupcon* of Jacobinism. Whatever be the truth Mollendorff is certainly to succeed him but whether he is to have additional troops or the *debris* only of the present Army the issue of the present negociations must determine. But to pass from more general Politics to what concerns more particularly ourselves. If you do me the favor to write me might I request you to give me some account of this late *soi disant* Convention[11] at Edinr and what appear to be the prevailing sentiment of the Country in respect to reform upon which much may be said on both sides. For he who is really and sincerely attached to the present Constitution may say with truth, the more the elections are popularized the greater is the tendency to Republicanism. Whereas on the other hand as the French revolution notwithstanding its atrocities has produced a kind of revolution in the human mind in Europe, and mankind think on many points as they never thought before. Government therefore by resisting all reform may risk to be taken by assault and the Country exposed to all the horrors of a revolution.

The Society of Dresden is this winter much improved by the arrival of many Polish refugees of the first distinction. We have at present Marechal Potocsky[12] the principal leader of the party which carried the late revolution into execution. His Brother the General, General Zabiello,[13] Prince Czartorisky[14] and several other members of the celebrated patriotic Diet. They are all most excellent characters

---

Mollendorff in 1794 on the left bank of the Rhine, becoming a field-marshal in 1807 and governor of Berlin, 1814.

[11] The Convention of the Delegates of the People at Edinburgh in December 1792, attended by delegates from some 70 Scottish societies, at which resolutions in favour of parliamentary reform and establishment of contact with London radical organisations were discussed (Carl B. Cone, *The English Jacobins*, New York, 1968, pp. 167–8, 172, 174).

[12] Stanislav Felix Potocsky (1745–1805), Polish artillery commander, who was forced to leave Poland after the insurrection in 1794, but on its suppression returned there and became a field marshal in the Russian army.

[13] Zabiello was a 'hetman', a Polish administrative officer for military affairs. Accused of betraying Poland to the Russians he was executed by the patriots in 1794 (*Cambridge History of Poland, 1697–1935*, Cambridge, 1931 [1937?], p. 166).

[14] Prince Adam Kazimierz Czartoryski (1731–1823). See *Correspondence*, iv, 242 n. 2. Although he went to Vienna in 1794 he did not prevent Austria from taking a share in the partition of Poland in 1795.

and in the present extraordinary times are proscribed and calumni-
ated as criminals for having dared to sacrifice voluntarily a part of
their privileges and their property in order to promote a greater
degree of happiness among their fellow citizens. I have the happiness
to be frequently in their Society and from the anecdotes I hear
I cannot help regretting the favourable moment that we lost to
humble the ambition of that female Monster the success of whose
projects is so disgraceful to Humanity, and which might have
prevented many of the calamities which have since happened—
Abbé Piatoli[15] is also here. He had a principal hand in the Polish
revolution. He is busy drawing up an account of that affair from
the beginning to its fatal termination and perhaps on this subject
I may take the liberty at another time to take your opinion with
respect to the manner of introducing this detail to English notice—

   If your Brother is still with you I beg you will present him my
Compts. Accept of my best wishes & believe me to be with great
regard

Dear Sir
Your most obedt
and very humble Servt
D G —

943

To Samuel Bentham

30 January 1794 (Aet 45)

Hendon Thursday Jan. 30 – 1794.

Send on to all eternity, and be d——d. What! the plague? am
I never to see a paper any more because I talked once of coming
one of these days.

   I was thinking of putting you to Board Wages: but as you find
means to dine so often upon Charity, I will consider of it.

   Alexander the Great was not fit to black my shoes: I shall
conquer not only Parishes, but Towns and Counties—in short
the Dragon of Wantley[2] is my hero, and my model—I shall set up
not only a Settlement Fabrick, but a Vote-Fabrick. You shall be

---

[15] Scipione Piattoli (1749–1809).
943. [1] B.L. V: 492. Autograph. No signature, docket or address.
   Evidently a reply to a missing letter from Samuel.
   [2] *The Dragon at Wantley*, a humorous ballad about a Yorkshire monster that ate
cattle and children, but was eventually killed by a local hero.

Beadle to one of my Towns if you behave well—your Regimental Tau[3] will convert and serve for the Cape.

The Tuesdays papers which with your Letter I should have received on Tuesday I did not receive till this day, Thursday—owing to the Frost—and now with a pox to you I shan't get today's papers today. Send them therefore tomorrow by the Coach, on your allegiance. Alack this is King-killing day.[4] I borrowed a comb of the Horses today, to comb my favourite Hog with—Spot used to go out with me upon a Day's ⟨walk?⟩—but he is turned out as bad almost as Puss though in a different way.[5]

944

F R O M   J A M E S   T R A I L

1 February 1794

I have heard of your Defence of Usury,—of your Panopticon,— and of your Law Taxes,—all spoken of with approbation, without any intention of being civil to me, for it was without knowing of our acquaintance, and I must add, because truth compels me, without the least intention of applying any of the principles contained in your two last works to practice. The government must be convinced as well as the governors; and that is a work of time, to be accomplished only by books and conversation. Among the governed may be comprehended many, perhaps the great majority of governors: fifty or sixty years is not too much time to be allowed for a new idea, or principle, to be generally established and admitted. Indeed, if, as in France, the enthusiasm of the people can be

---

[3] Possibly a slang expression for the Russian 'paltau' (French *paletot*), meaning a cloak.

[4] January 30 was the anniversary of King Charles I's execution and was observed with fasting by high tories. On 30 January 1778 Bentham had written to his brother 'Did you fast or eat Calves head today?' (See *Correspondence*, ii, 86.)

[5] 'Spot' may be the 'beautiful pig' at Hendon, an animal that Bentham remembered 'took to following me like a dog'; 'Puss' may be the cat, 'which used to follow me about even in the street' (Bowring, xi, 80).

944. [1] Bowring, x, 300. Quotations, introduced by the statement: 'In a letter from Trail, dated from Dublin castle, 1st February 1794, he says:'

Between the two extracts is a summary by Bowring which reads: 'There is a sketch of Colonel Bentham in the same letter. Never was a mind more inventive—more creative,—but never was a mind less disposed to work out laboriously its own conceptions. The philosopher had a portion of the same frailty. New subjects often distracted his attention; but the distraction was not a permanent one. He reverted back to the abandoned topic, and was never satisfied till he had completed and exhausted it.'

Trail had gone to Ireland as Sylvester Douglas's private secretary.

inflamed, new opinions spread faster; but such rapid conversions are not very desirable. I hope you perceive by these observations that I have already imbibed an abundant portion of official prudence,—you will say indolence and quackery.

I request my best compliments and wishes to Sam, in whose mechanical labours (I should say inventions, for never was a term worse applied than labour to your worthy, indolent brother) I feel an uncommon interest,—being so perfectly sure, that any the least considerable of his numerous inventions would make his fortune, if he would only abjure all further improvements.

945

To Samuel Bentham

7 February 1794 (Aet 45)

Newspapers

Received	Not received
Monday 3	Monday
Morning Herald	Times
Tuesday 4	Morng Chron
All	
Wednesday 5	Wednesday 5
Morng Chron	Times
Herald	
Thursday 6	Thursday 6
Herald	Times
	Chronicle

By the above list, it appears that whatever you ordered or pretend to have ordered Pollard, said Pollard has done clean contrary: which is most to blame your utterance or said Pollards conception, the Lord above knows, to whom I beg leave to refer the dispute. When you and he have settled it which is to go turn to the other leaf where you will find all that the received Nos. of the Herald afford. I fear that for want of your having the Herald of yesterday, a good opportunity is lost. I have taken your opus and

945. ¹ B.L. X: 611–12. Autograph, except for the two advertisements at the end. No docket. Addressed: 'To / Colonel Bentham / Queen's Square Place / Westminster.' Franked: 'Claridge'.
Evidently a reply to a communication from Samuel about forwarding newspapers.

run the rowel of it into my guts: though there is not quite that reason for haste as you might imagine as I could prove to you were it worth while.

The £50 received from Mr Shergold[2] it were better to send to Martins[3] although you should the next day have occasion to draw for the amount. Take my word for it, till I explain it to you. But as tomorrow is drawing day, keep it till I come, and I will send it with other parcels in a mass.

Hendon Friday 7

Trail is an impertinent fellow[4]—I allow nobody to find fault with my Brother, guilty as he is, but myself. Let him look at home —he may take his brother, and the Revd Dean Pig here, and shake them in a bag.

I cant see at present work enough for beyond Sunday if so long— but we are all in the hands of Providence

Send me the Papers however on Saturday—missing ones and all—or by Jove and Jupiter, I wont come till Monday sennight

Herald Thursday Feb. 6[5]

As Servant to a single Gentleman or in a small regular family, either in or out of Livery, a young man, who can shave and dress hair, writes a good hand, understands accounts, has been used to do every part of the business of a family, and would be willing to make himself useful to his employer; he has no objection to a temporary situation, or to look after a couple of horses, with a single Gentlemen, and can have an undeniable character from his last place where he lived two years.

Direct to A.B. at No 20, George Street, Hanover Square.

Herald Wedny Feb 5

As upper Servant, in or out of Livery, a single Man, thirty years of age, who can dress hair, writes a good hand, understands accounts, knows his business, and can have an undeniable character from his last place, where he lived four years.

Direct to N.B. at Mr Appleyard's, Wimpole Street, Cavendish Square.

2 Perhaps Samuel Shergold, conveyancer, of 6 Lincoln's Inn Old Square.
3 Martin and Co., bankers, 68 Lombard Street.
4 Bentham had evidently sent Trail's letter of 1 February (letter 944) to his brother, despite the comments in it on Samuel; Trail's brother would be William (see *Correspondence*, iv, 80 n. 4).
5 The two copies of advertisements which follow are in another hand.

946

To Samuel Bentham

9 February 1794 (Aet 45)

Hendon Feb. 9 – 1794.

The inclosed Advertisement[2] will serve at least as a ground to build upon.
I am glad to hear of your Scotch Gardener.
I am glad you did not come if you had nothing particular.
I shan't come tomorrow, nor I believe Thursday—but probably the next day.
Send me things however on Tuesday.

947

To Samuel Bentham

14 February 1794 (Aet 45)

Feby. 1794

And so you are for hawling me home on purpose to turn your back upon me, and leave me all alone in a great large strange house among strangers. No you must not go tomorrow I shall certainly be at Q.S.P. then, but whether to breakfast or to dinner or not till after dinner I can not positively say. I believe however to dinner and am so confident of it that I could wish you to dine at home, and make the dinner capable of adjournment say till 6. If I find you gone or going to Portsmouth, I shall turn back так yac[2] and stay here till you come and fetch me. Portsmouth will keep till next week.

Tomorrow is your better's birthday[3]
Tuesday 14th
Feb 1794.

946. [1] B.L. V: 493. No docket. Addressed: 'Colonel Bentham.'
Samuel had evidently written again after receiving letter 945.
[2] Missing.
947. [1] B.L. V: 494. No docket or address.
It would seem Samuel had written again urging his brother to return to Queen's Square Place before Samuel's departure to Portsmouth.
[2] Anglice: 'at once'.
[3] Jeremy was born on 15 February 1748.

15

948

TO MR PEASE

[?]19 February 1794 (Aet 46)

Queens Square Place Westmr
Feby 1794

Sir

Do me the favour to present my respects to the Gentlemen of the Trust, and express my regrets that neither my Brother nor I have it in our power to profit by the honour of their invitation. My Brother is gone to Portsmouth for some days, and my own time, after a long absence from town, is so thoroughly filled by some urgent business of a public nature, that it would be impossible for me to spare enough of it, even for dining, at such a distance. Another year perhaps I might be more fortunate—I am,

Sir, Your very humble Servant
Jeremy Bentham

Mr Pease

949

TO SAMUEL BENTHAM

21 February 1794 (Aet 46)

Q.S.P. Feb. 21. 1794

Been at the Office[2] this day which is more than Nepean has. He is said to be but indifferent, but it is not that that has kept him —He sees nobody, I was told, today at his own house—This without my asking—He was at the Office yesterday evening—No reason to suppose but that he will be there tomorrow—Tomorrow therefore I go on heel-kicking.

Romilly, poor fellow, has no time to fight.[3] He is oppressed with business as I am, or as I may begin to say, have been: but notwithstanding that he looks out, and is [as] anxious to find faults as you could wish.

948. [1] U.C. CLXXIII: 61. Autograph. No docket or address: perhaps a copy.
  Pease has not been identified: perhaps he was Edward Pease (1767–1858) or another member of the philanthropic Quaker family of Darlington, Co. Durham.
949. [1] B.L. V: 495–6. Autograph. No docket. Addressed: 'To / Colonel Bentham / at A. Lindigrens Esq / Portsmouth'. Postmark: 'FE 21'.
  [2] The Home Office: Nepean was Under-Secretary of State.
  [3] That is in support of the Panopticon project.

I went to Nepean's with a quiet conscience, having arranged matters in my mind sufficiently for the purpose.

There came Cards from Lady Baring[4] to both of us for Cards. I wrote afterwards and sent an apology—Go and eat there if you will on Tuesday, but I dont think I shall.

The Cup I did not forget. There came an invitation in form, which I speared in form.

A parcel of things are come from Sheffield—Hutchinson[5] came to ask me whether I know any thing about [them?], for nobody else [does?]. My answer was in the negative.

950

To Samuel Bentham

22 February 1794 (Aet 46)

Q.S.P. Feb. 22, 1794

Nepean still ill—but I have seen King,[2] who was sociable and referred me to Huskison[3] the man whom I had a quarrel with, and who ever since has been so civil. I told him of the necessity I was under of begging a decision about the land in the first instance. He seemed to make no doubt about it—took the paper of reasons which you saw, promised to send it to Dundas (who is at Wimbledon) immediately, and to let me know the result.

951

From Samuel Romilly

9 March 1794

Dear Bentham

I return you the remainder of your bill[2] which I have read with great Attention tho I have not any objections to make or anything

[4] An invitation to play cards from the wife of Sir Francis Baring (see *Correspondence*, iv, 364 n. 1).

[5] Not identified.

950. [1] B.L. V: 497–8. Autograph. No docket. Addressed: 'To Colonel Bentham / at A. Lindigren's Esqr / Portsmouth.' Postmark: 'FE 22.'

[2] John King, under-secretary of state for the home department, 1791–1806.

[3] Probably William Huskisson (see *Correspondence*, iv, 417 n. 1).

951. [1] B.L. V: 499–500. Autograph. Docketed: '1794 Mar 9 / Panopt / Romilly Linc. Inn / to / J.B. Q.S.P. / Panopt. Bill.'
Addressed: 'Jeremy Bentham Esq.'

[2] The new Penitentiary Bill, which Bentham was drafting at the request of the administration.

to suggest to you upon it. There is a Chasm in the Series of numbers of the Section Friendly Guardians from 15 to 19 but as I see none of the other numbers are scratched out perhaps there may be nothing wanting.[3] There is a great deal too much merit in the bill for it to have the smallest chance of passing

Yrs ever affectly
S.R.

9 March 1794

952

FROM WILLIAM WICKHAM

9 March 1794

Dear Sir,

I have talked with Burton[2] upon the subject of the King's Power of confing. Prisoners in such places as he shall think right. I have also looked into the Books upon the subject this morning, where there is in truth very little to be found.

The result of both Inquiries is this, that tho' such an opinion of the Kings authority may formerly have prevailed and with reason, yet the practice of the courts has so certainly superseded it that it is now scarcely worth enquiring into.

It seldom happens that the Court which passes sentence of Imprisonment does not name the Gaol in which the punishment is to take place. If it does not, it is understood that the common Gaol of the County is intended. I would with great pleasure look out all the authorities on this point and send you an abstract of them, but I am at this moment particularly hurried and should not wish to do it unless you especially desired it. In that case I should think nothing of the trouble, and you might command me without scruple.

The truth is that they amount to so little and are so much

---

[3] Footnote in Bentham's hand: 'Not so: on examination §§ from 15 to 19 were with the rest.'

952. [1] B.L. V: 501–2. Autograph. Docketed: '1794 Mar 9 / Panopt / Wickham White-Chapel / to / J.B. Q.S.P.'

Addressed: 'To Jeremiah Bentham Esq / Queen Square Place / Westminster.' Postmark: 'MA.11.E.94'.

William Wickham (1761–1840), diplomat and politician, had been a friend of Charles Abbot's at Oxford. He was appointed superintendent of aliens in 1794 and sent on a secret mission to Switzerland in October. He became an M.P. in 1802, Chief Secretary for Ireland, 1802–4, and a member of the Treasury board, 1806–7.

[2] Francis Burton.

18

dispersed that I doubt much whether they would ever answer the trouble of the inquiry.

I thank you very much for the time and patience you were so good as afford me yesterday which I shall be anxious to repay by all the means in my power.

Mrs Wickham desires her compliments, and begs I will repeat to you that the violin must not be forgotten.

I should hope that no engagement would deprive us of the pleasure of your and Colonel Bentham's company on Thursday.[3]

I am with great truth
Dear Sir
your very faithfull servant
Willm Wickham

P.Office—W. Chapel
Sunday March 9th/94

953

TO EVAN NEPEAN

21 March 1794 (Aet 46)

Evan Nepean Esqr etc. etc. etc.
Friday March 21, 1794 – 4 o'clock

Sir

I have been at the Office of the Board of Works and by favour of Mr Craig[2] to whom your Letter was addressed and Sir W.

---

[3] Possibly the occasion of which Bentham spoke in his reminiscences to Bowring: 'He and Abbott had a project to make me fall in love with his sister. I went there once; and after dinner an appearance of business left me alone with his wife and daughter. The net was spread, but the fish was not caught' (Bowring, x, 285). Perhaps 'daughter' is a mistake for 'sister', since Wickham's daughter could only have been a child at this time.

953. [1] P.R.O., H.O. 42/29, unnumbered fos. Autograph. Docketed: 'Panopticon proposal and leading points of Panopticon Bill with letter.'

The enclosures consist of a memorandum in a copyist's hand, entitled 'Leading Points of the Panopticon Bill', with a further three pages of notes on 'Superannuation Annuities', 'Identification Marks' and 'reduction of expence'. This is followed by another memorandum of twelve pages, in Bentham's hand, entitled 'Proposal for maintaining and employing Convicts by means of a new-invented species of building, in which they will remain universally subject to uninterrupted inspection: by Jeremy Bentham of Lincolns Inn Esquire.'

Also in H.O. 42/29, presumably enclosed with Bentham's letter, is a further memorandum of sixteen pages, in a copyist's hand, dated in pencil '21 March 1794', and entitled 'Proposed Panopticon-Penitentiary-House. Reasons for adhering to the subsisting choice in favour of Battersea-Rise, as the Spot to build on.' The last four pages are headed 'Supplemental Price—not Valuation de Novo.'

[2] Charles Alexander Craig, resident clerk in the Office of Works; chief examining clerk, December 1793–1815.

19

Chambers[3] who happened to be there I have got a copy taken by my Draughtsman of the Plan in question. While the Draughtsman was at work, having on my part nothing to do, and seeing a Bundle or two of papers which in the course of the search made for the Plan were laid upon the Table, it occurred to me that it might not be amiss to profit by the opportunity in order to look them over and see whether there was any thing amongst them that might be of use to me. I accordingly asked leave of Mr Craig, and he was so obliging as to permitt me. Afterwards, Mr Craig and Sir William on talking the matter over with one another, and referring to your letter, observed that the Plan in question was the only object therein mentioned, and the result was a conclusion that they had gone too far in giving me the permission in question (as to any memorandums over and above the Plan you mentioned) and done what they might not be able to justify to the Lord Chamberlain. In the meantime, I had in addition to some minutes which they had seen, made partly on the same, and partly on another slip of paper—some minutes which they had not seen; in which occupation Mr Craig coming in after the departure of Sir William found me. He there-upon communicated to me the abovementioned result, expressing at the same time a sort of dissatisfaction that bringing a letter from you requesting one specific thing, I should avail myself of it to make a general search and take copies. My answer was that I had not seen your letter to him (which you may perhaps remember was the case) that I had done nothing which he had not permitted me to do—that as to any ideas which I might have it in my power to carry away in my mind the mischief was certainly irreparable, but that as to any written memorandum that I had taken I had none what I had taken openly and as it were under his eye, that *there* they were, and I would either take them or leave them as he thought proper. His answer was that for his and Sir W's justification I shall obtain from you a specific order specifying every paper of which I wished to have a copy. My reply was that I wished for nothing more than I had which were the short extracts I had made, the greatest part of which he had allowed of, after reading to Sir W. as much as they thought proper: that as to specifying what I wanted, it was what I could not do without having before me these very memorandums which contained all that I wanted, or as I believed ever should want. As a sort of *mezzo termine* it occurred

---

[3] Sir William Chambers (1726–96), architect, Comptroller of the Works from 1769, designer of Somerset House, London, and many other buildings, including parts of Cold Bath Fields prison in the 1790s.

to him to propose to me to seal up the papers before him, and leave them with him, adding that if *you* would write to him that they might be delivered to me, they should be sent to me according to my address which by his direction I put upon the cover. I did so accordingly, and the object of the trouble I am now giving you is to beg the favour of a letter for that purpose. (N.B. The copy of the Plan need not be mentioned, since that with Mr Craig's permission I took away).

The Minutes I took and which remain impounded were relative to
1. The Cut or Canal intended according to Mr Blackburn's Plan
2. Some proceedings of the Supervisors—a line or two only—
3. The prices at which different persons offered to undertake for Bricklayer's-work and digging—To the best of my recollection this was all.

In the back of one of my two scraps of paper my Draughtsman was copying a sort of scheme in this form [diagram] with a parcel of figures in it purporting according to the indorsement to relate to the *levels* of the ground. But the copy was not completed when Mr Craig came in, and without the explanation (for I had not found any with it) the Draughtsman was in doubt whether any body would be able to make anything of it: as for me, it was to me utterly unintelligible.

As to the Gentlemen above-mentioned I have no doubt of their being perfectly well-founded in their scruples: and think myself obliged to Mr Craig for the middle course he had the goodness to suggest: neither on my own part do I see any reason to blame myself for endeavouring to avail myself, under his permission, of the existing opportunity, especially since by *superseding* the occasion for any further applications, I was saving time, not only to myself, but eventually to you, Sir, as well as to them—I am, with all respect, Sir, yours etc.

Jeremy Bentham

954

TO EVAN NEPEAN

30 March 1794 (Aet 46)

Queen's Square Place Westminster March 30th 1794

The season is so far advanced, while the condition of the Panopticon plan, as far as I can collect, is so much worse than stationary, that I find myself under the necessity of requesting the favour of you to represent to Mr Pitt and Mr Dundas, how inevitably the final fate of it depends upon its receiving the sanction of Parliament before the Session is at an end.

It was some time before the close of the last Session, that, at the conclusion of an audience you had the goodness to obtain for me from Mr Dundas, after speaking of some official communications that remained to be made to other members of the Cabinet, you were pleased to add—'*And in the mean time Mr Bentham you may be making your arrangements.*' Mr Dundas, who was at your elbow, hearing and, as it seemed to me, signifying concurrence, though *as yet* not otherwise than by looks.

It was a considerable time *after* that, but still a considerable time *before* the close of the then subsisting Session, that I was honoured by your means, with a joint visit from Mr Dundas and Mr Pitt. What passed on that occasion it is the more necessary I should state to you, as it was in your absence that it passed, for you may remember that you left them at my house. 'Have you taken any arrangements (said Mr Dundas to me) in consequence of what passed t'other day?'—'No, Sir, I have *not*: I did not look upon myself as sufficiently warranted to take any material step in that view without receiving a more express authority than I have as yet been favoured with.'—'Very well then, *now* you *will*,' replied Mr Dundas: and added Mr Pitt, 'there are some matters of detail which

---

954. ¹ P.R.O., H.O. 42/29, unnumbered fos. Autograph. Docketed: 'Panopticon Proposal Supp.t'. In B.L. V: 503–6 is an autograph rough draft, docketed: '1794 Mar 30 / Panopt / J.B. Q.S.P. / to / Nepean Whitehall / Dundas and Pitt's authorisation stated / No staying beyond the Session / S.B.'s regiment gone.'

Additional note, in red ink, at end of draft: '1798 or 99 / Returned by Mr Henry Thornton by letter.' This suggests that Thornton was shown this draft, perhaps because Bentham had kept no other copy.

In H.O. 42/29, with the letter of 30 March 1794 are two other documents, the first in Bentham's hand:

1. 'Proposal for a new and less expensive mode of employing and reforming Convicts'.

2. 'Supplemental Elucidations, 1793 June 8.' This is endorsed: '30 March 1794. Dom'.

remain to be settled, and which you will settle with Mr Nepean. I have given him what papers I had for that *purpose.*' This at the very conclusion of the visit: this in my Garden under my study window: Mr Pitt standing close to Mr Dundas, my Brother close to *me.*

The plan having been thus accepted, it appeared as far as my Brother and I could judge, to be the wish of both gentlemen that the execution of it should be speedy: upon my mentioning *six months* as a term within which we were not altogether without hopes of seeing the building in a condition to receive some at least of its inhabitants, some marks of satisfaction, if my Brother's observation did not deceive him, were visible in the countenance of Mr Pitt. It was in consequence, as I conceived, of those dispositions, that when the Articles were, as I understood, all settled between you and me, and every thing agreed on, you urged me to engage for the completion of the business within that period, under a penalty of £5,000. My answer was, that it was so evidently my *interest* (to say nothing of my *wish*) to give it every degree of expedition in my power, that I saw no need of *penalties.* Upon your observing that the insertion of such penalties was as much in course as the levying them, where no wilful default appeared, was unexampled, I did submitt, I believe, to bind myself accordingly, not to six months indeed, but however to a year.

It will be sufficient here to glance at a variety of subsequent incidents—at the failure of the different views we had separately entertained, of beginning the business without the necessity of a recourse to Parliament—at the failure of the negotiation with Lord Spencer—at the putting off of the business for *that* Session—at the assurances I received from you, with authority to make use of them, (which I did to his Lordship) that a Bill for the purpose would be brought in early in the present Session—at your recommendation to me to have a Bill prepared in readiness—at the assurance you were pleased to give me that the money I had required in advance was ready at any time, and would be put into my hands the instant the articles were signed, which they could be the instant a consent had been signified by Lord Spencer, or the requisite authority obtained from Parliament.

Trusting to grounds of expectation which to me seemed so un-equivocal, I did '*take such arrangements*' as it was in my power to take, for making up by my exertions for whatever delays the business had met with, or might meet with, from other quarters. I sacrificed, in spite of the incessant reproaches of my most confiden-tial friends, the plan of *gradual* and *successive* establishment I had

23

settled with my Brother for his numerous inventions, and which was suited to the nature and extent of my private fortune. The number of workmen has accordingly been at least doubled:—a considerable House and Manufactory has been added to what you saw: —Materials for the perfected erection have been laid in: a part of it has even been put together. *Patent* has been added to *Patent* (an object of itself of between 600 and 700 pound:) while the term allotted to the exercise of those dear-bought privileges has been mouldering away. The duration which in my calculations I had assigned to this forced disbursement is on the point of elapsing: *I can continue it no longer.* As little can I *now* retreat into the original plan of limited expenditure. A person with whom I had agreed for the sale of an estate which was to fetch me about £7,000 has within these few days declared off: the circumstances of the times have left the execution of the agreement, he says, no longer in his power: the Sale of other estates I had allotted for the purpose is becoming more and more precarious. As to borrowing money upon them, there are circumstances which render it rather a difficult, and at any rate a tedious business, had I ever so much time to attend to it: and as to loans of *favour*, you may judge how far the failure of a great and apparently eccentric project, is an auspicious period, for making experiments on a large scale, upon the confidence of friends. On the other hand, money which had been lent me by persons of very ample ability for the declared purpose of my keeping it untill those estates should have been disposed of, is now on a diminution of that ability called in, although the estates remain unsold, and, for I know not how long, unsaleable.

Meantime my Brother, whose offer, to save the public 25 per Cent in the article of woodwork for the Navy, the Earl of Chatham was pleased to reject on the declared ground of his attachment to the Russian service, has lost by his confidence in his Lordship's Brother, his Regiment in that service: a provision which was not worth as little as £2,000 a year to him, and which was all he had to live upon. I have more than once had occasion to speak of such an event as probable: I have, as you may perhaps remember, sollicited, and sollicited in vain, a word or two, by which I conceived it *might* have been *averted*. Within these few days accident led me to the discovery of its having *taken place*, I can't tell when, spite of my Brother's endeavours to conceal it from me. As to the Russian Minister here, who was most zealously his friend, he has not been able to look him in the face this twelvemonth.

Under these circumstances, Sir, you will not be surprized to hear, that *adjournment* and *abandonment* will be two words for the same thing. My own *economical* plans have so absolute a dependence on my Brother's *mechanical* ones, that without *his* assistance, even with money at command, it would be impossible for me to go on, at least upon any terms like those agreed on: and for his part you will, I believe, allow, that it will be high time he were in Russia, trying to get back, if possible, a part of the bread he has been led to forfeit, and beginning the same sort of game at Petersburgh, that after two or three years rather unexpected practice, *I* have just *done* playing at Whitehall.

Upon receipt of your *official* answer, or rather upon the *non-*receipt of it within a week, for events that are absolutely inevitable will not wait for others that have been found so eminently precarious, my *new 'arrangements' will begin to be 'taken'*, not such as I was twice spontaneously *authorized* to take, but such as a power much stronger *obliges* me to take: a collection of *Workmen*, such as, I believe (especially after the course of instruction they have had) are not to be matched in London, nor consequently in the World, will be *paid off* and *dispersed*: the *Houses* which you saw, together with others which you have not seen, will be *shut up*: and if you happen to know of any body whom a place, like that I am dating from, might be likely to suit, I should be much obliged to you if you would have the goodness to recommend it. I have the honour to be,

> with all respect
> Sir, your most obedient
> and humble Servant
> Jeremy Bentham.

Evan Nepean Esqr
etc. etc. etc.

955

To Sir Charles Bunbury

7 April 1794 (Aet 46)

Queries for Mr Dundas April 7, 1794

1. Whether Mr B. was not twice called upon to *make his arrangements* on the supposition of the proposals being accepted: viz:

---

955. [1] B.L. V: 507–8. Autograph draft. Docketed: '1794 Apr. 7 / Panopt / J.B. Q.S.P. / to / Sir C. Bunbury / Pall Mall / Queries for Dundas.'
The numbers in the draft are written in pencil.

once by Mr Dundas and Mr Nepean, and once by Mr Pitt and
Mr Dundas.
2. Whether that was not before the conclusion of the last Session?
3. Whether Mr Bentham was not assured that the Bill would be
brought in by Administration early in the present Session, and
whether in his treaty with Lord Spencer he was not authorized
to declare as much?
4. Whether the terms of the contract were not discussed and settled
in every article so long ago as June or July last?
5. Whether Administration have not been apprised of the difficulties in which he is involved by this neglect of him, and of the
irremediable mischief that has already been the result of it.
6. Whether they are not apprised of the impossibility of his
undertaking to resume the business on the basis proposed if
put off beyond the present Session.
7. Whether they have anything to object to Mr B. in respect to the
business or in any other respect whatever?
8. [Whether Mr B. has not][2] been employed in incessant sollicitation
for these two months, without being able to get a single word,
with regard to any point whatever and whether in particular
a letter of the most pressing nature has not been lying unanswered for this week past /and whether in particular the letter
conceived in the most pressing terms has not been lying unanswered for this week past/?[3]

956

To Evan Nepean

13 April 1794 (Aet 46)

Hendon Sunday $\frac{1}{2}$ after 7 Apr. 13th 1794
Dear Sir,
My evil genius had sent me hither at the time when you were
kind enough to call for the purpose of catching the moment for
procuring the Panopticon Bill the honour of a perusal from Mr
Pitt. I came hither for the purpose of working for a few hours
without interruption at a financial resource which (after having

---

[2] Crossed out in the original Ms., but required to make sense.
[3] Clearly a reference to letter 954 above.
956. [1] P.R.O., H.O. 42/29, unnumbered fo. Autograph. Docketed: 'Hendon 13th
April 1794 / Mr Bentham.'
Draft in B.L. V: 509, with note: 'In answer to his note / written at Q.S.P. to find /
out Panopt. Bill.' Nepean's note is missing.

had it in contemplation at least these dozen years) I have had in preparation for some time past, with a view of using my endeavours one of these days to present it to his notice.

I learn from my Brother who has sent me your note hither by express that he looked out as well as he could and addressed to you a copy, the only legible one I have of the Bill, except one which is not yet compleated. I wish he may have been successful in his endeavors to get it up perfect—I am

Dear Sir
Ever your most obliged
Jeremy Bentham

Evan Nepean Esqr.

When I saw you yesterday, I put a question the object of which was to know whether there would be any possible use in my staying in town today: from your answer I unfortunately inferred the negative.

957

To Charles Abbot

15 April 1794 (Aet 46)

Tuesday morng Apr. 15th 94

Dear Charles

I hope to God you may have been able to do something with the S.G.:[2] if not, we perish—Just what you expected has happened: Mr. L.[3] is exercising a negative upon the Bill, a negative which I fear will be effectual. I have not seen him: but the Report from Mr Long[4] is that [he] is working and working to put it into a Parliamentary Shape (meaning always the short Bill which I left with you) but with little hope of being able to do it in time—I shall let

957. [1] B.L. V: 510–11. Autograph. Docketed: '1794 Apr 15 / Panopt / J.B. / to / C.A. Linc. Inn / To gain the Sollr Genl.'
Addressed: 'C. Abbott Esqr.'
[2] Sir John Mitford (1748–1830), later Freeman-Mitford, who replaced Sir John Scott (later Lord Eldon) as Solicitor-General on 13 February 1793. He subsequently became Attorney-General, Speaker of the House of Commons and Lord Chancellor of Ireland; in 1802 he was created Baron Redesdale.
[3] William Lowndes was parliamentary counsel to the Treasury, 1789–98; thereafter chairman of the Board of Taxes.
[4] This is the first mention in the *Correspondence* of Charles Long (1761–1838), later Baron Farnborough (1820). He was M.P. for various constituencies, 1789–1826, and held a number of public offices; at this time he was joint-secretary to the Treasury, 1791–1801.

27

him work undisturbed, and whatever he makes of it I shall not object to, unless the S.G. steps in to deliver me out of his hands. From the first and only objection that happened to break out, judge of the rest—To give the establishment a name! never was any thing so unparliamentary! never was such thing put into a Bill before. My answer was—not that in speaking of a thing there was a convenience in having a name to call it by—that would have been impertinent—but that the self same thing was done in the existing Act, from which I copied it. Oh, that Mr Long could say nothing to, for he had never looked into that Act. And now I was given to understand that if any thing in the shape of a Bill was to be brought in now, it would be not by Mr Pitt (as Mr Nepean had mentioned) but by Mr Dundas: and that what Mr Dundas did would depend upon the report of Mr L. and upon what Mr L. could do in the view of putting the matter into a Parliamentary shape, for which he much feared there would not be time.

I write this at your chambers, where I called for the first time about 1. Since then I have been lounging about in the Sun and it is now 3. From your having gone out a riding so early as 9, I much fear that the S.G. some how or other has been and will be invisible, and that nothing will be to be done with him.

I go from hence to the Office to endeavour to get to the speech of Nepean—I hope you will let me see you by some means or other as soon as possible—My Brother had asked Romilly to dinner and we had advanced the hour to $\frac{1}{4}$ after 4 i:e: $\frac{1}{2}$ after precisely for the sake of accommodating him. As that early hour would take away whatever chance I might have of seeing you at dinner time, for I think you will hardly be come from riding by that time, I shall put it off till our usual hour $\frac{1}{4}$ after 5, in hopes of your making one with us. For if anything be yet to be done, you will see that there is not a minute to be lost.

I leave the Paper mentioned in my note of last night.[5]

I left home (for the last time) about 20 minutes before *one*: and nothing at the time had come from you that I heard of.

As there was not time for asking Romilly's leave to show his letter[6] that I sent, you may as well avoid mentioning the incident before him.

[5] Missing.
[6] Not, it would seem, letter 951, but a later communication, which is missing.

958

To Charles Long

21 April 1794 (Aet 46)

Sir

By the terms of the Contract as agreed to I was to have had £27,000 in advance on condition of maintaining the Prisoners for the first year; viz: £10,000 on the signing of the Contract, £10,000 three months after, and the remaining £7,000 on notice given of being ready to receive the Prisoners. From the nature of the intended Building, which will be composed, as far as strength is concerned, solely of Cast Iron and Wood, in which the Iron will be greatly predominant, it happens that the greatest part of it could be prepared and even in the way of experiment put together, before the acquisition of the ground so as [to be] ready to be put up as soon as the Land can be got to receive it. Mr. Nepean, if I did not misunderstand him gave it as his opinion that on this consideration, if the Bill could not be got to go through this Session, Administration would have no objection to the executing the terms of the contract at any time with regard to the above advances of £10,000 and £10,000, I finding proper security that the money should be applied to the purposes of the intended establishment, and not otherwise. This accordingly I flatter myself, considering the circumstances stated in my letter of the 30th last to Mr Nepean,[2] and which Mr Pitt and Mr Dundas are in possession of, will be found not unreasonable: and on these terms the year's farther delay which would otherwise ensue from the apprehended postponement would be very considerably reduced.

---

958. [1] B.L. V: 512–13. Autograph draft. Docketed: '1794 Apr 21 / J.B. Q.S.P. / to / S.G. Long etc. etc. / For £2000. Expenditure upwards of £4600 / Reference to Letter to Nepean 30 March.'

In the Treasury Board Minutes, P.R.O., T. 29/66 p. 467, there is the following entry: 'Whitehall. Treasury Chambers. 31 May 1794.

Present: Mr Pitt, Earl of Mornington, Mr. Hopkins, Mr. Townshend, Mr. Smyth.'

—— 'Read Letter from Mr. Secretary Dundas, dated the 28th Instant, desiring that My Lords will receive His Majesty's Pleasure for Issuing the Sum of £2,000 to Mr. Jeremiah Bentham, to enable him to make Preparations for the Custody and Care of a Number of Convicts, which it is His Majesty's Design shall be placed under his Directions, provided the Bill now before Parliament shall pass into a Law; the same to be accounted for by Mr. Bentham in such a manner as My Lords may hereafter think fit to require.

Prepare a Warrant for an Issue of the said Sum out of the Civil List.'

[2] Letter 954.

But finding myself in want of a present supply to the amount of 2,000£ owing to deaths and other unexpected incidents which they are also apprised of, and for the relief of necessities which have been also stated, the purpose of my waiting on you this day was to request a supply to that amount immediately without being obliged to wait till the close of the Session, or for the signification of the pleasure of Administration with regard to the larger advances above mentioned. I don't know whether it may be necessary to state here, as I did to Mr. Nepean, that from a rough account which has been given in to me, and which I know is not yet compleat the money already expended upon the establishment amounts to upwards of £4660, the produce of which is obviously visible in a numerous assemblage of machines and materials ready for the purpose, a part of them, though they [are] but a small part seen by Pitt and Mr Dundas. I need scarcely add that any account or elucidation which you may be pleased to order will be of course at your command. Waiting with great anxiety the pleasure of Mr Pitt upon this business, I have the honour to be

Sir

959

TO EVAN NEPEAN

22 April 1794 (Aet 46)

April 22 1794

¾ after 1   I call again
in ½ an hour

Mr Pitt and Mr Dundas expressed to Mr Sylvester Douglas on Sunday their desire that a short Bill might be drawn for the present Session. 'Why cannot Mr Bentham draw a short Bill?' etc.

I have got from Mr Lowndes Heads of a Bill for the purpose according to his own ideas purely, with a recommendation to get a Bill drawn either by Mr. W. Bentham,[2] or Mr Crewse,[3] by Friday,

---

959. [1] B.L. V: 514. Autograph draft. Docketed: '1794 Apr. 22 / Panopt / J.B. Sectys Office / to / Nepean ibid. / Heads of Bill from Lowndes.'

[2] William Bentham, a distant cousin of Jeremy; he was like him a great-grandson of Bryan Bentham (b. 1657). (See the family tree in *Correspondence*, i, pp. xxxviii–xxxix.) At this time he was practising as a conveyancer at 10 New Square, Lincoln's Inn (*Brown's General Law List*, 1787, p. 23; 1797, p. 45).

[3] William Cruise, also a conveyancer; he had been called to the bar in 1791 and was practising at 3 Stone Buildings, Lincoln's Inn (Brown, op. cit., 1787, p. 23; 1797, p. 21).

30

which he Mr. L. has undertaken to peruse and settle in readiness to give in for Monday.

But for the purpose of describing the Land a copy of the Inquest of the Jury of 10th Septr 1782 is absolutely necessary: which Inquest was procured on my application from Mr White[4] and is now in the hands of Mr Blake.[5]

I have Mr Lowndes's Heads of a Bill in my pocket, and hope they will answer my purpose.

960

To William Bentham and William Cruise

22 April 1794 (Aet 46)

To draw a Bill according to the written instructions as sketched by Mr Lowndes of Pump-Court Temple. The Record of the Inquisition describing the parcels of the Land has been perused[2] (in the hands of Mr Blake of the Treasury) a copy applied for, and may be obtained by applying to Mr Nepean.

It is absolutely necessary that the Bill should be drawn by Friday next, that it may be transmitted early on that day to Mr Lowndes for him to peruse and settle, in readiness to be brought in on Monday.

Please to observe that upon the shortness of the Bill depends its chance of passing this Session, a failure in which would be attended with great private as well as public inconvenience.

W. Bentham
Mr. Cruise 5[3] Guineas

[4] Joseph White, Treasury Solicitor, 1794–1806.
[5] Roebuck Blake (d. 1813), extra-clerk at the Treasury, 1785–1813.
960. [1] B.L. V: 515. Autograph draft. Docketed: '1794 Apr. 22 / Panopt / Short Bill for Panopt / Instructions from J.B. to W.B. (W. Browne) / Brouillon.'
Besides several crossed-out passages in the text, there is a crossed-out footnote: 'If Mr Cruse cannot be found this evening or cannot undertake for it in time then Mr. W. Bentham of Linc. Inn. If he can not be found or cannot undertake for it in time then tomorrow morning to Mr Cruse'.
[2] Crossed-out marginal note: 'To Mr W. Browne   Mr Lowndes's paper to be shown at the time, but not left.'
[3] The figure '10' is crossed out in the draft.

961

FROM SIR CHARLES BUNBURY

24 April 1794

Barton
April 24th 1794

Dear Sr,

I saw Mr Dundas before I left London, and am happy to inform you that he seemed entirely to approve of a short Bill for the sole Purpose of securing the Ground being brought in immediately.

I am
yours sincerely
T. Cha⁵ Bunbury

962

FROM CHARLES LONG

6 May 1794

Sir

The Lords of the Treasury have ordered a Warrant[2] to be prepared for you for two thousand Pounds towards carrying your

961. [1] B.L. V: 516–17. Autograph. Docketed: '1794 April 24 / Panopt / Bunbury Barton / to / J.B. Q.S.P.'

Addressed: 'To Jeremy Bentham Esq. / Queen's Square Place, / Westminster.' Franked: 'Bury, April twenty four, 94 / Free / T. C. Bunbury'. Postmark: FREE C.A.P. 25.94'.

962. [1] B.L. V: 518–19. Autograph. Docketed: '1794 May 6 / Panopt. / Long Treasury / to / J.B. Q.S.P. / Warrant for £2000 ordered.'

There is a copy of this letter in Bentham's hand in B.L. V: 520. It has the following notes by Bentham:

'Money paid accordingly—see 3d Rept of Committee on Finance, Ao 1797. Appendix B.'

'This was in answer to a letter dated March 30 1794 addressed to Mr Nepean, stating the particulars of the repeated authority given me first by Mr Dundas and Mr Nepean—then by Mr Pitt and Mr Dundas to take my arrangements with many other particulars indicative of urgency on their part. J.B. 27 Feb. 1798.'

'This letter would have been sent now—but it is an illegible Brouillon, which would be necessary to be copied, and occupied 4 or 6 pages.'

In view of the endorsement on letter 954, it would seem that the 'Brouillon' of the letter of 30 March was in fact sent to Henry Thornton in 1798, as well as a copy of letter 962.

[2] The warrant was not actually authorised until 31 May 1794 (P.R.O., Treasury Board Minutes, T. 29/66, p. 467).

plan into execution, as it will necessarily be a short time before the
Bill can have passed into a Law.

I am Sir
yr very obedt humble Servt
Charles Long.

Treasury Chambers
May 6th 1794

963

FROM ETIENNE DUMONT

8 May 1794

(Translation.)

I want a word or two—only a word or two—and you must
conquer your repugnance. I want not finished labours, but hints.
Mark the way by a few posts, and I will follow you. Your ideas are
all in ready money; so I can draw on you at sight. But I must
consult you; for if I suspend my labours, the interest will cool,
ennui will seize me, and the devil will do the rest.

—pendent opera interrupta, minaeque
Murorum ingentes, aequataque machina coelo.

Virg. Æn. iv. 88–89.[2]

964

TO HENRY DUNDAS

7 June 1794 (Aet 46)

Queen's Square Place Westmr. June 7th 1794.

Sir

A measure of Administration, being deserted by Administration, was carried by *me* through the House of Commons. The fact

963. [1] Bowring, x, 300. Introduced by the statement: 'Dumont addresses Bentham
on the 8th May:'

[2] Rendered by John Dryden, in his translation of Virgil: 'The mounds, the works,
the walls neglected lie, short of their promised height, that seemed to threat the sky'.
A modern prose translation is: 'The buildings and the high, threatening walls were
interrupted, and the crane reaching to the sky was idle' (*Virgil*, trans. and ed. Kevin
Guinagh, rev. edn. 1970).

964. [1] P.R.O., H.O. 42/31, unnumbered fo. Autograph. Docketed: 'Queens Square
Place Westminr / 7th June 1794 / Mr Bentham / R.'
    A copy of this letter is printed in Bowring, xi, 112–13. The draft of it in B.L. V: 521–
522 has an additional passage at the end, after a gap: 'Mr. S⟨ewel?⟩ whose new-built
Villa is nearer to the spot than any other House except the above, refused to join the

is not more ridiculous than true. Mr *Long* brought Mr *Long*: chance brought *me* two private friends. An Opposition of *two* was thus subdued after a hard struggle. In the Lords, after lying by till the 3d Reading, Ld Spencer obtains an Order for the printing of the Bill, in other words opposes it: opposes it, after having held such language, (to yourself, Sir, I presume) as (according to Mr Long to whose frankness I am beholden for the communication) rendered it impossible for him to oppose it. When thus opposed, since it is to be opposed, in the *Lords*, how then is it to be defended?—as it was in the *Commons*?—Time at least has not been wanting for getting it through, or for exposing it to disasters, since I had the honour of an audience: the week spoken of, Sir, on that occasion has been already doubled. What other helps it was destined to receive remain yet to be discovered. A Secretary to the Treasury neither knew what had been done, nor what was to be done:—an Under Secretary of State asked *me.*—Indeed, Sir, *I* do not not know. One thing I *do* know, which is, that I am no match for Lord Spencer any where; especially in his own House: and unless some such person as a Secretary of State, or a first Lord of the Treasury, should happen to know of some means whereby a Treasury-Bill, after having passed the Commons, may be supported against a groundless opposition in the Lords, there is an end of my hopes, as well as of other things better glanced at than expressed.

I have the honour to be,
with all respect,
Sir,
Your most obedient
and humble Servant
Jeremy Bentham

Right Hon. H. Dundas etc. etc. etc.

965

T O   A R C H B I S H O P   M A R K H A M

9 June 1794 (Aet 46)

My Lord

    I had had the satisfaction of hearing more than once from Mr

Opposition, though no application had been made to him in favour of the measure.'
    'The principal complainants are Mr Dent and Mr Baldwin, both of Clapham, neither of whose houses are within a mile of the spot.' (See letter 977, p. 45 below.)
965. [1] B.L. V: 523–4. Autograph draft. Docketed: '1794 June 9 / Panopt / J.B. Q.S.P. / to Archbp of York S. Audley Street.'

Long of the Treasury as also from Mr Dundas who spoke in terms of eulogium of the liberality displayed by his Lordship on that [the] occasion that Lord Spencer had declared he should give no opposition to the Penitentiary House Bill. Your Grace will thence judge of my surprize at learning from the public prints that on Thursday last the Bill being at its last stage an order [was made] at his Lordship's instance for the printing of the Bill, an operation altogether useless but for the purpose of opposing it: which shows that on one side or other some misconception must have taken place. As Mr Hastings's trial renders your Grace, as I understand a pretty constant attendant at the House, and on which occasion your Grace would naturally hear something on that subject from his Lordship, it has been suggested to me by some friends of mine who have the honour to be numbered among those of your Grace.[2] Recalling to mind at this moment of alarm the kind assurances your Grace was pleased to give me, it occurred to /me/ some friends of mine who have the honour of being numbered among those of your Grace /that after such a lapse of time/ that it might be /after an interval of such length as easily to admitt in the course of such a business of this sort might easily have escaped out of any one's remembrance/ agreable to your Grace /not only/ to be reminded not only with the general tenor of those assurances but with the very words to save discussions and to serve as a short answer upon occasion to any thing that might be urged on the other side. I have the honour to be with all respect.

My Lord Your Graces most obedient
and much obliged humble servt
J.B.

The Paper which I take the liberty of inclosing[3] was drawn up for the purpose of encountering, had it been found necessary, an opposition which manifested itself in some degree in the Lower House.

[2] This sentence is unfinished in the draft and those which follow have been reworded to take in the reference to the trial of Warren Hastings; the final version may perhaps have read: '. . . it has been suggested to me by some friends of mine who have the honour to be numbered among those of your Grace, that after such a lapse of time it might be agreable to your Grace to be reminded not only of the general tenor of those assurances but of the very words . . .'

[3] Missing.

966

To Bishop Warren

10 June 1794 (Aet 46)

My Lord

/I am/ Being the person interested in the Penitentiary House Bill, I write this to ask permission to wait upon your Lordship for the purpose of learning some particulars respecting it.

/presents his respectful compliments to the Bishop of Bangor begging permission to wait on his Lordship as soon as consists with his Lordship's convenience, for the purpose of learning some particulars respecting it/ at the desire of some Lords who propose attending when it comes before the House. Neither of the Secretaries of the Treasury any more than Mr Cowper[2] the clerk of the House being in town.

Bp of Bangor

967

To the Duke of Dorset

10 June 1794 (Aet 46)

Q.S.P. June 10 1794.

My Lord Duke

Understanding from my Brother the kind part your Grace has been pleased to take in relation to the Penitentiary business, I take the liberty of inclosing a few more of the printed papers on account of a few particulars that have since been added in Ms.

The Bishop of Bangor who I understand has the charge of the

966. [1] B.L. V: 525–6. Autograph draft. Docketed: '1794 June 10 / Panopt / J.B. / to / Bishop of Bangor / D. of Dorset / E. Warwick.'

As the docket indicates Bentham was rounding up supporters for his Penitentiary House Bill in the House of Lords (see letter 967).

Dr John Warren (1730–1800) was the second son of an archdeacon and brother of Richard, the royal physician. He was successively bishop of St David's (1779) and Bangor (1783).

[2] Henry Cowper, clerk assistant to the House of Lords.

967. [1] B.L. V: 525–6. Autograph draft. Docketed: '1794 June 10 / Panopt / J.B. / to / Bishop of Bangor / D. of Dorset / E. Warwick.' The docket indicates that a similar letter was sent to the Earl of Warwick.

For John Frederick Sackville, 3rd Duke of Dorset (1745–99) see *Correspondence*, iv, 427 n. 3, and for the 2nd Earl of Warwick (1746–1816), the brother-in-law of Caroline Vernon, ibid., iv, 86 n. 3.

Bill has just appointed me to wait on him about it tomorrow evening² on which occasion I shall learn what I can about the probable time of its coming on, for the purpose of reporting it to your Grace

I have the honour to be with all respect
My Lord Duke
your Grace's most obliged
and most obedt humble Servt

968

FROM BISHOP WARREN

10 June 1794

The Bishop of Bangor presents his Compliments to Mr Bentham, and is very sorry that his engagements happen to be such that it will not be in his power to have an interview with Mr Bentham till tomorrow evening. The Bishop cannot now fix the Hour, but will take the liberty of giving Mr Bentham notice tomorrow as soon he is returned, and able to receive Mr Bentham

Tuesday afternoon
10th June

969

TO EVAN NEPEAN

11 June 1794 (Aet 46)

On Barracks

Queen's Square Place Westmr June 11th 1794

Sir

It was an observation that dropped spontaneously from Lord Chesterfield² on seeing the Panopticon Models t'other day, that

² See letter 968.

968. ¹ B.L. V: 527–8. Docketed: '1794 June 10 / Panopt / Bp of Bangor Great / George Street / to / J.B. Q.S.P.'
Addressed: Mr 'Bentham.'

969. ¹ P.R.O. H.O. 42/31, unnumbered fo. Autograph. Docketed: 'Queen Square 11 June 1794 / Mr Bentham / R. 12th.'
² Philip Stanhope, 5th Earl of Chesterfield (1755–1815), godson and successor of the celebrated 4th earl; nominally ambassador to Spain, 1784–7, but did not go to Madrid; held minor offices in Pitt's administration, including that of joint postmaster-general, 1790.

a building of that sort might be adapted with particular advantage to the purpose of *Barracks*. His Lordship's quickness followed up the observation with some reasons of details which my tardiness could not overtake.

Hearing it said just now that you were gone to Colonel Delancey[3] from Mr Pitt, it brought to mind a very short conversation I was honoured with some months ago, and which may not improbably have escaped your memory. I had declared my persuasion of its being in my Brother's power to put Government in a way of making very considerable savings under that expensive head. I should scarce expect so little as 50 per cent. You were thereupon pleased to intimate a disposition to consult with him on the subject, upon Colonel Delancey's return from a tour on which he had then recently set out.

I have the honour to be,
Sir,
Your most obedient
and humble Servant
Jeremy Bentham

Evan Nepean Esqr
etc. etc. etc.

970

To Samuel Bentham

12 June 1794 (Aet 46)

Nobody seems to entertain any apprehension about the fate of the Bill; the Bishop of Bangor included, whom I had the honour of waiting upon at his own House last night, as I said I should. His hypothesis is, that Ld Spencer will amuse himself with saying a few words, after which the Bill will pass, which he supposes may be tomorrow. In the event of a serious opposition he has undertaken to give me timely notice.

This day came a letter from Burket,[2] desiring that the Bureau may be evacuated, and the contents put into any Box.

---

[3] Oliver De Lancey (1749–1822), colonel, 17th regiment, Light Dragoons; promoted to major-general, 1794; in 1790 he was deputy adjutant-general at the Horse Guards and in 1794 appointed barrack-master general. He was M.P. for Maidstone, 1796–1802.
970. [1] B.L. V: 529–30. Autograph. No docket.
Addressed: 'To Colonel Bentham / Post Office / Derby.' Postmark: 'JU 12-A'.
[2] An inventive friend of Samuel's, known to him since at least 1773 (see *Correspondence*, i–iii passim, especially i, 158 n. 1 and iii, 1 n. 4).

Amidst the general joy, Citizen Stanhope[3] has had his windows completely demolished last night, either for non-illumination, or for suspicion of non-illuminatory dispositions.

Brian[4] told me at noon today that between 2 and 3 in the morning all the servants were up and in a great hubbub under the apprehension of a mandate to illuminate. Dumont and I lay very snug and knew nothing of the matter.

I write this from Mr Brownes,[5] who in the midst of all the joy was treated with a bullet, which came in at the window, he supposed from Grays Inn Lane where several vollies were fired.

As Mr Sheffield[6] etc. are an expence running on, I should think with submission the best economy would be to begin the casting subject to stoppage. It might be begun, as if for experiment's sake, and as soon as the Bill passed, the experiment might be declared successful, and an agreement made for right arnest.

June 12—1974

Citizen Stanhope, I hear, went out of town early this morning, at the recommendation of his friends.

Puss[7] goes to East Bourne as supposed for 5 or 6 weeks with the Royers tomorrow sennight.

[3] Charles, 3rd Earl Stanhope (1753–1816), 'Citizen Stanhope'. The illuminations in London on 11 June 1794 were to celebrate Earl Howe's victory over the French fleet on 'The Glorious First of June'. Citizen Stanhope's known French sympathies made his house a target for a patriotic mob, who smashed his windows, which were of 'beautiful designs in stained glass . . . collected with infinite care, and at great expence' (*Morning Chronicle*, 13 June 1794). 'Lord Stanhope escaped from personal injury only by being in the country' (*Oracle*, 13 June).

[4] A servant at Queen's Square Place.

[5] The family friend, William Browne, who lived at no. 9 Bedford Row, close to Gray's Inn Lane.

[6] In a later letter (978, p. 47 below) Bentham refers to a casting 'work' near Sheffield, to whose staff this would appear to be an allusion.

[7] 'Puss' may have been the same person as 'Mrs L.', who went to join the Royer family on 22 June (see p. 49 below). James Royer, a former page to King George II, owned several houses in Eastbourne. He was the author of *East-Bourne . . . and its environs*, 1787, and later edns. (see Reginald Graham, *Eastbourne recollections*, 1888).

971

FROM THE DUKE OF DORSET

13 June 1794

Dorset House June 13th 1794

The Duke of Dorset presents his compliments to Mr Bentham and wishes to see him tomorrow morning at eleven o'clock. The bill which he interests himself about is to be considered *tomorrow* at *one* o'clock. The D. of Dorset thinks Lord Grenville[2] had better be apprised of it, as the D. of D. thinks it probable that both Mr Pitt and Mr Dundas have consulted his Lordship upon it. The D. of D. believes that Lord Spencer has some objection to the Bill.[3]

972

FROM THE EARL OF WARWICK

14 June 1794

Lord Warwick presents his Compliments to Mr Bentham and is extremely sorry that having returned from Town yesterday Evening it is not in his power to attend today at 1 o'clock in the House which he should have done with the greatest pleasure had not particular business detained him in the Country.—

Saturday
  June 14th
    1794

971. [1] B.L. V: 531–2. Docketed: '1794 June 13 / Panopt / D. of Dorset Whitehall / to / J.B. Q.S.P.'

Addressed: 'Jeremy Bentham Esqre'. Franked by impressed seal of the duke, almost intact.

[2] William Wyndham Grenville, Baron Grenville (1759–1834), Foreign Secretary, 1791–1801. See *Correspondence*, iv, 230 n. 1.

[3] The Panopticon Bill.

972. [1] B.L. V: 533–4. Docketed: '1794 June 14 / Panopt / Ld Warwick Isleworth / to / J.B. Q.S.P. / Excuse non-attendance.'

Addressed: 'J. Bentham Esq., / Queen Square Place, / Westminster.' Franked: 'Isleworth / June fourteenth 1794 / Warwick'. Postmark: 'FREE C. JU.16.94'.

973

FROM THE DUKE OF DORSET

15 June 1794

Dorset House June 15th 1794

The D. of Dorset's best compliments to Mr Bentham, and sends him enclosed the two letters[2] he received from him, they were of *great use in the business* of yesterday. The D. of Dorset thinks Mr B had better see Mr Charles Long tomorrow (of the Treasury), the D. of Dorset has no doubt but that the bill will pass *of course*, but it is better not to lose sight of it *a moment* as the Parliament will in all probability rise on Thursday next.

974

FROM SIR CHARLES BUNBURY

15 June 1794

Pall Mall
Sunday Evening
(June 15 1794)

Dear Sir,
　　After calling four Times I met with Ld Spencer at last;
　　He said he had no Objection to the Bill, except his Dislike to having the Buildings on his Ground: I told him that Intention was given up. He seemed satisfied but replied, Some Alterations were then necessary in the wording of the Bill. I hear it passed yesterday in the Lords with a few Amendments.
　　I will attend at the House of Commons tomorrow, when it will [be] brought there.

Yrs sincerely
T. Cha[s] Bunbury

973. [1] B.L. V: 535–6. Docketed: '1794 June 15 / Panopt / D. of Dorset Whitehall / to / J.B. Q.S.P.'
[2] Missing; perhaps copies of Bentham's letters to Nepean and Dundas.
974. [1] B.L. V: 537–8. Autograph. Docketed: '1794 June 15 / Panopt / Sir C. Bunbury / Pall Mall / to / J.B. Q.S.P. / Ld Spencer has no objections to the Bill only its being on *his* ground.'
Addressed: 'To Jeremy Bentham Esqre.'

975

To Samuel Bentham

c. 15 June 1794 (Aet 46)

S.B.[2]

Delighted as I am to find the Bill is safe, I am a little less so that the safety of it is owing in a manner solely to your Grace. This I hear in so many words from my Brother: and this is all I hear from him: he pretends he has not time to write but promises me against we meet a curious history of sudden turns and surprizes. So thick and so close drawn as the curtain has been in this business how fortunate has it been for us to have a friend to whom a peep behind it could not be refused.

*   *   *

After what is past, it is something more than form, and by no means out of the sphere of credibility, to say that I am with the most affectionate gratitude

Your Grace's most obliged
S.B.

Q.S.P. 3 o'clock

Well—the Bill is safe, but as it has been botched, the new Bill which of course must be brought in can not pass till Thursday, on which day the Duke tells me I may consider it as secure.[3] He takes the whole merit of its salvation: so much the better: the more he takes of it, the more it shows him to be pleased at the thoughts of serving you. Lord Spencer it seems has talked very adversely: so much the better again: he has set the Duke against him, and the Ministry eke also. If I may believe the Duke, whose idea is much corroborated by circumstances, Lord Spencer had gained the Chancellor,[4] who afterwards after having Pitt's fist held to his throat, was forced to turn against Ld Spencer and give him a kicked arse as if they had been at daggers drawn from the beginning. He

---

975. [1] B.L. V: 553. Autograph, with draft of letter for Samuel to send to the Duke of Dorset. No docket.

Addressed: 'To / Colonel Bentham / Post Office / Derby.' Postmark: 'JU ⟨...⟩ 94A'.

[2] The first part of this communication to Samuel, headed 'S.B.', is clearly a draft of a letter which Jeremy wishes his brother to send to the Duke of Dorset.

[3] This reference to Dorset's letter of 15 June (letter 973) enables the present one to be dated.

[4] Alexander Wedderburn, Baron Loughborough.

knocked down a parcel of mischievous amendments of Ld Spencer's, admitting such only as I hope will prove harmless ones. I think we shall have the Land yet: at the worst we shall be so much injured as to have the injurers at our feet.

Now begin and *cast* away.[4] Ramus[5] tells me the warrant money will be in readiness either in the course of the day, or at the worst on Monday. Adieu I go to meet Dumont Romilly and Chauvet[6] at an Inn by Putney Bridge.

Notwithstanding the warning they (Ministry) could not believe that Lord Spencer would be adverse. I am satisfied my dose of salts or cantharides if you please to Dundas did them no harm. Pitt assured the Duke I should have every satisfaction. They sent for Ld Grenville in a panic: and as he by some accident did not come, the Chancellor was forced to be Ld Grenville's deputy, eating his own words, one of the highest seasoned of *humble pies*.

I saw Pitt shewing me with a smile to my old friend the new Ld Camden[7]—They were going from the Horse Guards into the Treasury. Pole Carew has been very zealous and attentive—— hovering about in the Lords, as whilom in the Commons.

976

To Samuel Bentham

17 June 1794 (Aet 46)

Mr Bentham on account of his uncertainty with regard to his Brothers motions takes the liberty of directing this to Mr Evans.[2]

Q.S.P. Tuesday June 17 1794.

Well—after all—the Bill is passed—praised be the Lord therefore! Yea, the Bill, the very botched Bill, botched by the Lords, has passed the Commons, and by them been sent up to the

---

[4] Bentham is again urging his brother to begin casting iron (see letter 970, p. 39 above).

[5] George Edward Ramus (d. 1808), chief clerk in the Treasury, 1785–1808.

[6] David Chauvet. See above, p. 2 n. 3.

[7] John Jeffrys Pratt, M.P. (1759–1840), 2nd Earl Camden (1794), a close political associate of Pitt; Bentham had first met him at Bowood in 1781 (see *Correspondence*, iii, 82–3).

976. [1] B.L. V: 539–40. Autograph. Docketed: '1794 June / J.B.–S.B. / The bill is passed / Earl Spencer's land for / Panopticon not likely to / be accorded by him.' Addressed: 'To / — Evans Esqr: Banker / Derby.' Postmark: 'J⟨U⟩17.94.C.'

[2] Inserted at the top of the letter in small writing. Walter, William and Samuel Evans were, with John Bingham, bankers at St Mary's Gate, Derby.

Lords, there to receive the sacred touch of the Royal Sceptre.[3] Three amendments I think there were, all separately agreed to. I heard them mumbled—but you must not ask me what they were. Not pretty little Mr Hobart[4]—nor good Serjeant Watson[5] but Anstruther[6] took charge of the bantling and carried it to the Lords —Long, then Scotch Anstruther, a friend of Wilson's, and Trail's and Douglas's, and Ld Chancellor's, and all other Scotchmen's. How he came by it the Lord knows. I had been waiting in great despondency to hear the probable fate of it from Long—having waited near two hours in vain—thought I, I'll e'en saunter to the Commons, and take my chance for hearing it with my own ears. In great despondency said I—and certainly with great reason—for so late as yesterday peeping into the Commons and seeing nobody but Mr Hobart, whom I accosted, taking him for one of the Clerks, I learnt from him that 'Gentlemen were by no means unanimous about it, and that the probability was that it would go over to another Session'—Going to the Duke's with the sad news, found he had set off for Knowle not to return till Wednesday (viz: tomorrow).

Hovering about the Lords just now, saw Smith[7] of the Treasury, from whom I learnt for a certainty that the Lords' power over the Bill is at an end, and that nothing can hurt it now.—He said he would come and see me—asked me where it viz: Panopticon was to be—I told him that was the very thing I wished to know—He spoke of Dent and Thornton's objections as frivolous—when I told him it was not there that the matter stuck, but with Ld Spencer whose land it was, he drew up—as who should say—ah, c'est une autre affaire.

No—indeed I do not think we shall have the land and so, Mr Reprobate, not my righteous will, but thy wicked will, will be done.

---

[3] The progress of the bill through Parliament had begun on 9 May 1794, when Dundas successfully moved for leave to bring in a bill for the erection of a penitentiary house in Battersea (*Parliamentary Register*, xxxviii, 236); on 14 May the vicar of Battersea presented petitions against the bill (*Oracle*, 15 May); on 22 May it received its second reading and was ordered to be reported, which happened on the 22nd, when the bill was ordered to be engrossed; on 28 May it received its third reading; on 14 June it was considered by the Lords and passed, subject to amendments; on 17 June the Commons agreed to the amendments (*Oracle*, 19, 23, 27, 29 May, 18 June 1794, *Morning Chronicle*, 17 June 1794).

[4] Perhaps Robert Hobart (1760–1816), M.P., the future 4th Earl of Buckinghamshire (1804).

[5] James Watson (c. 1748–96), barrister, M.P. 1790–6, knighted 1795, judge of the Supreme Court of Judicature.

[6] Sir John Anstruther (1753–1811), M.P., 1790–6, Chief Justice of Bengal and baronet (1797).

[7] Probably Joseph Smith, junior clerk in the Treasury (1782–94) and private secretary to Pitt (1787–1801), but possibly William Edward Smith, under clerk of revenue (1776–97).

As to the money, not forthcoming yet—notwithstanding the assurances mentioned in my last—but it has got a step farther, Mitford tells me, viz: Ld Grenville's signature, and on Thursday there is to be a Board of Treasury, and then forsooth it is to be done. I suspect that the doubt about the Bill's passing was the cause of the delay.

⟨I wrote?⟩ to you on Saturday—I wrote to you a few days before —inclosing the Extray. Gazette of Lord Howe's victory—both[8] letters were directed to you, Post-Office, Derby, as you desired. I received from you the letter about your Coach falling-off accident: item yesterday yours of Sunday[9] about wheel-carriages, zoonomia,[10] Panopticon Canal etc.

I met Mr Wilberforce in the Treasury passage this morng a little before I went to the Commons. He was but just returned from the Country where he had been almost ever since we dined with him. He gave me some little hopes by informing me that money Bills botched by the Lords were sometimes received by the Commons, sometimes not, according to the existing *circumstances.*

977

FROM SIR CHARLES BUNBURY

17 June 1794

Pallmall
Tuesday Morning
June 17th 1794

Dear Sir,

I recd your's,[2] and am much concerned to find I have been in an Error for some Time past, for I conceived that the Concession to the opponents of your Bill in the House of Commons, vizl. Mr. Thornton,[3] Mr Dent[4] etc. which was made by Mr Dundas as I

---

[8] 'The Glorious First of June' (see letter 970, p. 39).

[9] Both of the letters from Samuel mentioned are missing.

[10] Perhaps a reference to Erasmus Darwin's *Zoonomia, or The Laws of Life*, 2 vols., 1794–6. The first volume appeared in 1794.

977. [1] B.L. V: 541–2. Autograph. Docketed: '1794 June 17 / Sir C. Bunbury / Pall-Mall / to / J.B. Q.S.P. / Opponents consent to two other spots in Battersea and Wandsworth—both are approved by Bunbury etc.'
Addressed: 'To Jeremy Bentham Esqre'.   [2] Missing.

[3] Henry Thornton (1760–1815), banker, economist, philanthropist and 'Claphamite'; M.P. for Southwark, 1782–1815; William Wilberforce, the anti-slavery campaigner, resided with him at Battersea Rise until Thornton's marriage.

[4] John Dent (1760–1826), M.P., who had a vested interest in Battersea (see above, p. 34 n. 1).

understood from them, (and which seemed I confess necessary to make, or the Bill would have been lost) had been with your Acquiescence at least if not your Approbation, under which Idea I assented to it, and the Bill passed the Commons. I was not in Town when the Bill passed the Committee because I understood the opponents had agreed to let the Bill pass *on Condition* the Buildings were not to be erected on that particular spot belonging to Ld Spencer and the See of York called *Battersea Rise*, or *Lavender Hill* but on any other eligible spot in the Parishes of Battersea or Wandsworth which the Commissioners should fix upon, and there are two others which appeared proper to Sr G. Eliot, Mr Bowdler, and myself when we viewed them, and which I hoped would meet with your approbation.

In Consequence of their Agreement I understood that some words were inserted in the Bill to this Effect viz: 'or *any other* Place' and I am therefore much surprised, and concerned to hear that this Alteration is Novel, or in the least disagreable to you.

I am Yours sincerely

T. Chas Bunbury

978

To Evan Nepean

18 June 1794 (Aet 46)

Queen Square Place Westmr June 18 1794

Sir

Under the following circumstances, (the Bill having yesterday passed both Houses) there will, I flatter myself, be no objection to the making *immediate* application from your office to the Treasury for the first advance to the amount of £10,000 which by the terms agreed on about a twelvemonth ago was to have been made immediately upon the signature of the contract an operation which waited for nothing but that of fixing upon the land.

  Cast iron, as I have already had occasion to state will constitute a very large proportion of the building. A very considerable progress may thence be made in the operation of building at any distance from the land: a circumstance peculiarly fortunate where the possession not to say the choice of the land is at so unfortunate a distance.

978. [1] B.L. V: 543–4. Autograph draft, with a few words altered in another hand. Docketed: '1794 June 18 / Panopt / J.B. Q.S.P. / to / Nepean Whitehall / For £10,000 on the Bill passing the Lords. Iron casting begun.'

My Brother (attended by a man of peculiar experience and ability at a guinea a day besides expences together with two other men at Foreman's wages) has for these ten days past been at the only Work of the kind (a Work near Sheffield) which upon searching the island through was found to be eligible for the purpose. Waiting the decision of Parliament he had put the People off till they would be put off no longer which reduced us to the alternative of beginning the business at all hazards or losing the season. This alone is an affair of several thousand pounds. Timber for flooring and other works which may likewise be begun upon immediately without waiting for the Land will come to several thousands more. Meantime the Contract, I apprehend, can not be made out in form at least not *signed* till after my own and several other appointments have passed the offices, nor even perhaps till possession of the land has been secured, events the waiting for which, if they were to be waited for, would again be productive of the loss of the season, a delay which Administration I presume would not be displeased to save.

What renders it the more incumbent upon me to be thus early in this my humble application is that this is the 18th of June, and that at this day not a penny of the supply applied for in relief of exigencies made known in March and for which immediate relief was announced before the end of April has yet found its way in to my hands. I have the honour to be

Sir
Your most obedient
and humble Servant
Jeremy Bentham

Evan Nepean Esqr
etc. etc. etc.

979

From Archbishop Markham

22 June 1794

Bishopsthorpe June 22 1794.

Dear Sir

    After visiting some Parts of my Diocese I am lately arrived at this Place and I find myself favour'd with your Letter.[2]

---

979. [1] B.L. V: 545–6. Autograph. Docketed: '1794 June 22 / Panopt / Archp of York Bishopsthorpe / to / J.B. Q.S.P.'
[2] Perhaps that of 9 June (letter 965).

I am much mistaken if I did not before say to you, that Ld. Spencers Interests were concerned much more nearly than mine that I took it for granted that the Rights of the See would at all Events be taken care of, and that my Conduct shou'd be perfectly passive. I have accordingly never taken any step except directing my Attorney Mr. Boodle³ in Lower Brook Str. to watch the Progress of the Bill, and occasionally to confer with Ld. Spencers Steward. Since that time I have not received any Information upon the Subject.

You desired me to return to you some papers. I trust I shall find them here and will send them. I am dear Sir

yr most faithful and obedt Sert
W. Ebor

980

To Samuel Bentham

22 June 1794 (Aet 46)

Q.S.P. June 22. 1794 Monday

Mr Bentham takes the liberty once more of addressing this to Mr Evans, who will deliver it, forward it or burn it, according to what he happens to know of Col. B's motions.

Nepean took me just now to Col. Delancey at his house and office now fitting up in New Street Spring Gardens No 21 and 22. His place is that of Barrack Master-General. He goes to Portsmouth tomorrow but will return in a few days.

They had a messenger this morning between 10 and 11—No news —they know not whether Ypres is or is not taken.²

Pitt and Dundas have read the Bill and a letter of mine that was sent out with it to them at Wimbledon on Saturday—but Nepean has not yet had opportunity of speaking to them about it, this and

---

³ Edward Boodle (1750–1828), attorney, of 41 Lower Brook Street, Grosvenor Square. He acted as agent for the archbishop of York and later for Richard, 1st Earl Grosvenor and his son, Lord Belgrave, both of whom opposed Bentham's scheme for a penitentiary in Tothill Fields.

980. ¹ B.L. V: 547–8. Autograph. No docket. Addressed: 'To / — Evans Esqr / Banker / Derby.' Postmark: 'JU. 23 94 A'.

² The rumour that Ypres had been captured by the French on 20 June reached London on the 22nd and was fully confirmed by the 28th (*Morning Chronicle*, 23, 25, 26, 28 June 1794).

that and t'other business which G.[3] detailed to me having successively intervened to render them invisible.

Mrs L.[4] went out of town this morning to Mr Royer's at East
Bourne for 6 weeks.

981

To the Marquis of Lansdowne

26 June 1794 (Aet 46)

June 26th 1794

On the| |[2] instant Mr Abbot[3] saw Lord Wycombe on the
road near Schaffhausen on foot, in very good health, in haste to
pass the dog-days under an Italian sky. It was on the 12th day
after his departure from England. Mr. Abbot and Mrs. Bentham
were bending their course to Vienna, where it is supposed they are
by this time.

Great gratitude at Q.S.P. for Lord L's kind offer about the proxy.
The Bill out of danger, but the Bastille still hanging in the Air, for
want of land to be set down upon. Col. B. out this fortnight first
upon an iron-casting expedition to Sheffield—expected back in
a day or two. His brother in an unintermitting fit of rage, plying
Messrs P. and D.[4] with letters *a la Chinoise*.

982

From Samuel Romilly

27 June 1794

Dear Bentham

Anstruther[2] wishes much to see the Panopticon and I told him

[3] Probably Garthshore (see p. 89 n. 1).
[4] Perhaps the lady referred to as 'Puss' in letter 970.

981. [1] Lansdowne Mss. Autograph. No signature, docket or address.
[2] Blank in original.
[3] Probably Bentham's step-brother, John Farr Abbot, who was travelling abroad
with his mother for his health; he returned to England in August and died on 22
September 1794 (*Diary and Correspondence of Charles Abbot, Lord Colchester*, 3 vols.,
1861, vol. i, p. xvii; *Gentleman's Magazine*, liv, October 1794, p. 960).
[4] Pitt and Dundas.

982. [1] B.L. V: 549–50. Autograph. Docketed: '1794 June 27 / Panopt / Romilly Linc.
Inn / to / J.B. Q.S.P. / Anstruther's visit announced.'
Addressed: 'Jeremy Bentham Esqr / Queen's Square Place / Westminster.' Stamped:
'Post pd.' Postmark: '10 o'clock 28 Ju 94 MORN OUTGN. 3'.
[2] Sir John Anstruther.

I would use my Interest with you to procure him a sight of it and we have agreed if it is not inconvenient to you to call at your House on Tuesday when the Court of Chancery rises which will be about 2 or perhaps 3 o clock. As A. is very intimate with the Chancellor and has considerable influence on him I am anxious that he should be sensible of all the merit of the Panopticon

Yours ever
S.R.

27 June. If it should be inconvenient to you that we should call on Tuesday pray let me know.

983

FROM ETIENNE DUMONT

July 1794

Je n'ai pas été hier chez vous, mon cher Bentham, parce que je rencontrai Romilly à Hyde park corner qui venoit diner à Kensington et qui m'apprit que nous etions contremandés. Vous oubliez de me marquer le jour de votre retour de Hendon, mais Romilly ne revenant des Sessions que mercredi, je suppose que notre appointement à Q.S.P. sera vers la fin de la semaine prochaine. J'ai laissé la traduction, j'en suis très sûr, cherchez et vous trouverez. Cependant, j'irai demain matin à Londres, et si par hazard, je l'avois rapportée à L. house, elle sera remise avant midi à Q.S.P., mais c'est une chance infiniment petite. Votre homme m'a remis les papiers sur la recompense,[2] et je vous promets que cette besogne sera très vite depêchée, car je suis tout ardent pour finir, vû la possibilité qui se présente de faire un usage réel du Code même. mes amitiés au Colonel. Tout à vous.

Et. D.

Kensington.
vendredi
1 heure

983. [1] B.L. V: 552. Autograph. Docketed: '1794 July / Dumont Kensington Square / to / J.B. Q.S.P. / Receives "Recompenses".' The exact date is not given: the Fridays in July were 3, 10, 17, 24 and 31.

[2] As far back as February 1787 Bentham had told George Wilson, 'I am marginal-contenting *Essai sur les Recompenses*' (see *Correspondence*, iii, 524), but the material was first published as *Théorie des peines et des récompenses* . . . *Redigé en françois d'apres les manuscrits*, par M. Et. Dumont, 2 vols., London, B. Dulau, 1811. A translation by Richard Smith appeared as *The Rationale of Reward*, London, J. and H. L. Hunt, 1825, and this was reprinted in Bowring, ii, 192–266.

984

To Samuel Bentham

1 August 1794 (Aet 46)

Q.S.P. 1 Aug. 1794

Sir John Sinclair[2] sent me yesterday a note on the cover whereof was written *Board of Agriculture* desiring to see me today or tomorrow between 10 and 12. I went about 12 today: it was (as it turned out upon his cross examination) at the instigation of Lowndes from whose account of things he supposed that our establishment might be made useful to the public in the way of making agricultural machines. The post does not leave me time for details: the conclusion is, that he comes tomorrow at 11 to see the glories, and as he proposes to go to Scotland Wednesday or Thursday I told him if he would get fed on Tuesday I would hawl you back to town on that day, to help feed him. We were both of us a little in a hurry, and we agreed that he should tell me about that tomorrow. He seems really a pleasant man: infinitely more so than I expected, and infinitely more so than his picture speaks him.

When I reached Rose's[3] door yesterday, I found it open with a man standing at it to make me an excuse saying that he had a sudden call in the country, but would let me know in the course of the day when he should be able to see me. On returning home I found he had sent a verbal Message (as I was told at his House) to Q.S.P. to the same effect: that day is over, this day almost over, but nothing from Mr Rose.

M[es?]sant[4] left a card for you.

A letter from Street[5] about price of Glass. The essential part illegible. I shall ⟨write?⟩ for explanation.

984. [1] B.L. V: 554. Autograph. No docket. Addressed: 'To / Colonel Bentham / At / Andrew Lindegren's Esq / Portsmouth.'
Postmark: 'AU.1.94 A'.
[2] Sir John Sinclair, 1st bart. (1754–1834), president of the Board of Agriculture. See *Correspondence*, iv, 296 and n. 2.
[3] George Rose.
[4] Name partly illegible.
[5] Probably James Street, painter and glazier, 17 Bedford Court, Covent Garden.

985

To Samuel Bentham

2 August 1794 (Aet 46)

Q.S.P. Aug. 2. 1794

Sir John Sinclair has been with me today, stared, was awe-struck, but shewed he knew nothing about the matter. He dines here on *Wednesday*, and *you* and I are to be with him at 4 that day to see his stuffed sheep, his models of machines, and whatever else he has to shew.

Poor dear Mr Rose has met with an accident: no wonder he has never sent me word, as he was to have done. He has got a fall from his Horse, hurt his leg and shoulder, but they say not dangerously. I have just heard it at the Treasury, and just sent in consequence to his House to know how he does after his accident, which will more-over serve in a civil way to remind him of my existence.[2] But you see what a spite all sorts of wicked Fairies and black Enchanters owe us.

Answer come: his compliments, and is a good deal better—blessed be God! As to his compliments, they are no proof of his having heard of the message.

Invitation for us to Sir John Hort's[3] for tomorrow—Answer: you out of town, I going, which (for the day) shall or may be the case.

---

985. [1] B.L. V: 555–6. Autograph. No docket. Addressed: 'To / Colonel Bentham / at Andrew Lindegren's Esq / Portsmouth'.

[2] In B.L. V: 557 is the draft of a formal note, dated 5 August, in which Bentham 'having the pleasure of hearing, that Mr Rose was so well recovered yesterday as to go abroad, hopes he will have the goodness to forgive the liberty taken by Mr Bentham in begging his recollection for the Penitentiary business'. The draft is, however, docketed: 'Not sent'. Another, longer, draft, written on the same day, asking 'to be relieved at any price from the state of suspense in which I have been lingering for so many years' is also docketed 'Not sent' (B.L. V: 574). There is also a draft of a letter to Nepean, composed a day or so later, which begins 'Not knowing when Mr Rose would see me, or whether he ever meant to see me, the project moreover (to say nothing of the projector) being in the Road to Ruin, my only resource was in Mr Long. I told him how matters stood—he said he would see you about it and appointed me tomorrow at ½ after 1, to hear the result'. This draft is docketed 'Not finished nor sent' (B.L. V: 575–6).

[3] Bentham had met Hort at Lansdowne House in 1791 (see *Correspondence*, iv, 99 n. 6).

986

FROM SIR JOHN SINCLAIR

10 August 1794

Dear Sir

I happen'd to dine in company with Mr. Jay[2] the American
minister, Mr Pulteney,[3] Sir John Macpherson,[4] etc., and having
mentioned the Panopticon, they expressed a strong desire to see it.
If therefore it is not inconvenient for you, I shall take the liberty
of bringing them to Queen's Square Place, on Tuesday at $\frac{1}{2}$ past
12.   With regard
                    believe me—
                       Yours
                   John Sinclair
Whitehall,
Sunday morning

987

TO WILLIAM PULTENEY

15 August 1794 (Aet 46)

Mr. Pulteney having expressed to *Colonel* Bentham a curiosity
to know something of the history of the Panopticon business, *Mr*

986. [1] B.L. V: 558–9. Autograph. Docketed: '1794 Aug 10 / Panopt / Sir J. Sinclair
Whitehall / to / J.B. Q.S.P. / for Pulteney, Jay etc. to see Panopt.'
Addressed: 'Jeremy Bentham Esqr / Queen's Square Place'.
[2] John Jay (1745–1829), American statesman and diplomat, one of the negotiators
of the peace in 1783; U.S. Secretary for Foreign Affairs, 1784–9, and in 1789 Chief
Justice; in 1794 he was in England concluding with Lord Grenville the Jay Treaty; he
returned to America to become governor of New York, 1795—1801. Visits by Jay to
the Benthams to see the Panopticon model and 'a number of curious and very useful
machines to be introduced into the penitentiary' are mentioned in *Correspondence and
Public Papers of John Jay, 1791–1826*, ed. Henry P. Johnston, 4 vols., 1893, iv, 46–7.
[3] (Sir) William Pulteney (1729–1805), Scottish advocate and M.P., 1768–74 and
1775–1805. He had changed his name from Johnstone in 1767, when his wife inherited
the estates of the earl of Bath. His title came in September 1794, when he succeeded to
the baronetcy of his brother, Sir George Johnstone, who had been governor of West
Florida, 1763–7 (see *Correspondence*, ii, 102 and n, 103–5).
[4] Sir John Macpherson, 1st bart. (1745–1821), temporarily governor-general of
India, 1785–6; M.P., 1779–82 and 1796–1802; a crony of the Prince of Wales, with a
dubious reputation.
987. [1] B.L. V: 560. Autograph draft. Docketed: '1794 Aug. 5 / Panopt / J.B. Q.S.P. /
to / Pulteney Picadilly / with Panopticon Book / and Proposal.'

Bentham takes the liberty of begging his acceptance of a copy of the book, and accompanies it with a copy of the original proposal in manuscript which has in substance been accepted, begging the favour of Mr Pulteney to return the manuscript when perused. As to the plates, they together with the impression were nearly destroy'd by a fire: Plates I and II are superseded by the improved construction which Mr Pulteney saw: of Plate III Mr Bentham sends a copy which is at Mr Pulteney's service if he wishes to keep it, otherwise he will have the goodness to return it.

Queen's Square Place Westmr Aug. 15. 1794

988

To Henry Dundas

16 August 1794 (Aet 46)

Queen's Square Place Westminster
August 16th 1794.

Sir

On Saturday last I was favoured with an audience of a few minutes by Mr Long, on the subject of the Penitentiary business: and as the result was, a recommendation on his part, to state to you at large, what I was ready to have stated equally at large, and did in part state to him, it becomes necessary for me to trouble you in some measure with what passed on that occasion between that gentleman and me.

His proposition was, that two Surveyors should be appointed, by a day he mentioned, to make choice, under the Act, of a spot for the purpose, intimating that it was with a view of finding out some other spot to serve in lieu of the present one: and, if I did not misunderstand him, he proposed to be present on the occasion as well as

---

988. [1] U.C. cxviii: 41–2 and 68–80. Autograph, signed, fair copy of letter and postscript, with Memorial to the Lords of the Treasury and Table of Contents in copyist's hand in between (fos. 43–66). There are autograph drafts of parts of the letter and memorial in U.C. cxviii: 2–40, and an incomplete second fair copy in fos. 110–22. There is another partial draft, including the table of contents, in B.L. V: 561–8. Dundas complained of the form and length of the letter and memorial, which together amounted to 80 pages in manuscript, and this signed fair copy may have been the one returned to Bentham from Dundas on 25 September (see letter 999).

Only the letter and the postscript part of the communication of 16 August are printed below, together with the Table of Contents (989), which sufficiently indicates the scope of the returned Memorial. The much shorter Memorial, which Bentham drew up in October at the suggestion of Dundas, is noted below (letter 1020).

myself.[2] My answer was, that as I could not hold myself concluded by the judgment of any two Surveyors, and I was satisfied by experiment that every search after an attainable spot that should in my judgment be '*as proper and convenient*' (to use the words of the Act) would be fruitless, I should not think myself justified, in concurring with the proposition, of his putting himself to any such trouble: and that, if it was the decision of Administration to refuse the old spot, I thought I could not be too early in begging leave to drop the business altogether: adding, what was most true, that my resolution to that effect was not the result of the whim or ill humour of the moment, but of a long-continued and most deliberate reflection, grounded on reasons which I was ready to submitt to him at large. It was thereupon that he gave it as his opinion, from which I saw no reason to withhold my acquiescence, that you, Sir, were the person to whom any such determination, as well as the reasons on which it was grounded, would with most propriety be submitted in the first instance.

It is for this purpose that I take the liberty of troubling you, Sir, with the following Memorial, which I had been preparing for the Lords of the Treasury, which had the business of the Land principally for its object, and which was nearly finished, when information was given me of a disposition, which I had flattered myself, would have rendered any such address unnecessary.[3]

*   *   *

Here, Sir, ends the intended Memorial. But in the course of my conversation with Mr Long, some hints fell from that gentleman, which could not, as it seems to me, be with equal propriety taken notice of in any such paper, and which at the same time seemed too material not to be reported, Sir, to you. His notion was, that there might be a spot found, such as is or might be made equally eligible, somewhere on Hounslow Heath, inasmuch as it has, or is at one time or other to have, the benefit of water carriage. My answer was, that such a spot, if it does exist (for I know of no navigable canal as yet existing on Hounslow Heath) would not by any means be equally eligible: not with a view to the public service, for want of equal vicinity to the great seat of public inspection, the Metropolis: not with a view to my own private economy (an object essentially connected with the public service) for want of equal vicinity to that great depôt of raw materials and finished goods.

[2] Marginal addition in pencil: 'By a subsequent letter of his it appears that as to his *presence*, I did misunderstand him.'
[3] The Memorial follows at this point.

On my speaking of the faith of the engagement, and of the old spot as the basis of the proposal that had been accepted, he had thereupon the candour to admitt, that certainly whatever were the terms contained in it, I could not be considered as bound by those terms, were the old spot to be taken from me: and that if it were, I should as certainly be at liberty to propose new terms, such as might be sufficient to indemnify me for the difference. My answer was, that with regard to *vicinity to the seat of public inspection*, I did not conceive it proper for me to barter away, for any emolument to myself, an advantage of such importance to the public service: that with regard to the *vicinity to the market*, I was altogether incapable of finding *data* whereon to fix the quantum of indemnification I was to require: and that moreover, in my conception, any such demand would be useless, since Administration never would comply with it: they ought not, therefore, said I, they would not. Mr Long.—They ought not?—*that* surely is a matter for them to judge of: if they should think otherwise, what concern is that of your's?

Mr Bentham.—Certainly it is for them to judge of: and were I already apprized of their judgment, and that it was to that effect, inference would be at an end. But till I *am* apprized of such their judgment, the consideration of what in my humble conception they *ought* to do, is the only means I have of judging what they *will* do: and, as to the conclusion, that if they ought not they will not, I hope it is not an unfair one.—If, for example, I were to demand £15 a year a head (which I declare beforehand I would not take) instead of the £12, that is, for the thousand men £3,000 for my life at least, and perhaps for ever, could Administration be justified in saddling the nation with that expence, merely to oblige a set of individuals, who cry out against what has been submitted to without a murmur by as many sets of individuals as there are prisons in the kingdom?

Mr Long, who had not the circumstances of the case, as stated in the above Memorial, present to his mind, seemed to think at the moment, there might be no impropriety in such a transaction: but, as it was agreed between us, that any thing more on the subject, addressed to him at that time, would be lost labour, I spared him the trouble of hearing the greatest part, of what, I am sorry, I can not avoid being so troublesome, Sir, as to address to you.

In the case I was putting to Mr Long, I spoke only of the thousand men, for which by the agreement I am to be paid at all events. But what if all the prisoners, who would otherwise go to the Hulks or to New South Wales, were to be consigned to the Penitentiary establishment? They have been frequently about 2,000: they may be more: call them 2,000 at a time. This number would, I presume, sooner or later be given me: for while Penitentiary management is to be had at £12 a head, Hulk-management at £21 a head, or even New-South-Wales management at I don't know how much more per head, will, in regard to sentences for short terms at least, hardly be preferred. Here then £6,000 a year at the least, instead of the £3,000, is the amount of the expence the public would be put to, to afford me an indemnification even upon this narrow scale, so narrow that I declare at the same time it would not satisfy me. This, annually: and that without a farthing abatement in the expence of purchase-money, since, as I have stated in the Memorial, if there be a farthing's-worth less of new land given me than what the old land would have come to, justice is not done me. *Number*, you will be pleased to observe, Sir, makes no abatement in this part of the expence: if one man works up in a year as much wood or stone as it will cost £3 to convey from the length of Battersea to Hounslow Heath and back again, 2000 men will work up as much as comes to £6,000.—£200,000 is the property invested on the part of the gentlemen at Clapham etc.: £200,000 is accordingly the loss apprehended by those gentlemen, supposing the whole value of all those Villas to be destroyed by the first stroke of the first pickax employ'd in opening ground for the Penitentiary-House, as compleatly as if it were by an earthquake. The gentlemen alluded to reckon at £200,000, a depretiation which I reckon at nothing. I reckon at £100,000 the £6,000 a year, supposed (though insufficient) to be paid by way of indemnity, for the real damage proposed to be created for the sake of saving the gentlemen from that (as I call it) ideal loss. Which calculation then, that of the £200,000, or that of the £100,000, would in your conception, Sir, come nearest to the truth? You, Sir, who have been pleased to declare that you, for your own part, should have no objection to see the establishment set down at Wimbledon, close to your own residence, you, Sir, being judge, can you bring yourself to conceive, that, if set down at Battersea Rise, it should effect the utter destruction, or the de-struction to any thing like £100,000, of the value of the houses at Clapham a mile off?

But this is not all. This charge for difference of carriage of raw materials and finished work being a standing one, the indemnifi-cation for it comes in the shape of *interest*: but there is another charge, which comes in immediately, and for which the indemnifi-cation would call for a large sum at once in the shape of capital. I mean the charge of conveying the materials of the building with

57

all its appendages for the distance which forms the difference between the near spot and the proposed remote one. Four hundred tons of iron now casting form but a small part of the load. Timber, to an amount in point of weight which unless ordered I will not attempt to calculate, form another. Bricks and Mortar, for aught I know, yet another. For the surrounding wall alone (to say nothing of foundation-wall and Out-houses) 2,000 feet of walling 12 foot high. *Et-cæteras*—but I will not trouble you, Sir, with *et-cæteras*.

Now then, Sir, in addition to what I was observing to Mr Long with regard to the improbability of Administration's acceding to any proposal, for an adequate indemnification to me, for the loss of the spot that had been engaged to me, an improbability grounded on the impropriety of any such arrangement on the part of Administration, I will beg leave to consider it with regard to the propriety of the part which *I* should have to act in such a business. As to this matter, Administration, Sir, are certainly the judges, and in the first instance the sole judges of what it may be proper for them to grant: but I, Sir, in my humble sphere am a proper judge, and in the first instance at any rate the sole judge, (Mr Long will not dispute it) of what it may be fit for me to sue for.

Be pleased, Sir, for a moment to consider in what light such a transaction would shew itself to the world; and that, not to the censorious part only, but, I should much fear, to the discerning part of it in general, even the candid part not excepted.

A spot of land, that had been pitched upon for a public establishment, and, by the most unexceptionable and most competent tribunal in the kingdom, had been pronounced the fittest for the purpose, happens to be in the tenure of a noble person of high rank, immense fortune, and great weight in the scale of politics: a weight which for a course of years he had been in the habit of throwing into the scale of opposition. This person, being applied to with all humility to suffer the law to take its course, refuses, and resists as long as it appears to be in his power. Understanding from competent authority that resistance will be unavailing, he at length testifies his acquiescence: and elogiums are now bestowed upon him for a facility, which his superior in tenure, the Archbishop of York had manifested a twelvemonth before, and at the first word. In the course of this business, the Noble Earl finds reason for accepting a seat in Administration. He now retracts his acquiescence. Viewing the proposed establishment from this new elevation, he now regards it again with a disapprobation, of which he makes no secret. He terms the plan 'speculative and visionary': and without vouchsafing to see what the Ministers who thought it otherwise had seen of it, he does what depends upon him to make it so. Being himself a party, he scruples not to stand up against it as a Judge. He stands up against it, and stands alone. He stops it in his own House: he stops it for reasons of which not even that House, much less the public, are let into the confidence. He gets a Q put to it: and this Q consigns it to oblivion for weeks: for weeks after the time, when, according to the representation one of his Majesty's Secretaries of State was pleased to make to the Author of the plan, the delay of a day might have been fatal to it. Another noble person,[4] observing the Bill at the last gasp, and ready to sink under this treatment, forces the attention of Administration to the subject, and thus the Act, after a little parliamentary manufacturing, administered to it in whispers by its noble opponent, at length crawls into existence.—The noble Earl is now dispatched upon an extraordinary mission, as the chosen interpreter of the plans and sentiments of an Administration from which almost till the moment he had kept at a hostile distance. The name of the noble Earl is now no longer mentioned as an opponent to the measure: it need not. In person he is no longer present: but his influence is not the less active and irresistible. An opposition is now brought forward, grounded on objections already negatived by the 12 Judges, whose decision the Lords of the Treasury are called upon to overthrow. They do accordingly dispose themselves to overthrow it: but the claims of the projector of the establishment to whom the first Lord of the Treasury and the principal Secretary of State had pledged themselves to give this very land, to whom they had declared over and over again he should have the land, stare them in the face. This man's mouth was therefore to be stopped: and it is stopped accordingly. He asks £6,000 a year, and £6,000 a year is given him. The contracting Jailor gets his sop: the noble convert to Administration preserves himself from the hardship, of not being exempted from the common lot of subjects: the prospect of a prison is removed from the privileged purlieus of Battersea-Rise: it costs the public no more than £6,000 a year to produce all this accommodation:—and thus every body is satisfied.

Such are the colours in which, according to my humble conception, an arrangement of this stamp would go abroad into the world. I do not say they would in every particular be the true ones: in my own instance I am sure they are not: for no such arrangement, though the £6,000 a year were all clear gain to me, would satisfy me. I do not say they are the true ones: but they have so much the

[4] Perhaps the Duke of Dorset is meant.

59

appearance of being true, and the imputation convey'd by them is at least so plausible, that I must confess, I can not stand it. Were my inclination ever so ductile, I could not bring myself to take a step so perfectly in the teeth of all my former professions and all my former practice: forgive me, Sir, but I have not nerves for it. In Lord Spencer's conception, I understand, his Lordship's receptacle of possible Villas is a sort of Naboth's Vineyard: and myself a sort of would-be David in miniature. According to him, it is the possible Villa that is my great object. Sir, the possible Villa is an object to me, it is true: so was the value of the handkerchief an object to Othello: an object of three and sixpence. Bating a fancy proportioned to an object of some such amount, my humble residence, the little *rus in urbe* that you saw, satisfies me: if it did not, the supposed £6,000 a year, or some such sum, which I beg leave to decline accepting, would, I suppose, be sufficient to procure me a site for a Villa, not inferior even to the so much envied one so highly prized by the noble Earl, who neither intends it for his own residence, nor, for want of certainty of tenure, has it in his power to adapt it in that quality to the residence of others. But what an annuity of £6,000 a year would not purchase for me, were it all clear gain, is that peace of mind and honest pride which I must bid adieu to, were I to betray my trust at the instant of accepting it, by sacrificing in so essential a point the manifest and acknowledged interests of the public service.

I say, *acknowledged*: for really, Sir, this about the importance of the circumstance of vicinity to the capital, as the great seat of inspection, is not an opinion of my *own* starting: it is no new-fangled concept of mine: it has been, without any exception that I know of, the opinion of every man who has turned his thoughts (and great numbers of very respectable men have turned their thoughts) to this part of the subject. It was the opinion (whatsoever difference might arise on the application of it to a particular spot) it was the opinion of all the Judges: it was the opinion of all the Supervisors (and it may be in your recollection, Sir, that there were different sets of them) that were successively appointed for the originally intended Penitentiary-House. It was the opinion of every Committee of the House of Commons that ever sat upon the measure. It was the opinion of Mr Howard, of Mr Whately,[5] and of Dr Fothergill,[6] who

---

[5] George Whatley (d. 1791) was, with Howard and Fothergill, appointed a supervisor of the buildings to be erected under the Penitentiary Act of 1779. He was treasurer of the Foundling Hospital, 1779–91 (see R. H. Nichols, *History of the Foundling Hospital*, 1935).

[6] John Fothergill (1712–80), physician, botanist and philanthropist.

delivered it into the bosom of Mr Howard, sealed with the dying breath of Sir William Blackstone. It was the opinion of Sir Charles Bunbury, Sir Gilbert Elliot and Dr. Bowdler, by whom the present spot was pitched upon for this cause: it was the opinion of the Committee of 1784 of which Sir Charles Bunbury was Chairman: and in whose Report among the advantages which recommended the spot in question to their repeated and maturest choice it occupies a distinguished place. It is, or at any rate very lately was, so much the opinion of Sir Charles Bunbury, that after perusing the paper before submitted to you, Sir, in defence of this very choice, he as pleased to pronounce it, I remember his very word, *unanswerable*.

Indeed, Sir, this sense of the value of authority in such a case is no grimace: and though the affection with which you observed me clinging to the robes of the Judges, drew a smile from you, as if something of affection had been betray'd by it, and though some awkwardness of expression in a situation rather new to me, afforded, I make no doubt, but too good a warrant, for any suspicions you might have conceived at the time, you will, I flatter myself, have been satisfied, by this time at least, that my reluctance to hazard any choice of my own, in competition with one that had received the sanction of such authority, was not without a practical and intelligible cause. That, if I were obliged to look out for a new spot, I should prefer leaving absolutely to the 12 Judges, the choice of the spot I was to lay out my money upon, to the choosing it myself, or even, that if I were obliged to stand by the choice of others, those Magistrates would be the persons of all others whom I should wish to commission for the purpose, is more, I trust, than I did say, more assuredly than I could mean to say. But, in the instance in question, I knew what their choice had been. I knew it was a good one, and so good an one, for myself as well as for the public, that not even the privilege of making a fresh choice of my own, was ever capable of drawing off my wishes, from a ready made one which nobody could blame me for, and nobody, as I thought, refuse me. Hard it would be upon me indeed, if the being so perfectly contented with the lot, which I conceived had fallen to me, should be considered as a ground of censure. What, if instead of being so contented as I am with this spot, for my thousand prisoners, for another thousand, or for any number I can have a prospect of, I had asked for another spot, in lieu of the old one, or, as the last set of Supervisors did, /Sir C. Bunbury at the head of them/,[7] in addition to it, as not think-

[7] This insertion is in pencil.

ing it large enough for the reception of 300 females in addition to the 600 males?

No, Sir, neither on this occasion nor on any other, do I give myself out as one, who, where honour is not concerned or some satisfaction that money will not buy, is in the smallest degree less attentive to personal interest, no not to pecuniary interest, than the passenger who is passing by your window: or that accordingly, were damage to happen to me, by the act of government, without any concurrence of mine, I should feel the smallest scruple of asking, any more than of receiving, the fullest indemnification. But that, Sir, with submission, is quite different from the present case. Damage, real damage, is to be created, created by Administration in the teeth of the decision of the law, created, in order to avoid creating an alledged damage, which the law had ordered to be created, and which the 12 Judges have decided to be no *injury*. I am to be a principal in creating this real damage, it is at my sollicitation that it is to be created, and thus it is that the justice of an indemnification, and of my claim to it is to arise. First I am to create the damage: and then I am to call for the indemnification. Sir, I can not do this, indeed I can not. I can not ask of government that which, not on pecuniary considerations only, but considerations of so much higher import, it seems to me so evident that government ought not to grant.

But, says Mr Long, *leave that to us, whose business it is: what concern is it of yours?*—With great submission to that gentleman, to whose candour I really feel myself much obliged, it is not impossible to a man to have public feelings, without being, or ever having been, or ever having thought of being, a member of any Jacobinical society, or of any other popular society, and at the same time without being in the pay of government: my whole life, if I must confess it, my whole life, obscure as it has been, has been made up of such feelings. There is scarce that nook or cranny in government that I have not pried into in my time, in every one with a wish, and in some of late with a hope, which now I am on the point of foregoing, of seeing economy, and that not as a mere inactive spectator, of seeing improved economy introduced into it. —Yes, Sir, if I may be allowed to say so, I felt for the public, and that with still more sensibility, perhaps, than I do now, before the Honourable gentleman had begun to feel for any thing. I will allow him without any dispute as much public zeal as he pleases to express, but I will not allow him the monopoly of it.— This is what I apprehended: this is what I expressed my apprehensions of from the very first: this comes of being a Contracting Jailor.

Mr Nepean, in the course of this negotiation, Mr Nepean, in observing my eagerness to take upon me some burthen, or to reject some benefit, has, in his good-humoured way, more than once called me an odd fellow, or told me I was mad. Sir, with equal good humour towards a man whom I love, and whom every body loves, permitt me to maintain, against him as well as all gainsayers, that a man may not only take up burthens, but push aside money, and yet be in his sober senses. He has seen yourself, Sir, for example, (with respect be it spoken) in addition to the burthen of the Treasurership of the Navy, in addition to the burthen of the chairmanship of the Board of Controul, take up the still heavier burthen of the Secretary-ship of State. He has seen you, at the same time that you were taking up the latter burthen, refusing the Salary that stood annexed to it. Yet, with submission to Mr Nepean, who to be sure has better opportunities of judging than I can boast of, with submission, I say, to Mr Nepean, I will not-withstanding be bold enough to maintain, though at my humble distance, that you, Sir, were then, and still are, (for if you are not I don't know who is) in your sober senses.

As to the disposal of the proposed indemnification-money, to be sure it does not belong to me to decide, but if the opinion of so obscure an individual may venture to peep forth, it is my humble apprehension that at a time like the present, some more necessary a use, than the giving it out in indemnifications for voluntary damage, might be found for it. But if I am wrong in this, and money must at any rate be given out to quiet matters, the persons on whom it might be bestowed, I should conceive, with most economy as well as propriety, are, not myself, who am so perfectly contented with the provision so long ago made by the law, but rather the gentlemen who are discontented with it. Were a number not more than half a dozen of them, for example, picked out for this purpose, and picked out with due selection, I would venture to undertake, Sir, there would not be a man left who would ever give you any trouble. I say, with most economy; for though I confess myself but indifferently qualified for entering into their conception of the damage, yet in their instance a douceur to rather less amount than the supposed £6,000 a year or £100,000 capital, (added to the unliquidated principal money) which would in my instance prove ineffectual, would, in the other instance, I should flatter myself, suffice. As to the proportions, an equal distribution, or if differences

63

be admitted, a gradation of douceur in proportion to the gradations of public situation and fortune, might at first sight be the most obvious plan. But, if I might be permitted to advise, as the abhorrence testified to the nuisance is, not in the inverse, but in the direct ratio of the distance, so should the quantum of douceur applied to conquer that abhorrence. And as to the persons who would be to have the nuisance under their very noses, as they are whimsical enough to be fond of it, and are ready to declare themselves so, as it is no nuisance to them, they would have no pretensions to diminish the fund created for the benefit of their nicer neighbours. But I beg pardon for applying so disrespectful an epithet as that of *whimsical* to such of the gentlemen as have the misfortune to be *un*discontented, for if I have not been misinformed, you, Sir, according to your declarations, would, as well as Mr Nepean, have been of the undiscontented party, had you been in their place. Convinced that under these circumstances, had they been all present to your mind, nothing but the importunity of such of the gentlemen whom you can not avoid seeing, and who have inevitable access to you in Parliament or elsewhere, could have prevailed upon you, so much as to think of departing, from an engagement so deliberately entered into, and so repeatedly confirmed, or of allowing claims of exemption so deliberately and unanimously disallowed by the 12 Judges, I can not, I say, help submitting to you, Sir, whether the gentlemen, by whom alone a complaint against the dispensations of the law has been preferred, are not the first from whom, if from any body, a claim for indemnification should be called for.

Now, Sir, as to my declining to accept the offer, obliging as it was, that was made me by Mr Long, with regard to the expedition for looking out for other land.—My expectation was, I must confess, Sir, either that Administration, after due consideration given to the case, would give up the idea of any further choice, and give me the old spot at the first word, or else that some particular spot, such as Administration, with or without hearing the gentlemen who oppose the existing choice had seen reason to be satisfied with, which they thought would be, or might be made to be, '*as proper and convenient*', (though I, without their knowledge, happened to be convinced of the contrary) and which was known to be in readiness to be taken possession of without opposition, would have been proffer'd to me. I was the more strongly impressed with this idea, in as much as I had repeatedly understood from Sir Charles Bunbury that there were two spots, both in Battersea Parish, and both of which he specified, which the gentlemen who refused me the other were (to my great surprize) ready to insure to me. Instead of that, no spot was in readiness, the four counties, or at least the environs of the navigation, actual and possible, were to be searched for some other spot, and my pretensions to the existing spot were to be given up, as a preliminary to the search after the possible one. In stating the matter in these terms, far be it for me to impute, for in my conscience I do not impute, any thing unreasonable to Mr Long: so far from it, that in his place I dont see what more favourable proposal to me he could have made. A very obliging one, I am sure, it was on his part: for, in addition to the two Surveyors, he was to have gone upon the wild-goose chace as well as I. /This it appears was a misapprehension on my part./[8] A wild-goose chace I call it, because having gone upon it myself I found it so: but this was more than he knew or could know.

Sir, I hope, and humbly conceive, I have now given you reasons enough, if you will be pleased to use them: and it is with this view that I propose printing the Memorial, that their Lordships, in the event of their deeming it fit to accede to the prayer respecting the Land, may, if such should be their pleasure, order copies to be given to the gentlemen concerned: or that in the other event I may possess the means of justifying myself, upon occasion, against any imputation of levity or imprudence in the eyes of the public and my friends.

It remains for me to beg leave to intimate to you, Sir, the necessity I feel myself under, a necessity which can not be expressed in too distinct language, and which is, that of declining to propose to their Lordships any other spot as equally '*proper and convenient*' with the old one: the consequence of which, unless their Lordships should be pleased either at your representation, Sir, to grant the prayer of the Memorial in this behalf, or else to offer me some equally proper and convenient spot, which it is clear to me they can not do, and which I do not expect they should think of doing, the consequence, I say, with respect to myself is, the relinquishment of the whole business, and the downfall of all my hopes. Anxious as I am to possess a place in your good opinion, Sir, however small an one I may be able to boast of in your favour, I hope I shall be permitted to observe, that even in this instance the caprice, if it be one, is not a caprice of mine. Steering by the light of precedent and authority, upon this occasion, as I am happy to do upon all

[8] Inserted in pencil.

occasions, where I do not see Reason clearly pointing the opposite way, a consideration that makes the affliction of this step sit the less heavy on me, is the reflection that in taking it, I do but follow the course chalked out for me by the good Howard. He too, when thwarted in this, which in every sense he regarded as the first point, he too conceived himself called upon to relinquish the object of his fondest hopes. Not that his inducements came near in point of cogency to mine. He quitted, because his opinion was crossed by the 12 Judges: I, because even that power is not strong enough to support me. He, because his particular notions of expediency were over-ruled by law: I, because in my instance law itself its over-power'd by favour. No Administration had engaged to him to give him the object of his preference: no imputation of sinister motives could have attached upon his acquiescence: I, besides sacrificing the acknowledged interests of the service, must either submitt to a breach of engagement, and such an one as would expose my capacity of fulfilling my part in it, to a peril which I can not calculate, or ask indemnity, for damage of my own creation, at the expence of my character and my conscience.

I wait your decision, Sir, with the anxiety that you may imagine, and my humble hope is, that as it is the *last* I shall have to trouble you for, it will not be a *tardy* one.—For it is time, indeed it is, Sir, that I should withdraw myself from this scene of uninterrupted anxiety and fruitless sollicitation, consult my health which has not been bettered by it, gather up the broken remnants of my fortune, and share them with my Brother whom I have ruined.

I have the honour to subscribe myself, with all respect,
Sir
Your most obedient
and most humble Servant
Jeremy Bentham.

Right Hon:ble H^y. Dundas
etc. etc. etc.

989

TO THE LORDS OF THE TREASURY

16 August 1794 (Aet 46)

Memorial Contents. 1794, July

I	1	7
Statement of the proceedings that have been had in the business.	Treaty between Memorialist and Administration wanting nothing but signature p. 1	1. Situation of Memorialist's Brother to whom he is indebted for the building and 2. the system of machinery for employ-ment p. 5.
II Prayer of the Memorial	2 Suspended on apprehension of want of parliamentary powers. p. 2	8 2. Advantageous undertaking foregone on this account. p. 6.
III Reasons why despatch is pray'd		
IV Reasons why the Memorialist should be the Feoffee.	3 Bill brought in accordingly and passed. p. 2.	9 3. Capital already expended £5,000
V Reasons why the old spot is pray'd for and that *instanter*	4 Powers given (inter alia) to Treasury by the Act. p. 3.	10 4. Irremediable pre-judice suffered by/ peculiar to/ Memorialist's Brother by the loss of his situation abroad. p. 7.
	5 Prayer in consequence 1. To fix on the *old* ground 2. To appoint the Memorialist *Feoffee* 3. To apply for the Kings Warrant for £10,000	11 5. Expence of keeping workmen together— £2000 a year. p. 8.
	6 Reasons for praying despatch p. 5.	12 6. £2,000 thus sunk irretrievably in the course of the year of suspense, besides the

---

989. [1] B.L. V: 567–8. Copy. Docketed: 'J.B. Q.S.P. / to / Lords of the Treasury / contents of Memorial / 1794. Aug 16'.

As noted on p. 54 n. 1, the Ms. summarises the long memorial contained in Bentham's letter to Dundas of 16 August (letter 988). The summary is arranged in nine columns in the original: I–V on the left, then, reading to the right, 1–9, 10–15, 16–22, 23–29, 29–33, 34–36, 37–38, 39–43. The last column is in rubbed pencil. In the other columns some of the numbering has been altered, and re-altered, in pencil.

profit that might have
been made from it if
applied to the private
undertaking sacrified to
this public one. p. 8.

13
7. The contract growing
irremediably worse and
worse in proportion to
delay. p. 8.

14
8. Work bespoken and
executing on the faith of
the treaty to the amount
of several thousand
pounds. p. 9.

15
Delay to an amount
very injurious to the
Memorialist may arise
out of the terms of the
Act notwithstanding
every despatch the
Board can give.

16
Reasons why the
Memorialist should be
appointed Feoffee
rather than another or
others.
p. 11
1. Dangers of
refractoriness on the
part of any third person
2. of disagreement if
they are several

17
Prayer for the land
confines itself to the old
spot – reasons why p. 13.

18
Reference to paper
given in to Mr Nepean
p. 14.

19. 20
No opposition on the

part of proprietors now
remaining p. 14.

21
Opposition in the
neighbourhood affords
no valid objection.
1. because it applies
equally to every other as
convenient and proper
spot. p. 15.

22
2. because already
over-ruled by the 12
Judges. p. 16.

23
No censure meant to be
cast on the opponents.
p. 17.

24
The principal opponents
are very distant
neighbours. p. 18.

25
The nearest neighbours
consent. p. 18.

26
Two other proposed
spots can not be
accepted. p. 20.

27
1. Not that by Battersea
Bridge. p. 20.

28
nor Battersea-Common
Field. p. 23.

29
nor any part of
Hounslow Heath.

29
Further reasons for
rejecting the latter—
1. Engagement to ensure
the lives of the
prisoners. p. 26.

30
2. Similarity of the spot
to that before rejected
at Limehouse. p. 28.

31
No other fit places. p. 29.

32
Inutility of hearing any
thing on the other side.
No parties to hear. p. 31.

33
Such a hearing would
on account of the delay
be pregnant with
injustice to the
Memorialist. p. 33.

34
Treasury bound by the
Treaty to fix upon the
old spot if claimed by
him. p. 34.

35
Though a hearing were
intended such fixation
ought in the mean time
to be made de bene esse
and instanter, as it could
not be conclusive. p. 35.

36
No agreement preclusive
of such a choice can
have been made by
Administration. p. 37.

37
The optional clause is
no proof of such an
agreement, but the
contrary. p. 39.

38
nor could /can/ it stand
if made. p. 43.

39
Magnitude of the price
above what was

expected no objection.
p. | |

[40?]

No [. . .?] to be
apprehended from
adhering to the old land
chosen

42
Great censure from
departing from it

43
Lordships will decide at
once if you see that no
good could result from

the enquiry, and a great
deal of inconvenience
could not but result
from it

990

To Samuel Bentham

20 August 1794 (Aet 46)

Hendon Wedny Aug. 20th 1794

As soon as you are returned to London, exhibit the light of
your countenance at Hendon. Pour passer le tems, I have been
amusing myself with forming plans and making calculations about
Luggage Ports:[2] and the profits are enormous: Panopticon is a
trifling business to it. What is best, the trial would not be out of the
reach of our faculties: even those immediately at command: and
as we have been prating to Sinclair about it, and Sinclair hears
prating in order to prate, I am apprehensive of rascals starting up,
and getting beforehand with us. We must have a patent: the first
plan itself would be sufficient to warrant one: but by way of dust
for people's eyes we will put in your divided axle-tree carts, with
some et ceteras, though certainly it would do with ordinary carts.
To speak in round numbers the money paid from London to
Edinburgh is £30,000 a year: expences in the Cart plan I do not
make much above £10,000: capital requisite from about £1000 to
£4000, according to circumstances. Here would be £20,000 a year
gained, say £15,000: add from Edinburgh to London £15,000, or
say only £10,000 more. This would make £25,000 a year for that
Road alone. This I can assure you is very sober: but come and see—
I have been collecting facts from Smith,[3] who was a Carter he says
40 year. Upsal[4] is likewise employ'd in fact—collecting as he will
tell you: he has just furnished useful facts from his experiences in
Russia. He is zealous, but a little hasty and inaccurate in his
conceptions.

---

990. [1] B.L. V: 569–70. Autograph. No docket. Addressed: 'To / Colonel Bentham.'
[2] That is, costs of portage.
[3] Not identified.
[4] Richard Upsal, the English sailor who had been in Russia with Samuel.

991

TO SAMUEL BENTHAM

21 August 1794 (Aet 46)

I can not make time to go to town today: you must absolutely come down to me this evening, and I will return with you tomorrow morning early: Upsal will escort you in the evening at least half way.

The case is, I wish you not to say anything to Lindegren or anybody till I see you: the business is too tempting to be trusted even to him without a Patent. I have no doubt of the validity of such Patent. I have since my last been more particular in my calculations. The result is

Road between Edinburgh and London, every other day from each place. Cart Caravan consisting of 5 carts each carrying a ton. Relays, 18: Stages, 36: Rests, 3, an hour each: rate of travelling 21 Miles a day each. Relay all the year round (which pr Smith can be done).

Sum necessary to be advanced for a Months trial, no more than	£900. 10. 0.
Capital for a whole year including the above	£2000
Receipt daily at £16 per ton instead of £22 the present charge and for 4 ton only, being only $\frac{4}{5}$ of a full freight	64. 0. 0.
Deduct daily expenditure interest of the above capital included	31. 6. 6.

Neat[2]	
Receipt per annum at the above rate at 312 days (Sundays being excluded) to the year	19,968. 0. 0.
Deduct expenditure per annum	9,765. 0. 0.
Remains neat	£10,203. 0. 0.

I have almost drawn out the account in form, but not quite enough to send you. I shall by the time you come, if you come this evening: and it is for the sake of conferring about the eligibility of displaying the whole to L.[3] that I want to talk to you: if you do

---

991. [1] B.L. V: 571–2. Autograph. No docket. Addressed: 'To / Colonel Bentham.'

[2] A variant of 'net' as opposed to 'gross'.

[3] Probably Andrew Lindigren.

70

not come, which would disappoint me very much, send me Upsal tomorrow so as to be here by 9. I have the whole plan ready cut and dry, and do not want a Lindegren, or any creature but myself to execute it.

Hendon Aug. 21. Thursday 1794

992

To Evan Nepean

26 August 1794 (Aet 46)

Queen's Square Place Tuesday Aug: 26. 1794

Dear Sir

Leaving my name at the door of your office just now, I was informed that you were very busy as well as unwell, for both which reasons I forbore attempting to trouble you. In the latter respect I sympathise with you the more sincerely as it happens to be in some measure my own case. I shall return to Hendon tomorrow morning early, and make another attempt on Friday, between which day and the present it may possibly be in your power to procure me the *Yes* or the *No*, to one or other of which, after what has passed, I cannot help conceiving myself to have some pretensions. My object in wishing to trouble you, being only to sollicit the one or the other answer in writing, (for on such occasion conversation in your office would amount to nothing elsewhere) if it should be in your power in the mean time to obtain for me and transmitt to me such official answer, it will not only put the speedier period to my sufferings but save you from a task which I am as fully sensible as you can be, can not in one event be of a very pleasant nature. In any event, be assured, I shall never cease to remember how much I have been,   Dear Sir

Your obliged humble Servant

Jeremy Bentham

Evan Nepean Esqr.

P.S. I take for granted my letter to Mr Dundas including a copy of my intended Memorial,[2] reached your hands. I directed it for

992. [1] B.L. V: 573. Autograph draft. Docketed: '1794. Aug. 26. / Panopt / J.B. Q.S.P. / to / Nepean Whitehall / Solliciting answer from Dundas to letter of 16th delivd 17th.'

[2] See letter 988, n. 1. There are two other draft letters dated August 1794, one addressed to Rose, the other to Nepean; both docketed 'not sent'. The former begins:

Mr Dundas, to your care and left it myself at your office on Sunday sennight.

993

TO SAMUEL BENTHAM

4 September 1794 (Aet 46)

Hendon, Thursday Sept. 4th 1794.

Poor unhappy divided-Axle-tree! Mr Smith's report of it is terribly unfavourable—never was so shaken in his life!—could scarcely bear it: and it draws heavier for the horse than a common cart. He goes to town with it to return it on Saturday morning: he sets out not later than 6 o'clock. Now if you will come here tomorrow and sleep here tomorrow night, you may return in it in the morning, and thence you will be the better able to judge how much there is of fact and how much of prejudice, and whether the defects, if real, are radical or curable.

I got no lift in it myself. I had a hard matter to crawl to my journey's end. Today the looseness is abated, but the nausea and listlessness not quite gone.

994

TO SAMUEL BENTHAM

9 September 1794 (Aet 46)

Hendon Tuesday Sept. 9th 1794

Send me todays and yesterdays Newspapers

Likewise Cooper's pamphlet[2] about the manner of settling in America.

'Having had the satisfaction of hearing yesterday morning of your being happily recovered to go abroad, I hope you will have the goodness to excuse the liberty I take in mentioning my business' (B.L. V: 574). The second begins: 'Not knowing when Mr Rose would see me, or whether he ever meant to see me, the project moreover (to say nothing of the projector) being in The Road to Ruin, my only resource was in Mr. Long . . .' (BL. V: 575–6).

993. [1] B.L. V: 577–8. Autograph. Addressed: 'To Colonel Bentham / Queen's Square Place / Westminster.' Stamped: 'Not pd'. Postmark: '7 o clock. SE.4. 94 EVEN'.

994. [1] B.L. V: 579. Autograph. Addressed: 'To Colonel Bentham.'

[2] *Some Information respecting America*, London, J. Johnson, 1794; 2nd edn., 1795, by Thomas Cooper (1759–1840), an Oxford graduate and barrister, who went to the United States in the winter of 1793–4 to find out the possibilities for a man like himself, with 'a small fortune, and a large family, to settle in America'. He decided to stay

Send the enclosed to Paynes[3]
Send the book herewith returned Romance of real life[4] to Fox's Library Dartmouth Street[5]
The Peerages in fee that go to females will answer the purpose to a T without calculation: and there are at least $\frac{1}{2}$ a dozen of them in Scotland alone[6]
I shall be in town probably tomorrow: either breakfast, dinner, or at night—If you have any thing to influence the choice, write me word.

995

FROM SIR JOHN SINCLAIR

10 September 1794

Edinburgh, 10th September, 1794.

Dear Sir,

I have already seen sheep with four horns, such as you describe, both from Sweden and Persia, and I have no doubt that they are of the primitive race; for one of them came from Mount Ararat, and the Armenians say, is the lineal descendant and representative of the ram that descended from the Ark of Noah. It will be necessary, however, to examine his tail as well as his horns, to ascertain whether he exactly resembles the sheep already in our possession. When he gets old, it would be a pity *not* to have him stuffed and preserved. I have ordered Cambridgeshire[2] to be sent to Queen Square Place. There is no doubt but that the Guinea grass might be assimilated to our climate in three generations. I hope that you will contrive to give it as fair a trial as possible. I set out in three or four weeks for the *Ultima Thule*, but return in about a month, and

there, partly because he preferred the political climate to that of contemporary Britain. He became a judge in Pennsylvania and later a professor of mineralogy and chemistry, publishing numerous works, including an encyclopedia of mineralogy.
[3] Missing; perhaps material for printing by Payne.
[4] *The Romance of Real Life*, 3 vols., London, T. Cadell, 1787, by Mrs Charlotte Smith: a collection of stories based on a translation of F. Guyot de Pitaval's *Les causes célèbres de tous les cours souveraines du royaume*, Paris, 1775–87. Charlotte Smith (1749–1806) was well-known by 1794 for her poems and five novels.
[5] James Fox, bookseller.
[6] Apparently a reply to an unknown query from Samuel.
995. [1] Bowring, x, 300–1. Introductory note: 'Sir John Sinclair writes:'. Clearly a reply to a missing letter from Bentham.
[2] Charles Vancouver, *General View of the Agriculture of the County of Cambridge*, 2 parts, 1794, one of the huge series of county surveys sponsored by the new Board of Agriculture, which came out in several editions for twenty years from 1793.

will then be happy to have the pleasure of meeting you at Edinburgh.[3]—Believe me, with regard, your very faithful, humble servant.

996

FROM PHILIP METCALFE

12 September 1794

Dear Adelphi,

How goes on, Panopticon? are you at work, or have you touched a little more of the ready by way of security? Tell me about the Chinese embassy, and, above all, give me a good account of yourself—

997

TO PHILIP METCALFE

14 September 1794 (Aet 46)

Hendon, Middlesex, Sept. 14, 1794.

Dear Metcalf,

Very badly; worse than badly: for it stands stock-still. A letter I had occasion to write by Long's suggestion to Dundas,[2] so long ago as this day month, has remained unnoticed, partly, I suppose, on account of Nepean's illness, whom I have not been able to get to the speech of in all this time.

Meantime, the whole undertaking does not know whether it is to live, or be starved to death. So long ago as August twelvemonth, I was to have had £10,000 from Government; three months afterwards, £10,000 more: it was all agreed upon—nothing wanting but signature, when the idea was started by Administration that Parliament was necessary. I have spent in one way or other about £6000 upon it; of which, after much ado, I got, as you know, £2000 Treasury currency—that is between £1800 and £1900. A letter

[3] There is no other indication that Bentham contemplated visiting Scotland at this time.

996. [1] Bowring, x, 301. A quotation from a letter to 'the brothers', contained in an explanation by Bowring of letter 997, beginning 'Bentham's answer to Philip Metcalf's inquiry, from Brighton, (of 12th September 1794,) which was in these terms'.

997. [1] Bowring, x, 301-2. A reply to letter 996 above.

[2] He probably means the letter and Memorial of 16 August (see letter 988 and the Table of Contents of the Memorial, p. 67 above).

I wrote to Pitt, at the suggestion of Nepean, for the first of the above instalments of £10,000, as soon as the bill had passed the Lords—that is, in June, remains unnoticed.[3]

It costs me at the rate of more than £2000 a-year merely to keep the men together; if one has the spare £2000 a-year, it is very well; but if he has not—?

Some of the men I have discharged already: the greatest part will be discharged in about three weeks more; we may go on lingering with the rest a little while longer. When they are dispersed, how we are to get such another set again, if we should want them, God knows. Such a set, after the instruction they have had, scarce exists in London, nor consequently, in the world.

Things standing thus, we are deliberating upon two projects,— one is to try to mortgage, and go on with some of his inventions on a contracted plan, and in a private way, if Panopticon should linger longer; the other is, for Sam to go back to Russia, where, though absence has lost him his regiment, (better than any two in his Majesty's service,) he is not without friends: a catastrophe of which, by the by, Mr Pitt had notice before it happened, and since it happened. Mr Pitt assured the D. of Dorset in June, that everything should be concluded to our satisfaction; the satisfaction, hitherto, has not been great. If Sam goes, there is an end of Panopticon in all its shapes, and of everything that hangs to it.

Sam flies to company for relief: I to solitude and scribbling. He is gone down to his friends at Portsmouth. Vexation has not been of service to either of our healths. Q.S.P., to both of us, is like school to a truant schoolboy. The only comfort is, I have just now got possession of a new channel for coming at Dundas, through which, I have some reason to hope, I shall get him to speak, I should say, to write, (for speaking is as good as nothing,) before many days are at an end.

As to the Chinese embassy, I know no more about it, than the Pope of Rome: had I been in sorts I should, before now, have known as much about it as other people. If I can muster up exertion enough, I will hunt out Staunton, and enable myself to give some satisfaction to your curiosity.[4] Sir J. Sinclair brought him to see our lions, when Sam only was at home. Then a party was made for us both to dine with him at a common friend's in the city, he wanting

---

[3] Missing, unless Bentham means the letter of 18 June, the surviving draft of which is addressed not to Pitt but to Nepean (see letter 978).

[4] Sir George Leonard Staunton, who had recently returned from Macartney's embassy to China.

to see the lions a second time, with the other lion-owner. He had with him a young Jay, little more than fledged, and Colonel Turnbull his secretary.[5] All of them seem pleasant people; with more sense and talent, or I am mistaken, than would easily be found in an equal set of English diplomatists. Turnbull, you know, I suppose, is a famous son of the brush, and has lived a good deal in England. Chief-justice Jay is a good chief-justice-like looking man, of a sensible, shrewd countenance, rather reserved, but not un-pleasantly so. He had been sitting up best part of the preceding night upon his despatches, which are to be made up by next Thursday; and under the urgency of the pressure he was obliged to miss the party he had made for Q.S.P. in the morning, and to leave dinner early. Sam and I both should like much to cultivate them all; but of course cannot attempt it before Thursday is over, and whether we can find spirits for it afterwards, must depend upon Dr Pitt.

Men who are somewhat in the way of knowing, say that Windham is going into the D. of Portland's place,[6] and the Duke into some other; but all this, if there be any truth in it, you must have heard of long ago from better quarters.

There was a grave assertion in the papers, not many days ago, of Broderick's[7] quitting, (which I should have been sorry for,) and Baldwin the Counsel taking his place. It was supposed to be a joke upon Baldwin,[8] not a shadow of truth in it.

Here you have your queries answered, and little over. Pros-perous or unprosperous—sick or well—weeping or exulting, I am, dear Phil, ever yours,

J.B.

[5] A mistake for 'Trumbull'; John Trumbull (1756–1843), an American artist, who had fought as a colonel in Washington's army and had been briefly imprisoned when he came to London in 1780 as a pupil of Benjamin West. He acted as Jay's private secretary during the treaty negotiations in 1794 and at the same time supervised the engravings of his paintings (see F. Monaghan, *John Jay*, New York, 1935, p. 369).

[6] The rumour that William Windham, who was Secretary at War, July 1794–1801, would replace Portland at the Home Office, proved unfounded. The Duke of Portland stayed in that post until 1801, was Lord President of the Council, 1801–6, and became prime minister, 1807–9.

[7] Thomas Brodrick (1756–95), barrister, Counsel for the Admiralty 1792–4, brought into the Home Office by Portland in 1794 as under-secretary, but became ill and lost the power of speech by early September (see R. R. Nelson, *The Home Office, 1782–1801*, Durham, N.C., 1969, p. 36).

[8] William Baldwin (c. 1737–1813), lawyer and M.P. 1795–8 and 1802–6. He acted as Counsel to the Home Office in matters of criminal law, but was not on the regular establishment. It was stated in *The Oracle and Public Advertiser*, 8 September 1794, that Portland had appointed Baldwin his private secretary (see also L. J. Hume, 'Bentham's Panopticon: an administrative history', *Historical Studies*, lxvi (1973), 710 n. 23).

998

FROM HENRY DUNDAS

21 September 1794

Walmer Castle 21st Septr 1794

Sir

I came here last night to enjoy with my family a few days of relaxation during an interval of official business. I have employed the morning of the first of those days in perusing the Letter from you which Mr Nepean sometime ago put into my hands: I regret the length of it because it prevented me during the pressure of my own business from giving an earlier consideration to it, and that regret is much increased from being satisfied that everything material to the object of it might have been compressed in eight in place of above eighty pages.[2]

I wish the superfluity of its contents had been my only objection to it, for I should then have had it in my power to transmit it with my sentiments upon it to the Duke of Portland and to the Commissioners of the Treasury to whose respective Departments the business belongs, but you have thought it expedient, for what reason I am at a loss to guess, to put your arguments into such a garb as would preclude me from receiving it as an official address, and therefore I cannot be the instrument of conveying it to His Majesty's Servants in other departments. I therefore return the paper[3] to you leaving it to yourself to judge how far you think it proper to transmit it in its present shape to either of the Departments I have mentioned, or whether you think it more proper to put your reasoning into a form more consonant to the Stile in which official business is usually treated.

It is with sincere concern that I feel myself under the necessity of returning such an answer to your Letter, for, if the belief that I am a real Friend to the project was the motive of Mr Long and you agreeing to transmit your ideas to me (from whom the business has now officially passed) you certainly was not mistaken. I profess myself an admirer of its ingenuity and enthusiastick in the belief that it may be turned to great national benefit, but to accomplish

---

998. [1] B.L. V: 584–5. Autograph. Docketed: '1794 Sept 21 / Panopt / Rt. Hon. H. Dundas Walmer / to / J.B. Q.S.P. / Reced at Q.S.P. through Secretary Long 25th Sept—at Hendon through S.B. and Upsal same evening'.
[2] The letter and Memorial of 16 August (see letters 988 and 989).
[3] It may be the fair copy in U.C. CXVIII: 41–80.

77

that purpose I am sure it must be treated of and digested into practice by temper and dispositions very different from those which have too often guided your pen in your proposed memorial to the Treasury and in the Letter you have addressed to me.[4]

I am
Sir
your most obedt humble Servant
Henry Dundas.

Jeremy Bentham Esqr

999

FROM CHARLES LONG

25 September 1794

Sir

I send you by Mr Dundas's desire the paper which accompanies this.[2] In perusing it which I have done very cursorily I was surprised to find that you had most unaccountably misunderstood me particularly in two points the first is not very material but when you suppose me to have intended to accompany the Surveyors to ascertain whether a spot of ground could be found more eligible than Battersea Rise for the Purpose of building a Penitentiary House you really suppose me to have made a proposal which never enter'd into my head. But Sir the other misconception is a little more serious and [one] wch. a very little of that Candour on your part which you are disposed to allow to me must have prevented. You represent me as saying that if government made with you a worse bargain for itself for building on any other Spot than Battersea Rise, it was no concern of yours—Now Sir I never said anything to this effect or ever meant to insinuate that Government would prefer a worse bargain to a better, but I said and still say that Government is to judge of what is the best bargain not you. If I am not to have

<hr/>

[4] Bentham had drafted on 14 September a letter to Dundas beginning: 'At Ld Spencer's return from the Continent you will have good news for him—Give you joy, my Lord—the establishment is knocked up, the fellows are ruined and your land is safe.' This draft is docketed: '1794 Sept. 14 / Panopt / J.B. Q.S.P. / to / Dundas / Pressing answer about Memorial sent 16 Augt / Not sent' (B.L. V: 580–1).

Bentham also drafted a strong letter of protest to Pitt, dated 16 September 1794, but this is also docketed 'Not sent' (B.L. V: 582–3).

999. [1] B.L. V: 586–7. Docketed: '1794 Sept. 25 / Panopt / C. Long Treasury / to / J.B. Q.S.P.'

[2] The letter and Memorial of 16 August, which Dundas wished to have returned to Bentham (see letter 998).

Battersea rise say you I will have nothing—I reply that there seems to me no reason for such a determination perhaps you cannot work it at so low a rate per man elsewhere, but first let Surveyors ascertain under the Act whether the Penitentiary House is to be built there or elsewhere, if elsewhere—make new proposals, those you have made apply only to Battersea Rise and cannot conclude you for another Spot—but cannot you conceive it possible that it may be more eligible and more economical too upon the whole for Government to give you higher terms per Head in another place, the original Cost of the Land may be so much higher in one place than another as alone to make the whole difference. But instead of considering what I said in this Light in which I thought I had sufficiently explained it you chuse to suppose me to mean that to please an Individual Government would make a bad bargain instead of a good one, an Idea very far indeed from my thoughts and which if you had been disposed to consider with fairness what I said you would not have imputed to me.

It is unnecessary for me to say anything upon your reasoning on these misconstructions but you seem to suppose me an enemy to your plan and wishing to obstruct the progress of it. I assure you I know not what business I have had to meddle in it all except as a promoter of it. I admir'd its ingenuity and thought it would be beneficial to the public in that point of view I wish'd it and still wish it success, and with respect to the ground on which the building is to be erected I have no other wish than that the properest spot may be fix'd upon, and it seems to me that the first official step to be taken by the Treasury is the appointment of the Surveyors I proposed and as the Commissioners are directed by the Act.

I am sorry you have met with disappointment—but I shall be more so if the effect of that disappointment is either to make you relinquish the prosecution of your plan, or to proceed in it with a want of temper which cannot fail to obstruct its success

I am Sir
yr obedt Servt
Charles Long

Treasury Chambers
Sept. 25

1000

FROM SAMUEL BENTHAM

25 September 1794

You may imagine I could not receive packets with the name of Long and Dundas on them without opening them before I forwarded them[2] to you. The contents grieve me sorely. I first determined to bring them myself but after various reflections I thought it better to send Upsal with them and hear from you first by his return.

In the train my ideas run at present I do not see how you and they will draw together again so as for you to treat with them with any satisfaction. I suffer and I fear shall continue to suffer exceedingly at seeing you throw away with so much anxiety time you could employ so much more usefully and creditably. Hitherto for various reasons I have been averse to taking the principal part in the business but I now cannot help proposing that you should relinquish it altogether to me telling them you did so on account of what their delays had made you suffer. You would then be no longer responsible for any failure. What you have now should remain secure to you and as to the profits of this or any other undertaking of mine half of them as fast as they arise should be secured to you. With this do anything for your amusement—but if you have dealings with such people and commercial business to be so very anxious about, you never can be happy and I am sure I cannot.

My unfitness for this business very ordinary tallents will supply but I never shall bear to see you so occupied, because in one case of ten you might do the business better. Besides, that part which nobody but yourself could do is done. My invention with anv orderly man's management are now sufficient.

1000. [1] B.L. V: 588–9. Autograph, unsigned. Docketed: '1794 Sept 25 / Panopt / S.B. Q.S.P. / to J.B. Hendon / Rec'd same eveng through Upsal.'
Addressed: 'J. Bentham Esqr / Hendon.'
[2] Letters 998 and 999.

1001

To Henry Dundas

25 September 1794 (Aet 46)

Hendon, Middlesex, Sept. 25th 1794.

Sir

It is now upwards of five or six weeks (I forget which) that I took the liberty, at the suggestion of Mr Secretary Long, to address a letter to you which I left at your Office at the Horse Guards, directed to the care of Mr Nepean. In the mean time I have had two apprehensions to struggle with: the departure of my Brother for Russia, worn out with disappointment; and the dispersion of my men. The former has not been realized:—the latter *has*. The greater part are discharged already. To enable myself to linger on a while longer with the small remainder, I am parting with household servants: two are gone already: two more follow in a few days.

In this state of things it so happens that it would be of particular use to me, if I could but know of *any certain* period though it were but a day before the meeting of Parliament, by which I might *depend* upon having some sort of answer, to an application which I can not help looking upon as having some claim to one. The attempt to obtain any such favour may seem idle enough, but it is now made, and may e'en take its chance.

This letter will reach you, I understand, at Walmer: consequently with Mr Pitt:[2] to whom I attempted about three months ago to be equally troublesome, and with equal ill success.

> I have the honour to be
> with all respect,
> Sir
> Your most obedient
> and humble servant
> Jeremy Bentham

Right Hon:ble
Henry Dundas.

1001. [1] Scottish Record Office, Melville Castle Muniments, G.D.51/6/996/1. Autograph. No docket or address.

A draft of this letter is in B.L. V: 591; when he wrote it Bentham had of course not received letter 998 from Dundas.

[2] Pitt had been appointed by King George III to the lucrative sinecure post of Lord Warden of the Cinque Ports, made vacant by the death of the 2nd Earl of Guilford in August 1792. Walmer Castle was the official residence of the Lord Warden and Pitt stayed there quite frequently, but his visits in the summer of 1794 were brief and Dundas may well have been there during Pitt's absence.

1002

TO HENRY DUNDAS

26 September 1794 (Aet 46)

Hendon, Middlesex Sat:y morning
Sept. 26th 1794

Sir

Last night, Sept. 25th, I received at this place the honour of your letter dated Walmer Sept: 21, transmitted to my House at Westminster yesterday afternoon by Mr Long.

The object of the present address is, humbly to beg to know, Sir, whether, on the supposition of a Memorial the same in point of argument with that which has passed under your review, cleared only from those superfluities and reprehensible passages which have drawn upon it the misfortune of your censure, you would *then* be pleased to 'transmitt' *such* Memorial 'with your sentiments upon it to the respective Departments' alluded to by you, and whether those sentiments would be in favour of my wishes in respect of the land.

Thinking I could not better testify my respect for your pleasure once signified, than by the shortness of this address,

I remain, Sir,
Your most obedient
and humble Servant
Jeremy Bentham.

Right Hon:ble
Henry Dundas

1002. [1] Scottish Record Office, Melville Castle Muniments, G.D.51/6/996/2. Autograph. No docket or address.

A draft of this letter is in B.L. V: 600. It is docketed: '1794 Sept 26 / Panopt / J.B. Hendon / to / Dundas / To ask whether the Memorial would be presented, if castrated.' There are much longer drafts of 25–6 September, docketed 'Not sent' (B.L. V: 591–9), and another, shorter one, dated 25 September, concerned with the expense of purchasing the site at Battersea: that draft also is docketed 'Not sent' (B.L. V: 590).

1003

TO CHARLES LONG

26 September 1794 (Aet 46)

Hendon Middlesex Sept. 26 1794.

Sir[2]

Accept my best acknowledgements for the favour of your long and very obliging letter of yesterday afternoon transmitted me hither last night.

As to mistatements, believe me, Sir, I wanted only to know your own statement of your own sentiments and expressions to subscribe to it: designed they could not be, the appeal being all along really to yourself, conceiving myself to be writing under your eye. These are accidents almost inseparable from *vivâ voce* intercourse, which makes me so anxious for written subjects of reference where the nature of the case admitts of it.

I take the liberty of inclosing the copy of an answer I have just been writing to Mr Dundas.[3]

Mean time I will no longer resist the proposal which with a view of forwarding the business you are pleased to repeat with respect to the nomination of Surveyors: always understood that such Surveyors are not to be precluded from fixing upon the spot I wish for, that any claims I may conceive myself to have upon that spot are not precluded in any degree by my acquiescence in the measure, and that the judgment of such Surveyors is not to be conclusive upon me. Was it your meaning, or would you now think proper that I should accompany them? But since their employment is to report what is the properest ground for works of mine to be carried on upon my account, should not the nomination of one of them be in me? I have some notion from your proposing two that this was your intention.

As to economy, no other ground can possibly be so convenient to government as that I wish for. For rather than be deprived of it I would pay rent for the difference to the amount of the interest government borrow at, instead of accepting of other ground with an encrease of terms: therefore the reasons that could prevail on

---

1003. [1] B.L. V: 601–2. Autograph draft. Docketed: '1794 Sept 26 / Panopt. J.B. Q.S.P. / to / Long Treasury.' A pencil note at the top of the sheet reads: 'Panopt. To Long. Answer. 26 Sept. 1794. Sent.'

[2] Marginal note: 'Fair copy sent from Hendon by Upsal ½ after 12.'

[3] That is, a copy of letter 1002.

Administration to refuse the land must be of some other nature. Is there any secret in those reasons? for you will have the goodness to recollect that none have ever been declared to me. After all of the determination of Administration is formed in this particular, reasons may indeed be spared and reasoning is at an end. But is that determination formed? This is exactly what I wish to know. Either your instructions are already determinate on that head, and then you can inform me already: or if not, you can if you see no impropriety, oblige me so far as to ask for such determinate instructions, and then inform me. Surely dependent as I am altogether upon the pleasure of Administration there can be no impropriety in my wishing or asking to know that pleasure? And to what purpose should they wish for a moment to conceal it?

I will take the liberty of waiting on you on Tuesday, or if you command me for Monday so much the better. By that time you may perhaps be able to give me the answer above required or at least about the Surveyors. I do not ask for a written answer to every thing, it would in point of labour be too much for me to request. But in conversation whatever may seem material enough to be retained I shall require permission to take memorandums of in your presence to save me from any more misconceptions in addition to those which it has been my misfortune to fall into.

1004

To Samuel Bentham

26 September 1794 (Aet 46)

Hendon Saty morng
Sept. 26 – 1794

Barret,[2] Martin and Co.,[3] Dundas, Long, and though last not least S.B. have all together found me a tolerable stock of occupation. What you propose I had always in contemplation,[4] I must confess, as a *pis-aller*: to you it seems a *mieux aller*: or rather as the only course either attainable or to be wished for. The difference in point of judgment I fear is irreconcilable: that it may make no difference in point of affection, let it be our mutual care. A difference in point

1004. [1] B.L. V: 603–4. Autograph. Addressed: 'To / Colonel Bentham'.
[2] John Barrett, coal merchant, Queen's Square, Westminster.
[3] The bankers.
[4] That is, Samuel's offer to take over responsibility for the Panopticon project (see letter 1000, p. 80 above).

of affection to require to be guarded against! Poor human Nature! After having lived as we have done for seven and thirty years!

But I must not waste my spirits: the whole stock is called for by Messrs. Dundas and Long.

I can not tell exactly when I shall visit Q.S.P. it depends on circumstances: probably not till Monday morning. Do not come unless I send to you for fear of interrupting me. But probably I may send to you. Keep yourself meantime if you can in a state of requisition—possibly I may come and fetch you if you are able to come.

P.S. I have dispatched all my business—therefore if you can come to me this afternoon or rather morning so much the better. At Q.S.P. I should have no ease.

Do come I beg and beseech you—but don't bring Upsal now, he would be a sad nuisance—Coaches you will meet with if you look out for them for Hampstead or Highgate.

1005

To Arthur Young

c. 26 September 1794 (Aet 46)

Hendon, Middlesex Sept. 1794.

Dear Sir,

Permitt my ignorance to draw upon your science on an occasion that happens just now to be a very material one to me. I have a sort of floating recollection of a calculation, so circumstanced, either in point of authority or argument, as to carry weight with it, in which the total value of the landed property in this country, Scotland (I believe) included, was reckoned at a thousand millions, and that of the moveable property at either a thousand millions or twelve hundred millions. Public debt did not come, I believe, at least it ought not to come, into the account: it being only so much owed by one part of the proprietors of the 2,000,000,000 or the 2,200,000,000 to another.

1005. ¹ Young Papers. B.L. Add Ms. 35127 fo. 338. Autograph. Addressed: 'To / Arthur Young Esqr / etc. etc. / near Bury / Suffolk.' Postmark (mostly illegible): 'SE⟨. . .⟩'.

Printed in *Autobiography of Arthur Young*, ed. M. Betham Edwards, 1898, 247–9. Quoted inaccurately in Bowring, x, 302–3.

As the dated letter of 30 September (1007 below) acknowledges a reply from Young, this one cannot have been sent later than 26 September.

Upon searching your book on France[2] which was the source from which I thought I had taken the idea, I can find no calculation of the value of the moveable property, nor even of the immoveable in an explicit form: on the contrary, in the instance of the *im*moveable, I find suppositions with which any such estimate appears to be incompatible. The Land-tax, at *4s*, I find you suppose, were it to be equal all over the country (it is of England only I believe that you speak) would be equivalent to as much as 3s: on which supposition the rental (the tax at 4 producing no more than 2,000,000) would amount to no more than £13,000,000, nor consequently the value at so many years purchase, say 28, to more [than] 364,000,000; or at 30, to 390,000,000: to which in order to compleat the calculation of the landed property of Great Britain, that of Scotland would be to be added.

The population of the 3 Kingdoms you reckon in two places at 11,000,000: but in another place at 15,000,000: is it that *15* was a slip of the pen or press, and should [it] have been *11* as in the other two places, or is it that in the two places *two* kingdoms (England and Scotland) only were in view, though *three* are mentioned. A circumstance that seems to favour the latter supposition is, that the population of Ireland is well known (if I do not much mis-recollect) from recent and authentic sources to be a little more than 4,000,000: and as Scotland turns out, I believe, to contain 1,500,000, this would leave 9½ for England, which I should suppose would quadrate in round numbers with Mr Howlet's[3] calculations, to which you refer: a book which from forgetfulness I have never made myself master of, and to which, being in the country, I have no speedy means of recurring.

Now what I wish for is as follows
1. A calculation /I should rather say the *result* of/ of the value of the *landed* property of *Great Britain* reckoned at | |[4] years purchase: (two prices, a peace price and a war price, could they

---

[2] Arthur Young had estimated the population of Great Britain and Ireland as not more than 15,000,000 in his *Travels during the Years 1787, 1788 and 1789. Undertaken more particularly with a View of ascertaining the Cultivation, Wealth, Resources, and National Prosperity of the Kingdom of France*, 2nd edn., 2 vols., Bury St Edmunds, 1794, i, 467. He had estimated the population of Great Britain (excluding Ireland) at ten million in *Letters concerning the Present State of the French Nation*, 1769, p. 394.

[3] John Howlett (1731–1804), Anglican clergyman and political economist. In his *Examination of Dr. Price's Essay . . . on the Population of England and Wales*, Maidstone, 1781, pp. 146, 152, he estimated the population of the two countries as just under 9 million, England alone over 8 million.

[4] Left thus blank in Ms.

be respectively of sufficient permanence to be ascertained, would be of use.)

2. Do. of the value of the personal i.e. *immoveable* property of *Great Britain*

3. The amount of the *population* of *Great Britain*

What I am a petitioner for, is, the benefit of your judgement and authority upon the three several subjects: by *reference*, if there be any *other* person's calculation that you are satisfied with: otherwise from your own notes: and in either case a word or two, just to indicate the *data* on which they are founded, the sources from which they are taken, would be an additional help and satisfaction.

The occasion of the trouble I am attempting to give you I expressly forbear mentioning: not only for want of space and time, but more particularly that it may be impossible, and might, upon occasion be known to be impossible, that the response of the Oracle should have received any bias from the consideration of the purpose for which it was consulted. I am, Dear Sir, with never-failing esteem and regard

Yours ever,
Jeremy Bentham

A. Young Esq.

1006

FROM SAMUEL ROMILLY

28 September 1794

Dear Bentham

You certainly did not lend me the book you mention I don't even remember having ever seen it at your house. I am sorry you are silent on a subject which you know interests me exceedingly I am afraid it is because you have no good news to tell me

yrs ever
Sam¹ Romilly

28 Sept. 1794

1006. ¹ Free Library of Philadelphia. Autograph. Docketed: '1794 Sept 28 / Romilly Bowood to J.B. Q.S.P.'

Addressed: 'Jeremy Bentham Esqr / Queen Square Place / Westminster.' Postmark: 'CALNE'.

Evidently a reply to a missing letter from Bentham.

87

1007

To Arthur Young

30 September 1794 (Aet 46)

Q.S.P. Septr 30th 1794

Dear Sir

A thousand thanks for your kind letter[2]—sorry you should fancy you have been bathing for health—hope it was not true—only idleness—we can't afford to have you otherwise than well.

Must pester you once more—'Rental of England 24 Mills: Good—but Houses, such as those in towns, and others that bear a separate Rent, are they included? I suppose not: since for them you would have given a separate and different price in no. of years purchase.—In one of your Tours you *guess* that article at 5 Millions—Do you abide by that guess?[3] I think the no. must have encreased since then considerably—that was I believe about 20 years ago—London and the environs must since then have increased I should think at least ¼ of a million—How many years purchase would you reckon houses at upon an average old and young together? Shall we say 16? —I should think at the outside. I am, Dear Sir,

Your much obliged
Jeremy Bentham

A. Young Esqr.

1008

To Charles Long

1 October 1794 (Aet 46)

Q.S.P., October 1st, 1794.

Dear Sir,

You are now a holiday-making,—I wish you as much sport as

1007. [1] Young Papers. B.L. Add. Ms. 35127 fo. 342–3. Autograph.

Addressed: 'To / Arthur Young Esqr / etc. etc. etc. / Bradfield / near Bury Suffolk.' Postmark: 'OC.1.9⟨4⟩. A.'

Also printed in Young's *Autobiography*, 249–50.

[2] Missing.   [3] See letter 1005 above, p. 86 n. 2.

1008. [1] Bowring, x, 303. Introduced by the statement: 'Bentham wrote two letters to Charles Long of the Treasury,—one announcing, and the other accompanying his pamphlet, "Supply without Burthen." ' This would appear to be the first one, but the letter of 13 October, which follows in Bowring, did not accompany a copy of this pamphlet, which was sent to the Treasury on 3 October (see letter 1011 n. 4).

88

you have afforded me satisfaction. To vary your pastime, which, perhaps, may be found not unsuitable to the place, permit me to present you with a riddle.

What is that pecuniary resource, of which the tenth part would be a tax, and that a heavy one, while the whole is no tax, and would not be felt by anybody?

The solution lies with the copyist; I hope it will be sent.[2] I am, dear sir, your most obedient and much obliged humble servant.

1009

FROM WILLIAM GARTHSHORE

4 October 1794

Copy

Dear Sir,
 Mr Dundas will present your Memorial[2] as you desire

Your obed: humble servant
W. Garthshore

Horse Guards Oct. 4th 1794.

1010

FROM ARTHUR YOUNG

5 October 1794

Bradfield, October 5th, 1794.

Dear Sir,
 I take the rental of England to be twenty-four millions, exclusive of houses, and the annual product of timber, mines, etc. Houses,—twelve years' purchase.

---

[2] That is, a copy of Bentham's manuscript of *Supply without Burthen; or Escheat vice Taxation: being a Proposal for a Saving in Taxes by an Extension of the Law of Escheat* . . ., first published in 1795, reprinted in Bowring, ii, 585–98.

1009. [1] B.L. V: 607. Copy. Addressed: 'Jeremy Bentham Esqr Hendon, Middlesex.' Included at the beginning of the letter of 7 October to Samuel Bentham (1011 below).
 William Garthshore (1764–1804) was at this time private secretary to Dundas; M.P., 1795–1804; he became a lord of the Admiralty, 1801–4.
 [2] That is, a shortened version of the Memorial sent to Dundas on 16 August (see letters 989 and 1002).

1010. [1] Bowring, x, 303. A reply to letter 1007.

No data strike me at present to discover the rental,—but these are questions I have not of late given my mind to.—
I am, dear sir, faithfully yours . . .
Apply to me on all occasions without apologies.

1011

TO SAMUEL BENTHAM

7 October 1794 (Aet 46)

Hendon Oct. 7. 1794.
Copy
Dear Sir,
Mr Dundas will present your Memorial as you desire[2]

Your obed: humb: servant
W. Garthshore
Horse Guards Oct. 4th 1794.

Direction Jeremy Bentham Esqr Hendon, Middlesex
It came by the Penny Post and not till this afternoon Oct. 7th.

Now Mr Sir, What do you think of Panopticon Hill? By its being written on Saturday (I mean the letter, not the Hill),[3] and not before Saturday it affords a fraction of a probability that *Escheat* which went on Friday morning may have been liked, and operated towards the Dundassian determination.[4]

Annuity—dealing—Supply[5] is almost dispatched: it turns out a noble and ample field: your Price's and Mazeres's[6] and Rose-

1011. [1] B.L. V: 607–8. Autograph. Docketed (by Mrs Samuel Bentham, at a later date): '1794 Oct. 7 / Jeremy Bentham / to his brother / Mary Sophia Bentham.' Addressed: 'To / Colonel Bentham.'
[2] The letter begins with this copy of the brief note from Garthshore, which has also been printed separately above (letter 1009).
[3] In both cases the word is clearly 'Hill' not 'Bill'; the brothers seem to have referred humorously to the site on Battersea Rise as the 'Panopticon Hill'.
[4] The manuscript copy of the pamphlet, *Supply without Burthen*, which Bentham promised on 1 October to send to Long (see letter 1008), perhaps under its alternative title of 'Escheat vice Taxation'.
[5] Probably the other proposals for raising revenue which Bentham sent to Long on 13 October (see below, letter 1014).
[6] Price and Maseres had collaborated in *The Principles of the Doctrine of Life-Annuities*, by Francis Maseres, 1783, with 'Directions for using the tables,' by Dr Richard Price.

Lowndes's[7] and Amicable Society[8] Gentry have been but gleaners. Bankers too are almost in readiness to be plucked—The project turns out not only promising in point of product, but justifiable beyond expectation.[9] Less hardly dealt with than Landed men: and an *indemnity* for them too which will make them amends, if they will have a little patience.

I see by the Times of today (7th Octr) that optical experiments with a view to Telegraph are actually making at Woolwich. I have written to J. Peake[10] at Woolwich to watch them.

1012

To Henry Dundas

7 October 1794 (Aet 46)

Hendon Middlesex Tuesday afternoon
Oct 7th 1794.

Sir

The Post has but just brought to this place a note[2] of so early a date as the 4th from Mr Garthshore, communicating your intention 'to transmitt my Memorial, as I desire.'

In declining to transmitt that paper in its *former* state, you acquitted yourself, Sir, to yourself; not to mention the Honourable Board to whom it purported to be addressed. In consenting to transmitt it in its *future* state, you acquitt yourself to the public, in respect to a measure which promises to be a beneficial one, and as such has been honoured by your patronage. As to the individual whose lot happens to be involved in it, he can no otherwise lay claim to notice, than as one who embraces the earliest opportunity

[7] George Rose has just published *Observations on the Act for the Relief and Encouragement of Friendly Societies*, 1794, perhaps with assistance from William Lowndes, who was also at the Treasury.

[8] The Amicable Society for a Perpetual Assurance Office received its charter in 1706. Jeremiah Bentham had been a member and was one of the twelve directors in the late 1770s and early 80s. (See *A List of the Members of the Corporation of the Amicable Society*, 1778 and 1783 edns.)

[9] These remarks indicate that Bentham was already beginning to draft material for what was to become his *Annuity-Note Plan* and the proposal to raise revenue by taxing the profits of bankers (Bowring, ii, 599).

[10] Jack Peake, son of Henry, the shipwright.

1012. [1] Scottish Record Office, Melville Castle Muniments, G.D.51/6/996/3. Autograph. A draft in B.L. V: 605–6 is docketed: '1794 Oct. 7 / Panopt / J.B. Hendon / to Rt. Hon. H. Dundas Horseguards / Thanks for promise to / Transmitt Memorial / Sent by Jack Oct 8 at 8 A.M.'

[2] Letter 1009.

of begging your acceptance of his most humble thanks.—I have the honour to be,

with all respect,
Sir
Your most obedient
and humble servant
Jeremy Bentham

Right Hon:ble Henry Dundas

1013

FROM ARTHUR YOUNG

10 October 1794

Dear Sir

I recd. your favour,[2] and yesterday attended a committee of Justices to examine plans, when we reduced the candidates to two, Mr Alexander[3] one—and the rest were rejected because they were not on the Panopticon principle wch I write you as I think yo should have the satisfaction of knowing how much yr ideas are approved.

yrs faithfully
A. Young.

Bradf. Oct. 10 94.

1014

TO CHARLES LONG

13 October 1794 (Aet 46)

Hendon, Middlesex, October 13th, 1794.

Sir,

If the pecuniary resource I ventured t'other day to submit to you,[2] should be deemed ineligible or impracticable, perhaps in some other instance I may be more fortunate. I have two other such resources upon the anvil,—the one involving a burthen indeed, but

1013. [1] B.L. V: 609–10. Autograph. Docketed: '1794 Oct 10 / Panopt / A. Young Bradfield / to / J.B. Hendon / Rec'd Oct 17 / Panopticon plan approved / by Bury Justices.'
Addressed: 'Jeremy Bentham Esq / Hendon / Middlesex.' Postmark: 'OC.17.94.B'.
[2] Missing.
[3] Daniel Asher Alexander, the architect (1768–1846). See *Correspondence*, iv, 404 n. 4.
1014. [1] Bowring, x, 303.
[2] See letter 1008, n. 1, and letter 1011, n. 4.

that burthen coupled with an indemnity capable of balancing it, and sooner or later even of outweighing it: the other absolutely pure from all burthen from the very beginning. The first is already with the copyist: the principle of it has been exemplified in the first instance upon a single denomination of persons: but it is a pregnant one, and if approved may yield a score or two of other taxes. The other has been already travelled through, and wants only to be digested a little. Neither will trespass so much upon your patience, in point of quantity of reading, as the proposal about escheat: both together will not equal it in produce. Proposing without justifying is nothing: I could not bring myself to hazard either proposal, till I had, to my own conception, established it upon principles. Resources new *in specie* are hardly to be found; but it will be something if any such as are justly approved *in specie* can be rendered new in point of *extent*, or any that have undergone unmerited disgrace can be restored to favour and to practice by being placed in a new light.

On the former occasion I trespassed on the gravity of your situation by the present of a *riddle*. Permit me now to reconduct you to the style of the subject by a grave apophthegm,—*Supply without burthen is victory without blood.* The application of it is what I have been pushing as far as time and faculties would carry me.

Thus occupied, I have thought it an escape not to have received a summons as yet about my own particular business: it has been laid upon the shelf for the chance, faint as it may be, of being of use by your assistance in a line of superior importance. I would, therefore, beg the favour of you to allow me *two clear days* notice: for it will take me one day to abridge the memorial, and another to get it copied.[3]

On the former occasion I trespassed on the gravity of your situation by the present of a *riddle*. Permit me now to reconduct you to the style of the subject by a grave apophthegm,—*Supply without burthen is victory without blood.* The application of it is what I have been pushing as far as time and faculties would carry me.

If either use or amusement should, on your part, have paid for the trouble of reading all this, mine in writing it will have been over-paid.—I have the honour to be, with all respect, dear sir, your most obedient and humble servant.

[3] That is, the shorter Memorial concerning the Panopticon scheme which Dundas was now willing to transmit to the Treasury (see letter 1009).

1015

To Samuel Bentham

14 October 1794 (Aet 46)

Hendon Oct. 14 – 1794

Send me by the next conveyance a list of Bankers for 1783. You will find one in the directory that we studied for Post Caravans—O no you wont it was for 1791–1792. Yet if it be for 1792, send it— for it was returned from hence—I mean the unbound one in blue paper. For the 1793 Bankers we must be beholden to Browne's Court Calendar.[2]

I am an object of compassion—Miss F's Marianne[3] almost read— not enough to last me from here to London—and no other novel in the room of it. See whether she can take pity of me and find one another such—the Paysan parvenu by the same Author[4] I have read—The rest of Charlotte Smiths novels I do not care to consume, reserving them against a rainy day, i:e: a day of trouble, such as illness or misfortune.

1015. [1] B.L. V: 611–12. Autograph. Addressed: 'To / Colonel Bentham / Queen's Square Place / Westminster.' Stamped: 'Not pd'. Postmark illegible.
[2] Information concerning banking 'collected for J.B. by Miss Fordyce and R. Till' is in U.C. cxv: 33–9. Richard Till (c. 1748–1824) was for many years principal clerk to the commissioners of the land tax for the city of London, and agent of the proprietors of the London Bridge Waterworks. He had a reputation for 'accuracy and assiduity' (Gentleman's Magazine, January 1824, xciv, 92). For the Court Calendar, see letter 1016, n. 4.
[3] That is, a copy of Charlotte Smith's novel, Marianne, belonging to Miss Mary Sophia Fordyce, the future wife of Samuel Bentham, whom she married in October 1796.
[4] Charlotte Smith, already noticed, was a prolific writer, but not the author of La paysanne parvenue, ou Les Mémoires de Mme la marquise de L.V., 3 vols., Paris, 1735– 1736, frequently reprinted: this was a novel written by the French romancer, Charles de Fieux, chevalier de Mouhy (1701–84).

1016

To Samuel Bentham

16 October 1794 (Aet 46)

Hendon Thursday eveng 7 – Oct 16, 1794.

Who to invite with Justice Lawrence?[2]—What say you to Butler?[3]—One use of his seeing the Lions is, that when he has seen them, he may be for shewing them to Ld Thurlow.

Remember you are to dine here on Sunday—and you chose to have the hour kept at 9. We will jog on to Q.S.P. then with one accord on Monday morning.

Send me the newspapers on Saturday notwithstanding, and if you can get the Court Calendars[4] of 1792 and 1793 for the sake of the Bankers list from Browne's so much the better: I hope Miss Fordyce has returned those she got from Browne's for me: if not, see that she does:—Upsal will manage this.

1017

From James Trail

23 October 1794

Lincoln's Inn.

Dear Bentham,

I have a thousand apologies to make for not having sooner

1016. [1] B.L. V: 613. Autograph. Docketed: '1794 Oct. 16 / J.B. Hendon / to / S.B. Q.S.P.

[2] Sir Soulden Lawrence (1751–1814), the judge; in March 1794 he had become a Justice of the Common Pleas, with a knighthood; in June he moved to the Court of King's Bench; he was a member of the Special Commission which tried Thomas Hardy, Horne Tooke and others for high treason, 1794–6; a friend of Lord Ellenborough, his contemporary at St John's College, Cambridge, he differed with him in a King's Bench case in 1808 and returned to the Common Pleas until his retirement in 1812.

[3] Perhaps their friend Charles Butler, the Roman Catholic lawyer, but possibly a spelling mistake for Sir Francis Buller, bart. (1746–1800), the judge with whom Lawrence had changed courts in June 1794 and one likely to have contacts with Lord Thurlow.

[4] There were several calendars, published annually, which gave lists of officials, M.P.s, bankers and so on. The *Court Kalendar* had ceased publication by 1770 and Bentham may be referring either to the *Court and City Register*, or the *London Calendar*, or the *Royal Kalendar*, all appearing during these years.

1017. [1] Bowring, x, 305.

thanked you for the perusal of your paper on *Escheat*.[2] I have been scarcely an hour at home, except for sleep, since I received it. I ran it over very hastily, and having no prospect of more leisure for some time, I sent it to Wilson with all the cautions and injunctions you prescribed.[3]

The plan appears much more reasonable on your development of it, than I had conceived it possible to have made it. I feel still startled at the proposal to vest in a public officer all property of which the state will, by your plan, be entitled to any share; and I doubt if the example of an executor or administrator will reconcile people's feelings, or even their reason, to this part of the scheme. However, I am very glad you have written it, and sent it to Long, as it must impress every person that reads it, with a very favourable opinion of the faculties of the author. You labour, and with much ingenuity, but I doubt if with complete success, to prove that this mode of raising supplies will *appear* less burthensome or oppressive than a slight tax on collateral succession. After it has been established some time, that may really happen; but although you may convince a minister that it will happen, he cannot venture, on his own conviction, to make the experiment. You must convince the public, also, which, I fear, is impossible. The reluctance with which tithes, compared to rent, are paid, is a very strong illustration of your point. If the Church could occasionally be put into the actual possession of the tenth part of every field or farm, as the landlord occasionally is of the whole, the property in the Church would neither be disputed nor repined at.

---

[2] *Supply without Burthen, or Escheat vice Taxation* was not published in England until 1795, when it appeared together with the other pamphlet, *A Protest against Law Taxes*, which had been previously published in Ireland in 1793. Bentham says in the preface to this new edition that the *Protest* 'received from the Minister on whose plans it hazarded a comment, all the attention that candour could bestow; and if I do not misrecollect, the taxes complained against did not afterwards appear. The publication of it in this country was kept back, till a proposal for a substitute to the tax complained of should be brought into shape: upon the principle of the parliamentary notion, which forbids the producing an objection to a tax, without a proposal for a better on the back of it'.

In the preface to *Supply without Burthen*, Bentham states that his suggestion of escheat instead of a new tax 'was submitted to the proper authority in the month of September 1794, but was not fortunate enough to be deemed worth further notice'.

[3] A missing letter to Trail is indicated.

1018

To Samuel Bentham

25 October 1794 (Aet 46)

Hendon Oct 25 3 o'clock
the former went at 9[2]

I left behind Theardy's[3] eight-penny Tax Tables which I want—a very small but thick less than 12mo pamphlet, supposed to be on my new Chest of Drawers in my room—send it with the Newspapers

Lemons I have got—you need not send any. I have written to Trail offering to see Lady C.[4] if possible answering being writing a treatise that for want of *pro* and *con* necessarily an unsatisfactory one.

Another fatted calf with two legs and feathers is slaughtered for you.

1019

From Samuel Bentham

27 October 1794

I am just come from the Treasury where I was admitted to Mr Long's audience immediately on my sending in my name, although the introducer could not help very judiciously observing that I was not the Mr Bentham who was used to come there so frequently. Mr Long seemed very ready and friendly, but seemed rather to crave your consulting him about the castrations of the Memorial. He said you seemed to wish him to look at your Memorial before it was sent to Mr Dundas and that he was very willing to look at it whenever you would send it to him, and that he was sure that if you or I would read it over with a view of leaving out the exceptionable parts we should find no difficulty in fixing on them. He spoke a great deal of the reason you had to be vexed and out of

---

1018. [1] B.L. X: 595. Autograph. Addressed: 'To / Colonel Bentham / Queens Square Place / Westminster.' Postmark: '12 o'clock / OC.25 / 94 noon'.

[2] This indicates that another, missing, letter had been sent to Samuel the same day.

[3] Not identified.

[4] Not identified: the lady may have been named in a part of Trail's letter (1017 above) not quoted by Bowring. The answering letter from Bentham is missing.

1019. [1] B.L. V: 614–15. Autograph. No signature, docket or address.

humour but that it could not assist the business to make allusions to the private Character of the Members of administration, in short the old story over again.

He intends independant of the memorial to lay the act itself before the Lords of the Treasury at their first Board and remind them of the necessity of their acting accordingly. He said however that you had wished to remind them of it by the Memorial and that certainly Mr Dundas was the properest person for presenting it, notwithstanding it was no longer his official department. He observed also that Dundas was certainly a friend to the business: and that he himself regretted very much the delay. Upon the whole though Long seemed to me to speak of your desiring what in some instances I had understood from you were his suggestions, whichever way it be there can be no use in your reminding him any former expressions: though he waved appointing a meeting he was very ready to see and of course give you his opinion of your memorial and there seems no difficulty in seeing him at any time. Of your other business neither of us said anything. Jenkinson[2] and somebody else were announced as waiting his audience which made me shorten my stay.

I forgot to tell you that I told him with respect to my revising the Memorial that I had not read it which then was true: but I have now since I have been at home read it through and what occurred to me in the way of advice was to confine it entirely to the first nine pages supposing that it is *that* land and no other that will be fixed on. The good effect of all the rest I think must have been produced by Dundas and Long having read it who knew and will let others know (if they are at all disposed to hear) what strong arguments you have in store. In this case I think I should in sending it so reduced to Dundas, tell him you have complied with his advice respecting the *measure* by leaving out all arguments about the land, trusting that however the stile in which you had been induced to shorten the arguments in favour of that land to the exclusion of any other they could not but have appeared to him sufficiently strong.

But if you should think it absolutely necessary to suppose they mean to look for other land, the printed paper of Queries seem to

---

[2] Probably Robert Banks Jenkinson, 2nd Earl of Liverpool (1770–1828); since 1790 M.P. for Appleby and a member of the India Board; later he held several cabinet posts, including the foreign and home secretaryships, before becoming prime minister, 1812–1827. He was created Baron Hawkesbury in 1803 and succeeded his father as Earl of Liverpool in 1808.

afford matter enough in a single page to convince where conviction is possible.

Do pray come immediately and let the delay be no longer at your door. It seems probable from what Long said that other places must *be looked for* by them were it only that they might know that they could not find any so convenient and proper.

If anything were to remain in the Memorial about the looking for other land it might then be good to put in your proposal for acting as Feoffee in preparing of [for?] possession of this land *de bene esse* to save time. But I rather think everything about the land had better be left to verbal intercourse and the use of the Memorial is to show the suffering from delay and to give Dundas an opportunity of forwarding the business by his recommendations.

Q.S.P. Monday Octr 27th 94

1020

To Henry Dundas

31 October 1794 (Aet 46)

Queen's Square Place Westminster Oct. 31. 1794.

Sir

It would be needless for me to trouble you with the causes which have retarded the inclosed Memorial[2] for above a fortnight after the time when you might have been expecting it. The delay being to my own prejudice, and that in no small degree, you will easily believe it was not the result of choice on the part of a man who does not reckon inactivity in the number of his faults. I have the honour to be

with all respect
Sir
Your most obedient
and most humble Servant
Jeremy Bentham

Right Hon.ble Henry Dundas
etc. etc. etc.

1020. [1] B.L. V: 616–17. Autograph draft. Docketed: '1794 Oct. 31 / Panopt / J.B. / to / Right Hon. H. Dundas Horse Guards / with amended Memorial.'

[2] This Memorial, not printed here, is very much shorter than the one of 16 August. A fair copy, with Bentham's autograph signature, is in U.C. cxviii: 106–8. It is docketed: '1794 Oct. 31 / Panopt / Jy Bentham Esqr / to / The Lords of the Treasury / Memorial / Submitted to Mr Dundas / and by him transmitted / officially to the Treasury / Novr 1st or 2d.'

1021

To Samuel Bentham

2 November 1794 (Aet 46)

Hendon Novr 2 – 1794

This novel is such cursed caggmagg[2] I shall never be able to get through. Puss has got the '*Lounger*'[3]—send me that.

Exchequer Bills. I have been reading about them in Acts of Parliament. How shall I do to know about them what I know through you about Navy-Bills without coming to town on purpose and consuming a day or two upon it? Ayton and Dawes[4] Thread-needle Street behind the Change are the Brokers I used to employ. I forget whether you know them. They pimp for Exchequer Bills as well as other things, for those Bills are in the lists of the prices of Stocks. I find by the Act of Parliament they have or ought at least to have the edges indented being cut off from a correspondent leaf kept in a book—Size of Paper—and amount of the sum i:e: of the smallest sum they are offered for are what I want to know— item what the hieroglyphics mean that exhibit their prices among the Stocks in the Newspapers—the premium seems to be exactly the same as upon the India Bonds—interest I believe 4 per cent on both. There seem according to the Act to be some formalities required for conveying them—which if they exist must impede their circulation. These formalities I want to know. The Acts which prescribe the issuing of them are the Annual Malt-tax Acts which like the Land-Tax Acts are the exact transcripts of a line of Acts beginning perhaps as long ago as Queen Anns reign.

The price of New Navy is in the Times of Feb. 27–$1\frac{7}{8}$ a 2—What this refers to I know not—the shillings in the Exchequer Bills and India Bond[s] are so many above £100 which is the par. I fancy therefore £100 is the sum that Exchequer Bills are offered for.

The Navy bills require an assignment for which there is a printed form.[5]

1021. [1] B.L. V: 618–19. Autograph. Addressed: 'Colonel Bentham'.

[2] Probably a family variant of 'quagmire'. The novel would perhaps be one of those requested in letter 1015.

[3] *The Lounger*, a literary magazine, written by Henry Mackenzie (1745–1831) and others; published in Edinburgh 6 February 1785—6 January 1787. It was reissued in book form.

[4] Stockbrokers, 57 Threadneedle Street (*London Directory*, 1794, p. 16).

[5] A sentence added in pencil by Bentham.

1022

TO SAMUEL BENTHAM

11 November 1794 (Aet 46)

Hendon Tuesday Novr. 11. 1794

Bond[2] has taken his measurements, but I directed him to consult you and Lloyd about certain points such as the height of the Hood from the upper bar of the stove. It will look better arched than square: so ⊖ than ⊟ so: in other respects it will make no difference, I suppose. The higher the Hood, the higher it extends before it terminates in the funnel—had it better terminate *sooner* i:e: more abruptly, or later i:e: more gradually?—All this is a mystery to me. The higher the arch ∩⌢ the less the draught; but then does it not through[3] the heat more into the room when high than when low? *Il s'agit* to have the heat thrown out: one has *beau* to have heat produced if it is carried up the chimney—Another mystery.

If you had not been a Wolchek[4] you would have kept him till 12 or so, instead of letting him go at 11, whereby I get no letter from you, nor today's paper—nor books—I hope they come this evening or rather tomorrow morning (for I shan't get them this morning by the ordinary conveyance.

Send a bottle of Ink by the next conveyance—item a $\frac{1}{4}$ 100 of pens. Item some ruled paper—*not* that ruled column-wise: but what I call *composition* Paper.

1022. [1] Wellcome Institute for the History of Medicine, London. Autograph. Docketed (not by Bentham): 'JB to his / brother SB / Jeremy Bentham / Légiste anglais.' No address or postmark.
[2] Not identified.
[3] A slip for 'throw'.
[4] The reading is doubtful: apparently 'a stupid person'.

1023*a*

To Samuel Bentham

15 November 1794 (Aet 46)

Hendon Novr. 15 1794 Saty. afternoon

For greater privacy, and that I might *abscond* with less danger of interruption or observance instead of setting out the Park way, I went Dartmouth Street way—Every body knows what *nuts* it is to the Lord to disappoint the designs, great and small, of any body that has the misfortune to bear any relation to such a reprobate as thee. As I was brushing by the casa del Illustrissimo Signore Borghese,[2] out brushes the Illustrissimo himself—I looked as hard as I could drive the opposite way—that would not serve me he happened to be in a condescending mood, and would run after me and catch hold of me by the elbow. When he had me fast, nothing would serve him but he would take me to the /his/ new Office, to shew me the lines[?] thereof. We had not been in his room two minutes when up came a Messenger saying that Colonel Lenox[3] was below, desiring to speak to him—'Tell him I can't see him'—What hindered the great man's seeing him?—He was too busily engaged with me, explaining to me what I never asked him to explain the difference between a Lettre de Chancellerie and a *Lettre de Cachet* such as our own most gracious King, as he assured me (God bless his Majesty!) is in the daily habit of dispatching and shewing me upon a piece of blank paper with pack-thread and sealing wax the manufactory thereof. In the midst of these important communications he rings up a Messenger again and sends him to the Council Chamber to Fawkener[4] to tell him that he was there and ready or desirous I forget which to see him. Soon after in comes Fawkener, and not knowing that we were acquainted the Great Man begins naming us to each other. After handshaking and so forth, Fawkener began talking about you and his mechanical ladies, who it seems

---

1023a. [1] B.L. V: 621–2. Autograph. No signature, docket or address.

This missive and the next (1023*b*) may be considered as one letter in two parts. In paragraph 2 of 1023*a* Bentham tells his brother that after returning to Hendon from Queen's Square Place 'I have been writing this stuff, with some less frivolous stuff to you on another sheet' (B.L. V: 620).

[2] Dundas.

[3] Charles Lennox, lieutenant-colonel in the 35th (Dorsetshire) Regiment of Foot from 1789.

[4] William Augustus Fawkener, Clerk of the Council.

102

have not given up their designs upon you. He asked where you were gone, and I told him, and when you return he must have legal notice. He asked likewise with much apparent interest and impatience about the state of Panopticon. I returned his compliment with the short answer which I conceived was all that was desired, and pleading business, viz: their business, and my own quality of idle man and intruder made my escape—In going out the street (we had come in the Park Way) I passed through a line of people who I dare say all had their business, and whose business was to be postponed or sent to the Devil while I was getting my initiation into the diplomatic mysteries. Learn hence, young Man the nature of business: if I had happened to have had business with the illustrissimo he would no more have seen me than he would Colonel Lenox, or than Mr Long would *me*, I having business with him, the day before. What is most probable is that neither this familiarity nor any former distances or familiarities meant any thing except the illustrissimo's general versatility—what is possible is, that among the superior diplomacy, the Ld Spencers for instance or the Ld Grenvilles of the age he may have heard by accident that the opposition to the Land won't do and that the consummation of all things is approaching.

Emmeline the 1st[5] lasted me by God's providence exactly till I got housed—It is a delightful thing, and we must get acquainted somehow or other with Charlotte Smith. Since then I have been writing this stuff with some less frivolous stuff to you on another sheet, giving instruction to Jack for the first of a set of Tables for you, myself, and Miss F.,[6] each of us to have a copy of on column paper lying upon one of my desks to cast a glance at whenever occasion comes across, and which will contain whatever is of any use in Geometry at a view. Table 1st in order of execution, because the chiefest in point of utility, though the last in Payne's[7] and Euclid's, in short in every body's order of tradition is the first that he begins with: it contains all Payne's problems in Mensuration: which by an example or two I shall I believe make Jack convert into Theorems, as being shorter—and now I am going to do a little *Paper* currency: from all which you will understand that yesterday's

[5] *Emmeline, or the Orphan of the Castle*, 4 vols. 1788, was the first of Charlotte Smith's novels, praised by Sir Walter Scott in his short appreciation of her.
[6] Mary Sophia Fordyce, who was apparently teaching 'Jack' to write and count.
[7] Probably a reference to William Payne's *Introduction to Geometry, containing the most useful Propositions in Euclid and other Authors*, 1767. He also issued *An Introduction to the Mesuration of Superficies and Solids*, 1768, and *Elements of Trigonometry, Plain and Spherical*, 1772, which contains 'A table of logarithms, etc.'

intellectual impotence is pretty well gone off, as I had the honour of promising you it would.

Miss F. has replaced Chinnery[8] perfectly in favour, by shewing me some very good writing of her son's as I call him who learnt of him—but that's nothing at all—I should have said by telling me how she had learnt of him and found him the only one of a multitude of great masters who taught by rule, he having in short mounted a system about the matter which is more perhaps than even the great Smyrnoff[9] has done notwithstanding his specimens extracted from Russian paws by *spirit of stick*. Chinnery it seems neither wants for genius nor for communicativeness, only there is reason for thinking that the evening the time which has fallen to Jack's share, is not the time in which it develops itself to most advantage. The thing I am this moment longing for, as if I were with child is the dear dying book: and that after a violent struggle, I determined to leave with Upsal for Miss F.

1023*b*

To Samuel Bentham

15 November 1794 (Aet 46)

Hendon Novr. 15th 1794
Saty. afternoon

Considering the risk we are running of losing the atmospherical business[2] every day by a variety of causes—a business not inferior perhaps to uniformation I can not bear the thought of delaying the Patent any longer. On the other leaf[3] are some specimens of

[8] William Chinnery, writing master, author of *Writing and Drawing made easy, amusing and instructive, c.* 1750.

[9] Yakov Ivanovich Smirnov was chaplain to the Russian embassy in London, but the reference is more probably to a Russian schoolmaster of the same name.

1023b. [1] B.L. V: 620. Autograph. The second part of what was really one letter (see letter 1023a, n. 1).

[2] Lady Bentham thus describes this invention of Samuel's: 'He had conceived, even during the time of his apprenticeship, that many chemical and manufacturing effects might be better produced, and more economically also, *in vacuo*, than by the usual modes of operation. Much of his time and many of his thoughts were occupied for more than a twelvemonth in directing experiments that were made in a receiver exhausted by a common air-pump, but the receiver and connected apparatus he adapted to the various operations to be performed. The experiments, it is true, were made on a small scale, but they were sufficient to exhibit the soundness of his opinions on the subject, and to enable him to take [out] a patent for the inventions' (M. S. Bentham, *Life of Sir Samuel Bentham*, 1862, p. 101).

[3] Missing.

wording which if you approve of I could talk over with Mr Poole,[4] not giving him that which *lets the cat out of the bag* unless he gives me reason for apprehending the more general and mysterious form would be insufficient. Why not sufficient as well as 'divers new modes of working in wood stone iron and other materials' etc.?

As to the money, could not you in your own name, or in my name or in both our names apply to Lindegreen,[5] and ask him to accommodate us with the £200 stating for what purpose, till the first moneys come in from Government? If it should not be convenient to him just now, the assurance of having it within this month or even these 6 weeks would be sufficient. Poole you know never wants it all at once, and what he wants to begin with we could borrow from the existing Panopticon money if we were sure of its being replaced. Supposing for arguments sake that Panopticon were to go to the Devil, it is impossible to suppose that there would not be at least a dozen applications of the principle each of which would be a marketable commodity without disposing of the others: or if all other resources failed I would give him any security he chose. As we are so likely to be so particularly connected with him, and as he probably has ready money to much more than that amount at command without prejudice to his business, it is better I think to try him than any body else.

If an assurance of the money was obtained something might possibly be done, some time be gained, before *swearing* time, and consequently in your absence, without waiting for your return—I could at any rate talk the matter over with Mr Poole and without letting puss out of the bag learn from him what patents had been taken out of late, and thence whether there be among them any thing touching upon our ground.

1024

FROM ETIENNE DUMONT

November 1794

Je vous prie, mon cher Benth⟨am⟩ de m'envoyer les manuscrits sur le droit civil que vous m'aviez montré avant mon départ

---

[4] Perhaps Henry Poole.
[5] Lindigren, their friend in Portsmouth.
1024. [1] B.L. V: 623. Autograph. Docketed: '1794 Nov. / Dumont Lansd. House / to / J.B. Q.S.P.'
Addressed: 'Jer. Bentham Esq.'

pour Bowood.—Avez-vous fait quelque chose pour completter la table des délits?—Dès que je serai guéri d'un rhume, j'irai dejeûner avec vous. Adieu. J'ai fait votre commission à D'Yvernois.[2]

1025

To Henry Dundas

1 December 1794 (Aet 46)

Queens Square Place Westmr Dec:r 1 1794

Sir

I am sorry to /have/ be obliged to trouble you once more about my unfortunate business. My Memorial which with so obliging a degree of dispatch was transmitted by your order the 2nd day after its being received, that is now a month ago, together with an official letter under your signature recommending it as I understand to immediate notice remains still unanswered: being regularly presented to, and as regularly put aside by Mr Pitt. The object therefore of this my humble address is to entreat the further favour of you to employ your personal intercession for the purpose of obtaining that decision, the delay of which is so inexplicable and so distressing to me.

---

[2] François D'Ivernois (1757–1842), the Swiss economist and financier, who had been condemned to death by a revolutionary tribunal in Geneva and fled to England, where he was already well-known, in 1794. He received from George III an honorary knighthood for his services to politics and learning. In the changed conditions of 1814–15 he represented Geneva at the Congress of Vienna. See also notes to letters 1026 and 1027 below.

1025. [1] B.L. V: 624–5. Autograph rough draft. Docketed: 'Panopt / J.B. Q.S.P. / to / Rt. Hon. H. Dundas / Brouillon / Pitt puts by the Instrument with aversion as often as presented by Long.'

There is no reason to suppose that a letter based on this draft was not sent: three further paragraphs, giving particulars of the expenses already incurred by the Panopticon project, are completely crossed out and presumably were not included in the final version.

Bentham drafted two more letters to Dundas at the end of the month, but these were definitely not sent. One is docketed: '1794 Dec 31 / Panopt / J.B. Q.S.P. / to / Rt. Hon. H. Dundas / Difficulties about Battersea / Rise removed / Suppressed at the suggestion / of Mr Long as reporting more than he chose to be / known to have reported' (B.L. V: 626; another copy, not in Bentham's hand, is on fo. 627). The other draft letter of the same date is much longer (3 pp.) and is docketed: '1794 / Panopt / J.B. to Dundas / Not sent / Long's information / that there were objections now to Battersea Rise.'

1026

FROM FRANÇOIS D'IVERNOIS

c. 3 December 1794

I have thought it necessary to put my name to the work. I had
been silent, for it was natural for me to wish to withdraw both from
the literary and political scene; but as many readers have asked
whether it is not my object capriciously to blacken the French
Revolution,[2] I feel that I am bound to take upon myself the responsibility of an historian.

1027

TO BARON ST HELENS

5 December 1794 (Aet 46)

Q.S.P. December 5th, 1794.

My dear Lord,

On reading the enclosed, (D'Ivernois' work,)[2] it occurred to me
that the example of the tragedies it displays might possibly be of
use within the circle of your lordship's mission; and that some
member of the Government there might think it worth while to get
it translated and printed there with that view.[3] Two propositions
seem to be placed by it in a strong light: that French principles are
not more hostile to a monarchy than they are to any existing
commonwealth, and that the first authors of a revolution grounded
on such principles, or supported by such assistance, may depend
upon being the second victims. If I may believe the enclosed letter

1026. [1] Bowring, x, 305. A quotation, perhaps translated from French, introduced by
the statement: 'D'Ivernois, in sending to Bentham his volume on the French Revolution, expresses a wish that it should be known in Holland, and adds'
[2] His most recent book on the subject was *La Révolution francoise à Genève. Tableau
historique et politique de la France envers les Genevois depuis le mois d' Octobre 1792 au
mois d' Octobre 1794*, London, 1794. An English translation appeared in 1795 and also
a German translation at Leipzig (see Otto Karmin, *Sir Francis D'Ivernois, 1757–1842*,
Geneva, 1920, pp. 670–1). Karmin considers it astonishing that Bentham should have
been interested in the dissemination of this book, since of all the works of D'Ivernois
'aucune n'a été écrite avec une documentation aussi insuffisante, avec une mauvaise
foi plus complète, avec une haine moins dissimulée' (op. cit., p. 257 and n. 3).
1027. [1] Bowring, x, 305–6. Introduced by the statement: 'Lord St. Helens was at this
period our ambassador at the Hague, and Bentham thus addressed him:'.
[2] The identification in brackets is by Bowring. See above, letter 1026, n. 2.
[3] It was not translated into Dutch, as here suggested.

from the author, a man of good character, with whom I have a slight acquaintance, the same idea of the utility derivable from the publication, had occurred to and been recommended by, Mr Windham to your lordship. Should any steps have been taken in consequence, I hope the business will not be so advanced but that the corrections and additions, annexed to the present copy, may come in time. The other little pamphlet is by M. Chauvet, master of an academy of the higher order at Kennington.[4] Some months ago I took the liberty of giving a relation of mine by marriage, Mr Abbott, a letter of introduction to your lordship; whether he ever had an opportunity of delivering it, I do not as yet know; for soon after his return to his country, he followed his wife to her long home.[5]

As for my own—my own affair,—I mean the castle in the air—
'Tis now as whilom might be sung, adherent-stuck, suspended-hung;

coördinate as well as subordinate persons, well affected, and not unzealous, but the grand and universal damper and doer of nothing, who knows he is ruining me, and has ruined my brother, still insensible and immoveable.[6]

Mr Gally's court, I hear, has opened for the winter; but that one of us who attends courts, whether for want of legal notice or for what other cause, has not yet begun to do suit and service.

Believe me now and for evermore, with the most affectionate respect, my dear lord, your most devoted

J.B.

[4] Bentham is probably confusing two Swiss émigrés with the same surname. Peter Chauvet was a schoolmaster from Geneva who ran an academy at Kensington, not Kennington. He died on 16 September 1796 (*Gentleman's Magazine*, 1796, lxvi, p. 798). David Chauvet, who also lived in Kensington, is much more likely to have written the pamphlet.

[5] As already noted (above, p. 49 n. 3), John Farr Abbot, Bentham's step-brother, had died on 22 September 1794. His wife, Mary (*née* Pearce) had predeceased him.

[6] William Pitt.

1028

TO THE MARQUIS OF LANSDOWNE

11 December 1794 (Aet 46)

Q.S.P. Dec:r 11 1794.

My Lord

The most unfeeling and faithless of Ministers[2] and mankind has not left me bread to eat. If it were of any use my existence should be supported two or three days longer, you might pay, give or lend me a miserable £12, being the price of certain books sent in to the Library at Lansdown House, in obedience to your Lordship's commands in the year of the Christian Æra 1789. It was the collection of the Transactions of the French Provincial Assemblies in 20 Vols 4to or thereabouts.

Great debates whether to beg as thus, or to write a letter about blood and wounds, and putting of money into a *sartin place*, or to lay in wait and display the polish of a pistol, or to break into the Butler's room some favourable night, and lay hold of whatever it afforded. At last, among a number of courses equally scandalous, this was preferred, as steering clear of halters.

All this will seem a dream to you: but if you will enquire whether such books are in the library, you will probably find them there: and if you enquire from what Bookseller they came, you will hear of none unless Mr. Cross[3] should happen to have among his Bills one of Elmsly's to me for those books, and I think to that amount, which said bill I with this hand gave not long after into your Lordship's.

Were you to see me, you would find me looking as well as talking like Romeo's Apothecary:[4] yet still, (saving these my necessities)

Your Lordship's most devoted Servant
to command till death, that is for a few days,
Jeremy Bentham

Marquis of Lansdown

1028. [1] Lansdowne Mss. Autograph. No signature, docket or address.
Printed in Bowring, x, 306, with a few verbal differences, perhaps because a draft was used.
[2] William Pitt.
[3] An employee of Lansdowne's.
[4] 'In tatter'd weeds, with overwhelming brows,
Culling of simples; meagre were his looks,
Sharp misery had worn him to the bones'
(*Romeo and Juliet*, V, I, 39–41).

1029

FROM THE MARQUIS OF LANSDOWNE

12 December 1794

Friday Morning,
12th December, 1794.

Dear Bentham,

I do not think you deserve the enclosed, but when you are upon the point of the cliff, I will promise you as much more.[2] I have, I assure you, been in a great deal of pain for you, for I am afraid you have got among a set of r——s.[3] I have been perpetually thinking how I could be of use to you; but I do not see that I can, except, perhaps, a little advice about men, and as to what may happen. The ladies are out of town. Why will not you and your brother come and dine here some Saturday with Romilly and Dumont, when it can do you no harm to talk your affairs over?

Next Saturday I have a dinner of Americans, but the following Saturday is quite at your command.

I am, though you do not deserve it,
very sincerely yours.

1030

TO SAMUEL BENTHAM

8[?] January 1795 (Aet 46)

Q.S.P. 8 o'clock Thursday evening

Peake[2] has been here but does not sleep here. The moment that your business at the Society[3] is over, come here and sleep here. I have the most urgent need of you—urgent, very urgent indeed. No

---

1029. [1] Bowring, x, 306.
[2] Evidently money in some form.
[3] Probably 'rogues' was the word meant.
1030. [1] B.L. V: 628–9. Autograph. No signature, date or docket.
Addressed: 'To / Colonel Bentham / At the Society of Arts / Adelphi'.
A date early in January seems probable; the second Thursday was the 8th day of the month.
[2] Either Henry or 'Jack' Peake, who in 1796 became the secretary of Samuel Bentham in the new office of the Inspector-General of Naval Works (M. S. Bentham, *Life of Sir Samuel Bentham*, 1862, p. 118).
[3] The Royal Society of Arts, founded in 1754.

harm however happened, nor to happen, nor any thing, that need
make you wish to quit the society before the business is quite done.

1031

To Henry Dundas

12 January 1795 (Aet 46)

12 Jan:y 1795

Sir
    I understand that Mr Pitt waits only to be informed of the
opinion you had the goodness to announce to me on Friday, in
order to accede to it, but that he must be informed of it by *yourself*,
and that he has not thus been informed of it. I am sorry to be thus
repeatedly troublesome to you about my unfortunate business, but
you see how necessary it is that I should be so—   I have the
honour to be,

with all respect,
Sir,
Your most obedient
and humble Servant
Jeremy Bentham

Rt Hon.ble H.ʸ Dundas

1031. ¹ B.L. VI: 1–2. Autograph draft. Docketed: '1795 Jan 12 / Panopticon / J.B.
Q.S.P. / to / Dundas Somerset House / Brouillon.'
    Addressed: 'To / The Right Honble Henry Dundas / etc. etc. etc.'
    This letter reveals that Bentham had had an interview with Dundas on Friday, 9th
January, the prospect of which may account for his anxiety to consult his brother on
the 8th (see letter 1030).
    There is another draft of a letter to Dundas, dated 'Jan 15 or 16', beginning: 'Sir / I
now find that Mr Pitt, after having referred to you the decision on my business as you
yourself were pleased to inform me and received that decision has gone back from it
/refused to abide by it/ act /carry it into effect/ and adjourned the matter *sine die* . . .'
Bentham goes on to complain of the 'ruin' which the delays and uncertainty have
caused to his brother and will soon cause to himself. January 28th, he says, will be a
decisive day, for if a bill of £280 for cast iron is not met Samuel may have to go to
prison. If Pitt suffers this disgrace to fall upon them, Bentham's 'last and melancholy
appeal' must be to the justice of his country: 'in plain terms I must then bring my
notice against him for damages' (B.L. VI: 5). This draft is, however, docketed: 'Not
sent / Nepean told J.B. that Battersea Rise was fixed upon, and that he should have it
to announce in form the Monday.'

1032
FROM FRANÇOIS D'IVERNOIS
26 January 1795

Voici Monsieur le petit écrit que vous avez cru mériter une traduction,[2] et votre opinion à cet égard n'a pas peu contribué à me faire accepter l'offre obligeante de la personne qui s'en est chargé. J'y joins un double exemp[laire] pour Mr Burgess[3] que je ne connais point assez pour le lui adresser moi meme ce dont je vous prie de vouloir bien prendre le soin. Agréez Monsieur, l'assurance de tous les sentiments distingués que je vous ai voués.

D'Ivernois

Le 26 Janv. 1795
No. 36 St. James's Place.

1033
FROM WILLIAM WILBERFORCE
27 January 1795

My dear Sir,

Will you allow my friends Ld Muncaster[2] and Dr Milner[3] to see the Panopticon tomorrow. I beg you will not confine yourself to attend them, and indeed I am less interested in your doing so because I fear I shall not be able to accompany them—yours sincerely

W. Wilberforce

Pal Yd. Wedy. night.

1032. [1] B.L. VI: 6–7. Autograph. Docketed: '1795 Jan 26 / D'Ivernois / to / J.B. Q.S.P. / with translation of Tableau de Geneve.'

[2] *Tableau historique et politique des deux dernières révolutions de Genève*, 2 vols., London, 1789.

[3] Perhaps Sir James Bland Burges, afterwards Lamb (1752–1824), M.P., 1787–95; under-secretary for foreign affairs, 1789–95; he supported Wilberforce in the campaign against the slave trade and was interested in other reforms.

1033. [1] B.L. VI: 8–9. Autograph. Docketed: '1795 Jan 27 / Panopt / Wilberforce O. Pal Yd / to / S. or J.B. Q.S.P. / To show Panopt. to Ld Muncaster and Dr Milner.' Addressed: 'Col. Bentham or Jeremiah Bentham Esqr.'.

[2] Sir John Pennington, first Baron Muncaster (1737–1813), M.P. from 1781, supported Lord North and afterwards Pitt; created an Irish peer, 1783.

[3] Isaac Milner (1750–1820), divine and mathematician, F.R.S.; first professor of natural philosophy at Cambridge, 1783–92; president of Queen's College 1788–1820; vice-chancellor of the university, 1792, and again in 1809. He was a close friend of Wilberforce.

1034

To Viscount Sydney

3 or 4 February 1795 (Aet 46)

Queens Square Place Westmr. 3d Feb. 1795

My Lord

Understanding from Mr. D'Ivernois that your Lordship appeared to express a curiosity in relation to the intended species of building stiled a Panopticon, or Inspection-House and the plan for the confinement and employment of convicts that has been grounded on it, I take the liberty of begging the honour of your Lordship's acceptance for a copy of an unpublished Book in which the plan of management as well as construction is detailed at large as well as applied to several other purposes. In the book references are made to prints, but the plates together with the impression have been burned by accident at the Copper-plate Printers. The loss however is the less to be regretted, as the details of the construction have received very great improvement in the hands of my Brother, and in particular to such a degree in the article of expence, as enables me to save upon a moderate computation £200,000 to the public; since in addition to the capital I advance myself I receive for that purpose no more than £15,000. We have Models of the building in this /its/ improved state which supersede the greatest part of the 2d volume of the Book, and which we should be very proud of the honour of shewing at any time to your Lordship and any of your friends at my house as above, together with my Brothers mechanical inventions which superseding the necessity of either dexterity or good will on the part of the workmen enable us to employ the labour of convicts as well as other raw and unwilling hands of every description in every branch of Shipwright's Carpenters Joiners Cabinet makers Turners work as well as many branches of work in stone and metal and in that point of view formed the subject of a speech made by Mr Dundas on moving for leave to bring in the Penitentiary Bill, which passed into an Act last

1034. [1] B.L. VI: 10–11. Autograph draft. Docketed: '1795 Feb. 4 / Panopt / J.B. Q.S.P. / to / Ld Sydney 12 Grosvenor Square / with copy of Panopt.'

Thomas Townshend, first Viscount Sydney (1733–1800) had had a chequered parliamentary career, including service as Home Secretary under Shelburne (being created a baron in 1783) and again under Pitt, with whose India Bill he disagreed. He resigned in 1789, but was raised to a viscountcy, with a substantial income from sinecures. Bentham had met him in the Bowood circle in the 1780s (see *Correspondence*, iii, 198 and n. 5).

113

Session under the title of an Act for erecting a Penitentiary House or Houses for the confining and employing Convicts. (34 Geo: 3. ch. 84 7th July 1794.).

In the course of a few days I propose myself the honour to take the liberty of calling at your Lordship's /in Grosvenor Square/ to know whether it would be agreable to your Lordship to fix a day (for we should know beforehand) and shall have in my pocket a copy of my Proposal as accepted by Mr Pitt and Mr Dundas which gave occasion to the above Act. Recalling with pleasure the time when I had the honour of being better known to your Lordship than of late I beg leave to subscribe myself with unceasing respect.

My Lord
Yours Lordships most obedient
and most humble Servant
Jeremy Bentham
Ld Visct Sidney

1035

To Charles Long

5 February 1795 (Aet 46)

5 Feb. 1795 Thursday

Dear Sir

I saw Mr Dundas yesterday: he said he would speak again to Mr. Pitt, and appointed me to hear the result on Sunday. Your kindness I thought might possibly avail of the intelligence, to profit by any opportunities that may occurr, and follow up any impression that may have been made, in behalf of

Your much obliged
Jʸ Bentham

I have no need to bother your further at present unless you happen to have any commands for me.

1035. ¹ B.L. VI: 12. Autograph draft. Docketed: '1795 Feb. 5 / Panopt / J.B. / to / C. Long / Dundas promises to speak to Pitt. / Saw him afterwards—no news.'

1036

FROM THOMAS OSBERT MORDAUNT

6 February 1795

Gen Mordaunt presents His Comps to Ms Benthams. Begs leave to enclose this Note from Lord Lansdown. Any day that is convenient to Ms B—s G—M—t will do Himself the Honor to wait on them with Mr Prachy² in Queens Place.

If *tomorrow* is agreable G.M. will wait on them at any Hour most Convenient.

St. James's Place,
 Fryday—

1037

TO EVAN NEPEAN

6 February 1795 (Aet 46)

Q.S.P. 6 Feb. 95 Friday.

I hope you dont forget to give Mr Dundas a jog now and then against Sunday—I saw Mr Long yesterday at ½ past 3 he had not heard any thing from Mr Pitt.

If *distant* mischances have their proper effect, it will be to dispose him no longer to struggle against doing the good which it is so compleatly in his power to do *at home*, which on his part requires neither time nor study—nor any thing but one single *word*, which can not be either refused or delayed without trampling on every obligation of honour generosity and good faith. Mr Dundas saw a *billet-doux* from my *Banker*—When you hear next from me, it may probably be from some Jail, unless Mr. Dundas finds something substantial to tell me of by Sunday.

Can Mr Pitt so far delude himself as to believe, that when my

1036. ¹ B.L. VI: 13–14. Docketed: '1795 Feb. 6 / Panopt / Genl Mordaunt / St. James's Place / to / J. and S.B. Q.S.P. / To see Panopt etc. with note from Ld L.'
 Addressed: 'Jermʸ Bentham Esq— / or Col Bentham / Queens Square Place / Westminster.'
 Thomas Osbert Mordaunt was from 1778 a lieutenant-colonel in the 10th Regiment of Dragoons under General Sir John Mordaunt (1697–1780); he was promoted to major-general in 1782 and lieutenant-general on 12 October 1793.
 ² Not identified.

1037. ¹ B.L. VI: 15–16. Autograph draft. Docketed: '1795 Feb 6 / Panopt / J.B. Q.S.P. / to / Nepean Horse Guards.'

115

case comes to be known, either the Country or Parliament can be kept from drawing their inferences from *small* concerns to *great*?

1038

TO CHARLES LONG

9 February 1795 (Aet 46)

Q.S.P. Monday Morng Feb.

Dear Sir,

I have to regret the being the cause (though, as you may well believe the innocent one) of dragging you out thus early. The note from Mr Dundas, (to me a very unexpected one) requesting you to meet him at Mr Pitt's at ½ after 10 this morning, was shewn to me before it went. To provide for the contingency of your having any commands for me previous to the meeting I shall be in the Treasury Chambers ¼ before the time, and shall have in my pocket the Act of Parliament and the Instrument of appointment as approved and signed by Mr Lowndes.

1039

TO CHARLES LONG

9 February 1795 (Aet 46)

Q.S.P. 9 Feb. 95.

Dear Sir

Mr Dundas, I understand, sends to make another appointment with you for the same hour tomorrow. If your indisposition should unfortunately prevent your meeting him, I fear the business will be in a bad plight, for Mr Garthshore spoke of it as a matter of great difficulty and even uncertainty the getting Mr Dundas to make this second exertion on behalf of

Your most obedt

J.B.

1038. [1] B.L. VI: 19–20. Autograph draft. Docketed: '1795 Feb 9 / Panopt / J.B. Q.S.P. / to / C. Long, Grosvenor Place / Meeting at ½ after 10 at Pitts.'
1039. [1] B.L. VI: 17–18. Autograph draft. Docketed: '1795 Feb. 9 / Panopt / J.B. Q.S.P. / to / C. Long / Grosvenor Place.'
   This note was, it seems, written after letter 1038, because Long had failed to keep the appointment at 10.30 a.m. on the 9th.

1040

TO SAMUEL BENTHAM

10 February 1795 (Aet 46)

Q.S.P. 10 Feb –95

Just received yours[2]—but a moment for writing—your inclosed shall be forwarded.

This and yesterday morning spent at the Treasury Chambers—a second appointment made and kept by Dundas—broken by Long— though Dundas staid both times long after Long came. Pitt refusing to hear of the business without Dundas. Written by Longs recommendation a letter[3] to get Dundas to make a 3d appointment. Long has a cold which however does not prevent his coming out. His laziness was foretold me by Garthshore.

I dine a 2d time at Chalie's[4] (Garthshore's Father in Law) because Garthshore is to be there—so is Abbot—and I have a notice Mr and Mrs Rudge,[5] who having been speared will be nuisances—but there is no help for it. If Lin[6] can't find the thousand I hope he will a hundred or two upon a pinch for present use to keep us from starving and from going to Jail unless sent thither by the Bankers.

Colonel Mordaunt[7] (Ld Spencers man) has been sending to see Panopticon (inclosing a note from Ld L) and waits only for your arrival. I would not let him come till your return—unless he had not chosen to stay.

1040. [1] B.L. VI: 21–2. Autograph. No signature. Docketed: '1795 Feb / JB. SB / Panopticon.'
Addressed: 'To / Colonel Bentham / at A Lindegren's Esq. / Portsmouth.' Postmark: 'FE 10 95 E'.

[2] Missing.

[3] Letter 1041.

[4] John Chalié (d. 1803), whose daughter, Jane, had married Garthshore in 1794. He was a partner in the firm of John and Matthew Chalié, 29 Mincing Lane, and lived at 12 Bedford Square, London.

[5] Perhaps Edward Rudge and his wife, of 4 Russell Place, Tottenham Court Road, London.

[6] Lindigren.

[7] He was already a general. See letter 1036.

117

1041

TO HENRY DUNDAS

10 February 1795 (Aet 46)

Tuesday Feb. 10 1795.

Sir

Mr Long, who went to Mr Pitt's apartment this morning with my papers in his hand, reports that Mr Pitt is decided in his refusal to attend to the business which I have the misfortune to call mine unless when you are present. All this while I am witness to your having written to Mr Long two appointments for two successive days (today and yesterday) to meet you at Mr Pitt's at ½ after 10 each day, mine being the only business named, you are there accordingly on both days, at or before the time appointed, you stay till long after Mr Long's arrival and for anything I know to the contrary for no other business than mine. Mr Long being indisposed comes the first day at about 12, the second at ½ after eleven. Under these circumstances he recommends it to me to be a suitor to you for a third appointment for any day at your pleasure. I really do not know on what terms to state such a request, or to express my vexation at finding myself driven to be thus troublesome to you, or the difficulty I am under at conceiving how it should have happened that the two former ones should have had such a termination. It really looks like a jest, and if it were a jest it is rather a cruel one, to set an obscure, distressed /almost/ half ruined individual like myself to find out means for bringing together three such persons as a first Lord of the Treasury, a Secretary of the Treasury and a principal Secretary of State, every day seeing one another, and every day transacting all sorts of businesses but mine. All I can say is, that if such a thing as a third appointment were obtainable, there seems a danger to judge of the future by the past, that an hour earlier than twelve stands but an indifferent chance of being kept.

1041. ¹ B.L. VI: 23–4. Autograph draft, much corrected. Docketed: '1795 Feb. 10 / Panopt / J.B. Q.S.P. / to / Dundas Horse Guards / For second appointment   Delivered through Nepean / Afterwards Garthshore spoke to Dundas and got the 2d appointment accordingly.'

The docket indicates that a letter on these lines was sent, but whether the 'second' or 'third' appointment was kept is not clear from the text.

In great perplexity and distress, but with constant respect and gratitude,
Sir,
Your most obedient and humble Servt
Jeremy Bentham
Right Hon. H. Dundas.

1042

To Henry Dundas

12 February 1795 (Aet 46)

12 Feby 1795
Sir
A misconception between you and Mr Long, will if not set to rights, be fatal to both your wishes on my behalf. Mr Nepean and Mr Garthshore's conception was that Mr Long was to mention to Mr Pitt the proposition about his giving the authority to Mr Long and Mr Nepean for Sunday. Mr Long's notion was that you, Sir, were to mention it. Mr Long will mention it, if such be your commands: but his notion is that he is of all persons the least competent and you, Sir, the most competent, to propose him for a referee. It had already struck me so forcibly in the same point of view, that the idea of his being to be the bearer of such a proposal instead of you, had suggested to me the most alarming apprehensions. Mr Long was going over to you to adjust the matter, but his Messenger found you just stepping in to your carriage and unable to stay. The difference between the having and not having the benefit of your influence in support of such a proposition is so great, that I would much rather lose the day *proposed* than be deprived of that advantage. I am with all respect.

Sir,
Your most obedient Servt
Jy Bentham
Rt. Hon. H. Dundas.

1042. [1] B.L. VI: 25–6. Autograph draft. Docketed: '1795 Feb. 12 / Panopt / J.B. Q.S.P. / to / Rt. Hon. H. Dundas / Brouillon.'

1043

From Thomas Osbert Mordaunt

26 February 1795

Genl. Mordaunt presents his Comps. to Mr. Bentham and to Coll. Bentham.

If its is not inconvenient Mr Preehy[2] and Himself will do themselves the Honor to wait on them Saturday next between one and two o'Clock—

Thursday 26th inst.

1044

To the Marquis of Lansdowne

6 March 1795 (Aet 47)

You ask me, what success I have met with from the great man? meaning, I suppose, Mr Pitt. If I had met with success—that is, if I had settled with him—you would not have been four-and-twenty hours without hearing of it. The case is, that besides his procrastinating disposition, the chapter of accidents has been against me. On the 6th or 7th of last month, Mr Dundas, with the privity of Mr Pitt, wrote to Mr Long (Secretary to the Treasury) to meet him on the Monday, the 9th, at Mr Pitt's, at half after ten, to settle everything. Mr Long having a cold, and sore throat, did not come till half after eleven,—and so nothing was done. Mr Dundas, at my solicitation, wrote therefore to Mr Long, to make another appointment for the same hour the next day. Mr Long having still the same indisposition, did not come till twelve,—so that opportunity was likewise lost. Mr Dundas thereupon finding the difficulty there was to find a sufficient time that would suit the joint convenience of himself, Mr Pitt and Mr Long, proposed, in concurrence with Mr Nepean, (who had conducted the business with me originally, to the stage at which, for want of parliamentary authority, it stopped,)

1043. [1] B.L. VI: 27–8. Original. Docketed: '1795 Feb 26 / Panopt / Gen. Mordaunt St James Place / to / J. and S.B. Q.S.P. / To see Panopt. 28.'
  Addressed: 'Bentham Esq. / Queen's Square Place / Westminster.'
  [2] The unidentified 'Mr Praehy' mentioned in letter 1036, p. 115 above.
1044. [1] Bowring, x, 306–8. Introduced with the comment 'What follows, dated March 6, 1795, is rather an amusing, though, to the sufferer, a sufficiently annoying detail of official delays and difficulties:'

that power should be obtained from Mr Pitt for him (Mr Nepean) and Mr Long to settle the business; and Mr Nepean devoted to that purpose the then next Sunday, (February 15,) the only day his regular business could possibly allow him to spare; and Mr Dundas was so sure of Mr Pitt's coming into it, that he told me on the Friday before, I might take for granted the meeting would be held with me that day, and that the business would then be done. Mr Dundas, however, reckoned without his host; for on the Monday or Tuesday after, he told me that Mr Pitt would not turn it over to anybody else: but that he had promised him, that the first hour he could spare from those branches of public business that admitted of no delay, he would set about it himself—Sunday and the fast days that were then approaching; meaning the Wednesday and the occasional fast. These fast days, however, are over, and still the business is not done; yet everybody joins in assuring me, that Mr Pitt means really to do it. In the meantime, this unfortunate business of Ireland[2] has come across them, and cannot have failed to furnish extraordinary occupation to their thoughts. They show at the same time a readiness to admit of our services in other matters. Mr Nepean t'other day introduced my brother to the Duke of York as commander-in-chief, for the purpose of examining his invention of an amphibious baggage-wagon, to answer the purpose of wagon and boats without increase of weight.[3] My brother accordingly waited on the Duke, at York House, by appointment the next day, Sunday se'nnight, February 22, with the model. The Duke saw it,—approved it highly, and gave him orders for making some in the great, and talked of coming to Q.S.P. to see Panopticon and the other things. The very next day, without any warning, he came —saw—admired, and told Nepean afterwards that he should bring the king, who would probably have been here before this, if my brother had not desired a day's notice, which was accordingly

---

[2] As part of his bargain for the support of the Portland Whigs, Pitt had in January 1795 replaced Lord Westmorland by William Wentworth Fitzwilliam, 2nd Earl Fitzwilliam (1748–1833), as Lord Lieutenant of Ireland. He was, however, recalled early in March for exceeding his instructions by encouraging premature hopes of catholic emancipation.

[3] Frederick Augustus, Duke of York and Albany (1763–1827), second son of King George III, had commanded the British forces in Flanders, 1793–5, but did not become titular Commander-in-Chief until 1798. Lady Bentham supplies the information that the Duke of York 'having examined a small model of such a vehicle expressed a wish that a similar one of full size should be constructed on his account. It was accordingly completed and tried satisfactorily on the Thames'. She adds that subsequently Samuel's 'Engagements with the Admiralty precluded his attention and it still rests in abeyance' (M.S. Bentham, *Life of Sir Samuel Bentham*, 1862, pp. 116–17).

121

promised. No baggage wagons, however, will my brother make till he has got orders for them from Lord Cornwallis, the new master of the ordance, to whom Nepean has already spoken of him, and has promised to introduce him in person by the first opportunity for that purpose.[4] Mr Pitt and Mr Dundas have likewise intimated to Mr Nepean, a disposition to listen to my brother's plans of improvement in relation to the navy: and for a beginning, have declared their willingness to turn over to him the Orion of 74— known as the worst sailer in the navy, which he has undertaken to make the best. He has likewise been sounded about quitting the Empress's service, for the purpose of taking such a situation in our admiralty service, as would give him the power necessary for carrying his plans into effect. The arrangement of these matters waits for Nepean's removal from his present office to his new situation of principal Secretary to the Admiralty, where he is to have great influence.[5] We have already an order from the Board of Ordance to make wheels, but the present situation of the works does not admit great despatch in the execution of it. What is remarkable is, that Pitt and Dundas should undertake for the alteration in the Orion, before Lord Spencer had been consulted about it.[6] My brother's introduction to Lord Spencer, has been deferred till Nepean, who is to do it, has been seated in his new office, which will render him the proper man for it. We are all along assured, from a variety of quarters, (for many people of weight among Mr Pitt's friends have volunteered their services on the occasion,) that his procrastination has not proceeded from any dislike either to the men or to the measure; and it was but t'other day that Nepean said to my brother in so many words, 'there are not two men alive that Mr Pitt has a higher opinion of than you and your brother.'

[4] Charles Cornwallis, 2nd Earl and 1st Marquis Cornwallis (1738–1805) had become Master General of the Ordnance in February 1795.
[5] Evan Nepean became secretary of the Admiralty in March 1795.
[6] Earl Spencer had become First Lord of the Admiralty in December 1794, in succession to the Earl of Chatham, who took his place as Lord Privy Seal.

1045

To Henry Dundas

6 March 1795 (Aet 47)

Qn Sq. Place 6th March 1795

Mr Bentham requests the favour of Mr Dundas to submitt to Mr Pitt the following proposition. Let him fix a day, any day however distant, on or before which he will have done *one* or other of three things:—settled the business himself, turned it over to somebody else, or afforded Mr. B. a temporary supply of £2,000. The worst certainty is preferable to so ruinous an uncertainty as that under which Mr B has so long been labouring.

1046

From Mr Scott

23 March 1795

Mr. Scott presents his Compliments to Mr. Bentham and begs he will accept his Apologies and Thanks for the books he has been so kind as to send him. Mr. Scott hopes Mr. Bentham will believe that he should not have had the Impertinence to make such an application, and will set it down to the account of the Bookseller or Binder, where the Blame ought to lay. Mr. S. gave the Book Mr. B: was so good as to send him some years ago, to be bound: it was lost or mislaid and as he insisted upon their getting him another in the Difficulty of finding one they were induced to make this application to Mr. Bentham, which he has been so obliging as to comply with.

Wimpole Street March 23d 1795.

1045. ¹ B.L. VI: 29–30. Autograph draft. Docketed: '1795 Mar 6 / Panopt / J.B. Q.S.P. / to / Rt. Hon. H. Dundas / Proposing 3ple alternative / Copy sent to Nepean.'
1046. ¹ B.L. VI: 31–2. Original. Docketed: '1795 Mar 23 / Panopt / Scott Wimpole Street / to J.B. Q.S.P. / Thanks for 2nd Copy of Panopt.'
    Addressed: 'Jeremy Bentham Esqr / Queen's Square Place / Westminster. Wimpole St., / March 23d / 5 o'clock.' Stamped: 'Mary⟨leb⟩on St / Penny Post / unpaid'. Postmark: '8 o'clock / 24 MR / 95 MORN'.
    Mr Scott has not been identified.

1047

To the Marquis of Lansdowne

26 March 1795 (Aet 47)

Q.S.P. 26 March 1795

My Lord

A Lady, who, not to mention her quality and character, is at once a friend of your Lordship's and a Sister of Sir Francis Baring,[2] is a most difficult personage to deal with. The letter which I take the liberty to inclose for your Lordship's perusal, was on the day of its date returned to me from her house, being refused admittance. The story was that they did not know how to convey a letter to her Ladyship—that she had not been in town these two years—that she was continually removing from place to place, and that at present they knew not where she was. Your Lordship, I am inclined to think, will join with me in looking upon this as a strange history: strange if true, and equally strange to be reported if it were not so. Your Lordship, observing my situation, as it is most truly stated in the inclosed letter, will judge whether it admitts of my acquiescing in this refusal on the part of a lady whom I really can not suppose (endow'd and related as she is) to stand in need of any such for-bearance as that she /claims/ exacts and who, to judge from the whole tenor of his correspondence with her would be much more inclined to laugh at me in her own mind than thank me for it. Under these circumstances your Lordship will not wonder that it should be a determined object with me to obtain the supply which is so much my due and which I am so much in want of: any more than that it should be an equally determined object with me to save the Lady from every inconvenience which is not the un-avoidable result of the principal pursuit. Were the first the only one, nothing could be more efficacious or more expeditious as your Lordship knows than the remedy which the law puts into my hands. To save myself from the necessity of taking a step which would cast such a stain upon her Ladyship's dignity I have sometimes had thoughts of stating the case to Sir Francis: but as a disclosure of that sort might for aught I could tell be productive of family

---

1047. [1] U.C. Ogden Mss. 62 (2) 4. Autograph draft, with a number of obliterations. Docketed: '1795 Mar 26 / J.B. Q.S.P. / to / Ld L Berkeley Square.'

[2] His sister was Lady Ashburton, the widow of John Dunning, 1st Baron Ash-burton; she was a tenant of Bentham's leasehold house, number 14, Duke Street (see *Correspondence*, iv, 363 n. 2).

uneasinesses beyond the power of a stranger to estimate I have preferred as the least evil I could think of the making my humble resort to your Lordship for advice: and that the rather as /since/ because your Lordship having in former instances been troubled on the same subject, the present business /communication/ does not subject /expose/ the state of her Ladyships affairs to any new disclosure. Perhaps your Lordship might have the goodness to enable the letter to find its way into her hands.³ I have the honour to be

My Lord, with constant respect and
attachment
Your Lordships most obedient
and humble Servant
Jeremy Bentham

Marquis of Lansdown.

1048

FROM THE MARQUIS OF LANSDOWNE

27 March 1795 (Aet 47)

My dear Bentham

I have had a conversation with Mr. Baring,² and everything will be settl'd to your satisfaction without any necessity for the inclos'd.³ I wish your business with Ld Spencer was equally sure of being settl'd.⁴ It makes me uneasy whenever I think of it, which I assure you is very often.

I am
very truly
yrs
Lansdown

Fryday
5 o'clock p.m.

---

³ Missing; perhaps destroyed by Bentham after its return by Lord Lansdowne (see letter 1048).

1048. ¹ B.L. VI: 33–4. Autograph. Docketed: '1795 Mar 27 / Ld L Berkeley Sq / to / J.B. Q.S.P.'

² Lady Ashburton's eldest brother was John Baring, to whom this may refer.

³ Probably the letter, enclosed in 1047, which Bentham had wished to have conveyed to Lady Ashburton.

⁴ The difficulty over the proposed site of the Panopticon penitentiary on Lord Spencer's land at Battersea Rise.

1049

TO HENRY DUNDAS

27 March 1795 (Aet 47)

The fast days to which Mr. Bentham's hopes had been pointed by Mr Dundas, having produced nothing but the usual mortifications, he humbly begs leave to point out the approaching holydays[2] as a season that might if it were Mr Dundas's and Mr Pitt's pleasure, be made to yield better fruits.

1050

FROM SAMUEL BENTHAM

31 March 1795

Q.S.P. 31 March 1795

I have a great cold in my head by which I am so stupid that if I go to Mr Dundas I may make some blunder: besides I have no idea for what I was to go. To ask him if he received your letter—of course he did.

If he sees me he may ask me questions I cant answer. I can say nothing but that we are both distressed from the delay, and this he has heard often enough. If you see him you can ask to see Mr Pit[t] or talk of what you will be forced to do. I cant do this. If I gain admittance to him with nothing to say, it will be more difficult for you to get admittance another time however much you have to say.

A friend of Mr. Wilberforce's has talked a good deal with Mr Pitt about Panopticon and its delay. Mr. W. tells me there has been more obstacles than we are aware of and which he is not at liberty to mention but he is in hopes they are got over.

There is still time for you to come if you think it necessary to see Dundas today.

1049. [1] B.L. VI: 35–6. Autograph draft, with several phrases crossed out. Docketed: '1795 Mar 27 / J.B. Q.S.P. / to / Dundas Somerset Place / Left by Upsal.'
   [2] Easter Sunday was on 5 April 1795.
1050. [1] B.L. VI: 37–8. Autograph. No signature. Docketed: '1795 Mar. 31 / Panopt / S.B. Q.S.P. / to / J.B. Hendon / Secret obstacles per Wilberforce.'
   Addressed: 'J. Bentham Esq. / Hendon.'
   This letter seems to be a reply to a missing one from Bentham, asking his brother to interview Dundas on his behalf.

1051

To Samuel Bentham

3 April 1795 (Aet 47)

Q.S.P. 3 Apr 1795

They could not compleat your experiment,[2] they say yesterday: but tomorrow the tide, they say, will serve better for it, and then they make pretty sure of its being done. If it is, you shall have the history of it.

No letter for you except two, which by the hand appears to be Mrs Lindegren's[3] and Peake's.[4]

One from Till[5] to me, inviting *me* to meet Mr and Miss Reeve[6] on Thursday, taking for granted and regretting that you will not be back time enough to be of the party, which is more than I know.

1052

From Etienne Dumont

3 April 1795

3 April 1795[2]

Voilà, mon cher Bentham, l'original et la copie[3]—je n'ai pas eu le temps de la relire, ce qui auroit pu vous épargner quelques corrections—je preférerois pour celles d'une certaine étendue, que vous les écrivissiez avec la plume plutôt qu'avec le crayon qui fatigue terriblement ma vue et disparoit quelque fois tout à fait— et peut-être vaudroit-il mieux les mettre sur une feuille à part avec renvoi à la page—mais ceci n'est pas de grande importance.

1051. [1] University of Edinburgh. Autograph. Addressed: 'To / Coll Bentham / At A. Lindegren's Esqr / Portsmouth.' Postmark illegible.
[2] Evidently the trial of Samuel's amphibious baggage wagon on the Thames (see above, letter 1044, n. 3).
[3] She was the sister of Charles Hanbury, an English merchant in business at Hamburg (see *Correspondence*, ii, 302 n. 1).
[4] Henry (later Sir Henry) Peake, the master shipwright.
[5] Richard Till.
[6] Perhaps Edward Reeve, a schoolfellow of Bentham's, and his sister or daughter.
1052. [1] B.L. VI: 39–40. Autograph. Docketed: '1795. April 3 / Dumont Ln House / to / J.B. Q.S.P.'
Addressed: 'Jer. Bentham Esqr.'
[2] The date is added in Bentham's hand.
[3] Perhaps the material on *Récompenses* (see above, p. 50 n. 2).

Plus j'ai pensé à la fin de notre conversation, plus je me réconcilie avec l'idée que le François pourroit être moins complet pourvû que vous eussiez vraiment l'idée et le courage de donner une Edition Angloise. Il y auroit alors de quoi satisfaire des lecteurs de différentes forces.

Ld. Lansdown a la goutte et reste en ville—le temps est triste, un petit pelerinage à Hendon me plairoit beaucoup quand le printemps seroit plus avancé. Adieu——vale et me ama.

N.B. Vous avez certainemt. le Ms. original du 1er livre.

1053

To John Jay

8 April 1795 (Aet 47)

Queens Square Place Westmr
8 Apr 1795.

Dear Sir

I avail myself of the kind permission with which I understood myself to have been favoured, to trouble you with a memorandum or two on the other leaf.

I take this opportunity to beg the honour of your acceptance for two copies (one for yourself and the other for Mr Peter Jay)[2] of an unpublished and indeed unfinished work, which though prevented by some of the Members of the then Government of France from meeting with the reception which others wished to have given it, was a good deal noticed by Mirabeau, Brissot and other leading men and was attended, I was told, with some little effect in practice.[3] I could not resist the opportunity of putting it into the hands of the most competent Judges America can afford, and if at any time the perusal of it should suggest any thing in the way of correction or confirmation to any body of your acquaintance who has leisure enough to bestow on such a subject, I should be much gratified and obliged by the communication of his remarks. Not to load you too unmercifully I send at present but one spare copy for the reader I figure to myself: but if any other friends of yours should be disposed at any time to honour the work with a place upon their

1053. [1] Columbia University Libraries, New York. Autograph.

[2] Peter Augustus Jay (1776–1843), who acted as his father's secretary during the diplomatic mission of 1794–5; he became a successful lawyer and local politician in New England.

[3] Probably Bentham's *Draught of a New Plan for the Organisation of the Judicial Establishment in France*, March 1790. See Bowring, iv, 285–406.

shelves, I have several copies more which should be heartily at their service.

To the above should have been added an unpublished extract I have in print of an unpublished work on the *Tactics of Political Assemblies*, with an analytical sketch of the contents of the remainder, but upon examination I find my stock exhausted and it would be some time before it could be replenished.—No one of these articles nor of those I took the liberty of presenting you with before were ever sold: but I could send a few copies of each to the American Bookseller in question if he chose to have them.

I was flattering myself with the hopes of seeing you and Mr Peter Jay once more at Q.S.P. in company with our excellent and common friend Lord St. Helens and another gentleman or two in the diplomatic line: but I had the mortification of learning from his Lordship that your departure would be too speedy to leave me any chance.[4]

Accept my sincerest wishes for your prosperous voyage, and believe me with the greatest respect

> Dear Sir
> Your faithful humble Servant
> Jeremy Bentham

My Brother (who is but just returned from Portsmouth) and I were in hopes of being able to make another attempt to find you at home: but the variety of businesses we have upon our hands with the offices here etc. will I fear prevent us.

Hon. J. Jay.

> Queens Square Place Westminster
> 8th April 1795

Information requested on the part of Mr. Bentham.

1. —Bookseller or Booksellers in America to whom he may address himself for the purpose of having American publications sent him as they come out—Mode and time of conveyance—Usual mode and time of payment.

2. Persons in different States to whom Mr Jay would recommend it to Mr Bentham to address himself for Plants and Seeds—Mode and time of conveyance—Usual time and mode of payment— Catalogues of stock with prices desired by the first opportunity.

---

[4] John Jay left London for the United States of America in May 1795, arriving in New York on the 28th.

1054

FROM SIR JOHN PARNELL

10 April 1795

Dear Sir

I have requested of Mr Pelham[2] that he would represent to Lord Campden[3] my most cordial approbation of following the Example of England by contracting with you for the Employment of Persons now banished by Transportation.

I have hardly any doubt but that I shall be authorized in a very few days to write to you specifically on this subject.

Do not blame [on me?] a delay which has inevitably arisen from the circumstances of our Government—and continue to give me yr assistance in forwarding a beneficial and humane system and you will much oblige

yr Obedt
Huml Servt
J. Parnell

April 10th 1795
Dublin

1054. [1] B.L. VI: 41–2. Autograph. Docketed: '1795 Apr 10 / Panopt—Irish / Parnell Dublin / to / J.B. Q.S.P.'

Addressed: 'Jerh Bentham Esq / Queens Square / Westminster /London.' Stamped: 'IRELAND'. Postmark: 'AP 14.95.B'.

With the change of the senior members of the administration in Ireland, Parnell takes up again the Irish panopticon penitentiary project.

[2] The first mention in the *Correspondence* of Thomas Pelham, 2nd Earl of Chichester (1756–1826), with whom Bentham was later on to have considerable dealings. After being in opposition in Parliament he had gone over to support of Pitt, when the Portland Whigs joined forces with him in 1794. Pelham became Irish Secretary, 1795–8; and thereafter held several posts in the British administration in London.

[3] Sir John Jefferys Pratt, 2nd Earl and 1st Marquis of Camden (1759–1840), M.P. 1780–94, a lord of the Admiralty, 1782–88, and of the Treasury, 1789–94. Appointed Lord Lieutenant of Ireland in March 1795 he had the unpopular task of checking the reform legislation promised by Lord Fitzwilliam; he felt obliged to declare martial law in 1797 and when rebellion broke out in 1798 was at his own request replaced by a military man, Lord Cornwallis. He succeeded his father as an earl in 1794 and was created a marquis in 1806. Bentham had met him at Bowood in 1781 and made passing reference to him in June 1794 (see *Correspondence*, iii, 82–3 and above, p. 43).

1055
FROM ETIENNE DUMONT
15 April 1795 (Aet 47)

On devroit aller voir ses amis, mon cher Bentham, quand on sait qu'ils ont quelque chagrin petit ou grand sur le coeur, ne fut ce que pour les distraire un moment—cependant la crainte que si vous préfériez la solitude, vous ne vous fissiez un mauvais scrupule de me le dire, m'empêche de suivre cette impulsion.—mais je me suis reproché de ne vous avoir pas dit hier que s'il se joignoit à votre inquietude actuelle quelque léger embarras d'argent, j'avois à vos ordres cinquante l. st.[2] qui ne sauroient avoir une destination plus agréable pour moi. Je n'aurois pas songé à vous offrir une aussi petite somme si vous ne m'aviez parlé de votre affaire avec Ly As.[3] où il ne s'agissoit pas d'une plus grande. Adieu, mon cher Bentham, je suis tout à vous   Et. D.

Mercredi
15 avril

Observez que je ne prévois pas que j'eusse besoin de cet argent de longtemps et qu'ainsi vous ne me le rendriez qu' à votre plus grande commodité.

1056
FROM SIR JOHN PARNELL
16 April 1795

Dr Sir
   I mentioned your plan for employing convicts to Ld Campden

1055. [1] B.L. VI: 43–4. Autograph. Docketed: '1795 Apr 14 / Dumont Lansdn House / to / J.B. Q.S.P.'
   Addressed: 'Jer. Bentham Esqre / Queen's Square Place / Westminster.' Stamped: 'Penny Post pd Piccadilly'. Postmark: '7 o'clock / Even 15 Ap 95 / PENNY POST PAID'.
   [2] Whether Bentham accepted this proferred long-term loan of £50 sterling is not revealed by his or Dumont's papers.
   [3] Lady Ashburton, about whose tenancy of no. 14 Duke Street Bentham had been having trouble (see letters 1047 and 1048).
1056. [1] B.L. VI: 45–6. Autograph. Docketed: '1795 Apr 16 / Panopt Irish / Parnell Dublin / to / J.B. Q.S.P.'
   Addressed: 'Jery Bentham Esq / Queens Square Place / Westminster / London.' Stamped: 'IRELAND'. Postmark: 'AP.20.95.B'.

Mr Pelham and the principal officers of the Crown whom I met this day, they approved of it in general, spoke with much respect of its Author and desired me to prepare a clause in an Act of Parliament to empower the Ld Lieutn at his discretion to apply the money allotted for transporting convicts to employ them at labour —they have not gone further into the business but I am sure will receive very favourably the offers which you may propose. If you continue to be of the same opinion on this subject I would recommend it to you to write to Mr Pelham and also if you will favor me with a letter to be communicated I shall do everything in my power to forward yr plan. I have informed you of all that has passed on this subject. Our Parliament will continue sitting a month.

I have received no direct power to communicate more than I have done of course I can not on the part of Government suggest to you what you first had intended visiting this Country, however if under the circumstances you should choose to come here I should be happy in endeavouring to accommodate you and to give you every assistance in my power.

I am dr Sir

yrs

very truly

J. Parnell

Apr 16 1795

1057

FROM WILLIAM WILBERFORCE

17 April 1795

My dear Sir

I shall meet my friends at your House at one o'clock today—I hope you won't think I have brought too large a party: they are all good men and true and it seem'd quite ill natured when the subject happened to be mentioned to sit sulky and refuse what I knew would give a friend pleasure

yours sincerely

W.W—

Friday morn.

1057. [1] B.L. VI: 47–8. Autograph. Docketed: '1795 Apr 17 / Panopt / Wilberforce / to / J.B. Q.S.P. / To introduce Ld Harrowby etc. to see.'

Addressed: 'Jeremy Bentham Esq. or Col. Bentham.'

The lord mentioned in the docket was Nathaniel Ryder (1735–1803), created 1st Baron Harrowby in 1776. He had been M.P. for Tiverton, 1756–76.

1058

To Evan Nepean

24 April 1795 (Aet 47)

Q.S.P. April 24. 95

My dear Sir

It would be a real charity if you could indulge me with a quarter of an hour of your time—the sooner the better just for the purpose of certifying to Mr Long by the initials of your name in the margin the conformity of the Articles as drawn up fairly by me to the rough draft agreed upon between you and me, which I carefully preserve in statu quo.

Mr Long is unfortunately imprisoned in an Election Committee every day from 12 till 4. He declares his readiness to accede to every article agreed upon by you without reserve and as it is impossible therefore to conclude the business without troubling you with it in some way or other, I take the liberty of suggesting this mode as laying the lightest tax possible as well upon you as Mr Long. I am, My dear Sir, ever your most obliged

Jeremy Bentham

Evan Nepean Esq.

P.S. Accepted Bills for parts of the Building tumbling in upon me tomorrow sennight, and nothing to pay them. Banker overdrawn £600 three months ago.

Evan Nepean Esq
    etc. etc. etc.

1059

To Charles Long

24 April 1795 (Aet 47)

Q.S.P. Apr. 24 Friday

Mr Bentham hopes Mr Long will have the goodness to put the Draught of the instrument of appointment into the hands of the

1058. ¹ B.L. VI: 49–50. Autograph draft. Docketed: '1795 Apr. 24 / Panopt / J.B. Q.S.P. / to / Nepean Whitehall / To certify with regard to the terms of the intended contract as settled with him.'

1059. ¹ B.L. VI: 51–2. Autograph draft. Docketed: '1795 April 24 / Panopt / J.B. Q.S.P. / to / Long Treasury / Quere whether sent or the purport mentioned *viva voce*? Appointment of Feoffee approved by Lowndes.'

proper Clerk tomorrow morning to copy it upon the proper sort of paper for receiving the signature of the Board. Mr. Lowndes's signature and approbation in his own handwriting is the only part of the Draught which Mr Long, it is presumed, will think it necessary to trouble himself with looking at.

1060

FROM WILLIAM WILBERFORCE

[24]? April 1795

Dear Sir
Was there any mistake between us yesterday; I thought I was to have had the pleasure of seeing you here at 10 this morng and staid in for that Purpose. You will find me abt 11 tomorrow or I will endeavour to call on you abt that Hour—

yours siny
W.W—

Pal Yd
Friday Night

1061

FROM WILLIAM WILBERFORCE

5 May 1795

My dear Sir
I forgot before I left town today to execute my Intention of send'g you Word that I yesterday spoke to the Atty[2] and Solr. Genl.[3] The former I found had actually *done the needful*, and the

---

1060. [1] B.L. VI: 55–6. Autograph. Docketed: '1795 Apr / Panopt / Wilberforce Palace Yard / to / J.B. Q.S.P.'
Addressed: 'Jeremy Bentham Esq.'
No day of the month is given in the letter or docket, but the last Friday in April seems the most likely.

1061. [1] B.L. VI: 57–8. Autograph. Docketed: '1795 May 5 / Panopt / Wilberforce Clapham / to / J.B. Q.S.P. / Spoke to Atty and Sollr Genl about Appointment of Feoffee. Impressions not unfavourable.'
Addressed: 'Jeremy Bentham Esq. / Queen's Square Place.'
[2] The Attorney General from 1793 to 1799 was Sir John Scott (1751–1838), later Baron Eldon (1799) and 1st Earl of Eldon (1821). He served as Lord Chancellor, 1801–1806 and 1807–27.
[3] Sir John Mitford succeeded Scott as Solicitor-General in 1793 and as Attorney-General in 1799 (see letter 957 n. 2).

latter promis'd to proceed without delay. I discern'd nothing of that unfavourable Impression you had apprehended—

Yours sincerely
W. Wilberforce

Clapham
Tuesday night.

1062

FROM GEORGE WILSON

5 May 1795

Tuesday 3 o'clock

Dear Bentham

Since I wrote to you this morning[2] I met White[3] who says he has laid your contract before the Atty Genl and yesterday returned it to the Treasury with his Observations—and he added that there is a serious difficulty from the Atty Genl thinking that the two acts are incompatible—as the matter is now out of White's hands I did not think it necessary to enter into any discussion with him about this point, the business now being to convince the Atty Genl or rather the Lords of the Treasury—I mentioned it to Lowndes who makes very light of it and says the Atty Genl is always raising foolish objections—when you understand the objection I hope you will find it not insurmountable[4]—

Yours sincerely
George Wilson

1062. [1] B.L. VI: 59–60. Autograph. Docketed: '1795 May 5 / Panopt G.W. Linc. Inn / to / J.B. Q.S.P. / Atty Genl and White's Doubts.'

Addressed: 'Jeremy Bentham Esqr / Queen's Square Place / Westminster.' Stamped: 'Paid 1d'. Postmark: '7 o'clock Even. / 5 MA 95 / PENNY POST PAID. LINCS INN 3'.

[2] A missing letter.

[3] Joseph White, solicitor to the Treasury, 1 July 1794–21 February 1806.

[4] On 6 May Bentham drafted a letter to Charles Long beginning: 'It was a false alarm—the Draught, it will be seen has undergone Mr. Attorney's improvements, received his approbation, and that approbation a decided one.' The draft ends: 'Mr Bentham hopes Mr Long will have the goodness to set it a going without further stoppage.' There is a second copy of this draft, but both are docketed 'Not sent' (B.L. VI: 61–2, 63–4).

135

1063

TO SAMUEL BENTHAM

9 May 1795 (Aet 47)

Q.S.P. Sat. May 9th 1795

I understand from Mr Ramus, one of the Treasury Clerks, to whom the business of getting the instrument of appointment dispatched was committed by Mr Long, that in the natural course of things it would be dispatched by Monday. If it is, you will know of it from me by that day's post—that is I shall send a letter to you on that day, directed to you at Mr Peakes.

Admy Report[2] would have gone on faster than it has, had it not been retarded, partly by the whole trade of heel-kicking, partly by low spirits. Perhaps it might have I believe it would have gone on faster, had I been quite clear about your wishing it.

Your commands in relation to Hyde Park Corner are obey'd.[3] With regard to your going on to Plymouth or returning I can have nothing to say, unless it be on Monday—

1064

TO SAMUEL BENTHAM

12 May 1795 (Aet 47)

Q.S.P. Tuesday May 12. 95

The Board (Treasury Board) which was to have been held today has been put off till Thursday—consequently no *instruments of appointment*[2] signed. But it has been transmitted /remitted/ by

1063. [1] B.L. VI: 65–6. Autograph. Addressed: 'To / Brigadier General Bentham / at Mr Peake's Dockyard / Portsmouth / Need not be forwarded to him if gone.' Postmark: 'MA 9.95.D'.

[2] Probably a reference to the letter of 21 April 1795, which, according to Lady Bentham, Samuel addressed to the Secretary of the Admiralty and which led to his being authorised to visit Portsmouth dockyards and make a report: transmitted on 29 May (M. S. Bentham, *Life of Sir Samuel Bentham*, 1862, pp. 102–3).

[3] A missing letter from Samuel is indicated: perhaps concerning a house near Hyde Park Corner, London.

1064. [1] B.L. VI: 67–8. Autograph. Addressed: 'To / Brigadier General Bentham / At Mr Peake's / Dockyard / Portsmouth / Not to be sent on to Plymouth.' Post mark: 'MA 12.95.D'.

[2] The brothers were expecting the 'Instrument of Appointment for Battersea Rise', in which Samuel as well as Jeremy was involved.

/from/ Mr White: consequently the signing of it on Thursday may (under Providence) be regarded as a matter of course.

1065

TO SAMUEL BENTHAM

14 May 1795 (Aet 47)

Q.S.P. May 14. 95

The Devil is in the Matter of things, I think. The instrument is not signed. The Lords separated, said Mr. Ramus, before they had signed it, not having time. But it will be done in course—When? What was the next board day?—it would be done without a board day—probably, almost certainly tomorrow—I gave him in general terms an intimation of your waiting for it—a commission to execute for the Admiralty—public business of importance waiting for and suffering by it. This made the impression I wished it should —he promised of his own accord to get it dispatched, and send me instant word about it. He wished me if possible to delay writing to you till it was done.[2]

Would you have thought it—some time in the course of the summer was the time Mr Pitt has been talking to Mr Long as the time for dispatching the *contract*: but upon sending for the contract to Mr Long, wishing to add necessary observations to my copy, and make different uses of it, Mr Long declined sending it by my Messenger (Upsal) saying that I should have it in two or three days from which I am apt to think, that they are attempting, he and Dundas or somebody, to make Pitt attend to it.[3]

1065. [1] B.L. VI: 69–70. Autograph. Addressed: 'Brigadier General Bentham at / Mr. Peake's / DockYard / Portsmouth.' Postmark: 'MA.14.95.D'.
[2] This paragraph refers to the Instrument of Appointment for Battersea Rise, which the brothers were expecting (see letter 1066).
[3] This paragraph is concerned with the contract to build the Panopticon penitentiary.

1066

TO SAMUEL BENTHAM

15 May 1795 (Aet 47)

Q.S.P. May 15 1795 Friday

The signing of the Instrument of appointment was so far from being a matter of course, that Mr Pitt according to Mr Long whom I have just been talking with has not read it. True it is it had passed Mr Lowndes, and the Atty Genl. and the Sollicitor General, but Mr Pitt was still to read it before he signed. I see /found/ however no reason to suppose but that it will share the lot of other things which are presented as matter of course to be read and signed whenever there is a Board.

En revanche, the Contract which (as per last) was to be looked at by Mr Pitt some time or other in the course of the summer, has been looked at and as it appears looked over by him already. On sending for it to Mr Long yesterday for the purpose of copying from it Nepean's pencil notes upon another copy, Mr Long declined sending it then (by Upsal) giving a verbal message that I should have it in a few days. Now today upon my laying hold of Mr Long to to ask him about the instrument of appointment, he produced the copy of the Draught of the contract, with pencil marks upon it, made as he said by Mr Pitt, in the presence of (him) Mr Long. The discussion was interrupted by the appearance of Mr Dundas, who came on other business. The pencil marks Qus and +s seem to have been continued to the end.

With regard to the supplemental allowance, what Mr Long objected to (though Mr Nepean had not) and what he assured me beforehand Mr Pitt would object to, Mr Pitt did accordingly object to—not the thing itself but the mode: if an encrease was required an encreased sum could be demanded in the first instance: the task of subsequent liquidation was what they would not engage in.

Now then how to make the previous liquidation? a business at which the Contract would stick till that were settled, if it did not stick at anything else. Is is for this purpose at any rate that you will judge whether it would not be proper that you should come to

1066. [1] B.L. VI: 71–2. Autograph. Docketed: '1795 May 15 / Panopt / J.B. Q.S.P. / to / S.B. Portsmouth / Instrument of Appointment for Battersea Rise about to be signed. S.B. to furnish materials for liquidating the supplemental allowance.'

Addressed: 'To / General Bentham / At Mr Peake's / Dockyard / Portsmouth.'
Postmark: 'MA. 15. 95. E'.

town before you go to Portsmouth,[2] that is immediately. If the instrument of appointment gets signed tomorrow as we hope it will, so much the better.

1067

TO HENRY DUNDAS

1 June 1795 (Aet 47)

Queen Square Place Westm. 1 June/ 1795

Sir

Permitt me to sollicit your assistance in relation to an object very trifling to appearance, but of great importance to me, and in respect of which no man I believe, at least I hope, but myself would have found any need of sollicitation.

It is some weeks since Mr Long sent for me and informed me that Mr Pitt had come to a determination with regard to the contested spot at Battersea Rise and fixed upon it as a proper one. The draught of an instrument appointing me feoffee to treat for the land etc. which had been drawn by me and signed and approved by Mr Lowndes was accordingly sent by Mr Long to Mr White the Sollicitor of the Treasury and after having run its official run through the Law department was in process of time returned by Mr White as long ago as Saturday three weeks, engrossed and ready for signature. It had been expected before, and Mr Ramus, the Treasury Clerk to whom it came in charge had all along spoken to me of the signature of it as an event that would take place as of course upon the return of the instrument to the Treasury, and that without the necessity of so much as waiting for a regular Board. Instead of that, Board after Board has been held, the instrument I am told now lies with Mr Pitt, and with all my entreaties I have not been able to obtain the instrument signed, or to learn when it will be signed, or whether it will ever be signed at all.

The season, the third since the acceptance of my plan, and my having been bid to take my arrangements, is on the point of being lost, applications such as I took the liberty of shewing you a specimen of four months ago but more pressing are pouring in upon me,

2 A slip for 'Plymouth': Samuel was already at Portsmouth, inspecting the docks and planning to go on to Plymouth.

1067. [1] B.L. VI: 73–4. Autograph draft. Docketed: '1795 June 1 / Panopt / J.B. Q.S.P. / to / Dundas Rt Hon H / To sollicit signature of / Appointm.t of Feoffee Battersea Rise again promised some weeks before this / Appointment of Feoffee returned by / White to the Treasury Saty 3 weeks.'

and the materials of /for/ the building have crowded in upon me till [I have not got an inch of ground[2]].

Perhaps Sir, it may be in your power, and if it is, I am sure it will be in your inclination, to prevail with Mr Pitt to cease keeping business out of its course, for no other imaginable purpose than that of heaping distress upon a man who, years ago was thought to have had some reason to complain on the chapter of delay.

The Contract is another matter; and the terms of it may in regard to this or that article be *supposed* to admitt of deliberation: but in regard to the signature of the instrument, which must precede that of the Contract surely after what is passed deliberation is or ought to be at an end.

1068

FROM RICHARD FORD

16 June 1795

Whitehall 16. June 1795

Mr Ford presents his Compts. to Mr Bentham he has received directions from Mr. Long to look over the Drat. of the Articles of Agreement relative to the new penitentiary House proposed to be erected, and to settle such terms as may appear to him proper, Mr. F. would therefore be very glad to see Mr Bentham at the Duke of Portland's Office[2] on Thursday morning about one o'clock if convenient to him. Mr Ford has not yet seen the act of Parliament respecting this business, which, if Mr B. could favor him with tomorrow morning, he would be obliged to him.

Jeremy Bentham Esq.
    etc. etc. etc.

[2] The phrase in brackets is crossed out, but is required to make sense. A footnote apparently intended for insertion at this point, but later crossed out, reads: 'my Brother, who instead of proceeding on his commission from the Admiralty from Portsmouth to Plymouth is returned from Portsmouth in order to form / govern / his plans by a survey of the ground on the assurance of the signature of the instrument, is wasting his own and I am warranted to say the nations time.'

1068. [1] B.L. VI: 75–6. Original. Docketed: '1795 June 16 / Panopt. / Ford D. of Portds Office / to / J.B. Q.S.P. / Long refers to Ford the settling of the Contract / Answered 17—sent the Act.'

Richard Ford (1758–1806), a barrister, was M.P. for East Grinstead, 1789–90, and for Appleby, 1790–1. He became a magistrate at Bow Street police office: chief magistrate, 1800. He was knighted in 1801.

[2] William Henry Cavendish Bentinck, 3rd Duke of Portland (1738–1809), had become Home Secretary in 1794, when the group of Whigs that he led transferred their support to Pitt's administration.

1069

TO RICHARD FORD

17 June 1795 (Aet 47)

Mr Bentham presents his Compliments to Mr Ford, and will do himself the honor of waiting on him tomorrow, in obedience to his commands. On casting his eye over the Draught of the proposed Contract, Mr Ford will find that, to save trouble, the clauses of the Act have been recited in the articles which have been respectively grounded on them. A copy of the Act is herewith enclosed, as desired.

Q.S.P. 17th June 1795

1070

TO RICHARD FORD

23 June 1795 (Aet 47)

Mr Bentham presents his Compliments to Mr Ford, and begs leave to submitt to him, whether, to save time, the several articles of the contract might not be settled without waiting for the estimate. The estimate is preparing, with all the expedition Mr B. can give it, but the completion of it depends not upon himself, but upon other people, and a variety of other people. As the other articles have no connection with the estimate, the contract might even go through the law offices with a blank for the sum, or a sum put by conjecture in the place in question, and thus a delay which would answer no purpose and might be productive of much inconvenience might be saved.[2]

Q.S.P. 23 June – 95 – Tuesday.

1069. [1] B.L. VI: 77. In copyist's hand. Docketed: '1795 June 17 / Panopt. / J.B. Q.S.P. to / Ford D. of Portds Office.' A reply to letter 1068.

1070. [1] B.L. VI: 80. Autograph draft. Docketed: '1795 June 23 / Panopt / J.B. Q.S.P. / to / Mr Ford D. of Portl. Office / To settle before Estimates.'

[2] Bentham was collecting information for a revised estimate. In B.L. VI: 78–9 is a draft in his hand, but initialled 'J.L.L.' in Lloyd's hand, inquiring on behalf of Samuel Bentham, whether 'if he could have given you the order for the work now going on in March 1793, it would have made any and what difference in the price'. The letter was addressed to 'Booth Sheffield Yorks' and dated 20 June.

1071
FROM SIR CHARLES BUNBURY
10 July 1795

Great Barton
July 10th 1795

Dear Sir,

The Jailor at Bury has received an Order to carry his Convicts to the Hulks at Portsmouth, and he setts off on Sunday next. They will probably stop at *the Inn* of Newgate on Monday. There is amongst them a Prisoner of an unusual sort, a very sober industrious man, a skillfull Carpenter aged 42 who had a very good Character, till tempted by Avarice he plundered a Bureau he was sent for to repair.

Such a Workman, I conceive, may be useful to you, and assist in the Construction of a Panopticon Penitentiary House for his own Confinement, as well as that of others. Till you have a proper place to hold him, he might be left at the New Gilspur Street Prison near Newgate and be allowed to work for your Service. Thus instead of costing the Public sixty Pounds a year, he might be maintained at a small Expence, and atone for his Crimes by labouring for the State. His name is Richard Coates, and I write this Day that if you wish to apply for him, you may do so *immediately*, and stop him in his way to Portsmouth. I will with pleasure second your wishes, and in the mean Time by shewing this Letter to Mr King[2] at the D of Portland's office, he will, I dare say procure an Order for his remaining in a London Prison, *during Pleasure*, and in a short Time I shall have the Satisfaction of seeing you and Mr King in Town, and we can take such further steps in the Business as may appear necessary.

I beg my Compliments to your Brother and am
yours sincerely
T. Chas Bunbury

The name of the Jailor of Bury St Edmunds is Scott.[3] He gives the Prisoner a very good Character.

1071. [1] B.L. VI: 82–3. Autograph. Docketed: '1795 July 10 / Panopt / Bunbury Barton to J.B. Q.S.P.'
Addressed: 'to / Jeremy Bentham / Queen Square Place / Westminster.' Franked: 'Bury July ten, 95 / Free / C. Bunbury'. Postmark: 'FREE JY 11 95 / BURY S'.
[2] John King (1760–1830), permanent under-secretary at the Home Office, 1792–1806; then Secretary to the Treasury, 1806; and Comptroller of Army Accounts, 1806–30 (see R. R. Nelson, *The Home Office, 1782–1801*, 1969, pp. 34–6).
[3] Robert Scott (see letter 1073).

142

1072

FROM RICHARD FORD

10 July 1795

Whitehall 10. July 95

Mr Ford presents his Compts. to Mr Bentham he is sorry he has not had time to examine the last paper he has been favord. with so exactly as it requires, but from what he is able to judge of it, he does not think their can be any Objection to what Mr. B proposes in it, excepting in the 2d Article and in the last—Mr Long mentiond 30,000£, which in some measure binds Mr. Ford, unless he sees that a larger Sum is necessary, which he cannot well do without referring to an Estimate—in respect to the other point Mr. F. aprehends that Mr. Long understands it in the way Mr. Ford proposes, for when he read the observations to him, Mr. L. thought that particular one not necessary that matter having been in his Opinion before so settled. Mr. F. will in a day or two look more particularly into Mr. Bentham's answer upon that Subject, as he only wants to settle the Contract upon equally fair Terms.

1073

FROM SIR CHARLES BUNBURY

12 July 1795

Barton
Sunday Evening July 12th 1795

Dear Sr,

I received yours:[2] Mr Robert Scott the Jailor informs me he shall take *Richard Coates* with the other Prisoners to London *this* night by the Yarmouth Coach which will arrive tomorrow noon or by one o'clock at the Spread Eagle in Gracechurch Street, and he intends *keeping them at the Spread Eagle till five on Monday Evening,*

1072. [1] B.L. VI: 84–5. Original. Docketed: '1795 July 10 / Panopt. / Ford D. of Portds Office / to / J.B. Q.S.P.'

1073. [1] B.L. VI: 86–7. Autograph. Docketed: '1795 July 12 / Panopt./ Sir C. Bunbury Barton / to / J.B. Q.S.P. / about taking *Coates,* a Convict.'
Addressed: 'To Jeremy Bentham Esqre / Queen Square Place, Westminster / To be sent without delay.' The letter is re-addressed, in Bentham's hand, to 'R. Ford Esqr. / D. of Portland's Office / over the Treasury / Whitehall.'
[2] A missing reply to letter 1071.

when he means to take them by the Portsmouth Coach to the Hulks there or in Langston Harbour.

I have desired him to send you this Letter as soon as he arrives, that if you have obtained an Order to detain R^d Coates you may send it to him without delay—He would have waited upon you by my Desire but is obliged to stay to guard the Prisoners.

Yours sincerely
T. Chas Bunbury.

1074

To Evan Nepean

13 July 1795 (Aet 47)

Q.S.P. July 13 1795

Mr Ford, to whom Mr Long has turned over the Penitentiary Contract business, finding it necessary to refer to Mr Nepean in relation to a Matter of fact, Mr Bentham takes the liberty of troubling Mr Nepean with a paper exhibiting the state of the question, that Mr Nepean upon Mr F's applying to him may not be taken unprepared.

Mr B will abide most willingly by whatever Mr Nepe[a]n says upon the subject, and as there is nothing else in dispute, it is the last trouble he will have.

Q.S.P.[2] ½ after 5 July 13

Mr Ford is not at all adverse, and is prepared to give up his proposition, upon the slightest intimation from you of its being inconsistent with what had been agreed on. He would have done it at my word just now, at least he seems to make a motion that way, but I thought it prudent as well as decent, that he should have to say he had seen you.

1074. [1] B.L. VI: 88–9. In copyist's hand. Docketed: '1795 July 13 / Panopt. / J.B. Q.S.P. / to / Nepean Admiralty with Ford's Observations on Contract and J.B.'s Answer.'

[2] What follows is on the verso of the sheet.

1075

FROM THE DUC DE LIANCOURT

[?]July 1795

The Duke de Liancourt writes to Bentham from Philadelphia, of the delight with which he had been studying the machinery, and the results of their system of prison discipline. He says, that he felt relieved on reaching a country where public opinion judged tolerantly of the variety of religious and political creeds. But he desires that his name may not be mentioned as the author of the remarks, lest he should awaken an attention he desires to avoid. He says, that the admirable management of the Pennsylvanian prisons has already brought about benevolent modifications of the penal code. He admires the care,—the attention,—the tact of the keepers: says that the jailor's wife had succeeded to office on her husband's death, and the discipline was quite as perfectly preserved as before. Whether from fear,—from conviction,—or from habit, order was admirably kept. He is struck with the superiority of the prisons, to every other public establishments. One thing only shocked the duke, namely, the total separation of the black from the white prisoners. And yet, says he, the directors of the prison are mostly Quakers and Abolitionists! So contradictory is man!

1076

TO CHARLES LONG

8 August 1795 (Aet 47)

Queens S.P. 8 Aug. 1795

Mr Bentham begs the favour of Mr Long to cast an eye in the first place on the shorter letter:[2] should that be thought not suf-

1075. [1] Bowring, x, 308. Translated summary, without any indication of date. The letter would seem to have been the one to which Bentham replied on 11 October (see letter 1085), when he apologised for the delay in answering and mentioned that the duke's letter did not reach his hands 'till after the Metcalf family had left London for the summer', so that a date not later then July is likely.

1076. [1] B.L. VI: 92–3. Autograph copy. Docketed: '1795 Aug 8 / Panopt / J.B. Q.S.P. / to / Long Treasury / with 2 letters about the 1st Year's £27,000.'

Bentham had a few days earlier drafted another letter to Long, containing a wish that 'Mr Pitt would have the goodness to cast his eye over the paper I gave to Mr Ford in relation to the disputed article'. He ended: 'Let him but read the paper, whatever be his decision upon it, I will submit myself to his pleasure without reserve.' The draft is docketed: '1795 July or Aug / Panopt / J.B. Q.S.P. / Long Treasury / Not delivered—Paper proposed *viva voce* / Letter on purpose sent instead of the Paper within mentioned' (B.L. VI: 90–1).   [2] Letter 1077.

145

ficiently explicit, or conclusive, he must then be under the necessity of troubling him with the longer one,[3] which concludes with a reason bearing a very serious reference to the success of the whole plan.

1077

To Charles Long

8 August 1795 (Aet 47)

Queen's Square Place West:r 8 Aug. 1795

Sir—

Permit me to state to you the light in which I have all along understood the matter now in doubt: if in the opinion of Mr Pitt, it cannot in justice to the public be understood in that light, I submit to his decision without reserve.

The basis of my Proposal was what I then understood to be the Hulk price, for a thousand Prisoners. Give me, said I, that price for the first year, every year after I will do the business at a reduced price (£12,000). Expence of building I take upon myself.

Requiring Mr Campbel's price for one year, but for one year only, what idea could I have that *my* Representatives should be expected to account for a single penny of it any more than *his* for the price received by him?[2] What if I had required the same price for half a dozen years, or for the whole term? Could I suppose that I was to fare the worse for making the abatement so much the sooner?

Mr Campbel's first price was £38 a head: (= £38,000) There were many reasons in *my* instance why the first price should exceed the subsequent ones still more than in *his*; and that without adverting to the building. After the first year Furniture and Cloathing etc. will have been provided, the advantage of the labour too may be reckoned upon: for the first year very little can be depended upon on that score.

It could not surely be supposed that I meant to keep up the establishment for nothing *any* year: still less this first and heaviest of all years. What less then could I be supposed to expect than the whole of the very sum I was requiring for that very purpose?

[3] Letter 1078.
1077. [1] B.L. VI: 98–9. Draft in copyist's hand. Docketed by Bentham: '1795 Aug 8 / Panopt / J.B. Q.S.P. / to / Long Treasury / No. 1 / J.B.'s Representatives whether to refund?'
This is 'the shorter letter' to which Bentham refers in letter 1076.
[2] Duncan Campbell, superintendent of the Hulks.

Ground as well as building was then to have been mine: the Ground was not to have reverted to Government: no such conception could at that time have presented itself to me as that of having the ground or anything upon it taken from me by Government with or without a satisfaction.

It was impossible therefore I should have made any such distinction in my own mind with respect to the £27,000 as to say, £12,000 if it is to be given me absolutely, the remaining £15,000 only lent, with or without reference to the Building. No such condition having been ever intended on my part, will it be thought necessary in justice to the Public, *now* to force it on me?

I have the honour to be
with great respect
Sir
Your most obedient and
humble Servant

C. Long Esq
etc. etc. etc.

1078

To Charles Long

8 August 1795 (Aet 47)

Queen's Square Place Westm:r 8 Aug 1795

Sir
Indulge me a few words in elucidation of a preceding letter of this date. It was but too natural I must confess, that in your position or Mr Pitt's, anybody should have taken up the matter in precisely the light in which you stated it to me. 'Between the allowance you required for every year after the first, (£12,000) and the allowance you required for that first year (£27,000) there is,' (it may be observed to me) 'a difference of no less than £15,000. This £15,000 which you required of government, it is plain that (however you might have talked of erecting the building at your

---

1078. [1] B.L. VI: 94–7. Fair copy, the first page in Bentham's hand, the remainder in a copyist's hand with corrections in Bentham's. Docketed by Bentham: '1795 Aug 8 / Panopt / J.B. Q.S.P. / to / Long Treasury / No 2 / J.B.'s Representatives whether to refund?'

This is the 'longer' letter to which Bentham refers in letter 1076. There is an autograph rough draft of it in B.L. VI: 101–3. It is described in the docket as 'Brouillon / on the unexpected alterations made by Mr. Pitt in the terms of the Contract / N.B. Fair copy of letter as delivered on another paper.'

147

own expence) it must all along have been your intention to lay out upon the building. But in a year or two (nobody can say how soon your Brother and you may be both dead): then comes the satisfaction you require for your representatives for *this* as well as whatever other money you happen to have laid out of your own upon the land. Now then, whatever money you have laid out of your own upon this government land, we are content your representatives should be satisfied for, when the land reverts to Government. But this £15,000 is none of your's: it is so much government money: how can you expect this to be included in the satisfaction.'

My answer is—Most certainly this £15,000 will have been Government money, but as certainly it will have ceased to be so, so soon as I have maintained the prisoners for a year: just as much as the £12,000 will: for though this argument divides the £27,000 into two sums, and makes a distinction between the destination of these two sums, neither did my Proposal or the former agreement grounded on it make any such distinction or division, nor did it ever so much as enter into my conception that any such would be made. The words of my original Proposal are 'taking on himself the *whole* expence of building, without any advance to be made by Government for that purpose'—The interpretation I am contending against, requires the considering this £15,000 as an advance to be made for that purpose:- the Proposal, you see, puts a negative upon any such ideas in express terms.

'But did not you in your own mind mean after receiving the money to apply more or less of it to that purpose'?—This is a question which I can have no sort of objection to answering, except its being so perfectly immaterial—Was it *granted* for this purpose? that is the true question.—No:—it was *asked*, and so expressly stated, to be *not* for this purpose, but for another: and *as* it was *asked, so* it was granted, without the smallest objection or observation being ever made. Would it be necessary, or even fair, after that, for Government to come at this time of day and say to me— 'No:—we did not give it you for the purpose for which you asked it, but for the purpose for which you declared yourself *not* to ask it',—merely that what was required on the footing of payment may be converted into a loan?

I spoke of the other question as immaterial: and surely nothing can be more so: for so long as the building is a fit one, what signifies it to anybody whether it is paid for with one parcel of money or another?

When to the words last quoted I immediately subjoined—

'requiring only that the abatement and deduction shall be suspended for the first year,' my meaning was, that my *reduced* price should not take the place of the abovementioned *Hulk* price till after such first year.—That the word *only* did not glance at the expence of the building, and that too even in my own conception, is more than I will take upon me to say: I should rather suppose it did: if so, all I *could* mean by it was this: that as to the Building, either Government gets it built absolutely with my own original money, or if *any part* of the expence is defray'd out of money that came originally from Government, it will be only out of a saving made by myself out of what I require for the keep of the Prisoners for the first year, and what would otherwise have been paid for that single purpose to Mr Campbel, who has nothing to do with building.

Another confession, it is true, I must make is that afterwards when the original Proposal came to be reduced to form, my expression was (Art 4) *'£27,000 to be advanced to the Proposer: for which he engages to maintain any number of Convicts not exceeding one thousand for the first year.'* *Possibly* then from the word *advanced* Mr Nepean as well as Mr Pitt, may have understood *advanced in the way of loan only*: and that at some future period it was to be refunded: though if they had gone further and looked for any period at which such refunding could have been called for, they would not, I believe, have found one. My meaning was not lent in advance, but *paid* in advance: i:e: according to the instalments then and ever since stipulated for, and before any Prisoners had been kept for it: in contradistinction to the *£12,000* required—*'for every other year,'*—which I only required (Art 7) *'to be paid quarterly'* as Mr Campbel's money is—

True it is, that had I been aware of any such distinction as is now suggested I might very likely have said *'paid in advance'* and perhaps too added other words for the purpose of putting if possible a still more decided negative upon it: but it has been seen, that I neither had, nor could have had any idea of any such distinction at either of those times. The interpretation I contend against refers to a subsequent state of things, which it was impossible I should have had in contemplation till full half a year afterwards.

The ground itself, as I have already stated, was to have been mine: bought with my money: legal power only for purchasing it to be furnished me by Government: afterwards indeed Government was to lend me *that* money, but still only for three years. These were the terms on which I was sent in my own name to treat with the Proprietors. It was not till (March or April 1794) that I was given to understand that the land could *not* be mine: that it must be Government property. This change I looked upon as highly disadvantageous to me: for so much of my property as I should find occasion to lay out upon the Land, so much was thus to be set afloat: but being announced to me as peremptory, submission was all that was left to me, and I submitted.

This disadvantage may be attended with serious danger to the plan itself. Aware of the accidents to which such new and extensive undertakings are exposed, aware in particular of the difference between estimated expence and eventual expence in building, I had all along trusted to the pledge which the land with such a property on it would afford, as a fund for extraordinary and unforeseeable expences, should any such arise. That pledge was weakened by taking from me the Ground: it would be shaken to pieces by taking from my Representatives the £15,000. What should I do if money ran short? would any individual be commonly safe in lending me any?—would Government lend me any? How much better then would it be on the part of Government to give up this claim to a possible allowance of £15,000, not to be made till at the end of two lives, nor except on the supposition of Government's neither choosing at that period to leave things in the train in which it finds them, nor being able to agree with my Representatives.

What is not disputed on the part of Government is that at the expiration of my term it gets the power of buying at prime cost, and that comparatively a very low price, a building which have [has] been keeping a number of Prisoners that otherwise were not to have been kept for less than £200,000, besides its having reduced the annual expence from £27,000 (now lately £21,000) to £12,000. What has been hitherto supposed on the part of Government is, that for this power it will on any construction be paying £15,000: what I humbly contend is, that it will at no time be paying for that power any such sum, but thus much only: viz: the interest of the £27,000 for the time during which it is to be in advance: viz: the year and something more, as may be found by a calculation not worth entering into: for that as to the £15,000 it is not be lent me on this account but *paid* to me (though in advance) on the same account as the remainder of the £12,000 from which it had never been distinguish'd by any act or thought of mine.

Once more then let me flatter myself, that Mr Pitt will not feel himself *compelled* in justice to the public to impose a condition so new to me: and that if not compelled he will not under these and all the other circumstances of the case feel any tendency so to do. But if his view of the matter is different, nothing is left for me but acquiescence.

I have the honour to be etc.

C. Long Esqr.
etc. etc. etc.

1079

To Joseph White

3 September 1795 (Aet 47)

Queens Square Place Westminster Thursday
3 Sept 1795

Mr Bentham presents his Compliments to Mr White, and is extremely sorry to hear of the trouble given him by Mr Browne.[2] Mr. Bentham's express instructions were, *not* to see Mr White, nor so much as to say a syllable to *any*body about dispatch, but merely to beg the favour of somebody in Mr. White's Office to let Mr Bentham know through Mr Browne of the time, whenever it should happen, of the Contracts being put from thence to the Treasury, it being material to him to have the earliest information of that event. Mr. Bentham had too grateful a recollection of the dispatch with which he was favoured on a former occasion to think necessary by any means to trouble Mr White with a similar application in the present instance: if he had he should not have employed a third person, but would have paid his respects to Mr White in person as before.

Mr Browne's account of the matter is that he accordingly addressed himself to the head Clerk, and that it was the Clerk that insisted upon his mentioning the business to Mr White.

1079. [1] B.L. VI: 104. Autograph draft. Docketed: '1795. Sept 3 / Panopt / J.B. Q.S.P. / to / White Linc. Inn.'
[2] William Browne, of 9 Bedford Row, the solicitor and family friend of the Benthams.

1080

To Samuel Bentham

17 September 1795 (Aet 47)

Hendon Thursday 17 Sept 1795

Upsal has just brought me your letter of the 15.[2] I have had a letter from Angerstein[3] telling me he has left an order with his partner Warren to let me have £1,000 on my note of hand for two months. He was to go out of town (into Lincolnshire) as [of] yesterday for 6 weeks. Of the £1,000 £200 or £250 must be stopped for Gen. Buckley[4] and other Duns. The rest you may conclude paid into Martins in your name tomorrow if you hear nothing to the contrary.

I thought you would like to hear of the above: but will it find its way to you?—that is the question—Will Mr Admiralty answer you, and when? Had I been let into the secret of the 'something' which he has to answer, I might have been able to give a rather better guess about the means of making a letter reach you than I possess at present. An *order* as Upsal calls it from the Admiralty to you (contents unknown to him) is already gone: possibly that is the order you have been expecting. If so, you are gone from Redbridge probably: and then this will perhaps reach you one of these days. I go to town to breakfast tomorrow to receive the money.

The communication from the Admiralty went by the post on Monday (Upsal tells me) directed to you at Peake's at Portsmouth.

Count Santi,[5] it seems, came to Q.S.P. on Tuesday where he occupies your little bed. He talks of staying a week or a fortnight. He came as Courier from the Fleet.

1080. [1] B.L. VI: 105–6. Autograph. Addressed: 'To John Poore Esqr / Redbridge / near Southampton / For Genl Bentham.' Postmark: 'SE 17.95.D'.

John Poore, perhaps related to Bentham's Oxford friend, Edward Poore; a John Poore acquired the manor of Leckford, Hants, in 1780; there was a younger John Poore (1778–1866), who was the son of Robert Poore of Redbridge.

[2] Missing.

[3] Angerstein, Lewis and Warren were brokers, 'over the Exchange', London. John Julius Angerstein (1795–1823) was the merchant, financier, philanthropist and art collector whose collection of pictures formed the basis of the National Gallery, London. The letter from Angerstein is missing.

[4] Felix Buckley, promoted major-general, 20 November 1782. He was a colonel of the 2nd Regiment of Life Guards and governor of Pendennis Castle, near Falmouth.

[5] Not identified.

1081

To Samuel Bentham

23 September 1795 (Aet 47)

Q.S.P. 23 Sept – 95

Keep Oliver[2] till I write for him—which I am not very likely to do. I wished you to have read D'Ivernois last pamphlet,[3] proving that the French Pandamonium must soon fall to pieces by the discredit of the Assignats (which already fetch no more than $\frac{1}{50}$ of their nominal value) that is, if we keep on the war whether we beat them or are beat—in order that if you had the same opinion about it that I am inclined to entertain you might put it into Ld Spencer's hands. At Portsmouth he will probably have now and then a few minutes upon his hands.

As he and his are for the continuance of the war they will probably like to see a publication which furnishes so strong an argument on their side—D'Ivernois is with Ld Sydney sometimes for days together.

1082

From Samuel Bentham

September 1795

I know nothing more of obstacles to Panopticon than what I told you of: but we then judged and still continue to judge very differently on the force of these obstacles. Ld Spencer's opposition to the giving up his ground you then made light of. I then thought his opposition unsurmountable and I have never heard anything from you or anybody else to make me think otherwise. That all the legal forms should procede in due order, till Mr Pitt's signature and

---

1081. [1] B.L. VI: 107–8. Autograph. Addressed: 'Sir Samuel Bentham'.
 [2] The manservant.
 [3] François D'Ivernois, *A Cursory View of the Assignats and remaining Resources of the French Finance*, London, 1795. Translated from his *Coup-d'oeil sur les assignats*.
1082. [1] B.L. VI: 109–10. Autograph. Docketed: '1795 Sept / Panopt / S.B. Portsmouth / to / J.B. Q.S.P. / Ld Spr's opposition unsurmountable.'
 Addressed: 'J. Bentham Esq., / Panop.'
 This is clearly a reply to a missing letter from Bentham inquiring whether his brother knows anything more about Lord Spencer's attitude to the Panopticon project. Through his Admiralty appointment Samuel was now in close touch with Spencer and his influential wife, Lavinia.

153

legal notice to Ld Spencer: does not I conceive forward the business. I can easily conceive Mr Pitt may *suffer* the business to go on in any way and that the one *only* time at which He and Ld S—spoke together on the subject, as neither spoke peremptorily, they dropt the subject as an unpleasant one and that the strength of the opposition was noways diminished. Independent of his influence the arguments Ld S used were too strong to be confuted without more pains than could be expected, even though the facts they were grounded on should be really untrue. What indemnification was Ld S to have for the loss of a perpetuity of 2,000£ per year?

From the time I heard from Ld S his determination of not giving up the ground if he could help it and which I immediately told you of I have not heard from him or from anybody else anything about his interference. Once I believe Ly Spencer[2] mentioned the business or it was spoken of by a third person in her presence, when I only said that I had had no further conversation with you on the subject: I think however I should have heard of it if he had acquiesced.

If you have heard of L.S being satisfied the case is very different, if not, I still think [we] will never get that ground.

1083

FROM LORD WYCOMBE

2, 5 October 1795

Naples, October 2, 1795.

My last was dated on the 24th ult., from Rome, which I quitted the same evening. On the 25th I passed through Terracina, which has been judged a proper residence for those whose lives the government has thought it not expedient to prolong, and which is situated at the extremity of the formidable *Palude* Pontini, now the *Ager* Pontinus, since the pope will have it so; for the good pontiff, with his usual vanity, pretends to have regenerated these swamps,

---

[2] Lavinia Bingham (1762–1831), eldest daughter of Charles Bingham, Baron Lucan (1776), who became Earl of Lucan in 1795. She married the future 2nd Earl Spencer in 1781 (see letter 1135, n. 4, p. 208 below).

1083. [1] Bowring, x, 309–12. As this long letter gives no information about Bentham, apart from the fact that he was receiving from Lord Wycombe long communications about his European travels, it is only quoted here from the full text, which Bowring printed with the introductory note: 'The following letter contains many curious particulars illustrative of Neapolitan politics and Italian customs:'

The original, or a copy of, the letter was evidently sent by Bentham to Lord St Helens, who returned it with his letter of 24 December (letter 1092).

and actually has created in them a job for the nephew, if not an accession to the state. . . .[2]

The nullity of the pope, the vacillation of the court, the false and unbecoming part which, through the intrigues of Lady E. M., it acted in the affair of Armfeldt,[3] the discovery of the correspondence carried on through Genoa, the affair of Medicis, the increase of imposts, the *insidious project with regard to Leghorn*, the jealousy which Acton[4] bore to Caramanico,[5] the change which has taken place in the *ostensible* existence of the former, and the death of the latter, are topics which cannot be new to you.

To these topics it appears to me that the history of Neapolitan intrigue may be confined; at least my information does not go beyond them. . . .

October 5.

The packet from Palermo arrived upon the 2d, and brought over a young man, nephew to the Prince of Campo Franco, who has been taken up for Jacobinism. Notwithstanding the time which has elapsed, nothing certain is known with regard to Caramanico, the sudden and peculiar circumstances of whose death make suspicion unavoidable.

I live most in habits with the Danish Minister,[6] whom I have

[2] Giovanni Angelo Braschi (1717–99), Pope Pius VI, 1775–99. He is best remembered in connexion with the establishment of the Vatican museum and his attempts to drain the Pontine marshes.

[3] Count Gustaf Mauritz Armfelt (1757–1814), Swedish statesman. A member of the council of regency after the death of King Gustavus III in 1792, he was appointed ambassador to Naples by the anti-Gustavian regent, Duke Charles, who wanted to get rid of him. While in Naples Armfelt urged the Empress Catherine II of Russia to intervene in Sweden in favour of the Gustavians, but his activities were discovered, and he escaped with the assistance of Queen Carolina Maria and fled to Russia. He was rehabilitated by Gustavus IV, and later held several major diplomatic and military posts.

[4] Sir John Francis Edward Acton, bart. (1736–1811), was born in France, the son of an English doctor. He entered the Tuscan naval service; he was recommended to Queen Carolina Maria by Prince Caramanico and entrusted with the reorganization of the Neapolitan navy, 1779. He became prime minister of Naples and worked in concert with Sir William Hamilton to substitute the influence of Austria and Britain for that of Spain at Naples. On the entry of the French into Naples in 1806 he fled to Sicily. He unexpectedly succeeded to a baronetcy and estates in 1791 on the death of a distant cousin. Lord Acton, the historian, was his grandson.

[5] Francesco d'Aquino, Prince of Caramanico (1736–95) was Sicilian envoy extraordinary and minister plenipotentiary to Britain, 1781–4; ambassador to France, 1784–5; Viceroy of Sicily, 1786–95. It was rumoured that he was either poisoned by Acton, or had committed suicide to avoid being charged with treason.

[6] Edmond von Bourke (1761–1821), was the Danish minister to Sicily, Dec. 1793–July 1797, and later had a distinguished career at Stockholm, Madrid, London and Paris. In 1795 he wrote *Notice sur les Ruines les plus remarquables de Naples et des environs*, published posthumously at Paris in 1823.

always known the same, and liked these ten years. He dines at home, almost every day, with Count Reydern,[7] not now employed, but whom you remember in England, and scarcely anybody else. I am also beholden to a society at Portici, consisting of Lady Hamilton,[8] who is not ignorant of the astonishment with which she strikes me; of the handsome Princess Vintemiglia,[9] who, born in France, unites, as I make no scruple of telling her, a Parisian tournure with the charms of southern countries; of the amiable Countess Corletti,[10] for whom I had a letter from her brother, the Chevalier de Saxe[11]; and of the Russian Minister's wife, who, if my old friend her husband may be taken at his word, is exceedingly devout, but whose eyes, if I may trust my skill in physiognomy, tell a different story.

The men, excepting a little commandeur who has seen the world, and the Russian, who is very gay, passably consequential, and communicative with a vengeance, are little better than mutes; I mean in that society. I must, however, do that Nestor in love and politics Sir W. H.,[12] the justice to say, that he is very particular in the mention of the obligations he owes to his friends.

Upon the 3d, I accompanied the Hamiltons to Monsieur Esterhazy[13]—a stupid, good sort of rich man, who plays whist, because he cannot bear to read; and told me he was *ambassadeur de famille*, with scarcely another idea in his head. In the meantime, he was doing the honours of a fête, at which the king[14] and queen[15] were present. I was presented to both: the former was as gracious as he could be, without speaking; the latter spoke to me different times

[7] Not identified.

[8] Emma, Lady Hamilton (1761?–1815), née Lyon. She had become Hamilton's mistress in 1786 and married him in 1791; she was a confidante of Queen Carolina Maria, who cultivated her as a means of gaining English support against France. Emma's claims to have rendered important political services at Naples were later endorsed by her lover, Lord Nelson, but ignored by the British ministry.

[9] Princess Ventimiglia was the wife of Giuseppe Belmonte, Prince of Ventimiglia (1767–1814), who married her in France, and returned to Sicily, where his opposition to King Ferdinand led to his imprisonment until 1812.

[10] Not otherwise identified.

[11] Joseph Xavier, Chevalier de Saxe (1767–1802), second son of Prince Xavier of Saxony, and a favourite of Queen Carolina; he served as a general in Sicily.

[12] Sir William Hamilton (1730–1803), diplomat and antiquary. He was M.P. for Midhurst, 1761–4, later envoy extraordinary and plenipotentiary at Naples, 1767–1800.

[13] Franz, Count von Esterhazy, Austrian ambassador to Sicily, 1792–1801.

[14] Ferdinand IV (1751–1825), King of Naples (Ferdinand III of Sicily and I of the two Sicilies).

[15] Carolina Maria (1752–1814), Queen of Naples, was a daughter of the Empress Maria Theresa of Austria and sister of Marie Antoinette. She married Ferdinand in 1768, and had a more effective influence on policy than her husband.

in the course of the evening, with the aire of a determined *maitresse femme*, and very well. . . . Lady Hamilton told me, that the queen had assured her that morning, there should be no peace but with the consent of England. She added, 'I could not think what a domestic, good-hearted woman the queen was!' The Russian minister's wife, who is no favourite at Court, was absent through an indigestion, the consequence of eating too much supper.

I am condemned to stay here till the departure of a ship, in which I mean to go to Sicily; and make a point of telling the ladies that I must quit Naples soon, lest I should grow to like it too well. In point of fact, I am impatient to breathe the sea air, uncontaminated with the breath of strumpets; but this is not so easy as you may imagine, for what with corsairs, quarantines, and French depredation, the Mediterranean has become an odious gulph.

The new Russian minister, Count Golowkin,[16] is a young man, born and educated at the Hague, who came to Russia not very long before I made an acquaintance with him, which was almost intimate for the time it lasted, at Moscow. . . .

It is now high time that I should apologize for having troubled you with this compilation of small talk. A more formal letter, however, might have conveyed a less accurate idea of the present situation of this residence, the business of which is conducted like that of an ill-regulated private family, in which an artful interloper finds a foolish husband in occupation and amusement, enabling, by such means, a dissipated wife to tyrannise over her household, spend the fortune of her family, and give loose to all her passions.

P.S. I am assured this will be conveyed safely to Rome, where it will be put into the post.

1084

TO SIR JOHN FREEMAN MITFORD

8 October 1795 (Aet 47)

Q.S.P. 8 Oct. 1795

Sir

Understanding that the draught of a Contract of mine with the Treasury as prepared by Mr White is, or is on the point of being,

[16] Feodor Gavrilovič, Count Golovkin, Russian envoy extraordinary and minister plenipotentiary to Sicily, 1795–6.
1084. [1] B.L. VI: 112–13. Autograph rough draft, much altered. Docketed: '1795 Oct 8 / Panopt / J.B. Q.S.P. / to / Mitford Sollr Genl / Begging communication of any difficulties relative to the Draught of the Contract.'

submitted to you previously to its engrossment, I take the liberty of requesting that in the possible event of your seeing reason to make any alterations in it or by which any further decision might be called for on the part of their Lordships (I say possible for I know of no special grounds for any such apprehension) I may be indulged with the permission of attending you on the subject before your opinion passes out of your hands. The motive for this my humble request is the hope that in the event of its being granted the matter may be adjusted, in the first instance, or at least I may at that earlier period see what I have to expect, whereas in the other event the business might stick at the Treasury for an indefinite length of time, at the end of which I might be referred to you for a hearing after all.

When you are apprised that my original proposal in relation to this business was delivered in as long ago as Jan 1791, that my amended proposal was accepted so long ago as July 1793, that in the course of that and the following month I was repeatedly called upon to 'take my arrangements' accordingly, that arrangements were accordingly taken by me at an expence still going on and amounting already to little short of £10,000, my anxiety to get clear of even the least chance /every further delay/ that can be avoided will certainly appear natural, and I hope will be thought excusable.

This general anxiety and not any apprehension of any doubts in particular liable to give occasion to doubts or difficulties is the sole reason for the provision I am thus endeavouring to make for the possibilities above alluded to, and not any apprehension of any particular points as liable to give occasion /likely to give rise to them/ to doubts or difficulties: nor does Mr White, in the wish he expresses that the draught may receive your sanction /refer to any reason of that nature for desiring it/ appear to entertain any presentiment of difficulty in the case.

1085

To the Duc de Liancourt

11 October 1795 (Aet 47)

Queen Square Place, Westminster,
Sunday, Oct. 11, 1795.

My dear Duke,
I have deferred the acknowledgment of your kind remembrance of me so long ago after the receipt of it,[2] that I begin to be apprehensive lest this letter should not reach the place you indicated to me time enough to find you there. The termination of my negotiations with our treasury, relative to the Penitentiary business, is an epoch of such importance to the remainder of my life, and will make so great a change in my position with relation to all sorts of objects, that I am got into the habit of deferring to that period all sorts of undertakings, permanent and transient, considerable and inconsiderable. Meantime, the intelligence of an opportunity for Boston that will not last beyond Wednesday next, is a warning to me not to postpone any longer the discharge of one of the most agreeable, as well as honorable of my debts.

Your present[3] has been of real use to me in the way of encouragement and self-satisfaction, and will be of use to me in the way of argument on more occasions than one. The injunction in which you are so earnest has prevented me, and, while it remains unrepealed, must continue to prevent me from giving the public the benefit of the work in any other shape. Statements, relative to matters of fact, depend for their reception upon their apparent title to credit, and their apparent title to credit depends upon a *name.*

Your letter did not reach my hands till after the Metcalf family had left London for the summer; and as they have not yet returned, I have not yet had the opportunity of communicating my treasures to the lady in question with the privacy you seem to require; for I am not sufficiently acquainted with the female branches of the family to know whether a letter directed by the post to one would reach

1085. [1] Bowring, x, 312–13. Headed: 'Bentham to the Duke de Liancourt (Boston, U.S.)'.
[2] Probably the letter of which the summary by Bowring is printed above (letter 1075).
[3] This suggests a present of an anonymous pamphlet, written by the duke, perhaps containing material supplied by Bentham and the 'remarks' mentioned in Letter 1075.

her hands without the cognizance of the rest.[4] The great probability is, that all this caution about a matter so well calculated for the public eye, is most perfectly superfluous, and that I am cheating more persons than one of a pleasure which it was not intended to deny them; but seeing explanations barred by the Atlantic, I chose to adhere to the safest side, and to let my *mandant*, though a Frenchman, see he had got a Spaniard for his *mandataire*.

I don't know whether you saw the *Draught* of my proposed *Contract* with Government, in which I inserted a clause for insuring, at my own risk, the lives of the prisoners,—a clause which, with great difficulty, I got allowed. In my *book*, you may have observed the *recommendation*, which, in my Contract I have got converted into an *obligation*, to debar them altogether from the taste of all *fermented* liquors. Judge how pleasant it was to find by your Report, that when prisoners are cut off from that source of corruption, they *live quietly* and *never die*.

As to my book on *Penal Legislation*, it is no more than upon a par, in point of forwardness, with half-a-dozen others in the same workshop; and I am inclined to think one on *Civil Legislation* will get the start of it, or at least accompany it. Whatever turns out at any time, the three copies you do me the honour to bespeak, shall be always at your service. Name me the two friends you allude to, and their copies shall be sent them from hence in the event of your departure. All the productions of that same workshop have been cruelly retarded by the dilatoriness, and (I won't say how many other pretty qualities besides) of our *higher powers*: two-thirds at least of the time that has elapsed since I had the honour of seeing you, has been consumed, in fighting them, or dangling after them in ante-chambers and passages. To save time on one hand, while so much was wasting on the other, the plan was, that *Dumont* should take my half-finished manuscripts as he found them—half English, half English-French, and make what he could of them in Genevan-French, without giving me any further trouble about the matter. Instead of that, the lazy rogue comes to me with everything that he writes, and teazes me to fill up every gap he has observed.[5]

---

[4] Philip Metcalfe was a bachelor, but he had three, possibly four, of his nieces living with him: Nelly, Margaret, Jane and Frederica Sophia Metcalfe, the last of whom, however, was probably married by this time.

[5] For Bentham's contact with Dumont earlier in that year, see letters 1052 and 1055, pp. 127 and 131 above. Romilly wrote to Dumont, who was at Bowood, on 27 October 1795: 'Bentham has been locking himself up at Hendon, and working, as he tells me, for you at his Civil Code. He has, too, a refutation of the French Declaration of Rights, which I encourage him to publish' (*Memoirs . . . of Samuel Romilly . . . with Correspondence*, 1840, ii, 54).

My contract, though every tittle has been agreed on, is not even yet *signed*: consequently, my brother's inventions (I mean those of the peaceable kind) have remained hitherto unemployed. In his military capacity, he is preparing some dishes for the entertainment of your countrymen, and my fellow-citizens, the *Pandemonians*. Talleyrand may perhaps be amongst them again by this time. I hope Beaumetz is of the party, if he wishes it; but I rather wish than hope they may find themselves as well off in their redintegration as you are, I hope, in your banishment. While I write, the news is arrived of the Sections and the Convention being employed in cannonading each other—the result not known, though the Sections appear to have [had] the worst.[6] Quiet seems now as far off as ever. I can see no issue to such a dispute. You may remember how the English *sang froid* was kept for year after year in a flame, upon the electors of one of the counties conceiving they had one single representative forced upon them to the prejudice of Wilkes, whom, after they had got him, and tried him, they turned their backs upon.

Apropos of my brother's inventions, do you know of anybody where you *are*, or where you *have* been, who would like to be taught how to stock all North America with all sorts of woodwork, without exception, (shipping not excepted,) besides a number of other et ceteras, by machinery, on the terms of allowing the inventor a share of the profits as they arise?—Wheels, for example. Small ones by way of models, were executed, I believe, when you were here last; now, we have full-sized ones, round, to a degree of perfection in point of rotundity, never before exemplified. If the preliminary steps that have been taken by the Admiralty terminate as is intended, he will soon have the direction of the whole system of naval works put into his hands, with the title of Inspector-general of the Navy. A plan which the Navy Board had devised, and proceeded a good way in the execution of, for the enlargement of the dockyard works at Portsmouth, has just been stopped by the Admiralty Board, and a very different one of his contrivance ordered to be substituted in the room of it. My paper is just out, to say nothing of your patience. By my gratitude for past communications, and attention to past commands, judge of the value I should set upon any future ones; and believe me, with the most cordial respect, yours ever.

[6] The French Convention had decreed that, in the first election under the 1795 Constitution, two-thirds of the Convention must be re-elected. This prompted the unsuccessful rising in Paris of 13 Vendémiaire (5 October 1795), in which some 200 people were killed.

The Irish Administration has applied to me once more to set up Panopticon there.

1086

FROM SIR JOHN FREEMAN MITFORD

14 October 1795

Lincs Inn
14 Oct. 1795

Sir

Mr. White having laid before me the draught of a contract for the purposes mentioned in your Note of the 8 instant, I have looked it over in the absence of the Attorney General, and made considerable alterations—Before I return it to Mr White, I send it to you,[2] that you may consider it and suggest any objections to my alterations, the principal objects of which have been to make the contract, as far as I could, free from legal objections, and explicit in its terms—

I have the honor to be
Yr. hble sert
John Mitford

Jeremy Bentham Esqr

1087

FROM SIR JOHN FREEMAN MITFORD

25 October 1795

25 Oct 1795

The Solicitor General presents his Compliments to Mr Bentham, and informs him that the packet he inquires after was delivered at the Chambers of the Attorney General who is out of town; but it has since been transmitted to the Solicitor, who will

1086. [1] B.L. VI: 114–15. Original. Docketed: '1795 Oct 14 / Panopt / Sollr Genl Linc Inn / to / J.B. Q.S.P. / with Draught of contract / Receved at Hendon 14th or 15 / Answered 18—by Jack.'

[2] An earlier letter sent by Joseph White to Charles Long is docketed by Bentham: '1795 Oct 2 / Panopt. / Josh. White Linc Inn to C. Long Treasury / Copy / with Draught of Penitentiary Contract' (B.L. VI: 111).

1087. [1] B.L. VI: 116–17. Copy. Docketed: '1795 Oct 25 / Panopt / Sollr Gen Linc Inn / to / J.B. Hendon / Copy / Original sent back to the Sollr Genl without any addition but the date 30 Dec underneath.'

Mitford acknowledged this letter and the reminder on 31 December (see letter 1094).

give it the earliest attention the extreme pressure of public business will permit—

Linc: Inn—
25 Oct 1795

1088

To Samuel Bentham

2 November 1795 (Aet 47)

Q.S.P. Novr 2. 1795 Monday

Nothing said at Nepean's yesterday about Panopt, or any kind of business.

News by one of the Princes of Orange[2] who arrived at Scarborough after 7 days stormy passage from Cuxhaven of three engagements in which the French lost from 20 to 30,000 men with 240 pieces of cannon—not absolutely out of doubt though confirmed by a letter from Paris reced by Thompson[3] whose intelligence has been suspected of Stock jobbery.

Arrived this day an augur for boring tree-nail holes.

Nepean persists in his projects upon your Tobacco—When he comes we must get St. Helens to meet him

$\frac{1}{2}$ after 2 just setting out for Collins's[4]

Jarvis[5] is going to the Mediterranean—was asked to meet us and regretted that he could not.

Company—Col Barré, Phipps[6] (an Irishman) with wife and daughter—an animal about 16 or 17 beautiful as an Angel—General Goldsworthy[7] of Vancouver—came in after dinner Colpoys.[8]

1088. [1] B.L. VI: 122–3. Autograph. Addressed: '/ Redbridge / Southampton / For Genl Bentham.' Postmark: 'NO.2.95.E'.

[2] On the night of 28 October 1795 Prince William George Frederick (1774–99), second son of William V, Prince of Orange, arrived at Scarborough in a lugger, after a passage of seven days from Hamburg (London *Star*, 31 October 1795).

[3] A London stockjobber, not identified.

[4] Perhaps the residence of William Collins, who had 'a beautiful house' at Greenwich (Bowring, x, 572).

[5] Admiral John Jervis, later Earl St Vincent (1735–1823), recently appointed commander-in-chief in the Mediterranean; in 1797 his defeat of the Spanish fleet off Cape St Vincent led to his earldom.

[6] Perhaps Sir Henry Phipps (1755–1831), afterwards 1st Earl of Mulgrave (1812). He was a military adviser of Pitt and rose to the rank of general (1809). He was also First Lord of the Admiralty in the Portland Ministry (1807).

[7] Philip Goldsworthy, Colonel of the First (or Royal) Dragoons, promoted major-general 1793; lieutenant-general, 1797; d. 1801.

[8] Sir John Colpoys, admiral (c. 1742–1821), one of those faced with the Spithead mutiny in 1797; later commander-in-chief, Plymouth and governor of Greenwich hospital.

The two letters you expected from the Admiralty came yesterday —Mr W.[9] as well as N.[10] very gracious—writing fine notes of thanks and apology about Mess [?].

1089

JOHN HEIDE KOE TO SAMUEL BENTHAM

9 November 1795 (Aet 47)

Q.S.P.   Nov 9 – 1795

Sir

Southampton Waggons do not go from any part of the Borough but on the other side of the water—Portsmouth Waggons which go from the Borough do not receive package for any part of Southampton.

Mr Edward Collins[2] has come to spend some time here.

The house received no harm and the garden no material injury by the late storm.

Mr Bentham's whole time is taken up in writing observations on the Treason Bill[3] or he would have written himself

The other parts of your letter will be duly attended to.

I shall go to make further enquiries concerning the Chest immediately.

I am
Sir
Your most obedient
and humble Servant
John Heide Koe

Gen. Bentham

[9] Perhaps Charles Wright, who was chief clerk at the Admiralty, 1796–1807.
[10] Evan Nepean, now Secretary of the Admiralty.
1089. [1] B.L. VI: 120–1. Original. Addressed: 'Gen. Bentham / Redbridge / Southampton'. Postmark: 'NO.9.95.E.'
Written on behalf of Jeremy Bentham by John Heide Koe, who began to act as his secretary at this time; not to be confused with his younger brother, John Herbert Koe (1783–1860), who acted some years later in the same capacity and ended as an eminent judge (1847) and treasurer of Lincoln's Inn (1860). They were the sons of a London businessman of Norwegian extraction, John Koe, who went bankrupt in 1778.
[2] Younger son of William Collins.
[3] Introduced into the House of Commons by Pitt in November 1795. See below, p. 165 n. 2.

1090

FROM BARON ST HELENS

27 November 1795

Gt Russel Street Friday 27th Novr

A thousand thanks to you, my Dear Sir, for the inclosed papers.[2] I have perused them from beginning to end, and extracted all the several Heads (12 in Number) which I purpose, unless you should forbid it, to communicate to Mr Wilberforce, who will probably apply them to some useful purpose. And this leads me to request further that you would enable me to impart to the House of Commons thro' the same very unexceptionable channel the benefit of any remarks that you may have made on the other Bill now before Parlt. commonly called the publick meeting Bill.[3] In fact this last seems to be the most exceptionable of the two, and to have contributed more than the other, to the bringing Mr Pitt and his *learned* advisers into their present entanglements. Pray don't give yourself the trouble of answering this, as I intend myself the pleasure of $\frac{1}{2}$ an hour chat with you tomorrow before the arrival of the rest of your Company.

yrs most sincerely
St Helens

1090. [1] U.C. Ogden MSS. 62 (1) 94. Autograph. Docketed: '1795 Nov 27 / Ld St Helens Gr Russel St / to / J.B. Q.S.P. /Treason Bill.'

[2] From the docket it would seem these concerned the Treasonable Practices Bill, introduced into the House of Lords by Grenville on 6 November and into the Commons by Pitt on 16 November. It passed on 10 December 1795 as *An Act for the Safety and Preservation of his Majesty's Person and Government against treasonable and seditious Practices and Attempts* (36 Geo. III, c. 7). Bentham sent to the *Morning Herald* his 'Observations on the Treason Bill', which were reprinted in Bowring, x, 320–2.

[3] What became the Seditious Meetings Act, 1795 (36 Geo. III, c. 8).

1091

FROM COUNT RUMFORD

10 December 1795

Count Rumford presents his Compliments to Mr Bentham, and returns him many thanks for the valuable and very acceptable present he has made him.[2] He promises himself much pleasure and a great deal of useful information from the perusal of his interesting Work.

Royal Hotel Pall Mall
December 10th 1795.

1092

FROM BARON ST HELENS

24 December 1795

My dear Sir,

I am just setting out for Hampshire, and if I find Mr Pelham there, or he shd be within my reach, I shall not fail to execute your Commission. Many thanks for your kind communication of the inclosed paper; which is indeed most extremely curious and interesting—particularly to myself who happen to be acquainted with most of the parties mentioned in it.[2] The writer seems to possess a great share of shrewdness and sagacity, and I am led to infer from this specimen that there is a strong similarity between his pursuits and turn of mind, and those of his father:[3] and that their understandings likewise are pretty much of the same

1091. [1] B.L. VI: 124–5. Original. Docketed: '1795 Dec 10 / Panopt / Count Rumford Royal Hotel Pall Mall / to / J.B. Q.S.P. / For Panopticon.'
Addressed: 'Mr Bentham Queens / Square Place / Westminster'.
Sir Benjamin Thompson, Count von Rumford (1753–1814), an American-born loyalist in the War of Independence; F.R.S., 1775; under-secretary for the colonies, 1780; lieutenant-colonel in George III's American Dragoons, 1782–3; in the service of the Elector of Bavaria, 1784–95, when he received his German titles; he became a social reformer in Britain, as well as an inventor; he founded the Royal Institution, 1799.
[2] A set of the *Panopticon* volumes.
1092. [1] B.L. VI: 126–7. Autograph. Docketed: '1795 Dec 24 / Ld St Helens Gr Russel St. / to / J.B. Q.S.P.'
[2] This clearly refers to the letter from Lord Wycombe to Bentham, quoted above (letter 1083).
[3] The Marquis of Lansdowne.

Calibre. I hope it is needless for me to assure you that I shall observe the strictest secrecy respecting what I shd call in official language this most private and confidential communication.

Adieu my Dear Sir—after my return which will be in about a fortnight, I shall certainly take the earliest opportunity of looking in upon you.

most sincerely yours
St. Helens

Gt Russel St.
Thursday 24th Decr.

1093

FROM BARON ST HELENS

27 December 1795

Broadlands Sunday 27th Decr. 95

My Dear Sir,

As Mr Pelham, who is here, assures me that he intends writing to you by this post, I send you these three lines merely to thank you for your letter of yesterday[2] and for the very friendly wish that you are so good as to express in it, and which shall certainly be gratified the very moment I return to London.

Mr Pelham talks of going to town in a day or two, however it is possible that he may change his mind, and in that case I shall be extremely happy to be your chargé d'affaires, if your business with him shd be of a nature to admit of or to be forwarded by my intervention. I shall stay here till Friday, and probably be in town on the Monday following.

ever yours, my Dear Sir,
most truly and faithfully
St. Helens

1093. [1] B.L. VI: 128–9. Autograph. Docketed: '1795 Dec 27 / Ld St. Helens Broadlands / to / J.B. Q.S.B.'

Addressed: 'To Jeremy Bentham Esqr / Queens Square Place / Westminster.' Franked: 'Romsey Decr Twenty seventh 1795 / Free / Palmerston'. Postmark: 'FREE DE.28.95.C'.

Broadlands was a country seat of the Temple family, and St Helens was visiting his friend, Henry Temple, 2nd Viscount Palmerston (1739–1802), M.P. and a former lord of the Treasury and of the Admiralty.

[2] Missing.

1094
FROM SIR JOHN FREEMAN MITFORD
31 December 1795

The Solicitor General presents his compliments to Mr Bentham. He presumes from receiving back a note dated 25. Octr. with the date 30 Decr underneath,[2] that Mr Bentham has not received from the treasury any information respecting the draught of the proposed contract. The Solicitor finally settled that draught very shortly, he thinks within two or three days, after the date of that note, and returned the draught so settled to the Solicitor for the Treasury. For what reason it has not been transmitted to Mr Bentham he is unable to guess. He can only say the delay not been with him, as he did when labouring under severe illness, and much oppressed by other public business, devote a considerable portion of his time to the dispatch of Mr Bentham's contract, and concluded it had been long ago completely arranged.
Lincoln's inn

Dec. 31 1795

1095
TO SIR JOHN FREEMAN MITFORD
31 December 1795 (Aet 47)

Q.S.P. 31 Decr 1795

Sir

It becomes me to lose no time in acknowledging the favour of your very obliging note.[2] The return of your former note had no other view than that of bringing myself to your remembrance in the shortest and the least obtrusive manner I could devise. It was indeed altogether beyond my hope that business in which I am concerned could have been dispatched at the very momentous as well as early

1094. [1] B.L. VI: 130–1. Original. Docketed: '1795 Dec 31 / Panopt / Soll. Gen. Linc. Inn / to / J.B. Q.S.P.'
    Addressed: 'Jeremy Bentham Esqr / Queen Square Place, Westminster.' Stamped: '8 oClock [—?] 31 [DE] PENNY POST PAID'. Postmark: 'Penny Post Pd 1d ⟨Chan⟩cery Lane'.
    [2] The original of letter 1087.
1095. [1] B.L. VI: 132–3. Autograph draft. Docketed: '1795 Dec 31 / Panopt / J.B. Q.S.P. / to / Soll Genl Linc Inn.'
    [2] Letter 1094.

period you speak of: the present being to appearance a time of comparative leisure, the season seemed to be returned at which my business, if present to your recollection, might obtain a chance— Mr. Whites chief Clerk having promised to give me immediate notice of the return of the Draught to his office and no such notice having ever come I could conceive no otherwise than that it remained still in yours. I cannot without compunction think of the pains you were taking about my business under the joint pressure of business of a superior order and ill health, nor is it without a mixture of remorse that I am now taking the benefits of a correspondence which your politeness has again imposed on you out of the ordinary course of things. I have the honour to be, with great respect

Sir
your most obliged
and most obedient Servt
Jeremy Bentham

Mr Sollicitor General

1096

To Charles Long

1 January 1796 (Aet 47)

Q.S.P. 1 Jan 1796

Sir,
    Permitt me to recall to your notice a business which some years ago was thought to have been too long delay'd, and in respect of which I have just received such intelligence as places me once more altogether in the dark. Full two months ago the Draught of the Penitentiary Contract was returned by the Sollicitor General. So I have just learned by a note from Mr Sollicitor, in which he has the goodness to inform me, that 'within 2 or 3 days', as he thinks 'after the 25 of October' he returned the draught finally settled to the Sollicitor for the Treasury, having dispatched it at a time 'when he was labouring under severe illness and much oppressed by other public business', observing that 'he is unable to guess for what reason it has not been transmitted to me', and that he had 'concluded it had been long ago completely arranged.'[2]

1096. [1] B.L. VI: 134–5. Autograph draft. Docketed: '1796 Jan / Panopt / J.B. Q.S.P. / to / C. Long Treasury / Draught of Contract still lying at Linc. Inn as supposed / though dispatched by Sollr Genl as long ago as 2 or 3 / days after 25 Octr.'
    [2] The quotations are from letter 1094.

169

My silence all this time had proceeded on the notion of the Draughts lying still with the Sollicitor General, to whom after he had had the goodness to give me a spontaneous assurance that the business should receive the 'earliest attention from him that the extreme pressure of public business would permitt', I thought it did not become me to be troublesome. Conceiving the present to be a moment of comparative leisure, I very fortunately took the liberty of bringing the business back to his recollection, and received an answer as above. Mr. White's Clerk having given me very particular assurances that he would give me immediate notice as soon as the Draught had been returned to his office, I had the improvidence to look upon myself as dispensed from a series of attendances of which I saw no certain end. Mr. White not being at his office, nor you at yours, and it appearing a matter of uncertainty to me how long it might be in this season of relaxation and fine weather before you resumed your respective stations, as also whether you might not be as much in the dark about the business as myself, I take the liberty of furnishing you with this memorandum, in hopes of your being the better prepared to favour me with some kind of intelligence by the time of my resuming my station in your ante-chamber. Mr White's Clerk informed mine just now that he had not received the Draught to ingross and that he supposed it had not been received from the Treasury. I have the honour to be,

with all respect
Sir, Your most obedient
and humble Servant
Jeremy Bentham

C. Long Esqr.
etc. etc. etc.

1097

TO SAMUEL BENTHAM

5 January 1796 (Aet 47)

Q.S.P. 5 Jan. 1796

The Herald,[2] according to your Generalship's orders, will be sent to your Generalship at Redbridge untill counter orders. Yet I observe the things are to be sent to Portsmouth, which a little puzzles me.

Your Generalship's orders about Philosopical Transactions[3] were so clear or clearly delivered that I have not known what to make of them. All 4 Vols were to go to Essex Street—according to Oliver. Yet two were to go to Dr Buchan[4] according to Jack; they are all four gone to Essex Street. It remains a mystery.

Your Cousin, Mrs Anderson,[5] has honoured me with an invitation to stand Godfather particularly desiring an answer as soon as possible. I am balancing whether to give no answer or a civil note saying it is the sort of thing I never did nor ever mean to do. Quere which would give least pain?—tell me what you would do by return of post.

On Sunday came a letter[6] from Browne saying that the tender must be pleaded and the money paid into Court supposing that if the tender[?] can be proved the Action will not proceed—that is supposing the Attorney not to be a thief which is a libellous supposition.

I will enquire about the notion of the necessity of the joint presence of all parties—it strikes me as a vulgar error.

1097. [1] New York Public Library, Manuscript Division, Miscellaneous Papers—Bentham, J. Autograph. Docketed: 'written by Jeremy Bentham—Mrs Bentham.' The docket is by Samuel's wife, the future Lady Bentham.
Addressed: 'To General Bentham / Redbridge / Southampton.' Postmark: 'JA.5.96'.
[2] The *Morning Herald*, a London newspaper issued daily (except Sundays), 1 November 1780–31 December 1869.
[3] The *Philosophical Transactions of the Royal Society*, started in 1665. The four most recent publications were volumes 82–5 (1792–5). The Fordyce family lived in Essex Street, Strand.
[4] Perhaps William Buchan (1729–1805) physician, who practised in London from 1778. His *Domestic Medicine, or the Family Physician*, 1769, went through 19 editions in his lifetime and was translated into the principal European languages; alternatively his son, Alexander Peter Buchan (1764–1824), who had studied medicine in London under George Fordyce and graduated M.D. at Leyden, 1793.
[5] Not identified.
[6] Missing. William Browne was their solicitor friend.

What concerns Lloyd[7] and Sadler[8] has been sent to them. Collins[9] wrote to you or Peake yesterday at Portsmouth with the Bill and particulars of your copper rattle traps.

1098

TO SAMUEL BENTHAM

6 January 1796 (Aet 47)

Q.S.P. Wedn. Jan 6 1796

Discord reigns in this garrison since the General has quitted the command. Mrs. W.[2] has just been breaking John's head with one of the dishes: and John has left the house, I suppose to get a warrant. Romilly happening to be here, we both heard the pother, though I did not then know the cause. Nuts to Oliver, who came with information of the affray, narrated with affected indifference.

Pole Carew called here yesterday to jaw about Es⟨cheat⟩.[3] He says that Pitt's Collateral Succession tax[4] must be given up. After a wrangle I got him to approve of Escheat to the extent of the quantum of Supply Pitt's tax is taken for. But as to anything further—his Aristocrace[5] makes him regard the inconveniences from the most oppressive tax as nothing in comparison of the peril to old families.

[7] John Lloyd, Clerk of the Survey, later Clerk of the Checque at Plymouth, 1762–1800. The Benthams had known him since 1778 (see *Correspondence*, ii, 160).

[8] James Sadler, who was later in Samuel Bentham's Inspector-General's office (see letter 1135, n. 7).

[9] William Collins, became closely associated with the work of Samuel Bentham at Portsmouth, and his son, Edward, assisted Jeremy (Bowring, x, 572–3).

1098. [1] B.L. VI: 136. Autograph. Addressed: 'To / General Bentham / Redbridge / near Southampton.' Postmark: 'JA.6.96.F.'

[2] Mrs Wilkinson, Jeremy's cook (see letter 1099).

[3] Bentham had printed his pamphlet on the subject in 1793 and published it, with notes added as late as 9 December 1795, at the end of that year. The full title was *Supply without Burden; or Escheat vice Taxation; being a Proposal for a Saving of Taxes by an Extension of the Law of Escheat, including Strictures on the Taxes on Collateral Succession comprised in the Budget of 7th December 1795*, reprinted in Bowring, ii, 585–98 (see letter 1017, n. 2).

[4] The Legacy Tax bill, one of several introduced by Pitt on 7 December 1795, passed its third reading in the House of Commons, 5 April 1796 (*Parliamentary Register*, xliii, 599–602; xliv, 362–3). It was a tax on 'that species of legacy, which, without taking in the lineal heirs, extended to collateral branches and to strangers'.

[5] Aristocratism.

1099

To Samuel Bentham

8, 9 January 1796 (Aet 47)

Q.S.P. Jan 8 1796

I have the weight of the house pressing upon my shoulders. Mrs. Wilkinson is gone off, and is not haveable but upon the terms of never having anybody else. She fell upon John upon the supposition of his stealing a spoon which was never lost, spit in his face several times, broke his head with a dish in which she was going to make a pie, and then followed up her blow with what remained of it in her hand. He gave her a blow or a shove against the door with such violence as to have produced either in the first instance or by a slip of hers in her endeavour to recover herself a black eye and a loss of sundry teeth. For this she got a warrant—had him taken up—is going to indict him, and he in consequence is held to Bail, Oliver by my consent being one of the Bail. The first Bell has rung and I have not time to give you any more particulars, except that I was before the Justices in Qn Sq. where I saw her for the first time, and the Justices who as well as myself would have made it up found her implacable. The maids (whom I have examined) seem good quiet animals, and I should rub on vastly well for some time were it not for the fear of Oliver and plunder before my eyes. Jack became Housekeeper as to keys, etc. by predestination without my interference, for to crown all I was not well yesterday nor the day before, but am now as usual, saving as to these plagues.

What I spoke of to you in my last[2] as being a vulgar error about the necessity of *mutual presence*, Romilly confirms.

A separate Bond will be the proper security for them to give over and above the Indenture. I could if necessary draw one for you and send you, but I had rather stay till your return.

What vicissitudes in Ireland! Pelham does not go back. Steele your friend Steele goes in his room: Abbot gives a good account of him.[3] They have had it for some time in the newspapers.

1099. [1] B.L. VI: 137–8. Autograph. Addressed: 'Gen. Bentham / at H. Peakes Esq. / Dock Yard / Portsmouth.' Postmark: 'JA.9.96.D.'

[2] He means his last letter but one (letter 1097, see p. 171 above).

[3] It was stated in *The Star*, 7 January 1796, and other newspapers, that the Right Hon. Thomas Steele would succeed Thomas Pelham as Irish secretary, but this did not happen. Pelham remained in the post until 1798. Thomas Steele (1753–1823) was M.P. for Chichester, 1780–1807; Secretary of the Treasury, 1783–91; Commissioner of the Board of Control, 1791–3; Joint Paymaster-General, 1791–1804. According to Pole

There was a report of Abbot's going to be married to a Miss Middleton,[4] sister of a great man in a fine castle in Wales. He denies it stating the origin: but recriminates by mentioning a match of yours. My answer was that we both went to the same place and went for Chemistry.[5]

It was impossible to have kept Mrs W.[6] even it we had turned off all the other servants: which would have been necessary, for I find clearly it is impossible for any Servants to live with her. She drinks too. The vexation is that her fidelity to us stands unquestioned, and she saluted me with benedictions as we left the office.

Panopticon—such incidents!—the prospect, however, though vexatious has nothing dark in it. I paid a visit yesterday to Puss,[7] who shewd me your letter.

Saturday 9

I let the post slip yesterday. Let me know how many Bonds you want and I will draw them and send them down. Of each Bond there will be only one part which you will keep. Of each Indenture there must be duplicates or triplicates. I will inquire which.

Ld St. Helens has just left me. He was over Portsmouth Yard 3 or 4 days ago with Pakenham,[8] who professed to explain to him your innovations.

1100

To Sir John Scott

11 January 1796 (Aet 47)

Q.S.P. 11 Jany 1796

Sir

Understanding that doubts have arisen in relation to my Contract with the Treasury since the Draught has passed from Mr

Carew he had more than once spoken to Pitt about the Panopticon project in 1791 (see *Correspondence*, iv, 282).

[4] Possibly the heiress, Charlotte Myddleton, who succeeded to the estates of her brother, Richard, in 1798 (*Dictionary of Welsh Biography*, Oxford, 1959).

[5] Samuel was courting Mary Sophia Fordyce at this time and this may refer to visits to her father's chemistry lectures at their house in Essex Street, Strand.

[6] Mrs Wilkinson, the cook.

[7] The mysterious lady, perhaps 'Mrs. L'., who has already appeared under this soubriquet (see letters 970 and 980).

[8] Probably Sir Thomas Pakenham (1757–1836), a naval commander distinguished at the Battle of the Glorious First of June, 1794; he became an admiral in 1810.

1100. [1] B.L. VI: 139–40. Autograph draft. Docketed: '1796 Jany 11 / Panopt / Brouillon / J.B. etc. etc. / Atty Genl Linc. Inn.'

Sollicitor General's hands into yours, I hope I may without impropriety request the indulgence of being permitted to attend you on the subject for the purpose of using my humble endeavours to remove any such doubts, and of being heard if necessary *pro interesse meo* before any Report is made to the Treasury importing any departure to my prejudice from the terms which appear upon the face of the Draught to have been agreed upon, beyond what has already resulted from the alterations which Mr Sollicitor found it necessary to make. Mr Sollicitor, to save circuity, was pleased in compliance with an application of mine similar to the present to transmitt to me his intended alterations previously to his returning the Draught to the Sollicitor to the Treasury.

When you are apprized, Sir, as Mr Sollicitor by a letter of mine of the 8th of October[2] was apprized 'that my original proposal in relation to this business was delivered so long ago as Jany 1791, that my amended proposal was accepted so long ago as July 1793, that in the course of that and the following months I was repeatedly called upon to '*take my arrangements*' accordingly—that arrangements were accordingly taken by me at an expence still going on and amounting already to upwards of £10,000 an advance not comprised in the conditions and such as my property will but ill bear either in respect of the nature or the extent of it, especially under the uncertainties that have been hanging over my head, my anxiety to embrace every possible chance of removing further delays and difficulties will I flatter myself not be received with less indulgence by Mr Attorney than it met with from Mr Sollicitor General. From a note of his dated 31 Decr[3] in which he expresses himself unable to guess for what reason it had not at that time been transmitted to me, adding that he concluded the business had been long ago compleatly arranged I find that the subject at that time at least had never happened to come upon the carpet betwixt you and him. If it were to become so, you might learn, Sir, if it were worth while, from the papers transmitted to him, other instances of hardship with which I forbear to trouble you—I have the honor to be with all respect

Sir Your most obedient
and humble Servant
Jeremy Bentham

Mr Atty Genl

[2] Letter 1084.
[3] Letter 1094.

1101
TO SAMUEL BENTHAM
c. 12 January 1796 (Aet 47)

Your undecypherable line[2] about newspapers might be meant
I thought to convey a desire on your part of receiving newspapers:
struck with remorse at having forgotten to send you a cargo the
last time on which I had notice of a parcel going to you from Lloyd,
I hereby send you those of the last week together with the Times
of today which has all the news of the others, the 2 others being
gone to Puss. Along with them and with this go certain pieces of
plate glass 6 doz: I believe at 3d procured by Mr Bunce.[3] Dont
forget to return the newspapers. The Chelmsford[4] [Chronicle] is sent
together with the whole week's compleat except that Frydays are
not as yet found.

Mr Bunce was sent for post-haste on Saturday by Ld Hugh,[5] and
likewise by Nepean for the purpose of attending the Board. They
had sent twice to his lodgings in Queen Street without being able
to find him. On Saturday when I thought him gone to the Admiralty
in consequence of Ld Hugh's message, he went by some misconception to his own lodgings in expectation of finding a message for
him there, and in the mean time Nepean's message came here.
Being just returned from his measuring work, I recommended it
to him to go to Nepean immediately (5 o'clock). He is gone accordingly. This looks like business. It looks as if they wanted to see
him for the purpose of ascertaining his consent, and putting his
name into some of the instruments.

Bunce is just returned. It was only for Ld Hugh, it seems, that
Nepean wanted him. He was accordingly sent to Ld Hugh's under
the notion of his being at home, but he not being at home nor
expected at any certain time Bunce came away settling it with the
Admiralty people there he should attend early tomorrow.

1101. [1] B.L. X: 617. Autograph, without date, docket or address.
[2] Missing.
[3] Samuel Bunce was a pupil of James Wyatt and exhibited at the Royal Academy,
1786–97. He joined Samuel's staff on 25 March 1796 as Architect and Engineer of
Naval Works, but died of a fever, 18 October 1802.
[4] *The Chelmsford Chronicle*, started 5 April 1771, contained local Essex news of
interest to the Benthams.
[5] Lord Hugh Seymour (1759–1801), son of the Marquis of Hertford, a vice-admiral
and a lord of the Admiralty, 1795–8; he was a crony of George, Prince of Wales.

Wilson[6] tells me he hears that Rose has read Escheat—I believe I told you that ministerial people say that the Collateral Succession Tax is not likely to go through.

Now as to Oliver—let me think about it on paper. If I discharge him, what shall I say to him? To discharge a servant without cause might increase that bad name the house has acquired through the enraged,[7] and make it difficult to get a good one in his room, especially on account of Barret, the coal merchant, who recommended him. An allegation of dishonesty would be worse than none, for I cannot prove any upon him, and just now he has been detecting an instance of dishonesty or mistake in the part of the Grocer. Shall I say it is for having given offence to you?—that would set him upon you—shall I say it is for having taken liberties with his tongue and made mischief⟨?⟩—that might set him to think what mischief, and so make more mischief. If you could have staid till the man comes from France the embarrassment might have been avoided: the change would then have been the natural result of prior negotiation (which is in some measure the case), without prejudice to Oliverian dignity. I can't discharge him without settling his accounts, nor can I settle his accounts without you, unless it be by paying him the balance without examination—what was it you agreed for? Discharging him would not break the thread of tittle-tattle without discharging John, who has given us no offence: nor would even the discharging John, without discharging the two maids i.e: the only remaining servants: and then how to get others?—and still there remains Barret who is undischargeable. If either Panopticon or Inspector Generalship had taken place we should not care 2 pence about all these put together, but at present they are plagues. When you have made a good launch and matters are ripe for Inspector Generalship, you wont mind facing the Protector,[8] at least for the purpose of dethroning him. After all the charge against him turns upon 2 or three words, not one of which, we may be pretty well assured was made use of by him: the subject could not have warranted such an appellation in the eyes of anybody: and the only evidence is the exaggerations if not the inventions of a woman half crazy with a mixture of rage and porter, and these communicated at second hand through a turbid troubled medium.

[6] George Wilson.
[7] The angry cook.
[8] A humorous nickname for the servant, Oliver.

177

1102

To Samuel Bentham

14 January 1796 (Act 47)

14 Jan 1796

A man of Lloyd's procurement has been here to look at Bond's fender, and values it at 26 Guineas. He said he would undertake to make as good an one for that money. Galloway's[2] action need not plague you—all will depend, I take for granted, either upon the agreement, or upon Lloyd's evidence.

The repairs done by Peniston[3] at Bell Yard[4] being to be valued according to custom, Bunce is to value on my part on Monday at 12. He does it as an act of condescension to oblige me. I thought it might prove a good occasion to form a just estimate of Peniston with a view to Panopticon.

You don't tell me how many Apprentices Indentures, nor how many Bonds. Tell me when, if any of the fish you angle for, are hooked.

You ought to have paid but 8d for your Newspapers, instead of 13d, it being but a double letter, unless the weight made it amount to so much—the free-passing of Newspapers has not yet commenced.

1103

To Samuel Bentham

21 January 1796 (Aet 47)

Morning Chron. 21 Jan 1796

'For the Naval Register—Shipbuilding—Mr Editor—That much is yet to be learnt in the art of Shipbuilding is agreed on all

---

1102. [1] B.L. VI: 141. Autograph. Addressed: 'To General Bentham / Redbridge / near Southampton.' Postmark: 'JA.14.96.D'.

[2] Thomas Galloway and his son were working for Samuel. See Bentham's memorandum of 6 March (letter 1117).

[3] Not identified; presumably a builder.

[4] Bell Yard was left to Bentham by his father. It was situated between Queen's Square Place and Petty France, and it included a public house, *The Bell*, and several tenements, coach houses and stables occupied by Thomas Jones or his sub-tenants (Will of Jeremiah Bentham, proved 5 April 1792, P.R.O., PROB. 11/1217, fo. 32).

1103. [1] B.L. VI: 146, Autograph. Addressed: 'To General Bentham / Redbridge / near / Southampton'.

hands—The following hints, lately transmitted from Admiral Sir Charles Middleton Bart[2] to the Society for the improvement of Naval Architecture will clearly demonstrate the fact, and prove the necessity of a legislative enquiry into these our defects, from which the enemy have derived considerable advantage in the superior sailing of their Ships of war, because they are evidently constructed on more scientific principles.' Then come his hints filling a column on the whole. Last but one 'To what extent that very ingenious and useful plan of Captn Schank,[3] on the advantages of sliding keels may be carried.'—It concludes: 'I am aware that some of these propositions do not literally come within the view of the Society: *but as they* have a connection with the subject, and *are more likely to be accurately examined by them than by any other body I am acquainted with, I have ventured to lay them before the Committee.* Charles Middleton'. Quere is '*body*' Scotch or English? *Body* in Scotch means an individual. In English, for an assemblage we seldom say *body* singly—it is usual to say *body of men?* This might be an occasion for introducing the intelligence of the Inspector-Generalship etc. if you wished it, in our own way—Skr.[4] might be set about it.

After all, there is nothing like your having the Paper itself.

There being but a Newspaper + this sheet—don't let them hoax you as they did before.

[2] Sir Charles Middleton, 1st Baron Barham (1726–1813), served at sea in the Seven Years War, became Comptroller of the Navy, 1778–90, was promoted to rear-admiral in 1783, vice-admiral in 1793 and admiral 1795; a lord commissioner of the Admiralty, 1794, and First Lord of the Admiralty, 1805. He was created a baronet in 1781 and Baron Barham in 1805. A leading evangelical, he was a friend of Wilberforce and an anti-slavery agitator. The Bentham brothers had been in touch with him about innovations in 1779 (see *Correspondence*, ii, 233–4, 354).

[3] Lady Bentham describes the 'sliding keels' of Captain Schank in her *Life of Sir Samuel Bentham*, p. 112. John Schank (1740–1823) entered the navy in 1758, was a captain by 1783, rear admiral in 1805 and admiral in 1821. He had built a ship with a sliding keel in Boston, Mass. during the 1770s when on service in American waters. At Plymouth in 1791, he superintended the completion of the cutter *Trial*, which had three such keels and successfully underwent her tests. Schank organised English coastal defences in the 1790s and superintended transport services for several expeditions. He became a commissioner of the Transport Board and a founder member of the Society for Improving Naval Architecture (see John Marshall, *Royal Naval Biography*, 12 vols., 1823–30, i, 324–32).

[4] Captain Lieutenant William Skinner, commissioned 1781; 9th Company of Marines at Plymouth (*List of the Officers of His Majesty's Marine Force*, 1782). Bentham recalled in 1827 that Skinner was 'an extraordinary man', who among other gifts had 'a talent for decyphering, which he possessed to perfection' (Bowring, x, 322–3). The Benthams had known of him as a 'wonderful decypherer', if not then personally acquainted, since 1783 (see *Correspondence*, iii, 232 and 250 n. 2).

1104

To Sir John Scott

22 January 1796 (Aet 47)

Sir

It is with great regret that I find myself reduced to the necessity of being so far troublesome to you in relation to my unfortunate business, as to beg permission to attend you in person for a few minutes. I know of no other possible mode of taking my chance for learning what is to become of the Penitentiary plan, its author, or the hopes that have been entertained of it.—With the benefit of the requested indulgence, I may hope to learn whether the difficulties that have presented themselves apply to the very *principle* of the Bill (viz: the extension of the powers of the existing Act from Lands in severalty to Waste-and-Common Land) or only to particular clauses—and in both cases whether the objections are such as are in the nature of them altogether unsurmountable. If not, I should hope to be favoured with some general intimation at least, by the help of which I might take the proper measures for getting them surmounted.

1105

From Sir John Scott

22 January 1796

Sir

I am at a loss to find a sufficient Apology for having so long delayed answering your Letter.[2] I think you must have been misinformed, if you understood that I have had any material difficulties respecting the drt. of the Contract, settled by Mr Solr General. There was nothing of any Importance, which it occurred to me to state, except that I thought that attending to an Act of Parlt, with which the Plan was connected, it would be necessary

---

1104. [1] B.L. VI: 144–5. Autograph draft. Docketed: '1796 Jan before 22 / Panopt / J.B. Q.S.P. / to / Atty Genl Linc Inn / About the Penitentiary *Waste* Bill—To ask interview.'

The docket on letter 1105 below indicates 22 January as the date of this letter.

1105. [1] B.L. VI: 142–3. Autograph. Docketed: '1795 ⟨6⟩ Jan 22 / Panopt / Atty Genl to J.B. Q.S.P. / In answer to letter of same date. May be called / out. Had never any material difficulties about the / Contract.'

[2] That of 11 January (letter 1100).

that His Majesty should *direct* those Things to be done, which the Contract of the Parties *stipulated shd be done*. It did not appear to me that such a Suggestion could occasion any difficulty.

If you will do me the Honor to call me out of the Court of Chancery any Morning during the Term at Westminster I shall be happy to explain any Thing to you that occurs as Matter of Difficulty occasioned by me.

I have the Honor to be, Sir, with Respect

Your obedt Servt
John Scott

January 22 1796
Jeremy Bentham Esq.

1106

To Charles Long

23 January 1796 (Aet 47)

23 January 1796
Q.S.P.

Sir

Underneath is a copy of a letter[2] I have been honored with by Mr Atty Gen.l together with a few words of observation which I take the liberty of submitting to you—being with all respect

Sir your most obed Servant
Jeremy Ben

Certainly at a future period: but not before the signature of the contract.[3] By § 1 the Contracting for the erection of the Penitentiary House is committed to the Lds of the Treasury and them only. On that occasion no mention is made of his Majesty: in that transaction he is neither expected nor empowered to bear a part. The period in which his Majesty's directions are to be taken for the first time is one that is not supposed likely to occurr till after the erection of the Penit.y House. Then it is that by § 3 his Majesty is empowered to appoint a Governor and to direct the Convicts to be delivered to him etc. reserving only a power of doing that part of the business if

1106. [1] B.L. VI: 147. Autograph rough draft. Docketed: '1796 Jan. 23 / Panopt / J.B. Q.S.P. / to / Long Treasury / with copy of Atty Genl's Opinion on draught of Contract.'
[2] Presumably a copy of letter 1105.
[3] A reference to the point made in Sir John Scott's letter that 'it would be necessary that His Majesty should *direct* those things to be done, which the Contract of the Parties *stipulated shd be done*'.

181

occasion should require. Therefore I humbly contend that at least it is not *necessary* that His Majesty should be troubled upon this subject before the signature of the Contract.

That the King his Majesty's commands upon the subject previous to the signature of the contract should be a means of expediting such signature seems according to my humble conception, difficult to suppose. The whole seems to rest entirely upon Mr. Pitts good pleasure.

N.B. What Mr Atty Genl says on the subject I know no otherwise than from the above letter not having seen the Draught since it came out of the hands of the Sollr Genl.

1107

To the Marquis of Lansdowne

9 February 1796 (Aet 47)

Queen's Square Place Westminster
9th Feby. 1796

My good Lord!

Permitt me thus humbly to sollicit your Lordship's assistance, if haply the matter should be found to be within the sphere of feasibility, in a business of cardinal importance. It would, I dare believe, have been recognized as such by your Lordship's late venerable friend, now a Saint in heaven, the Cardinal de Bernis.[2]—Cardinal Frampton (if I may yet avail myself of a privilege annexed to my quondam profession, and according to one of the rules established in virtue of that privilege speak of a thing as done which ought to have been done) I mean always the pious and learned luminary of our own Church, by whose grave and judicious estimates of men preferrable and things edible I have in days of yore been edified at your Lordship's table, Dr. Frampton[3] in a word, who, were this a world for merit and reward to meet in, *would have been* Cardinal, would, I am sure, have confirmed my humble conception of the importance of the subject by the sanction of his superior name, nor would his sympathetic feelings have disdained so far to descend

---

1107. [1] Lansdowne Mss. Autograph. No signature. No docket or address. Printed in Bowring, x, 313–15, with some phrases omitted and words changed.

[2] François Joachim de Pierres de Bernis (1715–94), French cardinal, poet and statesman.

[3] Perhaps Thomas Frampton, D.D. (c. 1725–1803), senior dean and sacrist of his college, St John's, Cambridge, in the 1760s; thereafter rector of various parishes in Suffolk, Norfolk and Pembrokeshire.

from his high dignity as to lend his support to the humble request which without further preface, having too just a sense of the value of a time, which constitutes so important a portion of the national property, to seek to encroach upon it by longwinded digressions or unnecessary preparations, I will venture to express.

That bread is dear—that I have none of it to eat, nor have had for a course of years, are unhappy truths, none of which can be a secret to your Lordship: in the mean time as is the custom with people in distress, I endeavour to support my drooping spirits by the brightest prospect I can figure to myself of better times. I had once, may it please your good Lordship, a French Cook,[4] who quitted me with reluctance, and whom her importunities have prevailed on me to say I would take back again, should that Providence which supplied the late Dr. Squintum[5] of reverend memory with leg of mutton and turnips vouchsafe at some future period to grant me any thing to cook: in the mean season, I should be glad to send her out any where, where she could pick up a few crumbs of science, as a man whose finances do not admitt of his keeping his horse in the stable the whole year round, is glad during a certain part of the year, to pack off the best to a Salt-marsh or a straw-yard.—Your Lordship's kitchen has ever been regarded by the best judges as one of the richest pastures in the kingdom for the sort of cattle I am speaking of: and could I be so fortunate as to obtain from your Lordship's kindness and from the patronage of your Lordships Chief Cook, free *ingress, egress* and *regress* for the same, doing as little damage as may be, into, out of, and upon the said pasture, videlicet during the day (for it is not necessary that she should be *levant* and *couchant* thereupon) my present distresses might, by a happy metamorphosis, become the fruitful sources of future comfort and advantage. She is not altogether destitute of that measure of science attainable by the *inferiority of her sex*[6] (a remark which I insert for the purpose of keeping this my humble application from straying into female hands) and upon great occasions, such as that of *Camacho's* wedding, or any other wedding,

---

[4] Probably Marie Duquesneau, the Frenchwoman who had been Bentham's cook in 1793 and was married to an emigré shoemaker. Bentham had intervened with Dundas, then Home Secretary, on her husband's behalf in February 1793, when he had been ordered to leave the country under the Aliens Act (see *Correspondence*, iv, 47).

[5] A character in Samuel Foote's play, *The Minor* (1760), through whom he ridiculed George Whitefield (1714–70), the Calvinistic Methodist preacher.

[6] Bowring has 'superiority', thereby missing the whole point of the remark: Bentham does not want the ladies of the household—Miss Fox or the Vernon sisters—to see his letter, so speaks of the 'inferiority of the female sex'.

might be not altogether unworthy of supporting the train of one of your Lordship's junior kitchen maids. Should your Lordship happen to possess influence enough, through any channel, however circuitous, over so distinguished a character as the one I have made bold to allude to, I will not permitt myself to doubt of its being exerted in my favour, and with prevailing efficacy.

In the utmost severity of my distresses, I have, through the kindness of neighbours, been preserved from absolute want in regard to the necessaries of life: my Butcher and Baker having humanely joined with a compassionate Barrow-woman at the end of the lane, in supplying me every Lord's Day with a shoulder of mutton supported upon a trivet, and forming a dripping canopy, distilling fatness over a mess of potatoes sufficiently ample to furnish satisfaction to the cravings of nature during the remainder of the week. Should some prosperous and scarce promisable turn in the wheel of fortune transform at any time the shoulder into a leg, and set the deeply rusted spit to retrace its once accustomed revolutions, what an addition would it be to my happiness, to present your Lordship, on some auspicious day, with the emanations of culinary science reflected from your own kitchen, and offer an apposite, however inferior, tribute of gratitude, on the board as well as from the bosom, of one who has the honour to be with everlasting respect,

My Lord!
Your Lordships most obedient
and most humble Servant
The distressed occupier of
Queens Square Place!

P.S. Not a doit this Christmas from a Noble Lady.[7] She has offered a *pot-de-vin*, Anglicé a pot of beer, (per favour of the Rev: Mr Du Barry) but an unliquidated one to let her off, and her project seems to be to starve me into compliance. But solvable tenants (solvent or no) are not let off for their *beaux yeux*, how *beaux* soever, when their turn is served, especially by impoverished heirs who would not make so much as legal interest, were it even regularly paid, for the money sunk upon the premises by imprudent Ancestors. General Buckley,[8] the Landlord paramount, never lets me rest unless he has his pound of flesh the moment it is due, nor would my utmost

---

[7] Lady Ashburton, Bentham's tenant in Duke Street.

[8] Lieutenant-General Felix Buckley, 10 Lower Grosvenor Street; he was promoted to general, 1801.

distress ever prevail upon him to wait as I have been made to wait by Noble Ladies, pleading their *beaux yeux*.—Even the baked shoulders must soon cease, unless some kind friend should whisper into one of the ears contiguous to the beaux yeux—not that Necessity has *no* Law (for that would be worse than nothing) but that Necessity *has* Law, and that John Doe[9] has a Long-Coach in waiting, into which he is ready at a moments warning to hand any Lady of his said Mother's recommending to him, on one of his tours through Middlesex.

1108

To Samuel Bentham

10 February 1796 (Aet 47)

You have heard by a letter from Collins, I suppose, that the man pitched upon by the Admiralty for the command of the Dart or the Arrow is a particular friend and I believe protegé of his.[2] He is burning with impatience to have his appointment, and Collins says that by getting it or appearing to get it for him a little the sooner you make him your own for ever. Collins gives him the highest of characters—says he will try everything, endure every-thing, and fight the Devil— that he is the best of all possible Seamen —⟨. . .⟩[3] understands Rigging, Chart-making etc. to perfec⟨tion⟩. ⟨. . .⟩ has been employed at Nootka, and the ⟨Calc⟩utta Whalery —was spoken of as mad by ⟨. . .⟩ *Mears*,[4] and made him eat his

---

[9] The imaginary name of the plaintiff in legal actions for ejectment between John Doe and Richard Roe.

1108. [1] B.L.VI: 148. Autograph. Addressed: 'Brigadier General Bentham / Redbridge / near / Southampton.' Postmark: 'FE.10.96.A. Tothill ⟨St⟩ Westm'. Stamped: 'DEAL'.
     One edge of the manuscript is torn off, removing several words at the end of lines, as indicated.

[2] The *Arrow* and the *Dart* were sloops of the same size, with sliding keels and armed with 28–32 carronades. Both were completed at Redbridge in 1796 (J. J. Colledge, *Ships of the Royal Navy: an historical index*, 2 vols., Newton Abbot, 1969, vol. i, pp. 52, 153). Nathaniel Portlock (d. 1817) was appointed commander of the *Arrow*, November 1796, and promoted to captain, 1799; Richard Raggett was appointed to the *Dart* at the same time and also promoted to captain, 1799 (*Naval Chronicle*, iii, 1800; Appendix, 'Commissioned Sea Officers of the Royal Navy').
     Portlock may have been the friend of Collins described: he had published an account of his *Voyage Round the World* (1789).

[3] The name is missing owing to the tear in the Ms.

[4] Probably not the shipwright the Benthams had known for many years (see *Correspondence*, ii, 247, n. 7), but John Meares (?1756–1809), naval commander and explorer. His mercantile schemes included the formation of a company at Calcutta for developing trade with north-west America. During the Nootka Sound crisis, 1789–90,

words—crossed the Spanish Main like Vancouver, and has made interesting Journals, which for fear of displaying the hostility and ill behaviour of the Spaniards the At.y will not let him publish.

It has not yet been intimated to him officially—but *my friend,* Sir Philip,[5] in giving him hopes for it said it was the greatest proof of confidence Ld Spencer could give. Your friend, *Sir William,*[6] who happens to have been his Guardian, *pitied* him—which has thrown Collins into an unceasing paroxysm of rage. C. says Sir W. and your Poore are hand in glove.

1109

TO SAMUEL BENTHAM

20 February 1796 (Aet 48)

Q.S.P. 20 Feb. 1796

Paper was sent to Essex Street yesterday—the people were all that while preparing it.

I have just seen Wilberforce—what he wants chiefly from us he says is—indications of employment—and of places to be hired for the purpose of working rooms on Rumford's plan.[2] I told him *employment* was a *difficult point* he seemed fully sensible of it. We are to have a breakfast on the subject.

He has read Rumford's Essay on the Poor and acknowledges there is not much in it.

Lloyd says the Treenail Engine[3] and Borer are more than half done, but will hardly be compleat these 3 weeks. The Engine he says will not cost so little as £30, nor the Borer less than £5, but

the Spanish had seized several of his merchant ships in those waters; he was promoted a naval commander, 1795.

[5] Sir Philip Stephens (1725–1809), Secretary of the Admiralty, 1763–95. He was M.P. for Liskeard, 1759–68 and for Sandwich, 1768–1809, but is not recorded as having ever spoken in the House of Commons. He was made a baronet in 1795 and a lord of the Admiralty.

[6] Probably Sir William Rule (d. 1815). He was Surveyor of the Navy, c. 1793–1813.

1109. [1] B.L. VI: 149. Autograph. Addressed: 'General Bentham / Redbridge near / Southampton.' Postmark: 'FE.20.96. / Oxford Street Unpaid / Penny Post'. Stamped: '⟨. . .⟩ clock 20 FE[B] NIGHT'.

[2] Count Rumford discussed employment of the poor in his essays entitled 'An account of an establishment for the poor at Munich' and 'Of the fundamental principles on which general relief of the poor may be formed in all countries' (*Essays, Political, Economical and Philosophical*, 1796, i, 1–112, 113–88).

[3] A 'treenail' or 'trenail' was a long, wooden pin used for fastening the planks of a ship to the timbers. Samuel did in fact introduce a machine for making such pins at the docks (see M. S. Bentham, *Life of Sir Samuel Bentham*, 1862, p. 156).

the Engine may afterwards be made for ½ the money—and the Borer for 1/3.

According to Lloyd there is an alarm among some of your men and their wives, about a supposed loss of a vessel, sent to you with timber and containing goods of theirs. The Timber-Merchant says that a timber vessel is really lost, but that it is not his. Give advice when yours arrives, or the time of its being lost.

Lloyd being in distress for money, I have squeezed out £30 which your Son-of-a-whore-ship will have the goodness to send me a draught for.

Written at Puss's which is a [. . .?].[4] No Puss till Tuesday. Letters have been forwarded [to] her at Col Borthwick's[5] Warren—Woolwich—none left here.

1110

To Samuel Bentham

24 February 1796 (Aet 48)

Q.S.P. 24 Feb 1796

I wrote to you yesterday[2]—

I know nothing to add today to the address which came last night from your *'affectionate friends'*

Except that *Poor Provision*[3] goes on swimmingly—rich in *sens*, and bidding fairer for engaging attention than even *Safeguard*,[4] to which it cannot be refused the preference.

[4] Illegible. These last three sentences are scribbled in pencil.
[5] William Borthwick (1760–1820) served in the royal artillery in Flanders and later in the Peninsular War; he became a major-general, 1812.
1110. [1] B.L. VI: 150. Autograph. Addressed: 'General Bentham / Redbridge / near Southampton.' Postmark: 'FE.24.96⟨—⟩. Tothill Street / Westminster'.
[2] A letter of 23 February is missing.
[3] The first mention of the 'Essays on the Poor Laws', which Bentham began to write this year. He got as far in 1796 as drafting a dedication of 'this little work' to William Wilberforce and William Morton Pitt ('Poor Dedication', U.C. cliiib: 361). In the following two years Bentham contributed his essays on 'The Situation and Relief of the Poor' to Arthur Young's *Annals of Agriculture*, xxix (1797), 393–426; xxx (1798), 89–176, 241–96, 457–504, xxxi (1798), 33–64, 169–200, 273–88. They were then reprinted, but not published, as *Outline of a Work entitled 'Pauper Management Improved'*. In 1812 they were published as *Pauper Management Improved: particularly by means of an Application of the Panopticon Principles of Construction*, which was later reprinted in Bowring, viii, 360–439.
[4] Probably material dealing with various 'safeguards', afterwards included in his works on Evidence, e.g. chapter 22 of *An Introductory View of the Rationale of Evidence* (Bowring, vi, 116–19), and chapter 9 of *The Rationale of Judicial Evidence* (Bowring, vii, 593–7).

1111

To William Pitt

28 February 1796 (Aet 48)

Panopticon for Poor Houses.   1796 Feb 28
                                                     To Pitt

Sir

Q.S.P. 28 Feb 1796

A Penitentiary Inspection House might afford an useful trial and exemplification of the Inspection plan, for the purpose of the Industry-Houses which it is your purpose to spread over the Kingdom.[2] Though there would be /are/ points of contrast, yet are there points of identity in abundance. By this the expence of building is believed to be reduced /brought down/ to its /the/ lowest pitch the advantages in every respect carried up to the highest: the first expence (the great stumbling block) brought as low as possible. Six months have elapsed since (after the minutest scrutiny,) at the end of a two years suspension every thing was understood to be settled but legal form: form has been long ago settled, after legal /the treasury of legal and official/ delay has been exhausted, and for this month and term the instrument has been lying on your table.[3] A single word only is wanting—how much longer will it be withholden? or is it never meant to be pronounced? Can the weeks not to say months bestowed or to be bestowed upon the new business be justly bestowed, while the moment wanting for the old business is refused?

1111. [1] U.C. cliib: 359. Autograph draft, among numerous drafts headed 'Poor plan', 'Observations on the poor bill', 'Pitt's poor bill', etc. There is no docket and this may indicate that no letter based on the draft was sent.

[2] Marginal insertion: 'by the excellent Bill which I have been /was/ favoured with in manuscript by a common friend'. On 16 February 1796 Pitt had announced his intention to bring in a poor relief bill and on 1 March he moved for leave to bring in a bill 'for the regulation of the laws relating to the relief and employment of the poor', which he hoped would be introduced and printed before Easter (*Parliamentary Register*, 2nd ser., xliv, 55, 212). No further action seems to have been taken until 22 December 1796, when Pitt moved to bring in a bill 'for the better support and maintenance of the poor' (ibid., 3rd ser., i, 517–19).

[3] Marginal insertion: 'In that interval twelve hundred pounds more have been disbursed /expended/ in testing the iron for the building.'

1112

TO WILLIAM MORTON PITT

1 March 1796 (Aet 48)

29 Feb 1796

Copy sent same day   To W. Moreton Pitt Esqr

Q.S.P. 1 March 1796

My dear Sir

Conscience has been haunting me all the time I have been suffering to remain unthanked the Statistical present with which you have honoured me.[2] It will be a sad disappointment to me if I do not find the model you have set turned to all possible account and the imitation of it made obligatory all over the kingdom by the depending Bill:[3]—the advantages that ought be derived from it are innumerable and unspeakable. Memora giving a copy to Britannia, with the epigraph Γνω θι δεαυτον[4], should be the frontis-piece.[5]

Poor Panopticon might ere this time have puffed up and shewn what use *might* be to made of it in the line of *PTOCHOCOMIAL*[6] economy—but *Diis aliter visum*. The contract, after having been settled in *terminis* 6 months ago at Whitehall and since then run the gauntlope among the Lawyers has been for this month past lying (without a metaphor) upon the table of your R. Hon. namesake, who finds it better economy to lavish months of fine speeches upon new business, than to bestow the word and the moment which is wanting to the old. Believe me, with the truest respect,

Dear Sir

Ever Yours

Jeremy Bentham

W. M. Pitt Esqr

1112. [1] U.C. cliiib: 360. Autograph draft.

William Morton Pitt (1754–1836), of Kingston Maurward, near Dorchester, was M.P. for Poole, 1780–90, and for Dorset, 1790–1826. A reformer and supporter of Lansdowne in Parliament, he tried to interest fellow-landowners in the problem of poverty and himself made many improvements in local social conditions.

[2] Evidently an unpublished pamphlet giving particulars of poor relief in Dorset.

[3] Pitt's poor relief bill (see above, letter 1111, n. 2).

[4] Anglice: 'Know thyself'.

[5] Marginal addition: 'Meantime would you like to see the example followed by Volunteers? Have you any more copies to spare for such a purpose. If you have and will favour me with a couple, a friend of mine will undertake to furnish you speedily with the state of two small Parishes—and perhaps I might meet with other Volunteers.'

[6] An invented compound word from the Greek: the economy of 'caring for paupers'.

1113
FROM WILLIAM WILBERFORCE
2 March 1796

My dear Sir,

Has your affair at length found its Way out of Downing Street —I have for several morn'gs been wantg to ask the Question but have been always and shall be this Morning prevented. I did mention it to Mr Pitt, but that was 10 days ago at least or perhaps more. I assure you very sincerely that the treatment you have met with grieves me and makes me ashamed for those who are the authors of it. That, however, is small Comfort.

yours very truly
W. Wilberforce.

Pal. Yd Tuesday Morng
2 March 1796[2]

1114
TO SIR JOHN FREEMAN MITFORD
3 March 1796 (Aet 48)

Mr. Bentham presents his respectful Compliments to Mr Sollr General and begs the honour of his acceptance for a copy of the unpublished work that gave rise to the Contract, which underwent his revision some time ago and which lies still upon Mr. Pitt's table where it has been lying for this month and more. The other copy Mr. B. takes the liberty of addressing by this opportunity to his old friend the Historian of Greece,[2] in whose remembrance the recent perusal of his admirable work revives his ambition of preserving a place.

1113. [1] B.L. VI: 151–2. Autograph. Docketed: '1796 Mar 2 / Panopt / Wilberforce O.P.Y. / to / J.B. Q.S.P. / Spoke to Pitt.'
Addressed: 'Jeremy Bentham / etc.'
[2] Date added in Bentham's hand.

1114. [1] B.L. VI: 153. Autograph draft. Docketed: '1796 Mar 3 / Panopt / J.B. Q.S.P. / to / Atty and Sollr Genl / with copies of Panopt etc. for W. Mitford. / Draught of Contract lying for a month past on Mr. Pitt's Table.'
[2] William Mitford (1744–1827), the brother of the Solicitor-General. His *History of Greece* started to appear in 1784 and was completed in 1810. A third edition of the first half appeared in six volumes, 1795–7.

1115

To Sir John Scott

3 March 1796 (Aet 48)

Mr. Bentham presents his respectful Compliments ⟨to⟩ Mr Attorney Genl and begs the honour of his acceptance for a copy of the unpublished work that gave rise to the Contract which underwent the /his/ revision some time ago and which still lies upon Mr. Pitt's table where it has been lying for this month and more.

1116

From Sir John Freeman Mitford

4 March 1796

The Solicitor General is much obliged to Mr Bentham for his copy of the unpublished work which gave rise to the proposed establishment to which Mr Bentham's note refers; and is extremely sorry to find the contract meets with any delay on the part of Government. He will send the other copy with which Mr Bentham has intrusted him to his brother, whom he daily expects in London, and who will be happy to acknowledge the remembrance of an old friend.

Adelphi
4 March 1796.

1117

Memorandum by Jeremy Bentham

6 March 1796 (Aet 48)

My Brother having called upon me to state what I remember in relation to his agreement with Galloway for himself and son my answer is as follows—

1115. ¹ B.L. VI: 153. Autograph draft, following immediately on letter 1114 and described by the same docket.
1116. ¹ B.L. VI: 154–5. Docketed: '1796 Mar 4 / Panopt / Sollr Gen. Adelphi / to J.B. Q.S.P. / Thanks for Panopticon. Sorry to find the contract delay'd.'
 Addressed: 'Jeremy Bentham Esqr. / Queen's Square Place, / Westminster.'
1117. ¹ B.L. VI: 156–7. In copyist's hand, except for the autograph signature and dating. Docketed: '1796 Galloway.'
 A sheet, dated 29 February 1796 (B.L. VI: 158–9) gives particulars of the dispute

191

Being more conversant than he in penmanship and matters of law, at his desire I drew up the agreement

The rate of wages struck me as being high, especially as he was to be bound to continue it during so long a period, whether the workmen continued to give satisfaction to his employer, or not. This my Brother admitted; but said, that what rendered it less high than I might at first sight suppose, was that Galloway was to give his *whole* time for the money, not being paid for *extra* time when he worked *extra hours* as the *other* men were for *their* extra hours. That this was his meaning at the time I am certain; as well from the observation of the words employed by me as from the recollection of the discussion that took place between us.

To that meaning I endeavoured to shape the agreement; and very much surprised indeed should I be, to find that I have not done so.

I really do not understand how they can (in the words of the agreement) have '*given up their whole time to Col. Bentham*' for the '*£3.10*' if there be any part of their time for which they are to be entitled to further payment.

If all the time intended to be engaged had been their *ordinary* time, in contradistinction to *extra* time, there would have been no use in saying any thing about time: for the whole amount of their ordinary time would have been engaged of course: they could not be understood to engage themselves for less than the whole of their ordinary time, if for any. But understanding clearly that it was the *whole* of their time that was meant to be engaged, viz: *ordinary* time and as much *extra time* as could reasonably be demanded of them, therefore it was that I accordingly put in the words '*their whole time.*'

To cut off all doubt about what *extra* time could *reasonably* be demanded, I added '*working as long as any other of his workmen work*'; concluding that, as it was by choice if at all, that the other workmen, who were paid by the week, would work extra time, they would take care for their own sakes not to work too much; and this would be a security to Galloway for his not being put to work more than a man can bear.

Jeremy Bentham

Queen's Square Place Westr. 6 March 1796.

between Samuel Bentham and Thomas Galloway. The latter claimed £67 for 'over work' during the time he was engaged by Samuel. For Alexander Galloway, see below, p. 324 n. 4.

1118

To William Wilberforce

8 March 1796 (Aet 48)

Q.S.P. 8 Mar. 1796

My dear Sir

A thousand thanks for your kind remembrance.[2] My business, for any thing I have heard, lies on the same table on which it has lain these six weeks. The Sollr. Genl., a perfect stranger, has in a recent letter, spontaneously expressed his concern on the same subject—Mr Dundas, by whom I was twice called upon 'to take *my arrangements,*' both times in the same terms, can not but entertain similar feelings (and they should naturally be stronger in degree) which indeed he has more than once expressed to me. Since the Contract, after having been settled with Mr Pitt through the medium of Mr Long *in terminis,* was transmitted by an official letter to Mr White, which I saw, '*to be prepared for their Lordships signature*' (now upwards of six months ago) I have found myself obliged to advance above £1200 on the business, in addition to the many thousands advanced before. I am warranted by deeds, as well as words, and looks that speak more than words, in adding Mr Moreton Pitt to the list of sympathizers. Surely the sentiments of such and so many friends can not be altogether indifferent to Mr Pitt.

The more I think of the System, which through your means,[3] is about to be set on foot, in relation to the Poor Laws, the more I am delighted with it. But to one clause a sheet of objections have presented themselves, which I take the liberty of submitting to you.

<hr>

1118. [1] Bodleian Library, Oxford. Wilberforce Mss. d.15/138. Autograph. Docketed: 'Jere: Bentham Cruelly us'd.'

Addressed: 'Mr. Wilberforce.'

Printed, with several mistakes, in R. I. and S. Wilberforce (eds.), *Correspondence of William Wilberforce,* 2 vols., 1840, i, 121–2.

[2] Perhaps Wilberforce's letter of 2 March (1113), although the docket uses a phrase not occurring in that letter and the reference to Morton Pitt, 'who, you tell me is a labourer in the same vineyard', also seems to suggest another communication from Wilberforce.

[3] Wilberforce had sent out to his friends a questionnaire under twenty-three headings, the answers to which provided him with information on the state of the poor in different parts of the country (see R. Furneaux, *William Wilberforce,* 1974, p. 208, and R. I. and S. Wilberforce, op. cit., i, Appendix i).

Possibly I may send another copy to Mr Moreton Pitt, who, you tell me, is a fellow-labourer in the same vineyard. Believe me,

My dear Sir
Ever your most obliged
Jeremy Bentham

1119

TO WILLIAM WILBERFORCE

24 March 1796 (Aet 48)

Q.S.P. 24 Mar. 96

My dear Sir,—

About a month [ago?], seeing Mr Long by accident, and exchanging a word or two with him, he called me back to say to me, 'that in *Easter Week* he thought he should be able to make Mr Pitt dispatch my business.' I take the liberty of forwarding to you this hint, for the chance that your kindness may be able to find an opportunity to avail yourself of it, and second his endeavours.

Ever yours most obliged
J.B.

P.S. I find that Heads of the Poor Bill are printed—Could you put me in a way of getting a Copy?—

Mr Wilberforce

1120

FROM THE MARQUIS OF LANSDOWNE

4 April 1796

Monday Morg

I send you the 4 Vol's you desire[2] and without attacking you on the score of punctuality I shall be glad of them, as soon as you have taken from them what you want, as I shall want in about ten days to look into them about Taxes.

1119. [1] B.L. VI: 163. In copyist's hand. Docketed by Bentham: '1796 Mar 24 / Panopt / J.B. Q.S.P. / to / Wilberforce O.P. Yard / Long's hopes of getting Pitt to dispatch in Easter Week.'
Easter Sunday was on 27 March 1796.
1120. [1] B.L. VI: 164–5. Autograph. Docketed: '1796 Apr 4 / Ld L Berkeley Square / to / J.B. Q.S.P. / Poor Laws.'
[2] A missing written request from Bentham is indicated.

Everything else which I have regarding the poor is at Bowood, where Mr Townsend[3] has had the ransacking them, but I believe there is nothing that applies.

From my own experience I do not incline to believe that any thing effectual can be done, till the municipal government of the country is revis'd and invigorated—a distinction should be made between the manufacturing and the Agricultural poor. The Friendly Societies might perhaps be enforc'd so as to include both. Public Houses should be in great measure abolish'd, except so many as are necessary to accomodate travellers, and wholesome malt liquor should be made accessible to the poor. Public Houses and Poaching you may depend upon it are the root of every evil. I speak from several years experience and observation—the present poor rate should be limited without delay, and finally abolish'd, unless the administration of it can be totally chang'd. The Ladys have expected you at dinner every day. I do not ask the General, because I take it for granted that he dines at the Admiralty every day. Surely there is great merit in several of Count Rumford's Ideas about the poor.[4]

1121

To Earl Spencer

18 April 1796 (Aet 48)

Queen's Square Place Westmr

My Lord
Understanding that the objections to the spot fixed upon by Mr Pitt for the Penitentiary House are grounded on an apprehended loss of property on your Lordships part, estimated by your Lordship's Steward at £2000 a year or thereabouts, which loss it is supposed would arise from the inability of finding Lessees for certain lands in the neighbourhood upon terms which several persons had already come into, who had afterwards demurred on

---

[3] Probably the Rev. Joseph Townsend (1739–1816), rector of Pewsey, Wilts. Bentham had met him at Bowood in 1781 and described him as a 'utilitarian', with similar interests to his own and as on 'a familiar footing at Bowood' (see *Correspondence*, iii *passim*, especially p. 57 n. 10, and p. 68).

[4] See letter 1109, n. 2.

1121. [1] B.L. VI: 166–7. Autograph draft. Docketed: '1796 Apr 18 / Panopt / J.B. Q.S.P. / to / Ld Spencer Admirty.'
   We know from letters 1127 and 1131 that a letter based on this much altered draft was sent.

hearing of the destination of the spot in question to the above purpose, I take the liberty of addressing myself to your Lordship for the purpose of saying that I should be perfectly willing to stand in the place of the persons in question with respect to the lands in question 'upon those same terms' on the supposition of the spots remaining attached to the business of the Penitentiary House. Not entertaining the same conception with regard to the apprehended depretiation, it is true that I should not expect any such /great/ loss to be the result: but supposing the loss certain, and reaching to the whole of that extent, my desire of submitting to it would remain unabated, as even on that supposition the disadvantage to me would be beyond comparison inferior to the unfathomable pre-judice which would result to me from the dereliction of that spot.

It is certainly not a proposition for me to make to your Lordship; to give up property to any such amount, without a compensation. But when your Lordship has been pleased to consider that it is now little less than three years since my proposition with regard to that spot (which I then considered as appropriated to the Measure) was accepted, by a minute which I have under Mr Pitt's own hand: that the instrument for the obtaining the possession of the Land after passing through the Law Officers lay engrossed ready for signature, I think it was not less than a twelve month ago: that the Contract relative to the whole business after long discussion was settled in terminis by Mr Pitt 8 months ago and has since passed through the Law Officers already upon the faith of which transactions I am already in advance upwards of £10,000, without any possibility of reimbursement but what depends on the completion of the Peni-tentiary business, your Lordships sympathy I can not but flatter myself will operate so far in my behalf as to bespeak some degree of favour for an expedient which if properly modified and adapted to the circumstance of the case may end in the removal of all difficulties, give effect to an Act of Parliament which for these two years has been a dead letter and give the public at length the benefit of an establishment, which many persons of high account as well as that part of his Majesty's administration to whose province it more particularly belongs have never ceased to regard as prom-ising service of very considerable import⟨ance⟩.

1122

To Evan Nepean

c. 19 April 1796 (Aet 48)

1. Objection—Mr. B may not be able to bear the loss.
Answer 40s a year more per man would indemnify him against it.
He has 2 grounds for asking for an addition
    1. The rise of prices since July 1793 when the price was fixed [at] £12 a head. It ought to be equal to the prices of that day to be at least £18 now. He would be content with £14. tho' £2 of it would go to Ld Sp. which would leave him without indemnity.
    2. Mr Long (in answer to what Mr B. had said upon the value of that particular land) said certainly if you like any other land you are not precluded from asking an addition to the price.
    3. The calculation and in short all the difficulties appear to come from the Steward, who having a House in the Neighbourhood conceives himself to have a personal interest in the business— Quere how to satisfy the Steward.
    4. Ld Sper not bound to adhere to his opposition in favour of the others—for their application had already been rejected—It was on Ld Sp's account and in consequence of his application that Mr Pitt made a stand after the Contract had been agreed upon *in terminis* and long after the fixation of the land had been announced to Mr B. in form and an instrument prepared by the Crown Lawyers in consequence and engrossed ready for signature.

1122. [1] B.L. VI: 175. Autograph draft. Docketed: '1796 Apr. / Panopt. / J.B. Admiralty to Nepean ibid / Memoranda of proposals to Ld Spencer for Panopticon Hill' [i.e. Battersea Rise].
    The docket suggests that this memorandum was written while Bentham was waiting for Lord Spencer, or his representative, at the Admiralty.

1123

FROM SIR CHARLES BUNBURY

20 April 1796

Pallmall
April 20th

Dear Sr.

I have no other Book here, or Paper, relative to the Veterinary College, but the enclosed.[2] I have in the Country a Book written by Mr St Bel[3] the late Professor, on the Diseases of Horses, and Shoeing, to which very probably, as an Introduction, may be prefixed some Account of the College. I can borrow this Book in Town, and send it to you, if you desire it.

Yours truly,
T. Cha[s]. Bunbury

1124

TO SIR FRANCIS BULLER

21 April 1796 (Aet 48)

Mr. Bentham, understanding from Mr. Moreton Pitt, that the new Penitentiary plan so long ago adopted by the Right Hon. Mr

1123. [1] B.L. VI: 168. Autograph. Docketed: '1796 Apr 20 / Sir C. Bunbury Pall mall / to / J.B. Q.S.P.'
Addressed: 'To Jeremy Bentham Esqre.'
[2] The enclosures are missing. Bentham must have written requesting information about the Veterinary College, which had been established on 8 April 1791 and marked the beginning of systematic medical treatment for animals in England, although horses were the only ones treated at first. The college was supported by subscriptions from members and also by parliamentary grants in its early years. Bunbury was one of eight vice-presidents. It became the Royal Veterinary College in 1844. (See the original prospectus of *The Veterinary College, London*, 1791, and the account in the *Prospectus of the Royal Veterinary College*, 1858. See also note 3 below.)
[3] Charles Vial de Saint Bel, or Sainbel (1753–93), founder of scientific veterinary surgery in England. He was born in Lyons and came to Britain in 1788, becoming the first professor at the Veterinary College in 1791. Bunbury had probably been reading his *Lectures on the Elements of Farriery; or the Art of Horse-shoeing, and on the Diseases of the Foot*, 1793. See *Works of C. V. de Sainbel. To which is prefaced a short Account of his Life, including also the Origin of the Veterinary College of London*, 1795.
1124. [1] B.L. VI: 169–70. Autograph draft. Docketed: '1796 Apr 21 / Panopt / J.B. Q.S.P. / to / Judge Buller.'
Sir Francis Buller (1746–1800) had been a justice of the King's Bench, 1778–94, and then became a justice of the Common Pleas, 1794–1800; he was created a baronet, 1790.

Pitt, and which gave occasion to a Statute passed at the close of the Session of 1794, had not till Mr. M. Pitt was mentioning it reached the ear of Mr Justice Buller, takes the liberty of inclosing a copy of the original proposal, that served as the basis of the Contract of which the former Draught having undergone the revision of the Atty & Sollr Genl. has been lying these 2 or 3 months at the Treasury waiting the signature of the Board, and consequently is not at Mr Benthams command. The above-mentioned Proposal is sent under the notion of its affording the concisest view that could be given of the plan: but Mr Bentham takes the further liberty of adding a copy of the unpublished work which gave occasion to the above Contract, that it may be found at hand should Mr Justice after casting an eye over the table of heads find time to honour the contents of any of them with his notice /after casting his eye over the list if he can find time/.[2]

Queens Square Place Westmr 21 April 1796

Mr Justice is requested to have the goodness to return the Ms paper at his leisure.

Mr B. need scarce add how proud he should be at any time to show the models or afford any elucidations which Mr Justice should find time or curiosity to command. The Machinery which had been viewed by many gentlemen of eminence at the Bar,[3] Lord Justice Waters, Mr Garrow, Mr Sylvester, Mr East and others, has been for some time laid up. Mr. Abbot, Mr G. Wilson, Mr Romilly and Mr Trail—all intimate friends of Mr Bentham would be capable of answering most inquiries.

[2] An alternative phrasing added in pencil.

[3] The lawyers in this list not previously mentioned in the *Correspondence* were: (Sir) William Garrow (1760–1840), K.C. 1793, Attorney General 1813, a baron of the Exchequer 1817–32, knighted 1812; Sir Jonathan Silvester (d. 1822), Recorder of London; (Sir) Edward Hyde East (1764–1847), barrister 1786, M.P. 1792–6 and 1823–1831, later a judge in India. East was created a baronet in 1823; he is best known for his reports of cases in the Court of King's Bench, 1785–1812, the first law reports to be published regularly at the end of each term.

1125

FROM ETIENNE DUMONT

23 April 1796

Mon cher Bentham

J'ai pris la résolution d'en appeller de l'air de l'Angleterre au climat de la Suisse pour juger le procès que je soutiens depuis quatre ou cinq mois contre une maladie. Tout incapable que je suis de m'appliquer à présent, j'aime à penser que je reprendrai plus de force en respirant l'air natal.[2] Parmi mes provisions d'amusement, j'ai pris quelques cahiers que je fais copier ici, et que je veux porter avec moi, soit pour les montrer (avec votre permission) à quelques amis dont je vous ai parlé, soit pour en inserer quelques fragments dans la bibliothèque britannique[3] qui se publie à prèsent à Geneve sous la direction de deux hommes d'un très grand mérite. Quelques

---

1125. [1] B.L. VI: 171–2. Autograph. Docketed: '1796 Apr 23 / Dumont Kensington / to /J.B. Q.S.P.'

Addressed: 'Jer. Bentham Esqr.'

An inaccurate translation of parts of this letter is printed in Bowring, x, 315.

[2] Dumont did not in fact go back to Switzerland this year; he tried instead the sea-air of Worthing in Sussex. He wrote to Romilly on 29 August: 'Je suis plus content de Worthing, mon cher Romilly, que je ne l'étois dans les premiers jours' (*Memoirs . . . of Romilly . . . with Correspondence*, 1840, ii, 57).

[3] The *Bibliothèque britannique* was a periodical started at Geneva in January 1796 and divided into three series: on literature, on the sciences and arts, and on agriculture. Between October 1796 and April 1798 eight articles giving extracts from J.'s works were published in the series entitled 'Littérature'. There were two headed 'MORALE. INTRODUCTION TO THE PRINCIPLES etc. Introduction aux principes de Morale et de Législation, par JÉRÉMIE BENTHAM, de Lincoln's-Inn Esq. in-4o. pages 335' (vol. iii, no. 2, October 1796, pp. 137–50, and no. 3, November 1796, pp. 265–83). These were followed by six articles in the form of letters from Dumont, four quoting Bentham on legislation and two on political economy. The first was headed: *Lettre aux Rédacteurs de la Bibliothèque Britannique* sur les ouvrages de BENTHAM', dated 'Londres, 1er Mai 1797' (vol. v, no. 2, June 1797, pp. 155–64). This was followed by three giving extracts from the *Civil Code*, headed: 'PRINCIPES DU CODE CIVIL: d'après les manuscrits de J. BENTHAM, Esq.' (vol. v, no. 3, July 1797, pp. 277–302, vol. vi, no. 1, September 1797, pp. 3–25, and no. 3, November 1797, pp. 281–306). The last two letters on political economy were headed: 'CINQUIEME LETTRE de Mr. DUMONT aux Auteurs de la BIBLIOTHEQUE BRITANNIQUE; sur les manuscrits de J. Bentham, Esq.' followed by 'EXTRAIT DU MANUEL D'ECONOMIE POLITIQUE DE MR. J. BENTHAM' (vol. vii, no. 2, February 1798, pp. 105–33), and finally the 'SIXIEME LETTRE de Mr. DUMONT aux Auteurs de la BIBLIOTHEQUE BRITAN-NIQUE; sur les manuscrits de J. BENTHAM, Esq.—Suite du Manuel d'Economie politique' (vol. vii, no. 4, April 1798, pp. 369–89).

The founders and conductors of the *Bibliothèque britannique* were Marc Auguste Pictet (1752–1825), his brother, Charles Pictet-de Rochemont (1755–1824), and Frédéric Guillaume Maurice (1750–1826); all were Swiss and had distinguished careers. The periodical continued under various titles until 1930.

essais jettés ainsi dans le public serviroient à sonder le terrein et à préparer le succès du grand ouvrage. Je vous prie en conséquence de m' envoyer aujourd'hui, si vous le pouvez, le premier livre du Code Civil,[4] en François, car c'est du Code Civil et du Manuel d'economie polit.[5] que je voudrois détacher quelques essais. Je vous renverrai ces papiers avec d'autres avant mon départ.

Je n'ai pas encore fixé l'epoque, et même il y a encore bien des difficultés à arranger, le choix de l'Allemagne ou de la France offre des inconvénients presque égaux, j'ai si peu de force d'esprit à présent que je laisserai décider à mes amis, ne pouvant pas décider pour moi même.

Si par hazard je viens à perdre le susdit procès, vous ne serez pas mécontent des arrangements que je prends par rapport à ceux de mes manuscrits auxquels vous pouvez vous intéresser. Adieu.

Je suis
Tout à vous
Et. DuMont

Samedi 23 avril Kensington

1126

From William Morton Pitt

29 April 1796

Dear Sir

Might it not be worth while to point out in stronger colours to the indolent, unthinking, cursory Reader, by *Italics* etc. that according to this plan,[2] the *whole** expense of *Building*, etc., is avoided by the *Public* and is defrayed by *yourselves,** that a *proportional part* (the blank was not filled up) of the *Hulk* expense

[4] Bentham had produced much material in French, headed 'Code civile', c. 1785–1790 (see U.C. xxii: 1–161; xxiii: 1–142; c: 34–89 and cxlvi: 1–8).

[5] Most of the material for the 'Manual of Political Economy' at University College London is in English (especially U.C. xvii: 13–353, but there are two sheets in French headed: 'Manuel d'économie politique, préface'). Photostats of the original Bentham legal and economic material among the Dumont papers, Geneva, which may be the basis of the articles in the *Bibliothèque britannique*, are in U.C. clxxvi. Dumont described to Romilly his difficulties in preparing for the *Bibliothèque britannique* Bentham materials 'fort obscurs et sans order' (Dumont Mss. Geneva, 17, fos. 106–7).

1126. [1] B.L. VI: 173–4. Autograph. Docketed: '1796 Apr 29 / Panopt / W. M. Pitt Arlington Street / to J.B. Q.S.P.'

Addressed: 'Jer. Bentham Esqr. Queen Square Place, Westminster.' Franked: 'W. M. Pitt'.

[2] The Panopticon penitentiary project.

* This word is underlined several times.

201

only is in future expected and the total expense of Botany Bay, or *as much of it* as may be thought proper avoided

Yr in great haste
W. M. Pitt

1127

TO EARL SPENCER

3 May 1796 (Aet 48)

Mr Bentham presents his respectful Compliments to Lord Spencer and begs the favour of being informed whether a letter of his to his Lordship, dated the 18th of last month, was received.[2]

Queen's Square Place 3d May 1796.

1128

FROM GEORGE ROSE

3 May 1796

Mr Rose presents his Compliments to Mr Bentham and will be glad to have the Time of seeing him tomorrow Morng at 8 if that is not too early for him.

Old Palace Yd
Tuesday May 3d

1129

TO CHARLES ABBOT

4 May 1796 (Aet 48)

It seems all very good—nothing strikes me as objectionable—nothing occurrs to me to add to it.[2] On pretence of looking into the

1127. [1] B.L. VI: 176. Autograph. Docketed: '1796 May 3 / Panopt / J.B. Q.S.P. / to / Lord Spencer / Asking for answer about Battersea Common.'
[2] Letter 1121.
1128. [1] B.L. VI: 177–8. Docketed: '1796 May 3 / Poor / Rose O. Palace Yard / to / J.B. Q.S.P. / Visurus'.
Addressed: 'Bentham Esq / Queen Square Place'. Franked: 'G. Rose'.
1129. [1] P.R.O. 30/9/31. Inserted into the Ms. Diary of Charles Abbot, Baron Colchester, for 1796, facing fo. 78.
[2] A select committee of the House of Commons had been set up on 12 April under the chairmanship of Abbot to examine the neglected subject of expired and expiring

expired and expiring Statutes, you have abused the state and arrangement of the Statutes in general—if people will bear this, so much the better—I suppose you find they *will* bear it, or you would not give it them. Mark forwards! Tally-ho! etc.

Do you ever take walks before breakfast? if you do I should like to take ½ an hour or an hour's stroll with you one morning, and would call upon you for that purpose. Rose has just given me the Heads of the Poor Bill—what stuff![3]

4th May 1796.
Q.S.P.

1130

From Thomas Powys

21 May 1796

Mr Powys presents his Complimts to Mr Bentham and is much obliged by the Communication of the interesting Papers which He returns with his best acknowledgements. Mr P. will be highly gratified by the perusal of any larger work of Mr Bs on this subject on his return to Town.

Albemarle Street
May 21st.

statutes. The committee reported on 12 May, making a number of practical suggestions, which were carried out and added greatly to Abbot's reputation as an administrative reformer (see R. B. Pugh, 'Charles Abbot and the Public Records: the first
phase', *Bulletin of the Institute of Historical Research*, xxxix (1966), pp. 69–85). This
letter suggests that he asked his step-brother to look at the draft report. (See also
letter 1202.)

[3] Pitt's bill for the relief of the poor (see letter 1111, n. 2, p. 188 above).

1130. [1] B.L. VI: 179–80. Docketed: '1796 May 21 / Poor / Powys Albemarle Street /
to / J.B. Q.S.P. / Returning *Poor* Papers / 1st parcel.'
A missing letter from Bentham, sending the papers to Powys, may be assumed. In
B.L. VI: 191–2 is a letter from Lavinia, Countess Spencer, to Samuel Bentham,
docketed by Jeremy: '1796 May'. It reads: 'Tuesday / Admiralty / I have spoken to
Mr Powis upon the subject of yr poor Bill and he will be happy to hear your *say* and to
pick your Brains when ever you chuse it. He woud rather call on you than give you the
trouble of calling on him. So now settle and fix your matters with him by a note—je
m'en lave les mains—my head is not good at these things. Adieu my dr Genl. / Lav.
Spencer.' The previous Tuesday to 21st May was the 17th, the probable date of her
letter.
Thomas Powys (1743–1800), M.P., 1774–97, was created Baron Lilford in 1797. His
London address was 20 Albemarle Street.
For Lavinia Spencer's friendship with Samuel Bentham see letter 1135, n. 4.

1131
To Samuel Bentham
24 May 1796 (Aet 48)

Your answer (i.e. Collins') I suppose will be that you are informed £600 is the least sum it will require to put them in tenantable repair—that this sum of course, or what less sum may be sufficient you expect will be laid out upon them. That (21) years is term you had in view, but that you are not as yet very decided nor consequently very tenacious /anxious/ as to the term but /and/ that it is impossible you should be decided about it till you know what term the *principal* is able and disposed to grant.

You being at such a distance, and there being so many *pourparlers* about it I will not swear but that for shortness sake I may personate Collins' friend and representative in this business—meantime write thou thy mind.

I think it was after your departure that the packet came back with a note from Powys[2]—'interesting papers'—'much obliged'—highly gratified by a sight of the remainder on his return to town.

You ran away six guineas in my debt—please to supply the deficiency by a draught.

I know not at this moment Tuesday 8 mg o'clock the event of Bond v. Bentham—very likely put off.

Greenwich May 23rd 1796[3]

Dear Sir

I have just reced the inclos'd from Mr Wilson in consequence of my calling upon him. you will perceive that I want your further instructions to enable me to treat. I am going into the country and shall return in the evening (by Queen Square) by wch time perhaps you will be prepared to say how much you mean to engage to

1131. [1] B.L. VI: 181–2. Autograph. Addressed: 'General Bentham / Redbridge near Southampton / or Portsmouth / To the care of Mr. Bunce.'
The Tuesday mentioned in the last sentence indicates 24 May as the date of Bentham's letter.
[2] Thomas Powys. See letter 1130, n. 1.
[3] The communication from William Collins to Samuel Bentham, which follows, is the original letter, with a copy of the letter from Edward Wilson to Collins below it on one side of a sheet of paper, and Bentham's comments to his brother, Samuel, on the other.

expend upon the premises and how long a term you wish to have them leased to you for

I am Dear Sir, Yrs truly
William Collins[4]

Copy

London Strand May 21 1796

Sir

If you'll have the goodness to call the first time you come to town, and explain the length of time you wish to take the premises in Queen's Square for—together with an intimation of the extent of improvement the premises would receive I will then obtain from the owner the proposals you desire

I am Sir Your obedt
hble Servt
Edwd Wilson[5]

1132

To Earl Spencer

24 May 1796 (Aet 48)

Mr Bentham presents his respectful Compliments to Ld Spencer and regrets very much the necessity he is under of being troublesome to his Lordship once more by begging leave to recall to his notice a letter of the 18 last[2]

Q.S.P. May 1796

1133

To Samuel Bentham

25 May 1796 (Aet 48)

Q.S.P. 25 May 1796

It happens by God's providence, that Collins has a kind of Welsh connection with your Upholstering Mr Wilson, the Agent for

---

[4] William Collins, as revealed by letter 1133, was acting for Samuel concerning the renting of a house on an island site in Queen's Square, close to his brother's house in Westminster.

[5] Edward Wilson, an upholsterer, was the landlord's agent.

1132. [1] B.L. VI: 193–4. Autograph draft. Docketed: '1796 May 24 / Panopt / J.B. Q.S.P. / to / Ld Spencer Admiralty.'

[2] Letter 1121, about which a reminder had already been sent on 3 May (letter 1127).

1133. [1] B.L. VI: 185–6. Autograph. No docket or address.

205

the Landlord of the Fortunate Island:[2] said Wilson being the great
Williams's, the great Coppersmith Williams's[3] Upholsterer!!!—
whereby said Wilson has undertaken that Collins shall have the
refusal of said Island. Said Wilson has accordingly written (at least
promised that he would write) by this day's post to his principal
for full powers: taking 21 Years for the hypothetical argumentative
term, and asking upon what terms (conditions) said Landlord
would let said Island—putting the matter in both ways with regard
to the laying out of the Repair-*gelt*—1st supposition Landlord to
lay out the money—rent so much more—2nd supposition, Tenant
to lay out the money—rent so much the less—

N.B. there might be a 3rd or medium or compound supposition—
Landlord to allow so much—Tenant to covenant to lay out so
much more, and in consideration thereof have the laying out of the
Landlord's quota, with the privity and if need be, approbation of
Landlord's surveyor—Therefore you Mr Inspector, first of all please
know your own mind—then and in the second place please communicate the same to

Sir

your humble Servt

to command

or anybody else.

Your friend Ld Spencer, instead of *writing* as he promised, has
upon receiving copy of the note of which you saw the Brouillon[4]
appointed me to call upon him tomorrow. Down upon your
marrow-bones and pray to God there may be no quarrelling.

J. Peake will probably tell you of Hoopers[5] draught being come
here for acceptance, £100.—J. Peake says you know of it—but
I hear of nobody's having any instructions about the matter—I
undertook that an answer should be here from you on Saturday.
Drawn at 20 days date—day marked as day when due 4 June.
Friths[?][6] have called here twice—and the 2d time took back the
note /Bill/.

---

[2] The house on the island site in Queen's Square.

[3] Probably Thomas Williams, Copper Office, Royal Exchange, London. On 7 May
1779 he patented a process for 'smelting copper-ore whereby the arsenic is extracted
from the metal, and it is brought to fine copper with less trouble and expense than by
the common process' (Bennet Woodcroft, *Alphabetical Index of Patentees of Inventions*,
1969 edn., p. 621).

[4] Presumably letter 1132.

[5] Not identified. Perhaps the same man as the one mentioned in letters 808, 809 and
812. Both the brothers were in financial difficulties at this time.

[6] Not identified: perhaps Friths were collectors of promissory notes and this may
refer to the same bill.

1134

MEMORANDUM BY JEREMY BENTHAM

26 May 1796 (Aet 48)

Barnes Common not objected to on the part of Ld Sp.
River between Battersea bridge and Lambeth what part of it
a matter of indifference to Ld Sp.—supposed, that the nearer to
Lambeth the less objectionable to the other parties

Thursday 26 May 1796 Q.S.P.

The above memorandum, having been taken by leave of Lord
Spencer, at an audience given me by his Lordship this day between
between 1 and 2 P.M. at a room in the Admiralty Office (nobody else
present) was at the same time shewn to his Lordship and approved
of by him.

1135

TO SAMUEL BENTHAM

27 May 1796 (Aet 48)

Q.S.P. 27 May 1796 Friday.
Your Inspector Generalship is much wanted here to inspect
the damned Marsh and see what is to be done with it. Your noble
friend vowing the most implacable opposition to Panopticon Hill,[2]
has offered me the cursed Marsh, or Barnes Common, of which he is
Lord of the Manor. Barnes Common I dont expect to find eligible,
for reasons not worth detailing, at least till I have enquired farther
into it. Meantime what he has said to me and allowed me to take
a memorandum of, in relation to the blasted Marsh, gives me a right
to swagger in it. Therefore the sooner you are here, to swagger with
me, and help me catch agues in it, the better.
It happens oddly enough that a square containing 80 acres (the
number we are intitled to claim) is exactly equal to a parallellogram
having $\frac{3}{4}$ of a mile for one of its sides: (Feet 2640) and $\frac{1}{4}$ of a mile

1134. [1] B.L. VI: 183–4. Autograph. Docketed: '1796 May 26 / Panopt / Ld Spencer
Admiralty / to / J.B. ibid. / Memorandum of consent to Barnes Common and Bank
between Lambeth and Battersea Bridge.'
1135. [1] B.L. VI: 187–8. Autograph. Addressed: 'To General Bentham / Redbridge /
near Southampton.' Postmark: 'MA.27.96.D'.
[2] That is, the Battersea Rise site.

for the other (Feet 1320). Edward[3] and I have been measuring F.2842/Feet/ = 947 Yards along the shore of the river which being free from all interruption would lie at your *bienséance*, and leave 1226 Feet = 409 Yards in depth from the river: a part of the depth which we partly measured and partly guessed at, (being interrupted by rain) appeared not to exceed that depth. Therefore it appears as if you might have from $\frac{1}{4}$ of a mile to a $\frac{3}{4}$ of a mile along the river, and at the same time have all the ground in depth from the River to the Road. Tomorrow I intend going to take correct measurements of the depth at different places, and if I do I will make you a Report accordingly. Now then if we had the execrable marsh, then, so long as you continued unpoisoned, you might scoop out Docks and Steps and cuts and canals, and all manner of holes in it and the more you made in it, and the sooner, the better, since the earth that came out would serve to heap up on the borders of the holes and so help to make the rest of the premises less poisonous and unhabitable. We might get some Woolwich Convicts perhaps to raise a mount to set down the building upon, and the hole left thereby would be a dock etc: that is you might have it of any shape and depth you pleased. Perhaps his Lordship and your Lavinia[4] might not dislike to have a Shipbuilding establishment for their amusement so much within their inspection: but this would require to be mentioned with caution, and probably not till

[3] Edward, son of William Collins.

[4] Earl Spencer and his wife, Lavinia. She was not only a beautiful and accomplished leader of London society but an influential supporter of her husband in his political and administrative duties. Many distinguished public men consulted her and her correspondence with them reveals her ability and tact, e.g. the letter to Samuel, quoted above, p. 203 n. 1. The future Lady Bentham said of her: 'Lady Spencer could not be accused of interference in political decisions, nor of meddling with her husband's department; yet many matters proceeded the more smoothly and more beneficially for the public service by her tact in indicating what would be agreeable, or at least tolerated, by those with whom Lord Spencer had to act.' She goes on to quote *in extenso* a letter from Samuel to Lady Spencer later in this year 1796, broaching the delicate subject of reforms in the administration of the Admiralty and the Navy, particularly in the keeping of accounts. The letter ends: 'In excuse for my troubling you with such a letter, let me once more observe that your ladyship is the only person to whom I dare address myself on such a subject.' From subsequent correspondence quoted by Lady Bentham, it is clear that the friendly collaboration went on for years, for instance the reply Lady Spencer wrote to Samuel's complaint in July 1799 that the promotion of his assistant, Henry Peake, was being obstructed: 'I am much mortified', she wrote, 'to find that all my persevering, hearty, eloquent scolds, have been entirely thrown away upon you,—and that you are as bad as ever, fretting, plaguing, worrying yourself to death, about what?—about nothing.' Lady Spencer significantly ends her letter: 'Now be quiet, and don't let Peake, or allow yourself to, open your lips on this subject from henceforward, and, everything will be right, not else—Adieu'. (M. S. Bentham, *Life of Sir Samuel Bentham*, 1862, pp. 170–2, 172–3.)

after the bargain was concluded with them for the land: lest they should regret the more the parting with it.

Observe that before my consent is given to his Lordship, or application made by me to the Treasury, your plans must be formed at least to a certain degree; therefore leave your nonsensical nonsense there quick, and come and pay your obeisance to your betters.

The refusal of the Island[5] seems perfectly secure to you: but the terms higher a good deal than I should have hoped. £160 a year has been refused for it, on a repairing base: viz: 30 years, and the Tenant to take upon him all expences of repair. But perhaps that or a little more would not now be refused. The choice of Collins was a fortunate one: the upholstering plenipo being a protegé of the great Williams! If you were to lay out £1,000 upon it that at 10 per cent (£100) would make the rent come to £260 even according to the price refund: though the income sunk at present upon the £1,000 would be no more than £50. Quere how to and where to get the £1,000?—Answer Багушка[6] would untie his purse strings for it.

Yesterday I communicated to Lloyd your Generalship's commands about the consultation with Sadler—I expected to have had a quick result to have given you by this day's post—but none such is yet come. Lloyd however said there could be no doubt of the feasibleness of it—and that it would be an easy matter. I mean the adopting Sadlers Engine[7] to the extracting of water from holes of variable depths made for docks.

Just now is come a Draught on you from Poor[8] dated 21 May for £100 at 30 days after date in favour of John Bailey.[9]

[5] The house on the island site in Queen Square.

[6] Anglice: 'father': perhaps Bentham thought Dr. Fordyce might produce the £1000 for his future son-in-law.

[7] An 'Engine for lessening the consumption of steam and fuel in steam or fire-engines', patented by James Sadler, 10 June 1791 (Bennet Woodcroft, *Alphabetical Index of Patentees of Inventions*, 1969 edn., p. 497).

[8] Perhaps Robert Poore of Redbridge, or one of his family.

[9] Not identified, possibly John Bailey (1750–1819), surveyor, engraver and writer on agriculture.

1136

TO WILLIAM WILBERFORCE

c. 28 May 1796 (Aet 48)

My dear Sir,

Enclosed is the paper which you gave me leave to trouble you with.[2] Observe the dates. It was after receiving a copy of it, together with a Memorial addressed to the Treasury Board, which he desired to have *pro forma*, that Mr Dundas, upon my meeting him at the outside-door of his office at the Horse Guards, said to me these words,—'Mr Bentham, I have just been saying to Mr Long, what I had before said to Mr Long and to Mr Pitt, *that it is impossible to change the land.*' Mr Dundas was addressed at that time in consequence of Mr Pitt's having signified his intention of resting his decision (as Mr Long told me) on the judgment of Mr Dundas, who, he observed, had the circumstances more on his mind than he (Mr P.) could have. Afterwards, Mr Long sent for me, and notified to me in form, that Mr Pitt had fixed upon the land in question as the proper spot,—and an instrument for the purpose was accordingly, by Mr Long's direction, drawn by me, approved and signed by Mr Long,—settled by the Attorney-general, and engrossed by Mr White, and when I heard last of it, about six weeks ago, was lying (so Mr Long told me) (together with the draught of the contract perused and settled by the Attorney and Solicitor General, and ready for engrossment) upon Mr Pitt's table. Lord Spencer has given up his opposition more than once: once, as I was informed by Mr Long, who called upon me at my house to congratulate me on it, and afterwards in conversation repeated to me that, after what Lord Spencer had said to him,—as I understood,—he certainly could not go back with honour,—honour was the word: another time, (after having been at my house, and seen what was to be seen,) as was notified on his part by Lord Hugh Seymour[3] to my brother, who came to me full of it at the time, but I doubt has since forgotten it.

Lord Spencer has since offered to me, through my brother, to

1136. [1] Bowring, xi, 113–14. No date is given, but internal evidence suggests that the letter was written about the end of May 1796, soon after the 'marsh' was offered as a site for Panopticon (see letters 1134 and 1135 above).

[2] Not printed by Bowring: perhaps a memorandum, sent with the shorter Memorial of October 1794 (see letter 1020, p. 99 above).

[3] See letter 1101, n. 5.

give up his opposition if I would accept of a *marsh*, admirably convenient for me in a pecuniary view, but as certainly pregnant with the destruction by hundreds in a year of those whom I would wish to reform, and not to poison, (I speak not from surmises, but *records*.) I wished to rid myself, once for all, of the temptation to commit safe murder for great gain; and, accordingly, after a hard struggle, prevailed to have retained in the contract the clause binding me (in consideration of what was deemed an adequate premium) to pay £100 for every death.

Lord Spencer, on the report of his steward, who I believe has been the private mover of all these vexations, estimates at between £2000 and £3000 a-year the detriment that may accrue to his son,[4] (to whom he pointed on the occasion,) by an adhesion to the old choice, quoting two instances in which persons who had been treating for taking land of him, on I know not what advantageous terms, had broke off on hearing of the Penitentiary House. Hopeless of justice, I would most gladly bind myself to take the land upon those terms, whatever they were, and, in short, indemnify this poor family from the apprehended injury, according to their own estimate of the extent of it.

It was in September last that the draught of the contract, after having been settled *in terminis* with Mr Pitt, through the medium of Mr Long, went to Mr White, with a letter signed by Mr Long, ordering it to be '*prepared for their Lordships' signature:*' since which I have been obliged to pay (*inter alia*) (in addition to £8000 or £9000 out of pocket before) £1140 for cast-iron, (materials for the building,) not to reckon some hundreds more, which by this time I am bound for. I am now lending my mind to the irksome task of drawing up my case with the vouchers for publication, that when those who take an interest in my fate become witnesses of my ruin, they may see it has not had imprudence for its cause, unless it be imprudence to have attributed common honesty to Mr Pitt. In this crisis you are my sheet-anchor,—*more orientali*!

P.S. What can I say more? I could read you a memorial to the Treasury, with Mr Dundas's answer, refusing to forward it, as being injurious to Lord Spencer, attributing to him what he has since avowed.—N. B. It attributed nothing, it was merely *hypothetical*,— that people would say how it would look, if, etc.

It was about the month of September above-mentioned, that Lord Spencer (according to his own account of the matter to my

---

[4] Presumably John Charles Spencer, Viscount Althorp, later 3rd Earl Spencer (1782–1845).

brother) signified his last, and still subsisting opposition to Mr Pitt, who all the while, either not meaning to sign the draught he had ordered to be prepared, or at least doubting whether he should sign it or no, has been suffering me (without vouchsafing the least hint of any such doubts) to amuse myself with putting it through all its stages, and laying out my money upon the faith of it.

1137

To Samuel Bentham

30 May 1796 (Aet 48)

Q.S.P. Monday May 30 – 1796

Lloyd says the loss by fruitless loading and then unloading of the Sawing apparatus will amount to not less than £10. The man talked of sailing as tomorrow (Tuesday) but Lloyd has scarce any expectation that he will be ready [in] time enough for that day, and at any rate he has promised, and it is necessary for him to call and see Lloyd before he sails. That opportunity will therefore be taken to stop the machinery according to your order. But now that you see how expensive it will be, we desire to have your peremptory orders by return of post; not waiting for your return. If the Machinery is to go to Portsmouth, there can be no use in stopping it: since the Vessel is sure to stop at Portsmouth. But I suspect you have in contemplation the employing it in your Dock-manufactory in the plague-manufacturing Marsh: if so, and there should be any means of paying for it, it would certainly be a great blessing to have it there. Indeed why should his Majesty not pay us for it? (God bless him!) He could have it put up in the land of mortality as soon as any where else, and I should scorn to charge him rent for the spot it was set up upon; and if he grew tired of it two or three years hence, Puss and I would buy it of him. You might transfer hither your whole strength from Redbridge, Boys and other Apprentices, to Contagion-town and they and the Felons might rot together.

I shall probably send you this letter separate from the Indres[2] though they go by the Mail Coach likewise: for this going by the

1137. [1] B.L. VI: 189–90. Autograph. Addressed: 'To Genl. Bentham, / Redbridge, / near Southampton.'

[2] The abbreviation would seem to be for the word 'Indentures', noted later in the letter as costing 15 shillings a pair for ten pairs, some containing 'the clause against Matrimony and Fornication'. Perhaps the indenture forms were for use in binding the apprentices mentioned in the previous paragraph.

Post like other letters will be sure of being delivered, which it is necessary it should be that I may have your definitive answer about stopping the Sawing-Rattle-traps: whereas the Indr̄es going in the form of a parcel may be delivered or not as God pleases.

Just now comes another Bill drawn by Poore in favour of David Thomas[3] for £180–13–0 due June 23d days, 30 after date from 21 May.

A Letter from Mrs Lindgren is with the Indr̄es 10 pr. price 15s a pair.[4] Observe that some of them *have* the clause against Matrimony and Fornication—others *not*. They were bought at 5 different shops.

The high wind which is not quite over has blown down several of the Trees in the Park.[5] The Garden Trees etc. have been sadly tormented and despoiled of several little branches—I hope nothing worse.

1138

FROM BARON ST HELENS

1 June 1796

Great Russel Street 1st June 1796

I return to you, my Dear Sir, your most valuable cahiers[2] with a thousand thanks and apologies for having kept them so long.

I entirely subscribe to the whole of your System, and admire in particular your fundamental principles, which appear to me to be not only unquestionably true, but exclusively so; by which I mean that they afford not only the best, but the only solid basis of a rational Code of Poor-Laws.

There is, however, one passage in that part of your work which perhaps requires some elucidation; I mean the Paragraphs 37 and 38 where you say that, 'in the case of *Adults, no* charge, beyond that for the amount of their individual expenditure, ought to be brought against them in the view of making up for any deficiency of supply arising from a deficiency of ability on the part of other individuals' —whereas in your Chapter of *Minors*, you contend and I think very justly, 'that individuals of that description, after having worked

---

[3] Presumably another creditor.
[4] See note 2.
[5] St James's Park, to which Queen's Square Place was adjacent.
1138. [1] B.L. VI: 195–6. Autograph. Docketed: '1796 June 2 / Poor / Ld St. Helens Grt Russel Stt. to / J.B. Q.S.P.'
[2] The draft essays on the poor law.

out their own individual expenditure etc., should also be charged with 1st their share of loss to the Establishment arising from premature Deaths of other Minors, and 2nd the probable amount of their own future maintenance in the contingency of *non-* or of imperfect ability.'

I am persuaded that you have good reasons for making this distinction; but I think they sh'd be explained, as otherwise it may be thought that adults are too favourably treated or Minors too harshly.

More when we meet which I intend shall be soon.

most faithfully yours
St Helens

1139

TO EARL SPENCER

4 June 1796 (Aet 48)

Q.S.P. 4 June 1796

My Lord,

To enable myself to speak with the more precision at the Treasury I take the liberty of requesting the favour of a sight of the Map of that part of your Lordship's estates which lies contiguous to the River between Lambeth and Battersea Bridge, and for this purpose would beg leave to wait upon your Lordship or to call upon Mr Harrison[2] (as may best suit your Lordship's convenience) I have the honour to be etc.

Earl Spencer

1140

FROM JOHN HARRISON

5 June 1796

Sir,

Lord Spencer has ordered me to inform you that his agent (my Father) will come to Town on Thursday next, and if you could conveniently call at his Lordship's office in Little St James's Street

1139. [1] B.L. VI: 197. Autograph draft. Docketed: '1796 June 4 / Panopt / J.B. Q.S.P. / to / Ld Spencer Admiralty / For sight of map.'

[2] Thomas Harrison, the land agent of Lord Spencer (see letters 979, 1121–2, 1136 and 1140–2).

1140. [1] B.L. VI: 198–9. Docketed: '1796 June 6 / Panopt / Harrison for Ld Spencer Admiralty / to / J.B. Q.S.P. / Map visend. Friday 11 and 12.'

on Friday morning about eleven or twelve o'clock you will have an opportunity of looking at the Plan of Battersea which is kept in that office

I have the Honour to be,
Sir,
Your most obedient
humble Servant
John Harrison

Admiralty 5 June 1796
  Sunday
Jeremy Bentham Esq:r

1141

To THOMAS HARRISON

15 June 1796 (Aet 48)

Queens Square Place Westmr 15 June 1796

Sir
Calling at your office this morning,[2] I found the copy not quite so extensive towards the Bridge, as I had expected to find it, not including for example any of the Gardener's Grounds, nor the large 4-acre Timber Dock (Hanks and Mill's, isn't it?).[3] I expected to have found it include (for example) the lands on both sides of the Lane which runs in a direction perpendicular to the River, with Walnut Trees on each side of it. Recollecting with acknowledgement your obliging facility with regard to the extent of the communication, I can no otherwise account for the difference between the extent comprized in the Draught, and the extent I expected to have found comprized in it, than by attributing it to a misconception on my part with regard to the parts of the ground respectively denoted by the parts of the Draught, a misconception, than which nothing could be more natural, on the part of one whose acquaintance with the place is so very slight as mine. If I do not misrecollect, your offer was so obligingly extensive, as to reach that way as far as the Bridge itself, and it was at my own desire (grounded on the

---

1141. [1] Spencer Mss, Althorp, 2nd Earl Misc. Box 21. Autograph. Docketed: 'Mr Jeremy Bentham 15 June 96 to T.H. / with copy of Harrison's reply. Ans. 17 June 96.' There is a draft, with a number of small differences, in B.L. VI: 200–3.

[2] The draft has, after the word 'morning', the following crossed-out passage: 'to see what had been done and exchanging a few words with Mr Stokes (that I think is the name of your principal assistant)'.

[3] Perhaps used by Richard Hanks of Limehouse, and Henry Mills, timber merchant, of Rotherhithe.

215

unwillingness to give unnecessary trouble) that the boundary line, as agreed on between us, was to be drawn so far short of the Bridge. It certainly does not accord with *my* opinion to carry the spot so far that way, nor, to my knowledge, with any wish or opinion entertained at the Treasury. Yet, as it is impossible to make any *definitive* selection in the present stage of the business, so that, on the side of the Bridge, any other boundary line than *that necessary* one would be arbitrary and premature, and as my wish is to go to the Treasury as fully prepared as possible, with the reasons for and against each part of the extent, if you would allow me to repeat, I wou'd be glad to accept of the latitude I understood to have been offered me, as above mentioned.

By a memorandum which I took in conversation with his Lordship, and which, to prevent all misconception, he had the goodness, of his own motion, to revise, I am warranted in saying, that to *him personally* what particular part the choice falls upon, within the whole extent of the River between Lambeth and the Bridge, is a matter of indifference. I should likewise *suppose*, though it be but my own surmize, that even the *quantity*, if it depended upon him, would be equally a matter of indifference: since, as there could be no fear of any inadequacy in the *quantum* of the compensation, the more he parted with in *that* quarter, where the property is a good deal intermixed, and the nature of the tenure adverse to improvement, the more ample the means he would acquire, of adding to his property in some *other quarter*, nearer to one or other of his residences, and where the addition may be attended with collateral advantages.

All this, which is matter of supposition only to me, is what you Sir, are perfect master of: and accordingly, if any reason bearing reference either to his Lordship's interests, or to those of any other party concerned, or to that branch of the public service in which I am more particularly concerned, should occurr to you for comprizing this or that spot, or for excluding this or that spot, from the choice, I should take it as an additional favour, if you would have the goodness to communicate to me your sentiments on the subject—

I am,

Sir,

Your very obedient

and humble Servant

Jeremy Bentham

—Harrison Esqr.

1142

FROM THOMAS HARRISON

17 June 1796

Earl Spencer's Office
Friday morning six o'clock
17 June 1796

Sir!

The sketch I had prepared began at the East End precisely at the point you noted, but Westwards did not extend quite so far as the spot at which you had begun to draw from the plan. That Sketch comprized 125 acres of land, a quantity which, from a comparison with a former occasion, I had presumed to think ample for the purpose (possibly it may be thought it was not my province to think about it) and a quantity which, it is probable, may not be given up without reluctance and perhaps some struggle, I do not mean from Lord Spencer, for that I submit entirely to his Lordship, his Land within that Sketch being a little less than half of the whole quantity. I should however be of opinion, that, for many reasons, his Lordship could not willingly consent to a nearer approach to the Bridge. One of which is, that a detachment of property Eastwards to a greater Extent than the present line effects, cut off and disjointed by your operation from the rest of the estate, could by no means be desirable. Another, I should presume would be, that looking forward to future wants, His Lordship would not willingly consent to be cut off from a Communication with *that* River for a length so considerable, particularly in that part, but to lose that communication in *any* part I conceive to be a matter of most serious importance.—To enumerate all the objections that present themselves, which are many, is not at this time necessary; and, as my instructions do not authorize me to furnish a Sketch of the land in question from one end to the other beginning at the Bridge and proceeding down the River, nor indeed to furnish any sketch or permit any to be taken, all I can further do in the matter now is to refer it to Lord Spencer at his return, which will not be many days. This Reference, lest I shod fall short, or over-act my part, will not I hope be unsatisfactory. The delay will not be much, and Lord

1142. [1] B.L. VI: 204–5. Docketed: '1796 June 17 / Panopt / Harrison Little James St. / to / J.B. Q.S.P.'

Addressed: 'Jeremy Bentham Esqr / Queen Square Place / Westminster.' Postmark: '7 o'clock / 17 JU 96 / NIGHT'. Stamped: 'ST. JAMES 2'.

Spencer will have the opportunity of acting for himself, which I the
more wish, as, till the rec.t of your letter, I was not informed that
the matter of Situation in the whole extent from the Bridge to
Lambeth was to his Lordship perfectly indifferent. Of this circumstance I freely own I entertain a different opinion, and it
therefore seems a fit question for his Lordship's own decision.—

Lord Spencer being a willing Buyer but an unwilling Seller, in
that and the adjoining Parish, the quantity certainly cannot be
a matter of indifference, as in the event of an Inclosure, for Instance, it would be a diminution, and in that respect a serious
prejudice of the Allotment his Lordship might expect in a situation
desireable to him, and it would be utterly impossible to replace it by
purchasing, because Lands to that extent are not there to be sold
and if they were, I beg leave to remark, that, without recurring to
the Sale in question, Lord Spencer has the means of accomplishing
any convenient purchases that may offer there or in any other
situation desirable to him.

I was yesterday out of Town the whole day from early morn. till
night, or you would have had this a day sooner, and am this
morning returning into the Country.

I am
Sir
Your most obedient
humble servant
Tho⁸ Harrison

Jeremy Bentham Esq.

1143

To Samuel Bentham

21 June 1796 (Aet 48)

Q.S.P. Tuesday June 21 1796
Arrived from the Admiralty
Letter from Wyat² proposing his tinned stuff instead of naked
copper for sheathing

1143. ¹ B.L. VI: 206. Autograph. Addressed: 'To / General Bentham / etc. etc. etc. /
Dock Yard / Portsmouth.' Postmark: 'JU.22.96.F'. Stamped: 'Tothill Street /
Westminster'.

² Charles Wyatt, tinned copper sheet manufacturer, 5 New Bridge Street, Blackfriars, London.

Letter from Wyat proposing a filtering apparatus for purifying Water.

Arrived from the Navy Board
Papers relative to Younger's Water-purifying proposal[3]
Quaere Report relative to Younger?
Suppose—that there is nothing new in the proposal—nothing that has not for several years been known to all chemists—but as he has the most of activity and promptitude in bringing it forward, if there be no other mode of application the mechanism of which is more advantageous than his, it may be proper to employ him in the business, if the profit he takes is no more than reasonable profit, untill the time should it ever arrive when some more advantageous mode shall have been suggested by anybody else, or untill Government should have thought proper to take the business of supplying itself with the article into its own hands.

1144

TO EARL SPENCER

23 June 1796 (Aet 48)

Q.S.P. Thursday June 23 1796

My Lord

As, upon your Lordship's return, Mr. Harrison may probably lay before your Lordship a letter[2] of mine to him, as a ground work for the observations he has to make upon the subject of it, I take the liberty in the present stage of the business to state to your Lordship a matter which is become an object of sollicitude with me that the necessity of troubling your Lordship on the subject may be as little repeated as possible.

The *Timber Docks*, which I, in my ignorance, was afraid of, and which your Lordship, as if by way of easing me of my apprehensions, seemed to hold cheap—turn out to be an object of the most serious importance. Not to your Lordship, I should hope, any more than so much rent from any other part of the land:—not even to the *occupiers*, I should likewise hope: for on the whole together the quantity of timber now lying is very inconsiderable, and in the

---

[3] Perhaps Thomas Younger, shipbuilder, 50 Rotherhithe (*Holden's Triennial Directory*, 1802–4).
1144. [1] B.L. VI: 207–8. Autograph draft, much corrected. Docketed: '1796 June 23 / Panopt / J.B. Q.S.P. / to / Earl Spencer Admiralty / Observations on Harrison's Letter / Timber Docks.'
[2] Letter 1141.

larger (consisting of 4 acres) there is not a single stick:—not to
myself, for any use that it occurs to me to make of them:—But to
the *establishment* in question, in respect of the health of the inhabitants, of the highest importance imaginable. Upon consulting
with the learned, I find everybody of opinion that the fitness of the
neighbourhood to afford human habitation to such a set of inhabitants and in such numbers depends absolutely upon the taking
of those parts of the shore out of the state of perpetual putridity to
which their present destination condemns them—an operation
which would require the property of them to be vested in the
establishment. Most, if not all of them, I believe, and the 4-acre
dock in particular (equal for ought I know to all the others put
together) turn out to be your Lordship's property. The line I took
the liberty of pointing out at a venture, and which Mr. Harrison
speaks of himself as having at first assented to, included, I *believe*
that large Dock, which is the farthest to the West, (that is towards
the Bridge) as well as the others: though as I was not, at *that time*,
so fully apprized of the importance of that part of the property in
the point of view above mentioned, it is more than I can be certain
of. I pointed to that part pretty much at a venture: not prepared to
form any opinion of my own, and expecting to find on Mr Harrisons
part, what at that time I accordingly thought I did find, a degree
of facility corresponding to that /the indulgence/ which your
Lordship had been pleased to express.

Mr Harrison seems as if he took the blame on himself for his
former facility in regard to the *particulars* of the land: a little farther
consideration will, I hope, satisfy him on the score. It is only in as
far as the particulars of this or that portion of it are known that it
can be presented to the Treasury as an object more or less suitable
to the purpose. More information than is necessary in this view I
have no motive for wishing for:—any that *is* necessary, Mr.
Harrison, I flatter myself, will not be instructed to refuse. The
including of this or that acre in the *communication* of the *particulars*,
sketch included, determines nothing with regard to the including it
in the *purchase*: but the *excluding* it from the communication,
excludes it from the purchase in the first instance.

The difficulty Mr Harrison alludes to relative to the future
probable *inclosure*, might admitt I should think of either of two
solutions: one is, the taking that contingency into account in the
adjustment of the purchase money: the other is, the reserving
the benefit of it (I mean of the annexation expected from it) in the
conveyance: the latter expedient strikes me at the moment as the

more eligible. By what I have heard of that gentleman, I am inclined to think I should have stood a better chance with him, had the land instead of being your Lordship's been his own. But, on that supposition, I flatter myself than when he has taken your Lordship's further commands on the subject, he will have learnt to consider it as his own for the present purpose.

I have the honor to be, with all respect,
My Lord, your Lordships most obed. and humble servant

J.B.

Earl Spencer

P.S. Lest for want of Mr Harrisons letter, the present one should in any part fail of being intelligible, I inclose a copy of his, which that I may not draw upon your Lordship for more time than the case may eventually appear to call for, I send *closed*.

1145

FROM EARL SPENCER

30 June 1796

Lord Spencer would be glad to see Mr Bentham at the Admiralty on Saturday at one o'clock on the Subject of his last Letter.

Adm:y 30 June 1796

1146

TO SAMUEL BENTHAM

2 July 1796 (Aet 48)

I don't know what to do, not I, with this Lord Spencer of yours, there is no fixing him to anything: nor did I ever hear any old woman in my life talk more irrelevantly or more irrationally. According to the memorandum[2] which of his motion he had revised

---

1145. [1] B.L. VI: 209. Docketed: '1796 June 30 / Panopt / Ld Spencer Admiralty / to / J.B. Q.S.P. / Appointment.'
1146. [1] B.L. VI: 210–11. Autograph. Docketed: 'July 2 1796.'
   Addressed: 'To Brigadier Genl Bentham / King's Dock Yard / Plymouth'. Postmark: 'JY.2.96.D'.
   [2] Jeremy Bentham's memorandum of 26 May (above, p. 207).

221

and assented to as correct, it was a matter of perfect indifference to
him where I took the land between the Bridge and Lambeth: now
it comes to this, that he is unwilling to give me an inch anywhere—
that he won't part with an inch any where that he can help parting
with, and he wishes (though without saying why) that the land
taken may be as far from the Bridge as possible. In conclusion he
gave me the Sketch I had desired of Harrison (beginning at the
bridge) but without the explanations which Harrison had begun
to make out, and without which what the sketch shews amounts to
nothing: and there he wanted me upon the spot to lay my finger
upon the paper, and tell him at once how much and what part of it
I would have. In conclusion we parted in tolerable good humour
with a sort of mutual laugh at the absurdities he had run into, in
charging me with plots to get possession of his land, for the sake of
selling it out piece-meal to other people: which I answered by
protesting that it was not out of malice to him that I proposed to
set up a Penitentiary House—that I did not mean to ruin him—
that I had more compassion for him than to think of any such thing
—and that I had no apprehension of its having any such effect. The
ridicule which was the best return I could make to his abundant
and unprovoked personalities was thus seasoned with a little
flattery administered to his opulence, which seemed to tickle him
and produce the designed effect, of enabling us to part on such
terms as would admitt of our meeting again.

What did I write all this to you for? and why would I wish to add
a thousand particularities that it will be impossible to me to add
without losing the post, and thence 2 days?—that you might judge
the better whether your presence here would or would not be of
use, and if it would, come post haste. Will you come to help me
prevent a quarrel, or stay away for the sake of keeping out of the
scrape. If I have any facility to hope for, it seems to be from his
fears: for while he expresses his wishes to dispute the ground with
me, he seems to admitt of his own accord that it is not in his power:
and the less civil I was to him the less uncivil he seemed to be to me.
For a long time I could get nothing from him but personal attacks,
all without the smallest provocation: at last I observed that I had
heard a good deal to the same effect before—that this was not what
I came for—that though I forebore to reply, it was not because
I was unable but out of respect for his Lordship's time, which was
the time of the public—and which I conceived might be better
employ'd than in hearing anything on that subject, that if he
thought otherwise I was ready to defend myself then or at any other

time and in any manner, according to his Lordship's pleasure. This seem'd to make the proper impression upon him, for he proceded immediately upon the business. Another time he was telling me of a parcel of things I had done, and none of which I had done: when he came to my having drawn the Bill and was proceeding to draw inferences from it, I said to him in so many words I did not draw the Bill my Lord, and thereupon he drew in his horns. After this you will acknowledge that it was something to get him into a sort of a smile approaching to a laugh, and to hear him say with a sort of frank bluntness what I want if that is what you want to know is to get rid of you altogether[3] confessing myself to be a nuisance, but adding that I took no pleasure in annoying him, and would annoy him as little as I could—But quere, how will it be in another interview? What I want is instead of the interview to get something from him upon paper in answer to the proposal /demand/ whatever it be that I make—I must conclude before I have half done, or lose the post.

Q.S.P. 2 July 1796
Come or write therefore immediately.

1147

To the Marquis of Lansdowne

c. 3 July 1796 (Aet 48)

THE GENEROUS FRIEND—A LINCOLN'S INN TALE

From the Sentimental Chronicle

A friend of Citizen Romilly's, calling on him one day, and observing a cloud upon his brow, ventured to ask the cause. 'The cause?' (exclaimed the citizen, pointing to the lacerated back of

---

[3] The lack of punctuation obscures the meaning: Lord Spencer appears to have said: 'What I want—if that is what you want to know—is to get rid of you altogether', to which Bentham replied 'I confess myself to be a nuisance' etc.

1147. [1] Bowring, x, 322. One of two quoted letters, introduced with the comment: 'Two specimens of epistolary communications, the first to Lord Lansdowne, the second to Miss F——, are remarkable for their oddity.' No dates are given, except the 'July 3' on the second quotation, but internal evidence strongly suggests early July 1796 for the dating of both letters. Lansdowne is clearly acknowledging receipt of this one in his letter of 25 July (letter 1154, p. 233 below) and apologises for not answering 'sooner'. The reference in Bentham's letter to a period 'Ever since a certain speech in a certain house' suggests a month or two after Lansdowne's speech in the House of Lords on 2 May 1796 (see note 3 below).

223

Chamfort.)² 'See there, and tell me whether I can ever look Lord Lansdowne in the face again?' The friend, in the handsomest manner imaginable, immediately offered to take the blame from off the shoulders of the citizen and set it upon his own, where it has been accordingly lying ever since.

THE MORAL

'Generosity like this, does it not deserve to be—rewarded, I was going to to say—I meant no more than to be rescued from infamy at least, to say nothing of oblivion? Ever since a certain speech, made in a certain house,³ it has been infamous not to have read the 'Attorney's Guide,' (not the 'Guide to the Practice of the King's Bench,' but) 'to the History of Florence,' and, at the same time impossible to obtain it—even to those who have money—*a fortiori* to those who have none. If then—some time within these two or three months—but the substance of an oration is sometimes contained in an expressive silence.'

1148

TO CAROLINE FOX

3 July 1796 (Aet 48)

July 3

Mr Bentham begs of Miss F——, to commission Lord Lansdowne to acquaint Miss F—— that he, the aforesaid Mr B., accepts with much acknowledgement, the favour to act upon the terms and conditions, and according to the true intent and meaning of the covenant proposed; *videlicet*, that, in proper time, a meeting of all

² A copy of *Maximes, pensées, caricatures et anecdotes* (Paris and London), by Sébastien Roch Nicolas Chamfort, was in Lansdowne's Library in 1806 (*Bibliotheca Lansdowniana*, p. 40, lot no. 1095). It would seem that Samuel Romilly had damaged the back of the borrowed book and Bentham had taken the blame. Chamfort (1741–94), French dramatist and essayist, had been secretary of the Jacobin Club in 1790–1 and director of the Bibliothèque Nationale in 1792. His witticisms gave offence and he was put under surveillance during the Terror. He died from self-inflicted wounds after a suicide attempt, about which Bentham may be making a grim joke.

³ The speech made by Lord Lansdowne in the House of Lords on Monday, 2 May 1796, on the conduct of the administration. Referring to 'the various papers upon the Table', he said 'They will certainly not be found so entertaining as Lorenzo de Medici' (*The Senator*, xv, 1583). *The Life of Lorenzo de' Medici*, 2 vols., Liverpool, 1795 [1796], by William Roscoe (1753–1831), at that time an attorney, had appeared in February 1796.

1148. ¹ Bowring, x, 322. The second specimen of Bentham's 'oddity' quoted by Bowring (see letter 1147, n.1).

224

proper parties shall be holden at the proper, and only proper place, at which a proper and distinct judgment of the proficiency of the intended pupil can be formed—proper security being previously given, by all proper and necessary parties, against all treasons, treacheries, conspiracies, deceits, impositions, snares, wiles, tricks, impostures, quirks, quibbles, equivocations, mental reservations, backslidings, tergiversations, and all other artifices, to wit, as well all and singular treasons, etc., set forth, and now remaining, etc., as of record, etc., in the Register Roll, etc., at Piepowder² Court, etc., in Albemarle Street, etc., entitled, *Liaisons Dangereuses*,³ as all other artifices, frauds, and contrivances whatsoever.

Mr Bentham begs of Miss F—— to desire Lord Lansdowne, to return Miss F—— innumerable thanks for the many thanks with which she has been pleased to overpay a humble tribute of ancient respect, far short of being worthy of so rich and unexpected, and for for many years, not to say ages, unprecedented a reward.⁴

1149

To J. P.

9 July 1796 (Aet 48)

Points to be ascertained from the Lease.

1. Years of commencement and expiration—especially the latter.

² Misprinted in Bowring 'Pixpowder:' it is clearly a reference to the ancient court of Piepowder, which had controlled markets and fairs.
³ The famous novel by Pierre Choderlos de Laclos (1741–1803), first published in 4 vols., Paris, 1782; it appeared in a two-volume London edition (in French) in 1796.
⁴ Indicating a missing letter from Bentham, either to Lord Lansdowne, or to Miss Fox herself.
1149. ¹ B.L. VI: 212–13. Autograph draft, much corrected. Docketed: '1796 July 9 / J.B. to J.P. / Instructions for Inquiries about Hanging Wood.'
The identity of 'J.P.' among Bentham's helpers has not been ascertained: possibly he was John Peake or John Poore, both of whom visited Woolwich from time to time.
On 1 July Bentham had drafted to Lord Spencer a long letter which is docketed 'not sent' (B.L. VI: 233–8). It begins: 'Since I had the honour of waiting on your Lordship I have taken a view of a situation at Woolwich which though in a very material point of vicinity to London it would [be] so much inferior to Battersea Marsh, yet in the great article of healthiness promises so well that if it were attainable, I think it not improbable but that I might find myself enabled to rid your Lordship of a negotiation in the unpleasantness of which I am most truly a sympathizer as well as a sharer . . .'
The unsent letter goes on to detail the advantages and disadvantages of the site beside Hanging Wood, mentioning that the owner is Sir Thomas Spencer Wilson, whose 'state of mental derangement' makes it necessary for his wife to manage the affairs of the family, which includes a grown-up son and a daughter married to Lord Arden. Part of the ground in question, Bentham adds, is leased to a person named Harding,

225

2. Extent of ground it includes: and whether any and what part of such ground is included under the name of wood.

3. Whether it conveys an unlimited power of following the vein of Sand, and thereby rooting out the trees—or whether the concurrence of the Landlord or his Agents is made necessary in any and what cases.

Say—That you had taken a friend of your's up to the spot by way of shewing him the prospect—that upon seeing it he had fallen in love with it, and conceived a sort of half-inclination of building a house upon some part or other of it if it were obtainable—that you had told him what you knew about it—and amongst other things that you imagined that even if he could persuade the Proprietor to sell a few acres or let a building here: it would not signify without his (H's)[2] concurrence—But that it occurred to you and you accordingly mentioned to your friend that very likely his (H's) concurrence might be obtained, for you did not suppose he (H) could want the whole wood, and that the opportunity of disposing of his brick, his lime and his sand for the building might be productive of considerable advantage to him (H)—and that he might be likely therefore to find his account in joining with your friend, especially as you understood that the business of sending the Sand to London was not a very advantageous one. Your friend thereupon hinted to you, that the house in question would probably not be the only occasion he should have of dealing with you for such materials.

If he manifests anything of a communicative disposition ask him for a sight of the Lease that you may be able to give the more certain information to your friend, and save him the trouble of making any unnecessary or fruitless application to Sir Th^s.[3]

H. will certainly be for asking who this friend is—but your answer will be that he said he had reasons for not caring his name should be mentioned on such an occasion, if the application came to nothing—and that you had thereupon promised not to mention it without his leave. This will be your constant answer and saving clause as often as he asks you any questions which it might puzzle you to answer.

who takes away the sand to such an extent that many trees have been destroyed. He would ask Lord Spencer 'for every assistance' in acquiring this site, although he would prefer the Battersea one.

2 Harding's.

3 Sir Thomas Spencer Wilson (see letter 1156 n. 1).

1150

FROM COUNT RUMFORD

10 July 1796

Royal Hotel Pall Mall
Monday Morning 7 'O Clock

My dear Sir,

Upon my arrival in Town last night from the Country I found your obliging letter,[2] and the Essays on the Poor-Laws which you have been so good as to permit me to peruse. You know my opinion of the importance of the subject, and if you do justice to my opinion of your merit as an author you will be persuaded that I am really very glad to see the subject in your hands. I wish it were in my power to devote as much time to the examination of your Plans as would be necessary to enable me to give the opinion of them which you desire, but really I am so very much engaged that I have hardly a moment I can call my own. I left directions when I went to Ireland to build a Kitchen for the Foundling Hospital[3]—when I came back I had the mortification to find that the workmen had totally misunderstood me. I am this moment going there to remedy their mistakes—that is to say—to pull down the kitchen and rebuild it, and for this operation I have only two days. You will judge of the rest. I *must* leave England the end of the Week.

If you are an early man, and will call on me any Morning this week between 7 and 8 o'clock I shall be glad to see you

With Sincere Regard and Esteem I have the honour to be

My dear Sir
Yours Most Sincerely
Rumford

1150. [1] B.L. VI: 214–15. Autograph. Docketed: '1796 July 10 / Poor / Count Rumford / Pall Mall / to / J.B. Q.S.P.'

[2] Missing.

[3] The Foundling Hospital in Bloomsbury, instituted by Captain Thomas Coram and opened in 1745; between 1760 and 1800 most infants were admitted on payment of £100 for each—no questions asked; before and after that period admission was free upon the personal application of mothers (see R. H. Nichols, *History of the Foundling Hospital*, 1935).

1151

TO EARL SPENCER

14 July 1796 (Aet 48)

Queen's Square Place 14 July 1796

My Lord

The spot which Mr Harrison had allotted me contained, according to his letter, 125 Acres: in point of quantity I shall not attempt to trespass upon your Lordship's indulgence any farther. But with regard to the necessity of taking in the Timber Docks, for the purpose of insuring the healthiness of the spot as a place of residence for such inhabitants, it is not in my power to change my opinion. This would require the beginning with the great dock as being the great source of putridity, and would carry the spot westward as far as the Walnut-tree walk, which is an existing boundary, and seems a natural and commodious one. To comprise all the Docks, that is all the repositories of putrescent mud, the allotment would require to extend to the East-ward as far as the small Houses called the the *White Houses* or thereabouts. These, any more than the Red House, or the Mills I don't very well see how I could propose to the Treasury to purchase, although your Lordship were inclined to part with them: which I should not expect to find the case, unless it were to save ground to the westward. But on my own private account I should have no objection to be your Lordship's tenant for the Houses, and I though they seem for some time to have gone a begging, should not think of offering less rent than the best they have ever fetched. If a tenant were wanting for the Mill, which, though it be a mere conjecture, I am inclined from circumstances to suspect may be the case, I think it not improbable I might conceive some means of making it worth my while to charge myself with the rent: not in any instance should I attempt to put any part of your Lordships estate in the worse plight for my intrusion into the neighbourhood of it. Not being informed of the rent, any more than of the means which a tenant has of making it out, it is of course impossible for me to speak with decision on the subject in the present stage of the business: what I have said, your Lordship will I hope have the goodness to receive as a testimony of my

1151. [1] B.L. VI: 216–17. Autograph draft. Docketed: '1796 July 14 / Panopt J.B. Q.S.P. / to / Earl Spencer Admiralty.'

228

wish to render the inconvenience, of which it is my misfortunate to become the instrument, as light as possible.

I understood it to be your Lordships wish when I had the honour of waiting on you, that I should even *then* if possible have given a precise description of the spot I wished for. But this was neither *then* possible, nor is it *now*. The sketch, in the state in which it had been originally made out, had been intended to be accompanied by a *particular*, which I saw making out for me at your Lordship's office. But this particular I have not received, and therefore remain in the dark as to the respective quantities of land in the several plots delineated in the sketch: which though a representation, and of course a correct one, of the *property*, is no picture of the appearance of the land which it includes: it exhibits boundary lines in multitudes, where there are no correspondent visible ones on the land: and it represents as terminating in No. 39 a road which runs nearly at right angles from the Walnut-tree Lane, and which in fact continues on across No. 39 as far or nearly as far as the Red House. The original map has a scale to it, I suppose: were this scale marked upon the sketch,[2] and the roads that run through it distinctly and compleatly represented (by a red line for example) with their names annexed, together with marks for the site of the Houses, these additions would enable me, I should hope, to obey your Lordships commands with regard to the marking out the spot desired, without troubling Mr Harrison for the particular abovementioned: It is in the hope of its receiving these little additions that I take the liberty of inclosing the sketch, begging the favour of the return of it, if your Lordship pleases, as soon as may consist with your Lordships convenience—I have the honour to be with all respect

> My Lord
> Your Lordship's most
> obedient and humble Servant
> Jeremy Bentham

Earl Spencer

[2] A copy of the the sketch is in B.L. VI: 218.

1152

TO CHARLES LONG

16 July 1796 (Aet 48)

(Copy)

July 16—1796

[2] From the Wall which bounds the Western extremity of *Woolwich Dock Yard*, runs a line of *marsh*, bounded on the *North* by the *River*, and on the *South* by the *Road* leading from *London* into *Woolwich Town*. This belongs to the *Bowwater* family,[3] who, if the report of the place is to be trusted to are, notwithstanding their large possessions, in a situation such as would render a little ready money likely to be not an unwelcome article—so much for the *bulk* of the land: but for the immediate *site* of the *building*, *elevation*, natural or artificial, I need scarcely repeat, may be regarded as indispensable. This elevation, would be presented, in a natural as well as very commodious form, by a small slice of *Hanging Wood*, which in its native wildness, skirts the Road (as you probably recollect) on the other side. The extent of the *whole* wood, is 120 acres: a portion, very conveniently marked out for the purpose in question by existing paths, appears to contain about 20 acres, to which would naturally be added a bare and unemployed spot, almost surrounded by the Wood, and containing 4 Acres.

Hanging Wood is the property of *Sir Thomas Spencer Wilson*: whose circumstances, family, and family connections, are probably much better known to you than myself. From such a mass of landed opulence and such a state of mind, consent *perfectly free*, seems hardly to be expected: but I need scarcely observe that the professed purpose of the Act, is to render such consent unnecessary. The spot is not 500 yards, I suppose, from the existing station of the *hulks*, on board of which the Convicts are exposed to view: it is a good *mile distant* from Sir Tho's *House*, and by the form of the ground and the thickness of the trees, even when the leaf is off, perfectly screened from the *view* of it. The spot I have in view for the

---

1152. [1] B.L. VI: 221–2. Fair copy. Docketed: '1796 July 16 / Panopt/J.B. Q.S.P. / to / Long Treasury / Hanging Wood proposed.' There is an autograph draft, with many alterations in B.L. VI: 219–20.

[2] The draft begins: 'Difficulties of the same nature with those which drove me from Battersea *Rise*, pursuing me to the Marsh a discovery has been made of a situation of *easy access* of which I should be content to profit, if it meets with your approbation or the sanction of Mr Pitt'.

[3] The Bowater family.

immediate site of the building (viz: part of the bare spot above-mentioned) is so happily embosomed in trees, that, if any part of the establishment were visible to any of the neighbouring *Villas*, it would only be the turret crowning it, or some such *frustrum*, which not presenting either the *persons* of the inhabitants, or any other object associated with the idea of *confinement*, would rather *add* to the pleasure of the prospect than *detract* from it. The *immediate* vicinity of the *Dock Yard* and the less immediate vicinity of the Military at the *Warren*, both within the reach of *signals* of both kinds, *visible* as well as *audible*, are circumstances of no small importance in point of *security*, or at least in respect of the *opinion* of security. It would in every *public* point of view be superior even to Battersea Rise, were it not for the *distance*, which places it comparatively out of the reach of the *great* seat of general inspection. In a *personal* point of view, I find (alas!) but too considerable articles of disadavantage:—but on these it is needless to insist.

The *inhabitants* of the *Town*, and even the *occupiers* of the neighbouring *Villas*, are too much familiarized with the *idea*, and even the *spectacle* of the *convicts*, in their present *squalid* state, to be alarmed by a change which would leave the obnoxious objects *less* exposed to view than at present.

As to the faculty of purchasing, there is a *protective* clause in the Act,[4] which, if the word '*planted*' ('*planted with wood*') had been changed into some such word as *covered*, *would have* exempted the greatest part of the necessary elevation from the *compulsive* power. But the Wood is fortunately an old *natural* wood, without the least sign of *plantation*, and even fenceless, and compleatly exposed to invaders of all kinds, four footed as well as two footed: and so far from its being or having been the object of any views of '*improvement*' in the character of '*pleasure ground*', it *is*, and for these six and forty years has been the subject (as to a considerable part of it unseparated and undiscernible from the rest) the subject I say, of what may literally be termed a *destroying* lease; under which the tenant has, in pursuit of a bed of sand, carried away soil, and rooted up trees, *ad libitum*, leaving the subjacent refuse in a state as compleatly *unproductive*, as any desert in Arabia.

Of the last of these destroying leases the Tenant has 16 years more to come: but so far is this remnant from being an object of importance, formidable in respect of the probable charge of indemnification, that the Tenant treats it openly as a concern that he is every now and then tempted to abandon, the number of men

[4] 34 George III, c. 84, § x.

employable on it having been gradually reduced from 200 to 20, and the number of horses from 70 to 10, and those employed about other concerns as well as this.[5]

1153

TO EARL SPENCER

19 July 1796 (Aet 48)

Qu. Squ. Place Tuesday
19 July 1796

My Lord

The trial in which Mr Long is a witness keeps him from Office for rather an uncertain time. A day or two is so material to me, that I can not keep myself from taking the liberty of apprizing your Lordship of this accident, for the chance of a word, (if in the mean-time any opportunity should present itself of dropping one clear of all impropriety) in favour of the proposed transplantation of a certain weed from Battersea to Woolwich.—What should hinder this for example, from whisking itself across the carpet amongst other still more trifling occurrences of the day, in the intervals of more important business?

Your Lordship is too good a classic not to know, that when the spear of *Telephus* had given a wound, nothing was found so effectual, as a gentle touch of the same powerful weapon, for the cure of it.[2]

I have the honour to be, with all respect
My Lord
Your Lordship's most obedient
and humble Servant
Jeremy Bentham

Earl Spencer.

[5] The fair copy omits the following significant passage at the end of the draft: 'Driven thus from two spots to a third, the accessibility of which has been matter of recent discovery, and which, in any public point of view but that of vicinity to the Metropolis has no equal but the first, I cast myself once more upon the equity of Mr. Pitt, in confidence that the change will, as far as depends upon him, not be attended with any prejudice to me and in particular in the article of *time*, in which every article of prejudice and hardship is involved. . .'

1153. 1 B.L. VI: 224–5. Autograph draft. Docketed: '1796 July 19 / Panopt / J.B. Q.S.P. / to / Ld Spencer Admiral⟨ty⟩ / Sent open under cover to Lady Spencer.' This last note suggests that Bentham expected and intended Lady Spencer to read the letter.

[2] Telephus, King of Mysia, was the legendary son of Hercules and Auge. He opposed the landing of the Greeks on the coast of Mysia and was wounded by the

1154

From the Marquis of Lansdowne

25 July 1796

Bowood Park
25th July 1796

Lord Lansdown presents his best compliments to Mr Bentham, and would have answer'd the honour of his note[2] sooner, if he had not had a slight attack of Bile, for which he is going this Evening to Bath for a fortnight. Mr Roscoe's book is out of print, but Ld. Lansdown is to have two copies of the new edition,[3] the first of which he has order'd to be carried to Mr Bentham before they go to their final destination. As to the other matter all that he can say is, that there appear'd a vast deal of bungling between a Gentleman and Lady about a Writ, which one was to write and the other to legalize.[4] If Mr Bentham wishes to know further, he would recommend to him to apply in person to them, when they are here in September, as they are both of his acquaintance, and can inform him much better than thro' the medium of a third person. The General seems to get the stone of the Philosopher.[5]

spear of Achilles; being warned by an oracle that he could only be cured by him who had inflicted the wound he went to the Greek camp and was healed by rust from the weapon. Achilles had been told by an oracle that the Greeks could not reach Troy without the aid of Telephus, who, in return for his cure, pointed out the best route. The legend is non-Homeric; it appears in the *Telephos* of Euripides and is mentioned by Pausanias in his *Guide to Greece*, trans. Peter Levi (1971), i, 21 and n. 46.

1154. [1] B.L. VI: 226–7. Autograph, but no signature. Docketed: '1796 July 25 / Ld L. Bowood / to / J.B. Q.S.P.'
[2] Letter 1147, p. 223 above.
[3] William Roscoe's *Lorenzo de' Medici*. See above, p. 224 n. 3.
[4] Perhaps the negotiation mentioned in the letter of 3 July to Caroline Fox (1148, p. 224 above).
[5] The success of Samuel Bentham at the Admiralty and the frustration experienced by his brother.

1155

TO EVAN NEPEAN

29 July 1796 (Aet 48)

Q.S.P. 29 July 1796

I observed you t'other day in close confabulation with Mr Sollicitor White, commonly called Lord White.[2] I happen just now to stand particularly in need of the protection of that great man, and shall continue so to do for an indefinite time. The Contract is at last sent back to him to get engrossed for signature: and then comes the business of getting the land which may be accomplished this century or the next, at his Lordship's pleasure. Are you in habits of society with his magnificence? If so, it would be an act of great Charity to your humble servant if you would get him to be replenished some day with your good things, while /your humble servant/ I eat dust under his feet. This would give your said humble servant occasion to offer to both of his honoured masters such humble fare, as the house of a man who has been so long starving may afford.

1155. [1] B.L. VI: 228–9. Autograph draft. Docketed: '1796 July 29 / Panopt / J.B. Q.S.P. / to / Nepean / Admiralty / For White.'
    In B.L. VI: 239 are copies of legal opinions on the draft of Bentham's Panopticon contract, viz. 'I approve of this Draught as altered by me. / John Mitford / Lincoln's Inn / 26 Oct. 1795'; and 'I think this Drt not liable to any material objection, if the Lords Commis. of the Treasury approve the Plan itself but I think that parts of what is herein convenanted to be done must also under the Act of Geo 3, be directed to be done by his Majesty—I think the 15 Article does not clearly express to whom the Annuity therein mentioned is to be paid which should be clearly expressed. / J. Scott / Lin. Inn Decr 31 1795'.
    These copies are headed by Bentham: '28 July 1796 Long to White sending Contract for engrossing', and the sheet is docketed by him: '1796 Aug 18 / Panopt / Copy / Atty and Sollr / Genl's opinion on draught of Contract / Sollr G. 26 Oct. Atty G. 31 Decr 1795 / Long to White ordering enquiry / 28 July 1796.'
    [2] Joseph White, Treasury solicitor, 1794–1806.

1156

TO SIR THOMAS SPENCER WILSON

30 July 1796 (Aet 48)

Queen's Square Place Westminster 30 July 1796

Sir—

The object of this address, from one who has not the honour of your acquaintance, is to request the favour of your concurrence to the purchase of a minute portion of your property, under general compulsive powers given for a public purpose by an Act of Parliament, a copy of which I enclose.[2] Being for the purpose in question put in the stead of the three gentlemen therein named (Sir G. Elliot, Sir C. Bunbury and Dr. Bowdler) the business of treating for the purchase devolves upon me. In lieu of the spot therein particularized, another spot, of which a small part is your property has, in virtue of the option given by the Act, been pitched upon, as being, all things considered, more *'proper and convenient'* for the purpose. The bulk of it will be composed of some land the property of the Bow-water family:[3] viz: some of the Marsh below Hanging Wood. But for the immediate site of the building itself, and a little necessary elbow-room around it, it has been deemed necessary on the score of health, to take some elevated ground, and for that purpose to trouble you for a small portion of the Wood itself, being the part most distant from your House,[4] say about 15 or 20 Acres: including the part which Mr Harding has so long been pulling to pieces, under the powers of his Lease.

Conceiving it but natural that landed possessions, of such very ample extent, should be accompanied with an inclination rather to add to that extent than to see it *diminished*, even for what would in a mercantile point of view be a full equivalent, I could have wished rather to have seen the lot fall upon some person of moderate

---

1156. 1 B.L. VI: 230–1. In hand of copyist, except for address and date at top. Docketed by Bentham: '1796 July 30 / Panopt / J.B. Q.S.P. / to / Sr. T. Spencer Wilson, Charlton.'

Sir Thomas Spencer Wilson, 6th bart. (1726–98) was an Army general, and colonel of the 50th Regiment; he owned Charlton manor through his wife, Jane, daughter and heiress of John Badger-Weller, of Charlton. Their only son, Sir Thomas Maryon Wilson, succeeded to the baronetcy.

2 34 George III, c. 84.

3 The Bowater family.

4 Charlton House, to the east of what became Greenwich Park, 'a splendid Jacobean mansion', now a library and museum.

fortune, to whom a trifle above the market price might have given the transaction the recommendation of personal advantage: as it is, in solliciting the favour of your acquiescence, and amicable concurrence in the execution of the powers created by the Act, the only foundation on which I can build my hopes, is the assurance of meeting with that sort of disposition which will naturally be looked for as the accompaniment of large property in liberal hands, a disposition to co-operate with those views of justice, humanity, moral reformation, and national economy, which gave birth to the Act; and to take a pride in embracing with alacrity the occasion of making one of those sacrifices of private inclination to public benefit, which every good subject is prepared to make, when properly called upon by government, in return for the protection he receives from it.

The building will not be visible from your House: but tho' designed for safe custody as well as industry, it will have so little the appearance of a *prison*, or rather will have an appearance so opposite to the idea one can scarce avoid connecting with the word *prison*, that I shall be much mistaken if the study of the neighbourhood round about should not be rather to catch a view of it, than to exclude it.

The inclosed is the Act of Parliament above alluded to: the parts that appeared to call more particularly for your attention are distinguished by scoring or by brackets.

In the protective clause (Sect X) the words '*planted with wood*' might possibly present themselves, to a hasty glance, as exempting the spot in question from the general powers of the Act. They certainly would, (all but the bare spot of 4 or 5 Acres comprized in the Lease to Mr Harding.) if instead of '*planted*' '*covered*' had been the word. But (without adverting to what actually was the intention of the Noble mover of that clause) it is sufficient to say, that as well from the meaning of the word *planted*, as from the obvious intent expressed by the words that immediately precede and follow it, *plantations*, and those made for pleasure, forming a Sort of extention of the pleasure-ground, were the only sort of woodland there in view: not *natural un*planted woods, how much soever prized by the owner on the score of pleasure, much less a wood which is so far from being considered in that light, as to be left without a fence, and (in a considerable part of its extent undistinguished from the rest) given up, by two successive leases of 31 years, to a Tenant, with an unlimited power of carrying away the soil and rooting out the trees: plain proofs that the ground in question has all along been considered merely upon the footing of any other outlying part of a gentleman's Estate, as an object of income not of pleasure.

This little remark I take the liberty, Sir, of submitting to you at the first opening of the business, not as apprehending it to be at all necessary for the guidance of your own particular opinion, but with a view of its meeting any doubts or difficulties that might chance to present themselves to any gentleman of the law, whose professional assistance you might happen to call in.

The natural course I believe, Sir, will be for *you* to nominate a Land Surveyor to meet a person of the same profession nominated by *me*, for the purpose of marking out the spot in question, and taking a valuation of it: the sooner you can make it convenient to take this step, the greater the obligation you will confer on me.

In the sincere hope that this application, however unexpected, will leave no unpleasant sensation in the breast of the respectable gentleman to whom it is addressed, and in the sincere determination that, as far as depends upon myself, it shall not at any period of the business, be productive of any such effect, I have the honour to subscribe myself

        Sir
           your most obedient and humble Servant
                Jeremy Bentham
Sir Tho[s] Spencer Wilson
    etc. etc. etc.

1157

To Charles Long

4 August 1796 (Aet 48)

                    Q.S.P. August 4 1796
Sir
    In consequence of a Letter of mine sent yesterday[2] to Sir Thomas Spencer Wilson, his Land Steward, Mr Stride,[3] a respectable Attorney in Carey Street, has just been with me on the part of *Lady* Wilson,[4] stating *her* repugnance. The spot forms the

1157. [1] B.L. VI: 240–1. Fair copy, not in Bentham's hand. Docketed by Bentham: '1796 Aug 4 / Panopt / J.B. Q.S.P. / to / Long Treasury / Lady Wilson.'

[2] He clearly means letter 1156, although that draft is dated 30 July.

[3] John Stride (c. 1745–1825), attorney, of 24 Carey Street, London (see *Gentleman's Magazine*, xcv, May 1825, p. 476).

[4] See above, letter 1156, n. 1.

termination of a favourite morning's walk of her Ladyship's:-
Offers made by individuals who wanted the spot to build on had
accordingly been refused:- Lord Cholmondeley,[5] I think, was mentioned, who had actually built on a spot not very far distant—What
seems to have been forgotten at the moment, tho' it was mentioned
afterwards, is, that the Law had been beforehand in the refusal:
the Estate being in strict Settlement.—No objections to the Penitentiary Plan in general—on the contrary, an enthusiastic approbation of it.—No alarm about the intended vicinity of the Prisoners:
—for in truth the favourite walk in question can never have been
taken without seeing them, and that in a state of less secure confinement, one may venture to say, than they would be in within the
four Walls of the intended House. But the loss of the *property* of the
favourite termination of the walk was the great, though only,
grievance.—A variety of spots offered in lieu, unfortunately none
but what are a mile at least from Water Carriage: Charlton Common
the most plausible—To make the argument the stronger, a fit of
illness undertaken for on the part of the Lady in the event of a
perseverance in the choice.—Decency seemed to require of me to
direct the complaint to the real source of authority, rather than
take upon me in appearance an authority that does not belong to
me. I accordingly referred the parties to the Treasury, recommending *paper* as the proper vehicle for their representations: but her
Ladyship's Sons in Law,[6] as in duty bound, will doubtless support
the paper with their voice.

If the part I have in the choice were to be kept out of sight, the
sort of sympathy which a man can't help feeling for a Lady in her
situation, might, at a proper time, give me a *chance*, at least, of
alleviating her reluctance, by such explanations, and even accomo-
dations, as the case may be found to admit of:—on the other hand,
were I to be considered as the author, nothing I could say or do,
would have any other effect on her uneasiness, than to encrease it.—
On *my own* account, you have seen too much of me, I believe, to
attribute to me a desire of shrinking from any responsibility that
belongs to me.

Sir Thomas, it is declared, never sees any body, but his own

[5] George James Cholmondeley, 4th Earl and 1st Marquess of Cholmondeley
(1749–1827), succeeded his father as earl, 1770, and was created a marquess, 1815.
[6] Three daughters of Sir Thomas and his wife all married influential husbands: the
eldest, Margaretta Elizabeth Wilson married (1787) Charles George Perceval, Baron
Arden (1756–1840); Jane married (1790) Spencer Perceval (1762–1812), the brother
of Lord Arden and the future prime minister, who was assassinated; Maria married
Sir John Trevelyan, 5th bart.

family, and this Steward Mr Stride; nor ever visits the spot in question, or any other spot without the circuit of his own walls. Whether he keeps it or parts with it, he remains equally a prey to morbid melancholy. The property of Mr Bowater (who happens just now to be in Town) was already (Mr Stride told me) intended to be disposed of. There is therefore but one repugnant party in the case: (the Tenant (Harden)[7] having declared himself passive, referring every thing to his Landlord, whom *he* expected to find equally so:) There is therefore, I say, but one repugnant party in the case: and if the considerations which plead in favour of the choice were to be deemed insufficient to support it against an opposition of that size, you will judge, Sir, whether the task of looking out for a fourth spot after three years struggle would appear worth engaging in. I have the honor to be, with great respect,

Sir
Your most obedient and
humble Servant

C. Long Esq.
  etc. etc. etc.

1158

FROM THE COUNTESS OF ELGIN

6 August 1796

Lady Elgin presents her Compts to Mr: and Col: Bentham, and thinks it very long since she had the pleasure of seeing either of them:—Their ingenious Labours for the benefit of the Publick she often thinks of, and if they will permitt her, she means to accompany the The Lord Chief Baron[2] and Lady Louisa Macdonald,[3] on tuesday or wednesday next, as may be most agreeable to the Messrs Benthams, to see the Model of the Jail he proposes. Lady Elgin was induced to take this liberty by hearing the Chief

---

[7] Elsewhere called 'Harding'.

1158. [1] B.L. VI: 242–3. Docketed: '1796 August 6 / Panopt. / Lady Elgin Down⟨ing⟩ Stre⟨et⟩ / to J. and S.B. Q.S.P.'
  Martha Bruce (née White), Countess of Elgin (d. 1810), was the widow of the 5th Earl; she was governess to Princess Charlotte of Wales and mother of the 6th and 7th Earls of Elgin.
  [2] Sir Archibald Macdonald, bart. (1747–1826), judge; M.P., 1777–93; Solicitor-General, 1784–8; Attorney-General, 1788–92; and Lord Chief Baron of the Exchequer, 1793–1813; he was knighted in 1788 and created a baronet, 1813.
  [3] Lady Louisa Macdonald, eldest daughter of Granville Leveson-Gower, 1st Marquess of Stafford.

239

Baron has express'd so much satisfaction in seeing the improvements made in the Jails by industry, in this his late Circuit and if tuesday or wensday morning about 12 o'Clock will suit the Mr Benthams—Lady Elgin is certain the Chief Baron will receive great Pleasure from what Mr. Bentham can shew him on that Subject—

Downing Street
  6 August 1796

1159

To Joseph White

10 August 1796 (Aet 48)

Queen's Square Westmr 10 Aug. 1796

Sir

As the change in the situation intended for the Penitentiary House will necessitate a correspondent change in the terms of the instrument of appointment for the nomination of the Feoffee, I take the liberty of sending you a Draught adapted to the purpose of the new spot whatever it may be. The first Draught having undergone the revisal of the Atty General as well as your's I avail myself of it as much as possible, making no other amendments in the way either of addition, omission, or substitution than what are necessitated by the substitution of a new spot. The parts that call for fresh consideration are shewn by the difference of Inks: the words copied literally from the Old Draught being in black ink: the additions marked in the new Draught in red ink: and such words of the Old Draught as required to be omitted to make way for the new matter are written in black ink, but marked as cancelled by red ink—This communication, though in some measure premature, might, I thought, be a means of saving /some/ a little breath on your part, and by waiting your leisure be productive of a little saving perhaps in point of time.

I am
Sir
Your very obedient
and humble Servant
Jeremy Bentham

Joseph White Esqr
Sollicitor to the Treasury

1159. ¹ B.L. VI: 244–5. Autograph draft. Docketed: '1796 Aug. 10 / Panopt. / J.B. Q.S.P. / to / White Linc. Inn / with fresh Draught of Appointment of Feoffee.'

1160

FROM BARON ARDEN

10 August 1796

Sir

 Sir Thomas Wilson has communicated to me a Letter[2] from you upon the Subject of a Penitentiary House proposed to be erected upon his Ground at Charlton and I have to request that you will allow me (before any further Steps are taken in the Business) to have some Conversation with you upon it, in which I shall hope to convince you that it is impossible to expect that he should consent to make so great a sacrifice of private Comfort as is required of him, so long as he or his Family have any Thoughts of continuing their Residence at Charlton. For this Purpose I will come to Town on Saturday Morning next or any subsequent Day that may be more convenient to you, and if it should suit you to call upon me at the Admiralty[3] at any Hour you please to fix, I shall be happy to have the Honour of seeing you, or will otherwise wait upon you at your own House.

I am Sir
your most obedient
humble Servant
Arden

Hook near Epsom
10th August 1796

1160. [1] B.L. VI: 246–7. Docketed: '1796 Aug 10 / Panopt. / Ld Arden near Epsom / to / J.B. Q.S.P. / Hanging Wood.'
 Charles George Perceval, Baron Arden (1756–1840) succeeded his mother, who had been created Baroness Arden of Lohort Castle, co. Cork, an Irish peerage which permitted her son and and successor to sit in the House of Commons as M.P. 1780–1802; in 1802 he was created Baron Arden of Arden, co. Warwick, and went into the House of Lords. He married (1787) Margaretta Elizabeth, eldest daughter of Sir Thomas Spencer Wilson.
 [2] Letter 1156.
 [3] Arden was a lord of the Admiralty, 1783–1801.

1161

TO BARON ARDEN

11 August 1796 (Aet 48)

Q.S.P. Aug. 11 – 1796

My Lord

It was with much concern that I was informed of Sir Thomas Wilson's repugnance by his Land Steward, Mr Stride, who called on me the next day after the date of the Letter which your Lordship speaks of. My answer was, that the choice resting exclusively with the Treasury Board, it was thither only that any application on the subject could be directed with any effect. This being the precise state of the case, it would be obeying the *Letter* to the prejudice of the *spirit*, of your Lordship's commands were I to put your Lordship to the trouble of coming to Town for the purpose mentioned.[2] The utmost I could do would be to convey to the Treasury the substance of your Lordship's representations. By passing thro' such a medium it is impossible they should gain any thing, nor could they undergo any alteration which would not be to their disadvantage. Should it be your Lordship's pleasure to intrust me with them in your own words and to make use of me as an instrument for conveying them in that form to the proper authority, the trust would be faithfully and promptly executed.

If after all it should chance to be the pleasure of the Treasury Board to abide by the choice (a matter about which I am entirely in the dark) it might then perhaps be in my powers, as it would most sincerely be my inclination, to alleviate very considerably, if not to avert altogether, whatever apprehensions may have been suggested by the idea of a vicinity, which to a first glance can scarcely do otherwise than appear formidable.

I have the honor to be—

Lord Arden

1161. [1] B.L. VI: 248–9. Fair copy, not in Bentham's hand. Docketed: '1796 Aug 11 / Copy / Panopt / J.B. Q.S.P. / to / Ld Arden Epsom.'
Autograph draft, B.L. VI: 250–1.
[2] But he did come to see Bentham (see below, p. 243).

1162

To Samuel Bentham

13 August 1796 (Aet 48)

11 Aug. Letter from Nepean. 'The Board of Ordnance are desired to cause experiments to be made on the abovementioned Guns and Carriages by the proper officers of their Department'— You are 'to communicate with that Board upon the subject, and fix a time for that purpose'.
12 Aug. Letter from Navy Board—Sending Plans of all the Yards except Plymouth which is to be sent afterwards—'the receipt of which you will please to acknowledge'!
13—from Nepean—Direction given to Victualling Board to furnish the Plans you requested.
Lord Arden (Devil take the fellow) spite of the spear would come, and John was blockhead enough to let him in upon me—Mutual civility but you may imagine little satisfaction on either side.[2]

1163

To Charles Long

14 August 1796 (Aet 48)

Q.S.P. Aug 14 1796.
Sir,
     A Noble Lord[2] after I had plainly, tho' gently, declined a visit, which could not possibly answer any good purpose, got into my house just now by surprise, for the purpose of telling me what Friends he had. This was just what I had no doubt about—what I wished not to have heard, were it only for his Lordships sake,— and what his Lordship chose notwithstanding to make me hear, it being one of those things that will not so well bear putting upon paper. I sympathized with him:—and through sympathy forebore

1162. [1] B.L. VI: 252–3. Autograph. Addressed: 'To / General Bentham / Dock Yard / Portsmouth / On his Majesty's Service.' Postmark: 'AU.13.96.D.'.
[2] The second page of the sheet (fo. 252) ends with the copy of a letter dated 13 August, addressed to Samuel by Col. J. Byde concerning the sale of a mare to him (cf. letter 1201, n. 3).
1163. [1] B.L. VI: 255. Fair copy, not in Bentham's hand. Docketed by Bentham: '1796 Aug 13 / Panopt / J.B. Q.S.P. / to / Long Treasury / Lord A's Visit.'
     Autograph draft, B.L. VI: 254.
[2] Lord Arden.

the expression of my other sentiment:—my sympathy would be double for *two repugnant* families *elsewhere,* and for *ten,* tenfold. I, upon his Lordship's word, admitted the *repugnance*:—he seemed to admit; that it was no great wonder that local circumstances should to a stranger have appeared rather unfavourable than otherwise to the supposition of repugnance. It would not have been easy to forebear admitting it. Several acres of the elevation, as much almost as is left, carried and *carrying* away, under a destroying lease:— therefore the *elevation not valued*:—other 17 Acres contiguous grubbed up within this year or two for the sake of a rent: therefore *the wood not valued*:—for hundreds of feet together by the side of the Road, not the least remnant of a fence: for other hundreds a scrap of a fence here and there: the interior of that part a common bog for vagrants, offensive to every sense: therefore *the condition of the place not valued*:—the ground about the mansion remarkably neat and closely walled in: the *neglect* therefore *not general but local.* Indifference excepted, two only possible causes of the abandonment, poverty or penury, both in the extreme:—as to poverty £18,000 a year, and no means of spending it.

I have the honor to be etc.

C. Long Esq.
etc. etc. etc.

1164

To Samuel Bentham

15 August 1796 (Aet 48)

Q.S.P. 15 Aug. 1796

Collins insults you, and says you don't know how to get Boys: he got five of them to one girl.[2]

Your invisible Master[3] got made infamous—I hope that is all he will get by his activity. Calling on Harries[4] this morning I found him in possession of the infamous-making letter which Long after

---

1164. [1] B.L. VI: 256–7. Autograph. Addressed: 'To / General Bentham / etc. etc. etc. / Dock Yard / Portsmouth / On his Majesty's service.' Postmark (partly blurred): 'AU.15.96.'

[2] A reference perhaps to Samuel's illegitimate daughters: it is known that he had two by a Mrs Maria Burton, who mentions them in a letter to John Herbert Koe, 24 April 1816 (Koe Mss in the possession of Mrs Hyde-Smith at Wilbraham Temple, near Cambridge).

[3] Lord Spencer.

[4] Not identified.

a flying visit of half an hour had (he said) put into his hands.[5] The
name not having been mentioned, he did not know who it was I
meant: being informed, he seemed to treat the opponent as lightly
as could have been wished. But you know how little dependence
is to be placed there.

Lord White[6] has taken me into his protection. Puss himself
(Sir Tho.)[7] could not have treated me with more condescension
than his Lordship did but now.

Letter from the Admiralty that your £2000 is ordered.

1165

To Charles Long

19 August 1796 (Aet 48)

Q.S.P. 19 Aug. 1796

Mr Bentham presents his respects to Mr Long, and earnestly
begs the inclosed[2] may, if necessary, be submitted to Mr Pitt. It
contains the substance of the Letters, with some additions.

1166

To Henry Dundas

21 August 1796 (Aet 48)

Mr Dundas's assistance is humbly and earnestly requested in
support of the inclosed concentrated representation, which is to be
laid before Mr Pitt this day on his return to Town—a last gasp after
a three year's struggle.[2]

[5] Presumably letter 1163.
[6] Bentham's way of referring to Joseph White.
[7] Not identified.

1165. [1] B.L. VI: 258–9. Autograph copy. Docketed: '1796 Aug. 19 and 21 / Panopt. /
Copies / J.B. Q.S.P. / to / Long Treasury / and / R. Hon. H. Dundas Parlt Street /
Hanging Wood / Left for Mr Long 20th / —Dundas 21st.'
   The docket covers both letters 1165 and 1166 below.
   [2] Perhaps the Memorandum, dated 18 August 1796, and headed: 'reasons *in
favour of the spot near Woolwich, as a site for the* penitentiary house' (printed in
Bowring, xi, 114–15). It concludes: 'A fit site, obtainable for *such* a purpose, *without
a dissentient voice,* is the site of the *Golden Tree* and the *Singing Water:* and after a
three years' consideration, I beg to be excused from searching for it.—J.B.'

1166. [1] B.L. VI: 258–9. Autograph draft. The docket given above for letter 1165
also covers 1166.
   [2] See above, letter 1165, n. 2.

1167

TO EARL SPENCER

26 August 1796 (Aet 48)

Queen's Square Place Westminster
August—26: 1796

My Lord

It is with the sincerest regret I find myself thrown back upon your Lordship's Marsh, spite of my utmost efforts to emerge from it. As to the quantity, I acknowledge with all thankfulness the liberality of the allotment proposed to me by Mr Harrison's Letter of the 17th June. But in regard to situation, I took the liberty of stating in my last Letter to your Lordship (dated 14 July) the apprehended necessity on the score of health of including all the Timber Docks: an arrangement which would allot for the Western boundary, the Walnut-tree-Lane, leaving consequently the use of that Lane, the only existing communication with the River, as free as at present.

The length of time is so great (no less than 3 months) since the memorandum was taken which has been the foundation of my hopes in this respect, that it may be necessary I should resubmit it to your Lordship, on pain of appearing presumptuous and unreasonable: especially as though for fear of misconception your Lordship had the goodness to revise it, you took no copy of it. It is of the 26th May and run[s] in these words '*River between Battersea Bridge and Lambeth—what part of it a matter of indifference to Lord Spencer, supposed that the nearer to Lambeth the less objectionable.*'

In obedience to Your Lordship's suggestion, I had already, before the Woolwich situation was suggested to me, paid a Visit to Barnes' Common: but could see no hopes of its being deemed obtainable.

After a five or six weeks superfluous cruize, I thus find myself wrecked upon your Lordship's Coast, and have no hopes of relief but what your Lordship's goodness may afford me, which I accordingly am reduced to beg the benefit of by the earliest convenience.

Mr Pitt, after a fresh reconsideration, has ordered the Contract

---

1167. [1] B.L. VI: 262. Fair copy, not in Bentham's hand.
    Autograph draft, much altered, fos. 260–1. Docketed: '1796 Aug 26 / Panopt / J.B. Q.S.P. to Ld Spencer.'

to be engrossed for signature: and as it is a month since the order
was communicated I hope it has by this time been obeyed.

> I have the honor to be
> with all respect My Lord
> Your Lordship's most obedient
> and humble Servant
> Jeremy Bentham

Earl Spencer
etc. etc. etc.

1168

FROM EARL SPENCER

29 August 1796

Sir

I can by no means allow the Statement made in your Letter of the
26th to be a fair one, as I always had and still continue to have
very strong objections against your pursuing your plans at Battersea; and I never sanctioned the making of any Proposal to you,
except in the Event of my being actually obliged to part with one
Portion or another of my Estate in that Parish—and in that Case
it is natural to suppose that of two great Evils, I should be disposed
to prefer the smaller one, as I clearly explained to you at our last
Conference on this subject. However, if you still persist in a plan
so directly contrary to my wishes, you must not be surprised at
being told that I am determined to keep my Estate unless compelled by law to give it up.

> I am, Sir,
> Your very obedient
> humble Servant
> Spencer

Admiralty 29 Aug.t 1796
Jeremy Bentham Esqr.

1168. ¹ B.L. VI: 264–5. Original. Docketed: '1796 Aug 29 / Panopt. / Ld Spencer
Admiralty / to / J.B. Q.S.P. / Brought to Q.S.P. between 6 and 7, Aug. 30. / Puts an
end to the Treaty.'

1169

TO JOHN STRIDE

29 August 1796 (Aet 48)

Queen's Square Place Westm:r 29 Aug. 1796

Sir,

Plumstead Heath, which you had the goodness to point out to me, proved unfortunately, upon a close examination, inapplicable to the purpose.

The difficulties that attend the pursuit of a fit spot for such a purpose are far greater than what any one who had not had the unpleasant experience of them that I have had, could easily conceive. Should the following very particular and certainly altogether unexpected offer fail of being sanctioned by Lady Wilson's acceptance, the act of submitting it to her, however, will therefore, I flatter myself, under the peculiar circumstances of the case, neither be considered as indicative of any want of respect, nor on any other account be productive of displeasure.

On the former footing, the land in question being to be bought on account of Government, the price would have been to be fixed by persons appointed in part by Government, or, in case of disagreement, by a Jury. The price which I would *now* beg the favour of you, Sir, to submitt to her Ladyship is—not an *extra* price in lieu of such *estimated* price, but a clear *addition* to it, in the shape of an annuity of £500 a year to her Ladyship for her life (I think it is to her that the Estate belongs) payable out of the £12,000 a year we /my Brother aged 39 and myself aged 48/ are entitled to for our lives by the terms of the Contract agreed upon with Government.

At first glance it will appear of course as if in return for this £500 a year a prodigious sacrifice would be to be made: a sacrifice of such a sort as to be incapable of being compensated for by any such pecuniary advantage: the loss I mean of the whole comfort and satisfaction attached to the enjoyment of so favourite and desirable a spot. On a nearer view you will join with me I believe, Sir, in thinking that her Ladyship would upon the whole, even in that very point of view be no loser by the change. Except about 300 or 400 foot square of the naked elevation (not above $\frac{2}{3}$ of it) that being the

1169. [1] B.L. VI: 266–8. Autograph draft. Docketed: '1796 Aug 29 / Panopt / J.B. Q.S.P. / to / Stride Carey Street.'

space which would be walled in, and within which the building would be placed, all the rest of the ground would, to every purpose of pleasure, remain at her Ladyship's command:—with this difference that the beauties of the spot instead of lying exposed, as at present, to intrusion and defilement from every dirty vagabond, would be shared by her with no more than a single individual, a sort of tenant by her favour, who would remain her debtor for it to the last moment of his life.

These beauties would, I flatter myself, receive no small addition from a Cut from the River, winding through the bare and broken extremity of the Wood to the steepest part of the precipice. The whole spot would be inclosed by an effectual fence: and the sharing the use of it with Lady Wilson by means of a Key at her disposal is a circumstance that instead of an incumbrance would be converted into a privilege, by the chance it would present me with of seeing my labours in the service of humanity now and then honoured by her presence. The naked and broken ground, the result of Mr. Harden's operations, would at a proper season require something to be done with it: and in considering what to do with it, it would be an additional advantage to me to have the benefit of her Ladyship's taste. She would thus have the spot improved in effect for her use, but without trouble or expense.

This circumstance you will observe is of itself sufficient to make a radical difference between the present offer and all those others, whatever they may have been, that you were alluding to as having been rejected. That a Nobleman, wishing to make purchase of a spot for his own personal accomodation, should submitt to see his use of it narrowed and controuled by any body else, is a condition as repugnant to the very nature of such a transaction as it would have been unlooked for and unprecedented: whereas in my peculiar situation, wanting the spot as I do, not for personal accommodation but for a public purpose, no condition that is not prejudicial to that purpose would be so much as regarded as a sacrifice.

Nor would her Ladyship's empire /Dominion/ be confined as now within the bounds of her present demesnes /territories/. A considerable portion of the Bank of the River underneath, gained from an adjoining Proprietor would be annexed to it: and though a part might come gradually to be demanded in the shape of Wharfs and Docks for the purposes of business, yet the greater part would necessarily remain susceptible of additional beauty in the shape of Walks and Plantations in which, as in every other case of Rural Economy, use and ornament might be made to go hand in hand.

As to the Building itself, whether, notwithstanding its desti-nation, it would not be an object still more agreeable to the eye, than even a Villa built upon any of the common plans, is a question, on which even now some judgment might be formed. The peculi-arities of the intended plan of construction have afforded amuse-ment to many Ladies of the first distinction, who have viewed the models at my House. If Lady Wilson would honour me so far as to add to the number, I should be happy to wait upon her at any time for that purpose, and upon you, Sir, in the mean time, to enable you to sollicit that honour for me to advantage.

As to the inhabitants, (who would be visible no otherwise than in case of a visit made on purpose, nor then but in a distant point of view, discoverable, like bees in a hive, in an upper Story or two where the view of them is not intercepted by the Walls) instead of being the dirty and frightful objects they are at present, they will in as far as they *are* seen, be seen occupied as Workmen, and habited with as much uniformity as Soldiers, and with at least equal neatness; but beyond comparison more perfectly under command, every man of them continuing exposed the whole time to the un-remitting inspection of a Chaplain, Surgeon, and other Officers, whose central situation enables them to exercise that authority over the whole numbers without stirring from their seats.

The surrounding Walls, by which all but the elevated parts of the Building would thus be screened, might either remain of their natural colour, be concealed by a coating of invisible green, or for the sake of enlivening the approach, upon a visit to that distant part of the Wood, they might be whitened on the outside, as they are designed to be within.

Should these particulars be ever seen in their true light, I should not despair of adding her Ladyship to the number of those of whom I could mention to you, Sir, more than one, who after being made acquainted with the plan, have actually, (with a mere view of amusement)[2] taken pains to procure the Establishment to be stationed in their own *near* neighbourhood, and in their own *full* view. For my own part I consider it as a sort of Bee-hive magnified: such it is not only in its destination, but in some measure even in form.

> I am, Sir
> Your most obedient humble Servant
> J.B.

[2] The words in brackets are inserted in pencil.

P.S. Were the Postscript[3] I have to add, an attempt to induce
Mr. Stride to make a sacrifice of any interests committed to his
charge, I have heard enough to be satisfied, that it could not any
where have been more compleatly misdirected. But the service
desired is precisely the reverse: A Lady, for want of sufficient
information, conceived a prejudice against a plan of acknowledged
public utility: it consists in the using his endeavours with her for
the purpose of engaging her to make a sacrifice of such her prejudice
to her own unquestioned interest and advantage. This being the
precise state of the case, I have no difficulty in saying, nor should
have the least scruple about being known to have said, that in case
of success in an enterprize of so much difficulty and delicacy,
I should consider an additional hundred a year for the Agency as
very well earnt and very happily employ'd.

J.B.

1170

FROM JOHN STRIDE

30 August 1796

Mr. Stride presents his respectful complim.ts to Mr Bentham.
He has reced his Letter of yesterdays date and will take the earliest
opportunity of laying it before Lady Wilson with a recommendn.
to her Ladyship to wait on Mr Bentham on the Subject—or Mr.
Stride will wait on him himself after he has seen her.

Carey Street 30th Aug.st 1796

³ The postscript, understandably intended for the eyes of Stride alone, has a
separate docket: '1796 Aug 29 / Panopt / J.B. Q.S.P. to Stride Carey Street / P.S.'
1170. ¹ B.L. VI: 269–70. Docketed: '1796 Aug 30 / Panopt / Stride Carey Street / to /
J.B. Q.S.P.'
    Addressed: 'J. Bentham Esqr / Queen Square Place / Westminster.' Postmark:
'7 o'clock / 30 AU / 96 NIGHT'. Stamped: '223 H. HOLBORN 223 / Unpaid Penny
Post / LINCS INN'.

1171

To William Wilberforce

1 September 1796 (Aet 48)

Queen's Square Place 1 Sept. 1796

My worthy friend

Extraordinary Crisises call for extraordinary measures: and may even throw a veil of gravity on what might otherwise seem ridiculous.—Read the Extract underneath: it may serve as a *text* for the *practical Discourse* that follows it.

'Paris 26 Thermidor 13 Aug. Executive Directory—Public Audience of the 20 Thermidor (7 Aug.)—(Extract from the) Speech of M. Vincent Spinola,[2] Envoy Extraordinary from the Republic of Genoa to that of France.—"My Fellow-Citizens have cast their eyes upon *me*: they have thought that he who has so often had *assurances of confidence* from the *Representatives* and Generals of the *French Republic*, will have, Citizens Directors, some *title to your's.*" Reply of the President of the Executive Directory, to M. Spinola— Concluding passage—"The Executive Directory sees with satisfaction that the Genoese Government has chosen for its *Representative with the French Republic* a Citizen who has *acquired* the *reputation* of being a *friend to humanity* and to the liberty of *French Republicans.*" '

Above you see the *occasional cause* of an idea, which, however whimsical, and whether practicable or no, proves at least to have something like a foundation in *precedent* and *experience.*—We must, sooner or later, have done fighting with Pandemonium: and upon that occasion may find it advisable to look out for some sort of a *Candle* to hold to the *Princes of the Devils.*—Waiving Devils and Candles, might it not contribute to smooth the approach to Peace, if in the steps taken, whatever they may be, towards that end, use were made, in some shape or other, of some person, the choice of whom might, upon the strength of some *conspicuous* and *incon-*

1171. [1] Bodleian Library, Oxford. Wilberforce Mss. d. 13, fo. 35. Autograph. Docketed: 'Jere: Bentham Proposes negotiatg.'

Printed, with a few inaccuracies, in Bowring, x, 315–18, and in *Correspondence of William Wilberforce*, ed. R.I. and S. Wilberforce, 2 vols., 1840, i, 139–47. There is an autograph draft in U.C. CLXXIII: 3–5; this is docketed: '1796 Sept. 1 / J.B. Q.S.P. to Wilberforce Buxton / Fr. Miss.' There was also a brouillon of the letter, apparently handed to Charles Long (see letter 1180, below p. 268 and n. 6).

[2] The Marquesa Vincent Spinola, envoy extraordinary on special mission from Genoa to France, 1796–7.

testible attribute, stamped, as it were, upon his forehead, appear intended purposely as a *compliment* to *them*, and indicative of a disposition to *humour* and *flatter* them?—Now then, my good friend, where is that *sort* of person, the choice of whom, for such a purpose, could be more likely to prove flattering to them, than that of one of the *chosen few*, on whom they took it in their heads to confer that sublimest of all earthly honours—that highest of all *degrees* in the *climax* of *Equality*, the title of *French Citizen*?—Looking over the list, among the 17 of which it is composed I observe 6 British: and, among these 6, none but *yourself* and your humble Servant, that are not *reputed Republicans*, unless it be your Journeyman Labourer in the Vineyard of the Slave Trade, Mr. Clarkson,[3] of whose sentiments in constitutional matters I am not apprised.— What say you then, to an expedition to Paris upon occasion— properly dubbed and armed—not *a la J——n*[4] to *devour* the country, but *a la Wilberforce* to *give peace* to it?—the knight of Yorkshire at any rate—his *fellow-Citizen*, if so please his Knightship, in quality of his humble Squire, to keep his *armour* in order, and brush his shoes?

As to yourself, every man, since *Thales*[5] gave him the hint, '*knows himself*' at least as *much* of himself as a man *likes* to know, and therefore *of yourself* speaking *to* yourself, I need say nothing.

As to your obscure and humble *would-be follower*, who has the *prophet-like* property of being still more unknown in his *own* country than in the *next*,[6] in addition to the grand article above spoken of, the following are the titles that might help recommend him to an embrace of condescending fraternity from the 5 Kings.

1. A sketch of the *Panopticon* plan, printed by order of their *second* Assembly, with a *letter* of mine before it:—a sort of *certificate of Civism*, such as no other *Non-Frenchman* that I know of could display.

2. An invitation in form, given me here by *Talleyran*[d], in the

---

[3] Thomas Clarkson (1760–1846), who worked closely with Wilberforce for the abolition of the slave trade and slavery; he had visited France in 1789–90 to urge abolition on the French government, but he was no republican.

[4] Left thus blank in the original: identified by a footnote in the *Correspondence of William Wilberforce*, i, 140, as 'Lord Hawkesbury (Jenkinson)', i.e. Robert Banks Jenkinson (1770–1828), later 2nd Earl of Liverpool and future prime minister; as an M.P. from 1790 he was strongly in favour of war à *l'outrance* with revolutionary France.

[5] One of the seven sages of ancient Greece; he flourished *c*. 600 B.C. and founded the Milesian school of philosophy.

[6] An allusion to the saying of Jesus: 'A prophet is not without honour, save in his own country, and in his own house' (Matthew, 13: 57. cf. Mark, 6: 4; Luke, 4: 24 and John, 4: 44).

name of the *Directory* of the then *Department* of Paris, during the *Duc de la Rochefoucault's* Presidentship, to go and set up Panopticons of different sorts *there*. *Witnesses* at least, and, for ought I know, the *Minute*, are still in existence.

3. In *Brissot's* as well as *Mirabeau's* Periodicals, flaming elogiums of some extracts translated from my papers on the *Judical Establishment*, which I sent to the *first* Assembly (before they had taken to plundering etc.) and which the Abbé *Sieyes* (proverbial there for jealousy and self-sufficency) prevented in spite of the endeavours of the *Duc de la Rochefoucault, Brissot* and others, (appearing in some measure from letters of theirs in my possession) prevented, I say, from being translated by authority, and printed.

4. An acquaintance made in London with *Brissot*, in the days of his obscurity and innocence, followed by marks of esteem and confidence on *his* part, evidenced by a *bundle* of *letters* of *his*, beginning 25 Jan:y 1783, ending 6th Nov:r 1790, relicks of that *Proto-Martyr*, which happen to remain unburnt, on which a Noble Scotch worshipper[7] of his is welcome, at any time, to kiss without a fee.

Brissot used his endeavours afterwards to get me *returned* to the *Convention*, and, but for the instances of a friend of mine, (who, happening to be there at the time, feared its drawing me into a scrape) was likely, as that friend afterwards told me, to have got my name added to those of *Payne* and *Priestly*: the whole business as perfectly strange to *me*, till months afterwards, as to the Pope of Rome.—Don't let it mortify you too much, but *we three* (*2 Ps* and a *B*) were made Grandees of the first class, set down *in petto* for *Solons*, fenced off from the *gens en sous-ordre* by a Semicolon, an *impayable* Semicolon;!—*we* being thus intrenched and enthroned, *after us* they let in a parcel of '*corn-consumers*,' the *Wilberforces*, and *Washingtons—fortemque Gyan, fortemque Cloanthum.*[8]

Some friends of mine (apropos of Brissot) used to be attacking me, in those early days, for having any thing to say to so poor a creature. My defence used to be—that he seemed a quiet good-humoured sort of man, and was of use to me in procuring Books and literary information.

5. The business your Excellency would have to do, would consist

[7] Identified in the *Correspondence of Wilberforce*, i. 142, as 'Lord Lauderdale': i.e. James Maitland, 8th Earl of Lauderdale (1759–1839), Scottish advocate and English barrister; M.P. 1784–89; Scottish representative peer, 1790; at first a strong opponent of Pitt and sympathiser with the moderate revolutionaries in France; he ended his political career as a Tory.

[8] 'As strong as Gyas and as strong as Cloanthus.' They were companions of Aeneas (Virgil, *Aeneid*, v, 118–22).

principally, I suppose, in chaffering about *Colonies*. As to *this* matter, which *vanity* would join with *duty*, in engaging us *both*, to strain every nerve in the endeavour to retain whatever you were instructed to haggle for, the printed opinion of your humble Servant would give him that sort of advantage in point of *argument* and afford him such a certificate of *sincerity* in the use of it, as can hardly be to be found elsewhere—What the *Minister* says to you now, is no more than what the *man* said to you at the beginning— *We* are an infatuated people—*you* a wise one—Give us what we want, you see it will be no loss to you.—In this point of view, how much fitter a man with such opinions, than a man who could never open his lips, without impressing people with the *importance* of the *very* objects, which it was his business to *prevail* upon *them* to *give up*!

True it is, that were they to see an *Analysis* I have by me of their *favourite Declaration of Rights,*[9] there is not perhaps that being upon earth that would be less welcome to them than I could ever hope to be:—but there it lies, with so many other papers that would be equally obnoxious to them, very quietly upon my shelf: and though no man can be more averse to *simulation*, even, in the best cause, yet no man, according to my conception, is bound to suppress any ideas that he happens to have *in common* with those whom his business is to *conciliate*, still less to fling at *their heads* any that he happens to entertain *in opposition* to theirs, because no man is bound to get his *own head* broke to no use. With these reserves, what renders everything of *simulation*, the less necessary in the case in question is, a general principle of human nature, a certain propensity we have, as often as we observe a man's ideas meeting our own in a *prominent point or two*, to jump to the like conclusion with regard to all manner of *other* points. But of *all* people the most remarkable for their precipitancy in *this* way are surely the *French*. I met with a Frenchman once, whom nothing would persuade, that *Priestly*, whom he had been talking with, was not an *Atheist*, as well as *himself*, because they happened to agree on some points relative to *matter* and *free-will*. Priestly foamed with *rage* at the *imputation*: but the Frenchman was not to be *taken in*. Priestly, on *his* part, was even with him: for he would no more believe the *Frenchman's Atheism*, than the Frenchman his *Theism*. If you and I, their

[9] There are various drafts under such heads as 'Observations on the Declaration of Rights', 1796, in U.C. cxlvi: 52–237: what became *Anarchical Fallacies* translated back into English from Dumont's French version, Bowring, ii, 489–529.

adopted Brethren with our recorded merits, were to go over and shake hands with them, and call them *Fellow-Citizens*, we might say what we would for the first month at least—they would no more believe it possible for us to '*honour the King*' who sent us, than the man believed it possible for Priestly to '*fear God*.'[10]

Were it to fall to *their* lot to send to *us* on a similar errand, who the Messenger were, so long as there were nothing about him particularly offensive, would *here*, I am apt to think, be regarded as a matter of very considerable indifference. But in *their* instance, the examples of the *vent* they give in this way to their humour, good or bad, are as abundant as they are notorious. This *Spinola*, and I believe many others, on the *one* side: on the *other*, *Carletti*[11] — the Swedish Envoy whom they shut the door against t'other day—the *Pope's Nuntio* and the *Sardinian Minister* whom they sent packing, with others who might be found, I dare say, in plenty, if there were any use in it.

Suppose them, on the *other* hand, applied to in the *ordinary* way —Suppose them in that case *refusing to treat* with *your great friend*[12]—Suppose their insolence to rise to such a pitch (and to what pitch may not French insolence rise?)—Would not his *option* be rather an *awkward* one?—to deprive the country of one of two things—the *benefit* of *his services*, or the *blessings* of *peace*! Would it not be a satisfaction to *you*, *before* the dilemma came upon him, to step in and save him from it?—However *slight* the *danger* on *one* hand—however *uncertain* the efficacy of the *preventive* on the *other*, yet, the expedient being so simple and so cheap, might it not be worth while to take the *chance* of it? Has not there been an instance? Tuscany was n't it?—(the events of the time succeed one another with such rapidity that without a particular call for attention the impression vanishes)—has not there been an instance, of their actually *forcing* a *Sovereign* to *discard* his *principal Minister*? There is some difference, indeed, between *that* country, whatever it may have been, and *this* country, it is true: and thence comes the hope, that in *our* instance they might be satisfied with that sort of complimentary *sub*mission proposed, (though an instance of mere common *civility*, and no more than what *good breeding* would join with *prudence* in dictating between *man* and *man*) whereas in the *other* case nothing short of dismission could be accepted.

---

[10] An allusion to the scriptural passage: 'Honour all men. Love the brotherhood. Fear God. Honour the King.' (I, Peter, 2: 7.)

[11] Francesco Saverio Carletti, Count (1750–1803), Italian statesman.

[12] William Pitt, the prime minister.

There is the *Invasion* too:—and, though at the long run I should not much expect, that many who came over on that errand would get back again, unless by a *Cartel*, yet, make the best of it, the *final destruction* on *one* side, would be but an indifferent compensation for the *intervening confusing* on the other.

On an occasion like *this*, it is impossible for me to avoid thinking of an excellent friend of mine, an acquaintance of your's to boot, a Veteran in the trade, who, in these hard times adds great dignity to great worth, without a morsel of bread.[13] I need scarce say how absurd it will be for me to name *myself* in company with *him*, were it not for the above mentioned *accidental peculiarities*, but for which, I should as soon have thought of offering myself for the *command of an army*, as for any such purpose as the *present*.—On the supposition of *your* declining the business, I would black *his* shoes with as much fidelity as *your's* and would black them literally, rather than see him a sufferer by my means.

Your *great Friend*, were this to reach his eye or his ear, might *smile*: but there are times, in which for a *chance*, how *faint* soever, of being of use, a man may be excused for *exposing* himself to a *smile*: and (if I may address myself to you, my good friend, as to a Confessor) when, looking round me, I observe those, who, taken from a situation which was *once my own*, without any such marked though accidental recommendations, have given satisfaction in this *very* line, I fear not to say to myself—*ed io anchio*—*I too am capable of going on an errand*.

Should the *general* idea happen to meet your approbation, make whatever you think *best* of it: nor let your friendship conceive, that because it is from *me* that the suggestion happens to have come, there is any necessity of *my* having any thing more to do with it. On the other hand, should I appear capable of being made useful, make use of me in *any* way without reason. Believe me, with the truest respect and affection

Your's ever
Jeremy Bentham

W. Wilberforce Esqr.

P.S. In the Papers of this *very* day I read the following articles. Times Sept. 1. 'From the Paris Papers Aug. 25–27. Italy Aug. 6. The French, it is said, require the *exclusion* of the *Chevalier Acton*[14] from the *Ministry* of the *Court of Naples*.'

[13] Lord St. Helens, who was, for the moment, not engaged on any diplomatic mission.
[14] Sir John Francis Edward Acton, 6th bart. (1736–1811). See letter 1083, above p. 155.

Herald Sept. 1. From the Paris Papers Aug 25–27. *Rome* July 27. Concluding sentence. . . . 'The Chevalier Azzara[15] was chosen by M. Miot, and Barbery was appointed to represent the Pope. But in the *first* day the conferences were broken up, and Mr. Azzara declared *he would not treat with Barbery*, whom he looked upon as *one of the principal causes of the ruin of the State.*'

1172

To John Stride

2 September 1796 (Aet 48)

Q.S.P. 2 Sept. 1796

Mr Bentham's Compliments to /wait upon/ Mr Stride, with two copies of a Paper, one of which if presented to Lady Wilson, may assist her Ladyships judgement respecting the Penitentiary business—as it exhibits the original sketch of the Plan of management and construction since agreed to by Government. Should her Ladyship have it in contemplation to honour him with a visit, he hopes he shall be indulged with a day's notice, otherwise beside the uncertainty of his being at home to wait upon her, she would find the models covered with dust, their size rendering it impossible to keep them habitually in a state fit for a Lady's eye. Mr Bentham hopes for the favour of hearing from her Ladyship as soon as it suits her convenience, being precluded in the meantime from taking measures which it becomes urgent for him to take in relation to another spot.

[15] Don José Nicolas d'Azara (1731–1804), Spanish diplomat and writer; minister plenipotentiary at Rome, 1785–98, and at Paris, 1798–9; he became Marquis of Nibbiano in 1801 and attended the peace congress of Amiens, 1802.

1172. [1] B.L. VI: 271–2. Autograph draft. Docketed: '1796 Sept 2 / Panopt / J.B. Q.S.P. / to / Stride Carey Street / With 2 Copies of Proposal.'

1173

FROM WILLIAM WILBERFORCE

3 September 1796

Buxton, Satr night
3d Sept. '96

My dear Sir,
     My eyes smart sadly, so I must only reply in the mercantile style—'Reced your Letter,[2] and note the contents.'
     There is much in what you say, and I will turn it in my mind; but I doubt if anything can be made of it, for Reasons which I should have no scruple to tell you, but which [I] don't care to *write*. You mention no more about your own affair, than if no such thing had ever existed: it was wrong; because you might be sure I should wish to know the state of it. I hope, yet I fear to draw the inference, that all is at length well over. Farewell—continue to think of me as of one who is, with every friendly wish, sincerely yours,

W.W.

P.S.—Do you in one part allude to Ld St Hns?[3] I have a reason for asking.

1174

TO CHARLES LONG

5 September 1796 (Aet 48)

Queen Square Place 5 Sept 1796

Sir
     I now take the liberty of pointing out a *fourth* spot for the Penitentiary-House. From one of the *pleasantest*, I descend at once to one of the *vilest*. I can descend no lower.

1173. [1] Bowring, x, 318–19, amended from a copy of the missing original in Bentham's letter to his brother of 12 September (letter 1180). There Bentham also quotes from his reply to Wilberforce of 6 September (letter 1175).
     [2] Letter 1171.
     [3] Lord St Helens (see letter 1171 n. 13, p. 257 above).
1174. [1] B.L. VI: 275. Fair copy, not in Bentham's hand. Docketed: 'Tothill Fields for Pan'. Another fair copy, VI: 276.
     Autograph draft, B.L. VI: 273–4. Docketed: '5 Sept. 1796 / Panopt. / J.B. Q.S.P. / to / Long / Treasury / Tothill Fields pointed out.'

Tothill Fields is the Lord's Waste. The quantity of ground according to a rough guess, assisted by stepping, is much upon a par with Battersea Rise 80 acres.[2] The Lords are the Dean and Chapter of Westminster. It does not bring in a single farthing to them. The only uses made of it are as follows—

1. The inhabitants of St. Margaret's and St. John's exercise the right of throwing down *Rubbish* in any quantity, subject to the controul of the Field Keeper as to the spot.
2. The Westminster Scholars, during a determinate portion of the year, make use of it for *Cricket.*
3. The Inhabitants of the above mentioned populous Parishes exercise the right of turning in all sorts of Cattle and Poultry without stint.

1. For *Rubbish*, I would reserve a spot amply sufficient.
2. The Cricket I would engage, not only to *reserve*, but to *keep* in proper *order* and embellish, a portion equal to the largest *inclosed* Cricket Ground, for the perpetual accommodation of my School-fellows.
3. As to the right of Pasture, being shared amongst so vast a *multitude* of Commoners, it has scarcely an assignable Value in the existence of any*one*. It is besides much diminished by Roads, by the indiscriminate dispersion of the Rubbish, and by extensive quagmires. Such as it is, they would, in respect of compensation, stand in the place of the Lessees and Occupiers of grounds enjoyed in severalty. The consideration-money to the Dean and Chapter would be so much clear gain to them.

To give the spot the indispensable communication with the *River* there would need no further purchase, other than that of a *Meadow*, in extent about 5 acres, in length from Tothill Fields to the River Wall not above 250 yards. It is bounded on the North (that is towards Westminster Bridge) by a Nursery Ground; on the South (that is towards Battersea Bridge) by a Meadow at the back of Campbell and White's Timber Wharf.[3] It is perfectly out of the view of *Ld Belgrave's House*,[4] being screened from it by *Buildings,*

[2] Marginal note in Bentham's hand: 'Scarce 60 I doubt'.
[3] Campbell and (John) White, timber merchants, Millbank.
[4] Robert Grosvenor, 2nd Earl Grosvenor and 1st Marquis of Westminster (1767–1845), succeeded his father as earl in 1802; at this time he was Viscount Belgrave; M.P., 1788–1802; a lord of the Admiralty, 1789–91, and a Commissioner of the Board of Control, 1793–1801. He acquired the Egerton estates by marriage, 1794, rebuilt Eaton Hall, Cheshire, and laid out Belgravia in London after 1826. He and his father, the 1st Earl, strongly opposed Bentham's scheme for Tothill Fields; see L. J. Hume, 'Bentham's Panopticon: an administrative history—I', *Historical Studies*, lxvi (1973), 714.

as well as by extensive and thickly planted Nursery Grounds and as far as I can guess not less than *half a mile* distant.[5] This which in the instance of a *Villa* might be termed vicinity, would hardly, I presume, be deemed so in the instance of a *Town* Residence: expecially a Town Residence set down so oddly and in so mean a neighbourhood.

There neither is nor used to be any sort of *communication*, even for Foot-passage between Tothill Fields and *Milbank*. No resort of Prison Company would therefore be drawn to the place last mentioned—Tothill Fields is a perfect *Cul-de-sac*: and so it might remain.[6]

Tothill Fields is a proverb, and ranks with *Hockly in the Hole*.[7] Nothing can well be meaner than the streets in its immediate vicinity. Close by has been *lately* built the Prison called *Tothill Fields Bridewell*: and the neighbourhood swarms with *Charity Schools* and *Alms Houses*—The neighbourhoods in which the *new* Prisons at *Newington Butts*, *St George's Fields* and *Cold Bath Fields* have so lately been set down, are much more respectable. In lieu of its present and primeval ugliness it would receive whatever degree of neatness and embellishment I might be capable of giving it.

I have the honour to be etc.

1175

To William Wilberforce

6 September 1796 (Aet 48)

Q.S.P. 6 Sept 96

Reading is worse for eyes than writing. Hence my Laconism. Hence too the suppression of the P.S. on the other side—nor would I mix microscopical objects with telescopical ones.

Your guess about the person alluded to was right. When do we see you *here*? Can't a Servant write for you?[2]

[5] Marginal note in Bentham's hand: '706 Yards'.
[6] Marginal note in Bentham's hand: 'True in substance, though not literally'.
[7] A disreputable district adjoining Clerkenwell, in London; the 'Hole' was the hollow through which the 'Hol-bourne' flowed—present-day Holborn.
1175. [1] B.L. VI: 288 and B.L. VI: 278. The originals of both this short letter to Wilberforce and the postscript are missing: the former is, however, quoted in Bentham's letter to his brother of 12 September (letter 1180), and there is an autograph draft of the postscript in B.L. VI: 278.
[2] In the letter to Samuel (1180) Bentham adds: 'There followed a newspaper article, about a Minister from Geneva, whom the Directory had been forcing away

To Wilb:
   Panopticon

P.S. As to *Panopticon*, it was a month since the Contract, after a fresh reconsideration by Mr Pitt,[3] was sent to Lincolns' Inn to be engrossed for signature: and in short, if it could be made to hang in the Air without hanging over any body's head, it might be built at any time. In exoneration of Ld Spencer's Marsh, which after having proffered itself groaned bitterly, I have just been making an attempt to hang it upon Hanging Wood, a few yards from the spot where the proposed inhabitants have been floating for so many years: the enclosed paper represents the *Reasons*:[4] As to the event, one of the Nymphs of the Wood is the Wife of Lord Arden, who descended in his own shape to drive me from that Paradise: so that there is no such veil over the *repulsive cause*, as covered Battersea Rise for so many years. As for you my friend, say nothing about the matter, for the decree[?] is passed.

6 Sept

Ld Spencer says now to me, and in writing—'*compel*' me to give you the *Rise*, and I will give you—*not that* but the *Marsh*: otherwise neither.

I seem likely now to get Tothill Fields: I shall perhaps know tomorrow: as soon as *I* know, *you* shall: but for fear of opposition, pray, pray keep silence.

1176

To Samuel Bentham

7 September 1796 (Aet 48)

Times   Wednesday – September 7 – 1796[2]

A Gentleman having formed a plan for a daily publication, wishes to engage with a Gentleman of character who can advance a few hundred Pounds to carry the Plan into execution: the nature

by "*declaring that his person was no longer agreable to them*". I had sent him another similar instance, the day before, without comment.'
   [3] Marginal addition: 'in confabulation, actual or intended, with the Chancellor, both converted by the drop of an impotent hand from Battersea Rise'.
   [4] A cross at this point refers to a note at the end of the postscript: 'Not sent'.
   1176. [1] B.L. VI: 279–80. First paragraph in copyist's hand, remainder in Bentham's.
   Addressed: 'To / General Bentham / etc. etc. / Redbridge / near Southampton.'
   Postmark: 'SE.7.96E'.
   [2] The paragraph which follows is copied from *The Times* newspaper of that date.

whereof is such, that with but little trouble and no risk it will produce many thousand pounds per annum and may from its obvious vast utility be extended not only all over Great Britain but also Ireland, an immense income will in that case result—The abovementioned plan would be beneficial to the proprietor of any Newspaper; and the Advertiser presumes it may be necessary to assure such of those Gentlemen as may not chuse to engage with him, that his plan cannot in the least injure their Publications, it being of such peculiarity, that nothing of the kind has ever been thought of by any person but himself. The Advertiser is aware that this Advertisement may excite mere curiosity in many and therefore desires he may not be troubled by any other but men of honour. Address post paid, to A.Z. at the Globe Tavern, Fleet Street.

The above alarmed me—you know why—supposing it mine how could he have got it—From any indiscretion of Jack's—From any treachery? He is so dark, and I am so perfectly unacquainted with his designs, that I can have no conviction of the negative.

About a month ago he had somebody call on him—and they were together in the Garden for a long time—part of the time when you and I were in consultation there—Who it was I did not see.

Last Sunday sennight or the Sunday before I don't know much— (I think it was on that day of the week but am not sure) he dined out. When he asked leave, I asked whether it was with his Mother? —No—It was with a Friend—Who the Friend was I did not ask, and accordingly do not know—I should like to know now, who it was—and who were of the party—just for the purpose of guessing whether it were likely my project[3] should have transpired by any such means—If you see any chance of getting satisfaction about it, do try—I know so well what the answer to a question put in that view would be, viz: the negative, howsoever the case were, that I should not think it worth while—or rather for fear of exciting his suspicion and putting him upon his guard, should avoid it. Jack had been occupied a good deal about the business in question, and had even gone through a whole weeks Papers, London and Country

---

[3] Bowring says that Bentham gave him in 1827 an account of this newspaper project: 'I considered that the number of advertisements was immense. No man had time to read every advertisement. The scheme was to publish every day a paper, called "The Indicator", the object of which was to lead to the paper where the advertisement was, but not to give information enough without reference to the original paper . . . The thing that cooled me was the knowledge that it could not go on without government. I mentioned it to George Rose, but he knew a peremptory refusal would meet any proposal of mine' (Bowring, x, 322–3). Material headed 'Indicator', a newspaper 'to index the whole body of national intelligence' is preserved in U.C. cviii: 2–99.

in that view—The only reason of my staying my hand was, the apprehension of risking money in the present state of pecuniary matters, after the uncertainties that Skinner had suggested from the experiences that had fallen within his observation of the arbitrariness of the Stamp-Office people—threatening prosecutions of periodical papers containing *no news*—nothing but mere Essays— and such accordingly he said, was Reeve's *Tomahawk*[4] for which the Editor was not only prosecuted but convicted.

Skinner, upon his own offer, on my showing him the advertisement, has been writing an answer in his own name, for the purpose of endeavouring to obtain an explanation.

Long is *mightily* pleased with the idea of Tothill Fields. I saw him while he read a letter about it, on *Monday*. He is to go there— but could not find time today nor will he, as I understand him, till he has mentioned it to Pitt, which however he is to do by the first opportunity. He supposes Pitt will come into it. Fortunately the owner of the Meadow of Communication is—not Ld Belgrave, but the Marqs of Salisbury[5] who is selling Estates in [a] great hurry and to a disadvantage. It was even before he knew this that Long expressed his approbation.

W. W. *Buxton* to J. B. Sept. 3.[6]

'There is much in what you urge, and I will turn it in my mind, but I doubt if anything can be made of it, for reasons which I should have no scruple to *tell* you, but which I don't care to *write*.'

P.S. Do you in one part allude to Ld St H.? I have a reason for asking.' Letter short because 'eyes smarting sadly'—the rest immaterial asking about Panopt.

Reced 6 Sept.—answered same day about Panopt. and that his *guess* was right.[7] Sent him another instance of a Minister sent packing (Reybas[8] the Genevan Resident Dumont's friend) because not agreable to the Directory.

Pears sent to Foulds[9]—and bringing *Eel* sent in return.

[4] *The Tomahawk, or Censor General*, a newspaper launched on 27 October 1795; it appeared daily from 29 October until 7 March 1796, when publication ceased owing to a prosecution by the stamp office.

[5] James Cecil, 7th Earl and 1st Marquis of Salisbury (1748–1823), M.P. 1774–80; succeeded his father, 1780; created a marquis, 1789. He held various minor offices, including that of Lord Chamberlain of the Household, 1783–1804, and joint Postmaster-General, 1816–23. He owned part of the Millbank estate where Bentham wanted to build his Panopticon.

[6] Quotations from the letter of Wilberforce printed above (letter 1173).

[7] That is, Wilberforce's guess that Bentham was alluding to Lord St Helens, in his letter of 1 September (1171).

[8] Letter 1175, including its postscripts. Reybaz, like Dumont, was a former member of Mirabeau's *atelier* (see *Correspondence*, iv, 93 n.).   [9] Not identified.

264

1177

FROM BARON ST HELENS

10 September 1796

Bath 10th Sept.r 96

Many thanks to you, my dear Sir, for your obliging communication of your epistle to Mr Wilberforce,[2] which I have perused
with much satisfaction and *relish*, it being perfectly in your own
inimitable style of *Cookery*, both as to flavour and seasoning. You
may be assured that there is nothing whatsoever in your project
that can exhibit you in the character of an *intrigant*, or in any other
colours than your true and proper ones of a most zealous and
disinterested Publicolist.[3] But, for the rest, tho' I am sincerely of
opinion, that, *quoad J.B.* nobody could be better fitted than yourself
for the Commission in question, I must confess that I have my
doubts whether your quality of Fr. Citn. instead of adding to your
recommendations as much as you seem to suppose, would not on
the contrary be somewhat of a draw-back. For tho', in ordinary
times, it is undoubtedly the part of a judicious Government to select
for it's agents abroad such persons as will probably be agreeable to
the Sovereigns to whom they are deputed: yet, in the present
circumstances and considering the present humour of the French,
it seems to me that a compliment of that sort would be wholly
unseasonable; since it would be next to impossible to prevent it's
wearing the appearance of a most unworthy and degrading compliance with their arrogant and unwarrantable pretensions. You
will perhaps make light of this scruple and reply to it by asking with
honest Flewellyn 'What! because the Enemy is an Ass and a Fool
and a prating Coxcomb, is it meet, look you, that we should also be
a Fool and an Ass, and a prating Coxcomb?'[4] I answer, Most
certainly not: but there is a wide difference between imitating the
extravagancies of an Enemy, and the refusing to give way to them;
and tho' I am ready to admit that in the course of events the
circumstances of the two countries might be such as to warrant the

1177. [1] B.L. VI: 281–2. Autograph. Docketed: '1796 Sept. 10 / Ld St Helens / Bath / to
J.B. Q.S.P. / Fr. Miss.'
Printed in Bowring, x, 319–20.
[2] Evidently a copy of letter 1171, sent with a missing letter from Bentham.
[3] *Publicola*, a Roman cognomen for 'a friend of the people'.
[4] An almost correct quotation of Fluellen's remark to Gower in Shakespeare's *King
Henry V*, IV, I.

French in imposing and our Govt in subscribing to highly disadvantageous terms of peace with respect to Territory etc., yet I do aver that no advantage of War could entitle them to interfere in the slightest Respect in our domestick Government; and that it would be our duty to resist any such pretention to the last gasp of our existence: and for this plain reason, that to submit to it would be in fact to cease to exist as an independant Nation. Accordingly, putting the case which you suppose, and which is in truth not unlikely to happen, that the French should require the dismission of Mr Pitt, as they have required that of the K. of Sardinia's Minister—the Comte de Hauteville,[5] I am persuaded that the consequence would be an unanimous address of both Houses to H.M. praying him to continue Mr. Pitt in office. Nay more, I have that opinion of Mr. Fox's character that I am more than half inclined to believe that he would be the very man to move the Resolution. There is, I own, a great deal of *ipse dixit* in all this; but I am the rather inclined to trust my own judgement upon the point in question, from my having had repeated occasion to observe that my feelings in matters of this kind, as compared with those of my Countrymen in general, are much more apt to be under than above the Standard *Spirit-Proof.*

I must moreover assure you that my objection as stated above does not arise from any jalousie de metier: for tho' I do not care to diminish the favourable opinion that you are pleased to entertain of me by any over-frank confession, and tho' if the Commission in question were tendered to me I should probably accept it, yet I am quite certain that I should be infinitely better pleased both in the publick account and on my own to see it entrusted either to yourself or to Mr Wilberforce.

I am just arrived from Bristol, where I have been, partly to visit a sick friend, and partly to try to get rid of a troublesome Cough which has been hanging upon me the whole summer. But those waters have done me no manner of service, and I have in truth little reason to hope that these will be more efficacious, and I therefore propose returning in about a fortnight to town, where I hope to have the pleasure of finding you.

believe me, Dr Sr, ever faithfully yrs

St. H.

[5] See letter 1171, p. 256.

1178

To Samuel Bentham

10 September 1796 (Aet 48)

Q.S.P. 10 Sept 1796

Your letter² to me on the back of that to Ld Spr had neither
time nor place—No more had the one to Ld Spr: but in this last
you spoke of observations made on the Gunboats at Portsmouth.
From this I collected that the letter was written at Portsmouth
(understanding Redbridge to have been the place you went to first)
and having I believe received a letter dated from thence. From
these data I concluded your said letters to have been written from
Portsmouth: Portsmouth therefore being the place to which you
wished to have your letter to Ld Sp. *'returned,'* 'by return of Post,'
Portsmouth was the place to which my packet of yesterday³ was
accordingly directed. Now this morning comes a short letter⁴ from
you dated from Redbridge.

My packet of Yesterday contained a copy of your Ld Spencerian
letter, with correction to one part, and a various lection for the
remainder: but in substance scarce any difference.

I therein also told you that *Crew*⁵ told Lloyd there would be no
money till next week: that the course would be Buller⁶ would call
to see the Carriages, and that if he reported them *proper*, then that
would be done whatever it was which would be proper to be done.

I saw Nepean just now by accident, who told me that an Imprest
Bill for £1000 was then lying upon his table. I begged him for God
sake to send it to you without delay—which he said he would do:
but whether it will be directed to Redbridge or to Portsmouth is
more than I can say.

Lloyd declares himself incapable of instructing Mr J. Peake
without seeing him.

I shall send duplicates of this: one to Portsmouth, the other to
Redbridge.

1178. ¹ B.L. VI: 283. Autograph. Addressed: 'To General Bentham / etc. etc. / Redbridge, near Southampton / On his Majesty's Service. Duplicate sent to Portsmouth.'
Postmark: 'SE.10.96.D.' Stamped: 'Tothill Stree[t] Westm.'
² Missing.
³ Packet, including the copy of Samuel's 'Ld Spencerian letter'. missing.
⁴ Also missing.
⁵ Not identified.
⁶ Not identified.

267

1179

FROM SAMUEL BENTHAM

11 September 1796

Portsmouth Sept. 11 1796

I came here chiefly for the purpose of finding your letter supposing you would send it to where my letter came from. I have just copied out and dispatched my letter to Ld Spencer[2] and am returning to Redbridge to dinner there I shall remain till Wednesday evening if I hear nothing otherwise from Ld S. Your friend Mr Rose and his friend Captn Mcintosh[3] have been to see my Vessels. I dine with him on Tuesday. He talked about Pan:[4] that it must be settled somewhere and was glad to hear of Tothill fields.

I began this letter on the road, am now at Redbridge, have rec'ed the Bill from Nepean and am going to return it directed to J. Martin Esqr M.P.[5] Lombard Street Sunday. I must send express to Southampton.

If you have any instructions for Rose write by return of Post.

1180

TO SAMUEL BENTHAM

12 September 1796 (Aet 48)

Q.S.P. 12 Sept. 1796

I have received your letter[2] written with the impression of the inconveniences resulting from the want of the *local* part of the date full in your mind, and still without date.—Can't you make it a

---

1179. [1] B.L. VI: 284–5. Autograph. Docketed: '1796 Sept 11 / Panopt T. Fds. / S.B. Redbridge to J.B. Q.S.P. / Rose. Tothill Fds.'
 Addressed: 'J. Bentham Esqr / Queen Square Place / Westminster.' Postmark: 'SE.12.96.B'. Stamped: 'SOUTHAMPTON'.
 [2] Presumably the corrected version mentioned in letter 1178.
 [3] Captain William Macintosh, who took part in Macartney's mission to China, and privately criticised it in a letter to Rose (*Diaries and Correspondence of George Rose*, ed. L. V. Harcourt, 2 vols. 1860, i, 124–6; see also J. L. Cranmer-Byng, ed., *An Embassy to China*, 1962, pp. 311–13).
 [4] The Panopticon penitentiary.
 [5] Probably James Martin (1730–1810), M.P. for Tewkesbury, 1776–1807, and a member of the banking family.
 1180. [1] B.L. VI: 288–9. Autograph. No docket or address.
 [2] Probably the short one, mentioned in letter 1176 above.

general rule, that the name of the place you write from shall be the
first word in every letter?—If you don't know where you are, ring
the Bell, and ask your Servant: Be so good to consider that this
pretty effusion of genius and fine-gentleman-ship cost me eight
and forty hours of uneasiness—that for a long time I did not know
what to do—and that when I bethought myself of the expedient,
being imprisoned in Long's Lobby, and not having time to make
the Duplicate myself, I was forced to expose your Wolchekism[3] to
Boys.[4] If this scolding makes you angry, so much the better: it will
give you the better chance for remembering it.

That cursed Long who was to have been at office today, is not nor
will be: but will be, they say, tomorrow. Unfitness for everything
else sets me a chattering to you on paper.

Let Paris mission be the theme. Finding the Times positive that
the appointment was made, and that young Jackson (you know
who he is) was the man,[5] I thought that nothing could be gained by
waiting for Wilberforce's meditations, nor any thing hazarded by
taking another chance. Accordingly on Friday (as I believe I hinted
to you) I put the Brouillon of the Letter[6] you read into his hands,
without telling him the subject, but with an apology for its being
a brouillon, viz: that if the requisite time were taken for copying
it, it might be too late to answer any purpose, if it were not already.
When I mentioned the word Brouillon—Oh says he, that does not
satisfy—I know what your Brouillons are—I am used to your
Brouillons—whether this was meant as a compliment or no I could
not tell—he told me he could not read it then—but would read it in
the carriage, when he went from thence, and return it me the next
morning. As he seemed to like my *Tothill Fields* Letter,[7] I thought
he might possibly like the *Mission* letter, which would be a slight
collateral use, the principal one going to the Devil of course. The
next day, Saturday, on my sending in my name a little after *12*, he
sent out word that he would see me presently—but the Devil a bit
did he send out to me till 3, when, being unable to stay longer on
account [of] an accepted Bill which made it necessary for me to go

[3] Stupidity?
[4] Perhaps he means the young men in the house who copied letters for him.
[5] *The Times* of 10 September 1796 incorrectly stated that whereas yesterday
morning's papers had said Thomas Grenville would be sent on a peace mission to
Paris, Jackson would be going. Actually it was Lord Malmesbury who went on an
unsuccessful peace mission in October. Francis James Jackson (1770–1814) had been
secretary of legation at Berlin and Madrid, and in fact was sent as ambassador to
Turkey later in 1796.
[6] That is, a draft of the letter to Wilberforce of 1 September (letter 1171).
[7] Probably letter 1174.

to a Bankers in the Borough, off I marched without his having the civility to send out to me, or I the courage to force myself in—there being always somebody else either with him or waiting for him. Wilberforce to J.B. Copy including the extract before given.[8]

Reced the above, 6 Sept. Answered same day as follows

Q.S.P. 6 Sept 96

Reading is worse for eyes than writing. Hence my Laconism. Hence too the suppression of the P.S. on the other side (It was about Hanging Wood etc.)—nor would I mix microscopical objects with telescopical ones.

Your guess about the person alluded to was right. When do we see you *here*?—Can't a Servant write for you?

There followed a newspaper article, about a Minister from Geneva, whom the Directory had been forcing away by '*declaring that his person was no longer agreable to them.*' I had sent him another similar instance, the day before, without comment.

From his silence after I had written as above, in answer to the question put to me, I am half inclined to think that he had been writing on the subject to town, and would not write again till he had taken time for seeing what effect his letter may have produced. On my mentioning his name to Long as privy to the business, Long said *he* had just been receiving a letter from him. He did not mention on what subject—it can hardly have been *that*.

All this while no letter from St. Helens. This silence rather chagrined me—fearing that some how or other the communication might have chagrined him. From this apprehension I was relieved just now by the following letter.[9]

I send a copy of the Tothill Fields letter for the chance of your being able to find means to make Rose mention the spot in a letter to Pitt: which will oblige Pitt to *read it*: whereas Long, while there is more pressing matter may be unable to make him hear of it. Caution Rose not to speak of it, lest there should be an opposition in

[8] A copy of the letter of 3 September follows: it is given in letter 1173 above, amended from the version printed by Bowring, and is not printed again here.

[9] An extract from the letter of 10 September from Lord St Helens (1177) follows, beginning 'Many thanks to you, my dear Sir, for your obliging communication. . .' and ending 'and for this plain reason to submit'. Bentham goes on 'What is between I omit for want of time' and he then quotes the last paragraph but one of the same letter, from 'I must moreover assure you . . .' to 'to yourself or to Mr Wilberforce'. Bentham adds '(Then follows about his health)'.

Parliament which would give trouble and consume time—Opposition elsewhere ⟨. . .⟩ to such a quantity of pecuniary interest in ⟨. . .⟩¹⁰

1181

To Baron St Helens

c. 12–13 September 1796 (Aet 48)

Q.S.P. September, 1796

My dear Lord,

Make yourself easy—no such tender will be made to you. The Ethiopian must have changed his skin, before anybody who is eminently fit for a business will be charged with it. Since, therefore, you will risk nothing by the promise, promise me, that if you go, you will take me with you; not as Secretary of Legation for the reasons that *you* mention, but without a title, character, and even for reasons that *I* will mention, without so much as my own name. My person, such as it is, has the honour to be sufficiently unknown to them; but my name in that conspicuous, and at the same time subordinate situation, might impregnate them with umbrage. An adopted French citoyen, the third man in the universe, after a natural one, put under a vile aristocrat, a malignant, who bears the mark of malignancy upon his very name—a colleague and confederate of the *ci-devant* monarchy, a crony and support of the *ancien régime*!

*   *   *²

French citizenship, no, never! My name is John Brown. I am sober and honest—capable of bringing a parcel from Paris to London, when it is made up; and even of copying a letter if bid, after a little instruction from a master, though not a writing one. My business would be to make myself master of the freshest discoveries in French chemistry, and my amusement to pick up what political intelligence I could from your lordship's *maitre d'hôtel*, and principal valet-de-chambre.

Your lordship's history of future contingents I admit to be correct

---

¹⁰ The rest of the sentence is written along the edge of the paper and is illegible at the two points indicated.

1181. ¹ Bowring, x, 320. A reply to letter 1177, which Bentham mentions receiving on 12 September (p. 270 above), so this one may be dated that day or the next.

² Footnote in Bowring: 'Here there is a partly obliterated Latin quotation, which which cannot be satisfactorily made out.'

as far as it goes; but my copy happens to have another page in it. The resolution was moved, carried, as yourself has it, by Mr Fox, (Mr Pitt being absent), and carried without any dissentient in the lower house; and without any but Lord Stanhope's in the upper. Message from his majesty full of satisfaction, firmness, and dignity. But then next day came Mr Pitt with a speech, the most brilliant of any upon record, expressing in proud language, his humble, but unalterable resolution, on no consideration whatever, to stand between his country and the blessings of peace.

As to the dukedom that he got, and the pensions and grants of land confirmed by parliament, and the cenotaph prepared for him by his father's side, with the most brilliant toasts of the speech sparkling in capitals on the pediment, are they not written in the chronicles of the kings of Johanni-taurinia?

1182

FROM SAMUEL BENTHAM

13 September 1796

Redbridge Sept. 13 – 96

Banks[2] and his wife were at Rose's.[3] They had been there two or three days. We talked about Tothill fields: both agreed in its being the best of all places. I read them 3 or 4 lines of your letter.[4] Banks was for your obtaining the *consent* of the Westminster boys, seeming seriously to think they ought to be consulted. I should think therefore the less you said on that subject the better. The giving them leave to play at Cricket and the making the place ornamental as a Cricket ground may be pleasant enough to do, but it may be inconvenient to make any engagement for so doing. Rose will be in Town on Monday and I suppose would rather be disposed

1182. [1] B.L. VI: 291. Autograph. Docketed: '1796 Sept 13 / Panopt. / S.B. Redbridge / to / J.B. Q.S.P. / Tothill Fields Rose and Banks.'
Addressed: 'J. Bentham Esqr / Queen Square Place / Westminster.' Postmark: 'SE.15.96.B'. Stamped: 'SOUTHAMPTON'.
[2] Probably Henry Bankes (1756–1834), M.P. for Corfe Castle, 1780–1826, and later for Dorset. He went to Westminster School, then to Cambridge University. His wife was Frances, daughter of William Woodley (1728–93), governor of the Leeward Islands. Bankes was a Pittite; he had long been known to Samuel (see *Correspondence*, iii, especially 152 and n. 2).
[3] George Rose had purchased an estate and house at 'Cuffnels' (Cuffnells or Cuffnalls) near Lyndhurst, Hants, in 1784. This became his principal country residence: he also had a small house at Christchurch.
[4] Letter 1180.

to help the business if it comes across him but I found no opportunity of making him take an active part.

I may possibly be in Town Fryday perhaps not till Sunday. I think as Ld St Helens with respect to making any parade to them about choosing out a person they are likely to approve; but yet that such a person would be preferable ⟨if?⟩ all such intentions were discussed. It should be from general abilities and confidence he should appear to be chosen, the other should be only a lucky accident, which should make it more difficult for them to find any personal objections to.

Nothing from Ld S.[5] I suppose I have promised too much and they think they should see something bef⟨ore⟩ they believe more.

1183

To Samuel Bentham

13-15 September 1796 (Aet 48)

J. H. Babb to J.B. Q.S. Place 13 Sept. 1796

Sir

'Wishing to accommodate Gen.l Bentham as soon as possible, I am now treating with a gentleman in the neighbourhood for a House—And my concluding with him will much depend upon your answer, whether it will be most convenient to you that I should quit your premises at Michaelmass or Christmas.'

I have been with him in consequence, and the House he is in treaty for, he tells me is Mr *Dive's*,[2] the House with 4 Windows looking upon and contiguous to the Q.S.P. Paddock, in a line with the end of the Island. This offer you see is quite explicit: and yet he does not know what the rent of the House is yet—is afraid of its being too high and seems determined not to give above £60, if so

[5] Lord Spencer.

1183. [1] B.L. VI: 290. Autograph, starting with a quotation from a letter of John H. Babb's, dated 13 September.

Addressed: 'To General Bentham / etc. etc. etc. / Redbridge / near Southampton / To be kept till / the General's return / if gone from Redbridge.' Postmark: 'SE.15. 96.F.'

[2] The Dive family had owned no. 1 Queen Square (later no. 40 Queen Anne's Gate) since 1726. John Dive had occupied it until 1767, then the Hon. Dorothy Dive, 1768–73; and after that another occupant, Louis George Dive, 1779–96. John H. Babb secured tenancy 1797 and was followed by Humphrey Babb, 1798–1801. Bentham himself then secured a lease and put in James Mill as the tenant, 1814–31, after which John Bowring occupied the house (see London County Council, *Survey of London*, vol. XI, *The Parish of Saint Margaret, Westminster*, part 1, L.C.C., 1926, pp. 106, 142).

much. I told him where you were, and engaged for his having an answer by return of post.

As to your answer, I wish most ardently you were settled and would therefore be proportionably glad that you had Babb's at the earliest period viz: Michaelmas, if that would accelerate it. But if there is nothing to do at Babb's till the work at Brigstone's[3] is finished, and that can not be finished before Christmas, it would be only flinging £10 away to take the House sooner: or rather taxes included £13, £14 or £15.

Saw Mr Long again. Has not seen Pitt since, but so sure of his consenting that he would almost take upon himself the ordering the requisite steps to be taken. He would have had me take the Land at once, and run the risk of consent and so forth: I said I would do any thing he would bear me out in, but when I observed, that if the Building was erected under a possession so acquired, any *Commoner* might pull it down, he acknowledged there must be a new Act, but with a long face: and said he would mention it to Mr Lowndes and if he approved of it give directions for a new Act. In conclusion I made him promise to speak to Pitt about it, the next time he saw him, which may be, he says, tomorrow.

I dine today at Metcalfe's, in consequence of an invitation sent to us both pretty early in last week, which I forgot to tell you of.

Your letter of yesterday is delivered to Capt. S.[4]

This was omitted to be sent on Tuesday (when written) by an accident, kept back purposely yesterday, on account of the not receiving any letter from you whence, you were concluded to be on the road.

Thursday Sept. 15.

It is now sent, your letter of yesterday[5] being received in which you speak of it as a matter of uncertainty whether you are here on Friday or not till Sunday.

[3] Presumably the name of a property.
[4] Not identified: possibly Schank.
[5] Letter 1182.

1184

TO SAMUEL BENTHAM

30 September 1796 (Aet 48)

Herald—30th Sepr 96—'This evening arrived and came into the harbour his Majesty's sloop Arrow, built on a new construction, with four sliding keels; She is to mount twenty-eight 18 pounders and is to be commanded by Captn Portlock; she will not carry any ballast, and will, when fitted, and four months stores on board, draw only ten feet water: her guns are not to go on carriages but are to be mounted on a screw, from a stock fastened to the deck, by which means the guns will only be turned round as a swivel instead of running in and out for loading.'

Morning Chronicle—30th Septr 96 and Times in the same words.

'The Arrow, a new ship of 28 thirty two pounders commanded by Captn Portlock, is this evening come into harbour, to be coppered and rigged. She was built at Buckler's Hard on a plan by General Bentham.'

Letter from Navy Board, inclosing Woolwich Plan signed 'J. Tovery'.[2]

Letter from Nepean dated 29 saying that money is ordered in consequence of S.B.'s of the 27th.

Park Guns fired—and Bells rung—I suppose for a Victory[3]

Peake's letter kept, as you have the writer.

The Guns having fired twice as they do when the King goes to the House, there is a Report that he has been by water. He did not go by the Park.

1184. [1] B.L. VI: 292. Autograph, apart from the newspaper extracts, which are in a copyist's hand.

Addressed: 'Gen. Bentham / Queen's Square Place / Westminster / London.' Postmark: 'SE.30.96.B'. Stamped: 'SOUTHAMPTON'.

Perhaps first sent by Jeremy to Southampton, with the letter of 1 October (1185), and forwarded to Queen's Square Place.

[2] John Tovery (sometimes spelt 'Tovrey'), master boatbuilder at Chatham, 1765–76 (when Samuel was there); assistant to master shipwright at Plymouth, 1779–93; master shipwright at Woolwich, 1793–1801.

[3] A wrong supposition; see letter 1185, p. 276 below.

1185

To Samuel Bentham

1 October 1796 (Aet 48)

Q.S.P. 1 Oct 1796

You are likely to be on the *pavement* for a Commander for your Dart. Now then is the time to think of Rogget.[2] Remember his ship is the Camel, a Storeship, and her station is at Portsmouth. This morning came Darch[3] with a letter from Nepean saying that Colnet[4] was appointed to the Dart: but with a conversation held since with Colnet, in which Colnet said, that he should have been to go as on Monday next to take the command, but that he had just been stopt at the Admiralty, being told that there was something in agitation for him of more importance.

This day came for payment a Bill drawn by Upsal, due yesterday, but not accepted, never having been presented for acceptance. Had I known that it had not been presented for acceptance I should have let it take its chance: but not knowing this, and fearing therefore a loss of credit, I recommended to Darch to go and see about it. He brings me word how it was circumstanced as above, and that by desire of the Bankers, with whom it lay, he went to Martin's about it, who upon hearing his story, he showing how it had been marked for payment in his memorandums, took upon them to pay it accordingly. This is mentioned to you at his suggestion, that when you return to them the paper that is to get the £1000, you may mention your approbation of what they have done.

The mysterious gun-firing was after all, nothing but the new Sheriffs going to Westminster Hall to be sworn.

Darch has called upon all your correspondents—but none being at home, has left appointments for them for Monday.

Collins goes to Plymouth the latter end of next week, taking

1185. [1] B.L. VI: 293. Autograph. No docket or address.

[2] Captain (later Admiral) Raggett was in fact given command of *The Dart* (see p. 185 above, n. 2).

[3] Thomas Darch (d. 1834), first clerk in the Naval Works Department, 1796–1800, and in other naval administrative posts thereafter.

[4] James Colnett (c. 1755–1806) was appointed to command of the *Dart*, Sept. 1796, but transferred to another ship in October and promoted to Captain; he left naval service in 1805. He wrote several journals and published *A Voyage to the South Atlantic and round Cape Horn into the Pacific Ocean*, 1798. F. W. Howay edited *The Journal of Captain James Colnett aboard the Argonaut, from April 26, 1789 to Nov. 3, 1791*, Toronto, 1940.

Edward[5] with him. We know not why, but suppose it is about some
Copper business. He has agreed for the purchase of *Sandhurst*, near
Blackwater, if the Title be approved of.

1186

To Samuel Bentham

3 October 1796 (Aet 48)

I am sorry the Arrow has so many Visitors: some of them will
be Informers. The French will reap the benefit of your inventions,
before Ld Spencer can muster up the courage—so said Sk[r2]—and
so fear I. Could not strangers be invited to keep away?—But now,
I suppose, it would be too late.

[3]Q.S.P. 3 Oct. 1796

Mr. Darch having been informed at the Bankers' this morning
that they had not received the imprest Bill, and having learnt in
Essex Street that it had not either been received by Genl. Bentham
at Portsmouth, has made enquiries respecting it at the Admiralty
and finds by Mr Nepean's Clerk that its inclosure was duly directed
to Genl. B. and sent the same Evening (Saturday) to Portsmouth in
the Commissioner's Packet.

Q.S.P. 3 Octr 1796

Lloyd is said to have set out yesterday morning by a public
Coach—I did not know there had been any Sunday ones.

I don't see how the mistake in the Herald about the weight of
metal should be of any bad consequence. It strikes me rather as
good by being in contradiction with the other accounts, and thence
helping to puzzle the French and make them consider /look upon/
the whole story as inaccurate. Besides that now it may be stated
(as from authority) as being erroneous etc.—in a word may receive
a sort of general contradiction, which I suppose it could not have
done otherwise.

I dine tomorrow, (by invitation to *both* of *us*) at Wilberforce's,
whose note mentions the having sent to invite St. Helens.

[5] Edward Collins, his son.
1186. [1] B.L. VI: 294. Autograph, except for the copied letter from Darch.
No docket or address. This letter seems to be in reply to one from Samuel.
[2] Skinner.
[3] The quoted letter from Darch which follows is in a copyist's hand.

Booth's[4] letter was brought to me *closed*, along with the other closed letter, which I sent you at the same time. I had no suspicion of your having seen it, much less of your having seen it, and left it for me. I did not know on what account the money was due. Since the Panopticon castings have ceased you have had other castings performed by Booth on the Admiralty account. You had told me a day or two before, what was then news to me, viz: that there was money owing to Booth on Panopticon account, £250 I think was the sum mentioned. But that this £250 was on that account did not appear upon the face of his letter at least I did not collect any such conclusion from thence. You sent me the letter very coolly, that I might be *prepared for the demand*. Prepared for the demand I am— that is prepared to go to Jail—I mean, (speaking with respect) prepared to see your Generalship go to Jail. For as to £200, I know just as well where to find 200 Devils. Please God and Mr Pitt, money may come from the Treasury by that time—but as to borrowing it is not at this day to be had from any body or by any body, for money or for love.[5]

1187

To Samuel Bentham

5 October 1796 (Aet 48)

Q.S.P. 5 Oct. 1796

The Ordnance Letter and the Admiralty Order to you in consequence of course threw me into a great rage. If war be to be made, here is Ink languishing to be shed.

Herald 5 Oct. 1796[2]

The French /Philistines/ will soon be upon us with good Gun boats by the hundred, we opposing them with floating batteries by the dozen. 'At Dunkirk, Gravelines and Ostend' 'vessels long and broad, so as not to draw above three foot water: those for the artillery are made to receive Field pieces with Horses, and at the Bow a bridge is fixed to fall down on the Beach, by which the

---

[4] Booth and Co., iron founders, Sheffield Park, Sheffield.

[5] A copy of an undated letter from Samuel Bentham to Booth follows, concerning the latter's having drawn on Samuel for £200, a draught which Samuel says he will be unable to honour, unless he shortly receives what he expects.

1187. [1] B.L. VI: 296. Autograph. No docket or address.

[2] The two paragraphs following are quotations from the *Morning Herald* newspaper.

Horses can trail the cannon on shore immediately. Each to receive from 100 to 150 men with arms and ammunition'—'All Merchant Vessels are put in requisition to carry troops ammunition and baggage'—50,000 stand of arms and Field Pieces brass from 12 to 6 pounders arrived at Ostend from the interior—before the Gentleman (arrived at *Hull* on Saty. last) had left the Country—He had made his escape from Ostend—having been a prisoner.

Flat bottomed boats at Boulogne—upon the whole coast, supposed about 500—Reported by the Captn of the French Active Privateer captured by our Racoon Sloop—examined before the Bailiff of Seaford on Friday—Others of the Prisoners reported 2 or 3,000—each boat to transport 80 men.

Two letters from Nepean—one referring to letter from another Water-purifier, Matthew Sheffield,[3] 85 Cannon Street, who gives no particulars but wants an interview. Another requiring you 'to report for their Lordship's information, the Amount of the Sums necessary to be inserted in the Extra Estimates for the ensuing year for the works to be carried on in his Maj's Yd at Portsmouth' agreable to the Plan proposed by you.

Wilberforce had heard at Pitt's table t'other day Tothill Fields mentioned as the place I was to have—Pitt said nothing—Wilberforce thought it best to say nothing then, lest the idea of partiality to me should operate to my prejudice. Hearing how matters stood between me and Long, he said of his own accord, he would go and speak to Pitt about it, without delay.

Morn Chron—Harwich Oct. 2.[4]

Orders given for erection of furnaces for heating red hot Balls along this coast, at Walton, Clackton and Holland, in Essex.

Herald 4 Oct.[5]

French improved Telegraph account from the French Decade Literaire et Politique[6]—It seems infinitely better than the English ones—and like S.B.'s is usable by individuals.

---

[3] Matthew Sheffield, poulterer.
[4] An item from the *Morning Chronicle* newspaper.
[5] A comment on an item in the *Morning Herald*.
[6] *La décade philosophique, littéraire et politique* was a periodical started in Paris 'par une Société de Républicains' in 1794. An article entitled: 'Des télégraphes, description de ceux du Louvre et des Tuileries à Paris, et de celui de l'Amirauté à Londres' appeared in no. 87 (16 Sept. 1796), pp. 525–33.

1188

TO SAMUEL BENTHAM

7 October 1796 (Aet 48)

Q.S.P. 7 Oct 1796

Herald 7 Oct. 1796

'Thursday last, in saluting the new Mayor of Yarmouth, Dover Colby Esqr. who was that day sworn into office, with a discharge of cannon, a man unfortunately had his arm shot off, and his eyes nearly blown out.'[2]

Eight or ten more Candidates have offered themselves—one or two tolerably promising.[3] One, an Usher, aged 28, professes Mathematics, writes a most beautiful hand, but a stiff stile.

I had no time to get any explanation of the cause of Pitt's silence. Perhaps he did not hear: perhaps he did not choose to speak: perhaps his silence imparted assent—in short it is a mystery. Nothing yet from Wilberforce: but where's the wonder. He laughed at Bankes's notion about the Boys: and undertook spontaneously to beat him out of it.[4] Thornton[5] was there, and did homage to Def. of Usury: others abused Colonies. Abbot there—more law-mending work ready cut and dry, he tells me.

The Alderman[6] dines here Saturday /tomorrow/. Old Collins has just been here, and clawed away Edward—Devil take him. It is for Williams[7] that he goes to Plymouth.

Grateful letter from your friend Mrs Wilkinson:[8] with a fowl and a goose 'of her own feeding,' from Petworth, Sussex, the place I gave her a character to. The goose won't keep beyond Sunday. I hope you will be here to take your share of the goose at least. As for Naval Works and Bruizes, it is all nonsense—The Bruizes prudence kept be [by me?] silent about, *quoad* Essex Street.

Letter from Mulford,[9] wanting you to take a Boy of Chandler's.

1188. [1] B.L. VI: 297. Autograph. No docket or address.
[2] A quotation from the *Morning Herald* newspaper.
[3] Perhaps for an appointment on Samuel's staff.
[4] Henry Bankes and the cricket ground for the Westminster School boys (see letter 1182, p. 272 above).
[5] Henry Thornton (1760–1815), the banker and economist; M.P. for Southwark, 1782–1815; a leading philanthropist and 'Claphamite'.
[6] Richard Clark, their father's friend.
[7] Perhaps Thomas Williams, Copper Office, London (see letter 1217, n. 5).
[8] The former truculent cook at Queen's Square Place.
[9] Their elderly distant cousin, John Mulford (1721–1814).

Be a good boy and come home immediately, I have got a novel for you that will delight you—the Chevalier de Faublois[10]

1189

TO WILLIAM WILBERFORCE

18 October 1796 (Aet 48)

Q.S.P. 18 Oct. – 96

4 Oct.r—
11 Oct.r 'Tothill Fields'?

P.S. A meadow of Ld Salisbury's[2] indispensable, for communication with the River—Ld S.'s Estates *all* on Sale, (per Lowndes). Lowndes—'Buy it this instant, or you are too late'—
J.B. 'No money—
No Authority—
No confidence—'

1190

FROM WILLIAM WILBERFORCE

18 October 1796

Indeed my dear Sir I am *quite hurt* that I cannot send you any definitive Intelligence, but it is not in my power—I have not had a convenient opportunity of mentioning it to Mr Pitt, but will lose none that really is such—and to bolt it out at an unseasonable moment would be to injure rather than serve your Cause. I realy am asham'd to see you—But what I can do I will do I would it were more—

yours very siny
W.W.

Tuesday night Octr

[10] Not identified.
1189. [1] Bodleian Library, Oxford. Wilberforce Mss. d. 15/140. Autograph. Docketed by Wilberforce: 'Jere Bentham suo more.' Copy in B.L. VI: 299.
[2] Owner of the Millbank estate. (See above, p. 264 n. 5).
1190. [1] B.L. VI: 300–1. Autograph. Docketed: '1796 Oct / Panopt / Wilberforce O.P. Yd to J.B. Q.S.P.'
Addressed: 'Jere: Bentham Esqr.'
This is evidently an immediate answer to Bentham's cryptic message of 18 October (letter 1189). The 18th was a Tuesday and Bentham replied the next day (letter 1191). He apparently received another, missing, note from Wilberforce on the 20th, to which he replied with letter 1192.

1191

TO WILLIAM WILBERFORCE

19 October 1796 (Aet 48)

Q.S.P. 19 Octr 1796

Not less obliged by your forbearance, the motive considered, than I should have been by your activity.

N.B. Octr 11. The engrossed copy of the Contract lodged at length by Mr White in the Treasury in readiness for signature. 5th Septr 1796. Letter to Mr Long, proposing Tothill Fields, with Reasons.

1192

TO WILLIAM WILBERFORCE

20 October 1796 (Aet 48)

Answer to note of same date   Q.S.P. 20 Oct.

A thousand thanks. Out when your note came.[2] A little indisposed—an obstacle to talking but not to hearing, or eating.

1193

TO EDMUND ESTCOURT

21 October 1796 (Aet 48)

Lincolns Inn Friday Oct 21st, 1796

Sir

Ld Salisbury has some property at Milbank, of which it might eventually be convenient to me to become a purchaser, if it were to be disposed of. At your Chambers (where I have just called in

1191. [1] B.L. VI: 298. Copy. Letter 1192 follows on the same sheet and the copy of 1189 on the following sheet, with a docket (fo. 299) covering all three: '1796 Oct 11, 18 and 19, 20 / Panopt / J.B. Q.S.P. / to / Wilberforce O.P. Yd / Tothill Fields.'

1192. [1] B.L. VI: 298–9. Copy by J.B. For the docket, see letter 1191, n. 1.
[2] A further, missing, letter from Wilberforce.

1193. [1] BL. VI: 302–3. Autograph draft. Docketed: '1796 Oct 21 / Panopt / T. Fields / J.B. Q.S.P. at Lincs. Inn / to / Estcourt.'

Edmund Estcourt (d. 1814) was an attorney, then at 2 Lincoln's Inn Stone Buildings. He became solicitor to the Stamp Office about 1797 and later on receiver-general for the county of Monmouth.

consequence of having heard that that property formed a part of what was allotted for Public Sale) I was informed that was not precisely the case: but it seemed not improbable to the Gentleman whom I saw on the occasion, that proposals might be listened to for more articles than what the particular exigency had been considered as extending to. The quantity that would suit me is not altogether determinate: it might depend in a considerable degree upon the price. Not knowing the extent or the parcels of his Lordship's Estates in that quarter, except in the instance of two or three articles, and being informed that you are not expected in town till the beginning of next month, I take the liberty of applying to you in this manner for the purpose of begging the favour of any information you could oblige me with on the subject in the mean time, for example by directing the Gentlemen in your office to show me any Maps or particulars that may happen to be in your custody, or by informing me where else the information may be obtained. Not having the honour, perhaps, to be known to you, it may be necessary for me to say that I am an old member of the Inn, that consequently we can not fail to have many acquaintances in common, among whom it may be sufficient to mention Mr Trail, who, I just happen to hear is a particular acquaintance of yours, and who is an old and very intimate friend of mine. It is in his chambers I should have written this, had he been at home: as it is I write it from the opposite Chambers, Mr Romilly's. Your answer if the mode were more satisfactory to yourself, might be addressed to either of them; or else as underneath. I should not have attempted giving you the trouble, if it had not been material to me to obtain the information in question without loss of time.—I have the honour to be,

> Sir,
>   Your most obedient humble Servant
>   Jeremy Bentham

Queen's Square Place
Westminster

1194

To Samuel Bentham

27 October 1796 (Aet 48)

Q.S.P. 27 Oct. 1796

I send a letter from an unknown person about an unknown matter from Rotherhithe. It might have been sent yesterday, but I thought you would be in no want of business.

Map of Elysian Fields traced from the large map of London in the Treasury.

Another plan from measurements by E. Collins and his Master[2] begun today, to be finished tomorrow morning.

Mr. Babb hopes to evacuate the middle of next week—say the end of it.

Your Daddy[3] dined with me yesterday—item Buchan[4] by invitation sent before the expectation of the other Guest. Daddy gave the *nouveaux mariés* after dinner,[5] and after Buchan was gone made a merit of his consent. I gave the merit on that score to the Law of the Land: but admitted his claim so far as concerned the Chapter of facilities.

Give my Sister,[6] by commission, a plentiful stock of the most cordial and affectionate fraternal kisses you can find out for me, in due subordination to the marital ones.

I treated the Doctor with an oration on the superior value of grandchildren in comparison of children—and seemed to have *gain de cause*.

1194. [1] B.L. VI: 308. Autograph. No docket or address.
[2] That is, Bentham himself.
[3] Samuel's father-in-law, Dr George Fordyce, whose daughter, Mary Sophia, he had married earlier in the month.
[4] See p. 171 n. 4 above.
[5] That is, proposed a toast to Samuel and his wife.
[6] Bentham's new sister-in-law, Mrs Samuel Bentham.

1195

FROM WILLIAM WILBERFORCE

28 October 1796

My dear Sir,
    Long authorizes me to say to you that the Treasury approves of the Situation of Tothill Fields. If therefore you think you can make anythg. of the Dean and Chapter you are warranted to say so to them or I will with all my Heart apply to the Bp. of Rochester[2] on the matter if you rather wish it. I apprehend however that after all, an Act of Parlt will be necessary—I could not get a Sight of Mr Pitt today in private—

Yours sincerely
W. Wilberforce

Friday night
28 Oct. 1796[3]

1196

TO SAMUEL BENTHAM

29 October 1796 (Aet 48)

Q.S.P. 29 Oct. 1796

    I hope the happiness you speak of does not depend absolutely upon the 8 forks.[2] You don't mean to be where you are above 2 or 3 weeks after which you go to Plymouth. Plate at Lodgings is an object of plunder and a subject of sollicitude. Nothing can be more contrary to my interest than that you should be comfortable anywhere but here. A deduction of 8 Forks from 24 would leave me under a disability of giving a dinner, and that for an indefinite time, during which the necessity of giving victuals may turn up. The paragraph about forks was written in a wrong hand. If there comes an order from them in the same hand that wrote the coaxing line,

1195. [1] B.L. VI: 304. Autograph. Docketed: '1796 Oct 28 / Panopt. Toth. F. / Wilberforce O.P. Yd / to / J.B. Q.S.P. / Authorisation / Long authorizes him to say that Tothill Fds. is approved of.'
    Addressed: 'Jere: Bentham Esqr'.
    [2] Samuel Horsley (1733–1806), bishop of Rochester and dean of Westminster.
    [3] Date added in Bentham's hand.
1196. [1] B.L. VI: 309–10. Autograph. Docketed: 'J.B. 29th Octr 96'.
    [2] Samuel had evidently written asking for eight table forks on loan.

285

they get sent instantly—otherwise not at all. So many months as you have been a housekeeper (instead of a lodger) at Redbridge, how have you managed to exist without silver forks, Mr 2-Shoes? Now you have got somebody to back you, you hold up your head, and grow pert.

I did or rather meant the generous thing by you in the article of Walnuts. All my industry could find but one, and that (suspecting it to be a rotten one,) I carried forthwith to Essex Street for you, where I arrived but a few minutes after you were moved. But the birds were flown, and nobody knew whither, nor where they were to be caught. In my way I peeped into St. Clements, and was but a minute or two too late. I had occasion to go to Bridge Street, to hunt books about Tothill Fields at Alderman Clark's.

The Dr[3] talked to me about Vines. Wishing to provide for him, I offered him the place of Sub Gardener, under Mrs Bentham. He accepted it with due gratitude. I shewed him the Map of his new-acquired territories. He is to call by day light to see the territories themselves. There are ideas of building a Bridge from the Q.S.P. Garden to the Pimlico Garden—now no longer a nuisance. All this was tête-a-tête: for Buchan got flung away at 8 o'clock: which you wanted ingenuity to imagine.

Wilberforce was with me this morning to report conversation with Pitt Long and Rose all together—Long had told him lies, as I suspected, and given him a false authority without ever having opened his mouth to Pitt on the subject. Now it is established that Pitt approves of the place, but Wilberforce had to fight him and quarrel with him about the mode of bringing it into Parliament. Particulars too tedious to give.

I took the opportunity of reading to him my letter to the Bishop.[4] He approved of it, subject to two or three omissions in which I went all along with him. It is to be sent on Monday, and he to pay his visit on Tuesday. Delighted to hear of my Colony pamphlet.[5] We are forming an alliance on that ground—he to furnish me with facts etc.

No answer haveable yet about the Tothill Fields House (Campbel and White's), Campbel being dead, and the Partnership business

---

[3] George Fordyce.
[4] Samuel Horsley.
[5] Perhaps Bentham was planning to expand his pamphlet, *J.B. to the National Convention of France*, first printed in 1793, but not published until 1830 under the revised title, *Emancipate your Colonies! Addressed to the National Convention of France, anno 1793, shewing the Uselessness and Mischievousness of Distant Dependencies to an European State* (Bowring, iv, 407–18).

to be arranged, which leaves the property in a state of uncertainty: this is unfortunate.

Ald. Clark is here waiting for his dinner. We have been to the *Fields* together—so pressed for time I know not what I write.

A parcel of woman's trumpery sent here by the Doctor without warning—the old organ, a Box, with I know not what besides. It will serve for a bonfire. This is one of his whims.

While Wilberforce was with me, comes Kluch[6] with a written letter in her hand in these words—'Would Mr Bentham be so good as to let me speak to him for minutes'—The message brought by Mr Du Quenay,[7] Wilberforce and I in my pigstie,—saying that there was a lady below, that brought it. My answer was as sudden as the occasion, and conformable to the truth—that I was that moment engaged with a gentleman about very particular business, and could not stir. Consequently miff and umbrage—What in hell could she want with me, being in habits with Skinner, to whom she might have said any thing?—Why come rather than write: or if an interview was so necessary, why not desire me to call on her, as if this were a time of all others for commencing an acquaintance. Then the burthen of the Song would be as before, my despising her, and my pride in so doing. This is Skinner's engagement day. Tomorrow morning early I shall desire him to call on her, and see what she wants. I have, and always have had, a dread of her tongue. The less she knows of me, the better: the more she knew of me the more umbrage she would take.

This and the disappointment about the Tothill Fields House, conspiring with other little momentary matters, put me out of humour, or you might have had your forks—not that I have had a moments time for sending them.

Corresponding with the Cat[8]—the Cat in a way to be tranquillized.

---

[6] Not identified.
[7] Neither the messenger, nor the lady friend of Skinner have been identified.
[8] Perhaps the same lady as 'Puss'.

287

1197

TO JONATHAN WHITE

29 October 1796 (Aet 48)

Q.S.P. Sat Oct. 29 1796

Sir,

On this day sennight, I transmitted to you a proposal relative to the empty House adjacent to your Wharf at Millbank, through the hands of our common friend Mr Foulds; who left it at your Counting House in Cannon Row.[2] I am so circumstanced that I must give up the matter, and betake myself to a different quarter, if it should not happen to suit you to favour me with an answer before Wednesday.

1198

FROM JONATHAN WHITE

29 October 1796

Cannon Row Westminster 29 Octr 1796

Sir,

When my Clerk shewed me your Letter I was much press'd for Time and desired him to write to Mr Folds saying from circumstance of my late partner Mr Campbell's death and the arrangements to be made in consequence I could at present come to no decision about the House at Thames Bank. I am concerned to find he has misunderstood me or you should not have [been] kept in suspense till this time.

I am Sir
Yr very humble Servt
J^{no} White

1197. [1] B.L. VI: 311. Autograph draft. Docketed: '1796 Oct 29 / Panopt. / Tothill Fields / J.B. Q.S.P. / to / White Cannon Row.'
    [2] The letter containing the proposal is missing.
1198. [1] B.L. VI: 312–13. Autograph. Docketed: '1796 Oct 29 / Panopt. Toth. / White Cannon Row / to / J.B. Q.S.P.'
    Addressed: 'Jeremy Bentham Esq / Queen Square Place.'

1199
TO BISHOP HORSLEY
31 October 1796 (Aet 48)

Queen's Square Place Westminster
31 Oct. 1796.

My Lord,

I have the honour of addressing myself to the Dean of West-minster,[2] on the part of the Treasury, on the subject of a Waste, in which the Dean or Chapter, in right of their Seigniory, possess a sort of honorary interest—I mean Tothill Fields.

An Act which passed at the close of the Session of 1794 may perhaps have afforded your Lordship a general intimation of the revival of the long suspended Penitentiary plan, and of the modifications it is destined to undergo in the hands of Mr Pitt. The inclosed paper will furnish any information of detail which may suggest itself as worth obtaining in relation to the origin of the present plan, or the leading features of it.

The site originally pitched upon for the Establishment in question was Battersea Rise. It is needless to trouble your Lordship with a history of the causes through the influence of which that choice came at length to be superseded.

It is sufficient for the present purpose to say, that Tothill Fields, a place already not strange to prisons or prison company, is the spot finally pitched upon by Mr Pitt as the place which, with proper consent and authority, he proposes shall be purchased for the Crown and appropriated to this use. Being for the purpose in question put in the stead of the three gentlemen named in the abovementioned Act (Sir Gilbert Elliott, Sir Charles Bunbury and Dr Bowdler) the business of treating for the purchase devolves upon me. Doubts having arisen whether the powers created by that Act extend to Wastes, a Bill to supply the deficiency is to be brought in as soon as possible.

The Act above alluded to, following the example of the original Penitentiary Act (19 Geo 3 ch. 74) and I believe of all former Acts having for their object the purchase of ground for purposes of this sort, is armed with general coercive powers: but, in the particular

1199. [1] B.L. VI: 314–17. Fair copy, corrected by Bentham and signed by him. Docketed: '1796 Oct. 31 / Panopt / Tothill Fields / J.B. Q.S.P. / to / Bp of Rochester.' Two other fair copies are at B.L. VI: 318–21 and 322–5.
[2] That is, he addresses the bishop in his other capacity of dean of Westminster.

case in question, the spot being already fixed on, and consequently the persons who are to be dealt with known, the respect inspired by the character of the Right Reverend Prelate who happens to be principally concerned in point of title, the confidence entertained of his disposition to lend an assisting hand to the beneficent designs of government, and the assurance of his meeting with the readiest concurrence on such an occasion on the part of the Reverend body of which he is the Head, all these considerations together have put so new a face upon the matter, that an application for previous consent and cooperation, in, as well as out of, Parliament, has been considered as the only sort of opening suited to the present complexion of the business.

As far as my information is correct, the uses made of Tothill Fields at present are as follows:

1. The Inhabitants of St Margaret's and St John's[3] exercise the right of depositing Rubbish in any quantity subject to the designation made by the Dean and Chapter's Bailiff or Field Keeper as to the particular spot on which the deposit shall be made in the instance of each Load.

2. The Inhabitants of these populous and extensive Parishes exercise the right of turning in all sorts of Cattle and Poultry without stint.

3. The Westminster Scholars make use of the ground for Cricket. No right of Turbary[4] or any right by the exercise of which any part of the soil would be carried away, is possessed by anybody: and under the authority of the Dean and Chapter, every act of that tendency is studiously interdicted.

4. At the farther end of the Waste, stands an old and decayed pile of mean Buildings, formerly a Pest House, now known by the name of the Five Chimneys, belonging to the parish of St Margaret, and made use of as a Poor House. It affords Lodging to 7 or 8 Families, besides the Dean and Chapter's Field Keeper. Several of the windows are altogether without glass, and the whole together exhibits [a] variety of wretchedness.

5. After these uses I can find neither actual profit nor possible source of profit, remaining to the Lords of the Waste, the Dean and Chapter.

So much as to the nature of the proprietary rights under the

---

[3] The two parishes which constituted the old city of Westminster; from 1536 to 1728 there was only the one parish, St Margaret's; they were reunited in 1888 for civil administration. Both parishes opposed the erection of a penitentiary in Tothill Fields.
[4] The right to take peat from another's ground.

existing state of things: now as to the arrangements to be made in the way of compensation in respect of the above rights.

1. As to the right of depositing Rubbish. This right might remain in full force, and with no other change, than the substitution of the Officer of the Crown to the Officer of the Dean and Chapter.

2. In compensation for the right to pasture, it has been proposed on the part of the Treasury, that a perpetual Annuity be granted to the Parishes by the Crown, proportioned to the principal money which the Land would be worth to be sold, subject to the rights reserved. The proper expedient for obviating the depretiation in the value of money, would of course be to be pursued—for instance that of a Corn Rent.

3. For the amusement of the Scholars, should the object in the judgement of the Dean and Chapter appear of sufficient importance to claim a provision on the part of Government, an allotment might be made, equal at least to the largest of the Cricket Grounds instituted expressly for the purpose. In the most celebrated of them, and as far as I can learn, the largest, (Lords Cricket ground,[5] Marybone, near the New Road) the gross content is called 8 Acres, in which space is included a considerable Kitchen Garden, occupying perhaps 2 Acres. My Schoolfellows, I have the satisfaction to think would, in every point of view, be no small gainers by the change. At present the best part they can pick out is rough uneven ground, exposed for want of fences to the unpleasant, not impossibly in some instances even corruptive, intrusion of promiscuous company. In the event supposed, the space allotted to this purpose would necessarily be inclosed, the access to it subject to such controul as the Dean and Chapter may deem competent to the occasion, and the mode of fencing might be such as would add embellishment to use. The maintenance, as well as institution, of this sequestered, and very dissimilar appendage to the principal establishment, would successively depend upon two old Members of the fraternity:[6] I mean myself, and the General my Younger Brother: so your Lordship will feel no difficulty in imagining the pleasure there would be in giving a new and improved face to a spot rendered interesting, in spite of aboriginal ugliness, by remembrances drawn from the morning of life.

4. The compensation due to the Parish for their almost ruined

---

[5] Founded by Thomas Lord (1757–1832) and already recognised as the principal cricket ground in London, although not formally opened, on a different site, as the headquarters of the Marylebone Cricket Club until 1814.

[6] That is, Old Westminster scholars.

Poor House, as well as to the Inhabitants of it for the loss of such of their comforts as could not be made to follow them to their new abodes, this, as well as the quantum of compensation in the former instance, would be proper matter of enquiry for Commissioners.

5. The Dean and Chapter would, according to the practice in these cases, receive a minute compensation for their unprofitable right. About $\frac{1}{15}$ or $\frac{1}{16}$, I understand, is, in case of division by Act of Parliament, the proportion usually allowed to the Lord upon the collective value of the subject to be divided. Whether to receive it in the form of an annual payment, such as a Rent charge, payable according to the price of corn, or in the shape of a gross sum to be laid out, will rest with the pleasure of the Dean and Chapter to determine. But the most valuable part of their recompense will be the honor and satisfaction of having cooperated with Government in a foundation of so much importance to the public service.

In point of prospect and appearance, the occupiers of the circumjacent Houses would have no small reason to congratulate themselves on the change. In the room of the existing ruin of a Poor House would rise a circular building of 180 diameter and between 50 and 60 feet in height, of an appearance which could scarcely have been more ornamental had ornament been the sole object of it. To the eyes of the nearest inhabitants, at the distance from which it will present itself to their view, there will be nothing about it that can so much as present the idea of a prison. The lower stories will be screened by a surrounding wall, inclosing a square of from 400 to 500 feet a side, guarded and watched on the outside in the manner stated in the printed paper which accompanies this address. The limits of the surrounding space will again be protected by an exterior inclosure.

As to prison-company, the Neighbourhood, instead of being exposed by the change to any annoyance from that source, will on the contrary be rescued from it. At present, if common fame be good evidence in such a case and a Playhouse Song good evidence of common fame,[7] company of this sort may be regarded as Masters of the spot. If, under the new arrangement, persons of this stamp ever gain admittance, it will be either in the character of prisoners, or on the footing of Prison Visitors at regulated times, and under

[7] Quoted in a footnote, which is crossed out:
'Ye Pads, Ye Scamps, Ye Divers
 And all upon the lay
In Tothill Fields gay Sheep Walks
 Like Lambs ye skip and play—etc.'

the same controul and inspection as the inhabitants. It will no longer be a *Place d'Armes* to them, with room to hold Councils and perform evolutions, as at present.

Under these circumstances, not the smallest particle of apprehension, I trust, can take place on the part of the neighbourhood, with regard to the value of property in general, or that of the Dean and Chapter in particular, as it if were liable to suffer in any respect by the proposed change.—Grosvenor House, the nearest residence of a rank capable of taking umbrage at such vicinity, is little if anything less than half a mile distant from the intended site. In the instances of the New Prisons lately set down at Clerkenwell and Newington Butts, the stile of the circumjacent houses was and is in general superior, the vicinity incomparably closer, the date more modern, and ever since the erection of those Prisons, new Streets almost in contact with them have been built.

In point of forwardness, the state of the plan is as follows: A Deed of Appointment, nominating a person to treat in the name of the Crown for the purchase of the spot, and take possession of it when purchased, has been lying ready engrossed for upwards of a twelvemonth at the Treasury: but this instrument, being exclusively adapted to the spot originally in contemplation, will now be of no use. A contract for the erection of the proposed Penitentiary House, and for the management of the Establishment when instituted, lies at the same place in a state of equal readiness, having lately undergone a last revisal on the part of Mr Pitt.

An expression of regret which happened to drop from me t'other day at Mr Wilberforce's, at the thoughts of not having the honour of being personally known to your Lordship, drew from my worthy friend the immediate offer of supplying that deficiency, by waiting upon your Lordship for the purpose of giving any of those explanations which are more satisfactorily obtained from third persons than from parties. He will accordingly wait upon your Lordship, either with this letter, or soon after it.[8]

> I have the honour to be, with all respect,
> My Lord,
> Your Lordship's most obedient
> and humble servant
> Jeremy Bentham

Bishop of Rochester

---

[8] Wilberforce reported on 5 November that he had so far failed to see the bishop (see letter 1203).

1200

FROM EDMUND ESTCOURT

1 November 1796

Sir
I am extremely sorry that by the uncertainty of my removing in the Country I was prevented from receiving your Letter[2] so soon as I otherwise should. It was sent after me, but did not reach me till my return. I shall be happy to see you upon the contents of it, and I will see if I can forward your wishes.[3]

I am
Sir
Your most Obt Sert
Edm[d] Estcourt

Lincolns Inn 1st Nov. 1796

1201

TO MARY SOPHIA BENTHAM

2 November 1796 (Aet 48)

Q.S.P. 2 Nov. 1796
Finding you corresponding already with fellows, I have intercepted the letter[2] for the honour of the family, and broke it open: that's what you have got by directing your letters to fellows under my nose.

I won't have my Sister's books touzzled and tumbled about in her absence. If your minxship will please to condescend to take up with my copy, Mrs What's your name, so:—you shall have no other.

1200. [1] B.L. VI: 326–7. Autograph. Docketed: '1796 Nov. 1 / Panopt / Tothill Fields Estcourt Linc Inn / to / J.B. Q.S.P.'
Addressed: 'Jeremy Bentham Esq. / Queen Square Place / Westminster.' Postmark: '7 o'clock. / 1.NO.96. / NIGHT'. Stamped: 'Penny Post Unpaid' ⟨rest illegible⟩.
[2] Letter 1193.
[3] Pencil note by Bentham at foot: 'The letter to which the above is an answer, begins thus   Oct 21 – 96
"Ld Salisbury has some property at Milbank of which it might eventually be convenient to me to become a purchaser, if it were to be disposed of—".'
1201. [1] B.L. VI: 328. Autograph. No docket or address.
[2] Evidently a missing letter to one of the young men in Bentham's household.

Who's that Mr. Bentham you speak of in your letter to that young fellow? Is that your Brother?

Col. Byde's[3] letter about a Coach Horse you will receive through Mr. Darch, who was to [go?] from hence this morning. This seemed to me to indicate the necessity of suspending the negotiation about Coach Horses, which otherwise I should have opened in Essex Street.

Mr. Darch had in charge to tell you that Mr. Babb's would be evacuated most probably by today, but to a certainty, by to-morrow. This intelligence I hope will have dispatched my Brother on his way hither before this letter reaches you: in assurances of which I suspend till I see him the letter he incloses, as well as everything else about the business.

A Bill of Upsal's for £56 on my Brother lies *due* at Moffat's, 20 Lombard Street.[4] Had it been presented for acceptance I should have accepted it for him payable at Martin's, in pursuance to his authority sent to Martin. As it is, I can not so much as attempt to do any thing in it, without begging favours of Martin's people, which it is by no means advisable for me to do.

Letter[5] from Essex Street to J.B. with a pair of gloves. Too late for Mr Darch, they shall be given to my Brother. Enquiry about a piece of flannel, whether it arrived in Q.S.P. last night.—Yes it did arrive. 'Has sent all the things for Redbridge which he had in charge'—At the same time here are a bushel of things which I am told by Mr. Koe are designed for Redbridge. How they are got thither—and how it happened they did not go to Essex Street and accompany the rest of the things that were sent thither, I don't know.

Gloves, Letter-paper etc. by my Brother when he comes.

[3] John Byde, of 27 Holles Street; colonel of the Coldstream Regiment of Footguards, 1783; equerry to the Duke of Clarence, 1789. He does not appear in Army lists after 1790. He had previously negotiated with Samuel about a mare. See letter 1162, n. 2.
[4] Moffat, Kensington and Styan, bankers, 20 Lombard Street.
[5] Missing.

1202
FROM CHARLES ABBOT
3 November 1796

Dear Jerry,
  You see I have got my Committee[2]—i.e. full liberty to plague myself as much as I please. I have intended every day to see you, but I have *others* to see who are more imperious in their authority. Some day I shall come and consult the oracle in Q.S.P. when I get forwarder.

Adieu
Ever Yrs
C.A.

Nov. 3.

1203
FROM WILLIAM WILBERFORCE
5 November 1796

My dear Sir
  I have in vain made repeated Efforts to meet the Bp of Rochester—but have now written to him to desire him to name a time on Tuesday or Wedy Morng for our Meeting. Have you receiv'd any answer from him, or how stands your affair in that Relation? Do be kind enough to inform me by a line to Pal. Yd, where I shall return of Monday.

Yours very sincerely
W. Wilberforce

Saty evg
  5 Nov '96[2]

1202. [1] B.L. VI: 329. Autograph. Docketed: '1796 Nov. 2. ⟨3⟩ / C.A. Pallmall / to J.B. Q.S.P. / Promulgation.'
  Addressed: 'Jeremy Bentham Esqr / Queen Square Place.'
  [2] Following his report on expiring acts (see above, p. 202 n. 2) Abbot had urged Speaker Addington that the methods of promulgating statutes should be improved; on 2 November 1796, he was appointed chairman of a committee on the subject, which reported on 5 December, with the result that the classifying, printing and distribution of copies of statutes was completely overhauled. (See *Diary and Correspondence of Charles Abbot, Lord Colchester*, 2 vols., 1861, i, 74; and R. B. Pugh, loc. cit., pp. 20–1.)
1203. [1] B.L. VI: 331. Autograph. Docketed: '1796 Nov 5 / Panopt. Toth. Fds / Wilberforce / O.P. Yd / to / J.B. Q.S.P.'
  [2] Date added in Bentham's hand.

1204

FROM CHARLES ABBOT

8 November 1796

Wed. Evn'

I will call upon you tomorrow after Court—and I suppose that will be about *one*.

Yrs ever
C.A.

1205

FROM WILLIAM WILBERFORCE

8 November 1796

My dear Sir,
I should like to see you for 5 minutes tomorw morng a little before 10 respecg. the Bp of Rochr.

Yours always
W.W.

Tuesday night

1206

FROM CHARLES ABBOT

14 November 1796

Wilberforce is not at home but his Servant says there is a *chance* of his being in Town today—and another chance of his being in Town tomorrow.

½ p. 12. Monday.

1204. [1] B.L. VI: 332. Autograph. Docketed: '1796 Nov 8 / Panopt. Toth. Fds / C.A. Pallmall / to / J.B. Q.S.P. / coming 9th.'
   Addressed: 'J. Bentham Esqr.'
1205. [1] B.L. VI: 333–4. Autograph. Docketed: '1796 Nov 8 / Panopt. Tothill Fields / Wilberforce O.P. Yd / to / J.B. Q.S.P. / Novr 9 J.B. called and heard of his / W's / interview with the Bishop.'
   Addressed: 'Jere: Bentham Esqr.'
1206. [1] B.L. VI: 335. Autograph. Docketed: '1796 Nov 14 / Panopt Toth Fds / C.A. Q. / to / J.B. Q.S.P.'

1207

TO WILLIAM WILBERFORCE

14 November 1796 (Aet 48)

Q.S.P. Monday ½ after 12 – 14 Nov. 96

Abbot has just seen Dr Smith[2] (one of the Prebends) to whom the communication with me was turned over by the Bishop. The Bishop wrote (time not mentioned) to Mr Pitt, to know whether it were a thing he really desired—On Saturday when Smith saw the Bishop, no answer. The Chapter meets on Wednesday at 11. The Parish to whom the Chapter has made communication of the business, has a meeting on the subject tomorrow. Smith when Abbot left him, was going again on the subject to the Bishop. Abbot is to see him again tomorrow at 1. Smith says that if the Bishop is fully impressed that Mr Pitt really wishes it, it will be done—otherwise not. You see how critical the situation of things is: now then, my good friend, once more, now or never is the time for your assistance, in order to get Mr Pitt to write such a letter before Wedy at 11, as may answer the purpose.

Since writing the above, Abbot called in O.P. Yard: item J.B. and from thence was sent to Clapham[3] where he arrived 20 minutes too late.

Wanted sadly at the Vestry tomorrow a Friend with a name, a character, and a tongue—to overcome the Tradesmen who govern the Parish and to prevent the interests or supposed interests of the present and active few from overbearing the interests of the absent many.

N.B. W.W. /My best friend being a Parishioner/ has as much right to take a part as any body.

1207. [1] B.L. VI: 336–7. Autograph draft. Docketed: '1796 Nov 14 / Panopt Tothill Fds / J.B. Q.S.P. to Wilberforce'.

Scribbled in pencil: 'Abingdon Tallow Chandler King Street / Mann Linen Draper Jones the Plumber Overseer Top of Tothill Street / Mr Drake ⟨illegible⟩ Vestry Clerk Opposite Palace Yard.'

[2] Samuel Smith (?1731–1808), educated at Trinity College, Cambridge; LL.D. 1764; ordained 1755; head master of Westminster School, 1764–88; prebend of Westminster, 1787–1808; prebend of Peterborough, 1787–1808; also rector of Walpole St. Andrew, 1762–1808, and of Daventry, 1795–1808. Bentham had known him when his brother, Samuel, was a boy at Westminster School (see *Correspondence*, i, 101 and n. 3, 151).

[3] Wilberforce divided his free time between his house in Old Palace Yard and Battersea Rise, where Henry Thornton built a residence for Wilberforce next to his own.

I don't know how the notices are distributed—None have come to me—that which I saw, I saw by enquiring just now at a shop in King Street next to the Church Yard—between the Church Yard and the Tinman's.

Churchwardens { Mann the Linen Draper
               {   Parlt Street
               { Abingdon Tallow chandler
               {   King Street

Overseer Jones the Plumber, Upper end of Tothill Street
Vestry Clerk Mr Drake—abode unknown.
The communication from the Chapter was made, it seems, last Wednesday, and now the meeting is to decide on it—a dead secret to me, till now.

Q.S.P. 6 o'clock.

1208

FROM MR ATWOOD

15 November 1796

Mr. Atwood presents Compliments to Mr. Bentham, and recollecting his Enquiries yesterday Evening respecting Mr Ellis[2] the Attorney, believes he mistook the person meant by Mr B.—Mr Ellis late Attorney Brother to Mr William and Charles Ellis died some time ago: but a Son of his succeded to him in his profession and is Mr A believes now employed in Parochial and other business in Westminster.

Tuesday Even.

1208. [1] B.L. VI: 338–9. Docketed: '1796 Nov 15 / Panopt. Toth. Fields / Atwood / to / J.B. Q.S.P.' The writer has not been positively identified.

[2] George Ellis and his son, George, were attorneys in North Street, near St John's church, Westminster; the son continued the business after his father's death.

1209

FROM CHARLES ABBOT

15 November 1796

The Bp of Rochester says that havg no answer to his first Letter, he has again written and if no Ans. comes to this, he shall *not* consider Mr B. as an agent of Govt.

Dr. S.[2] thinks *if an Avowal of the Authority comes*—the Chapter may probably concurr—tho' the Parishes are both adverse.

Dr /Smith's/ notion is—that it wod be fair and advantageous to all parties that the Fields shod be parcelled out,—viz. some part as a compensation to the Chapter—and some to the Parishes, and the rest sold to Govt.

Ld Grosvr's opposition is thought to be the most formidable.[3]

1210

TO SAMUEL BENTHAM

15 November 1796 (Aet 48)

Q.S.P. 15 Nov. 96

Things are in a fair train as to the general success—but I am sadly afraid of being pillaged of a deal of the land—at least it will not be the fault of the D. and Chapter if I am not.

I have been intriguing like Lucifer—and nothing but the most strenuous exertions could have saved me from the misfortune of

1209. [1] B.L. VI: 340. Autograph. Docketed: '1796 Nov. 15 / Panopt. Toth. Fds / C.A. / to / J.B. O.P. Yard.'
Addressed: 'For Mr Bentham / at / Mr Wilberforce's.'
In B.L. VI: 341 is the autograph draft of a letter from Bentham to Charles Abbot, dated 15 November 1796, but docketed: 'not sent', viz:
'I am obliged to keep vibrating between Wilberforce's and the Treasury—I wish much you could contrive to meet me at one or other—the Treasury the surest. The Parish have taken umbrage at the prior application made to the Chapter. Vestry today—nothing will be done today—Parish infinitely disgusted at the haughtiness of the Chapter—I have a thousand things to say—no time to write them—but the 1000 will be comprised in 10 minutes.'
[2] Dr Samuel Smith.
[3] Richard Grosvenor, 1st Earl Grosvenor (1731–1802). He was the greatest breeder of horse-racing stock of his day; M.P. 1754–61, created Baron, 1761, Viscount Belgrave and Earl Grosvenor, 1784. He and his son, Lord Belgrave, strongly opposed the scheme for a prison in Tothill Fields or Millbank (see letter 1174, n. 4).
1210. [1] B.L. VI: 342–3. Autograph. Docketed: '15th Nov. '96.'
Addressed: 'To General Bentham.'

being considered as an imposter through Pitt's sulkiness and silence —Rose has hazarded himself to save me—at the intercession of Wilberforce.

Wilberforce wonderfully cordial and confidential—but is laying plots for converting me—I was hard put to it this morning to parry him. Time will not admitt of any particulars.

I have two sets of Tallow Chandlers to buy—each of which think themselves greater than the Bishop and exasperated at my having applied to him first. I am putting on Sackcloth and Ashes.

The Bishop wrote a letter to Pitt—no answer—A second letter saying that if he did not hear before the Chapter Day (tomorrow Wedny) he should conclude Mr. B. was no Agent of Government. Rose has been writing to him speaking of Pitt's going out of town in such as hurry as did not admitt of his answering the letter but he Rose could take upon him from his own knowledge (and what he had heard Pitt say?) that it would be a real satisfaction to him (Pitt) to—I forget the expression—to see the Bishop come into it, and to have the Penitentiary House built in Tothill Fields. This he was to shew to Pitt if he came to town, otherwise send it without shewing. Pitt presently after did come to town, and Rose went down to him. He shewed me the letter, saying he should send it off immediately—Wilberforce present, who had gone in to Rose first, and then sent out for me to come to them.

That was in consequence of intelligence given by C.A.[2] as obtained that morning on a visit to Smith.

I wish you were at the Devil, both of you, for not being here. I want somebody sadly to keep up my spirits amongst all these struggles, especially at dinner time without being obliged to hunt about for company and that at an uncertainty.

1211

To George Rose

16 November 1796 (Aet 48)

Queen's Square Place Westmr 16 Novr 1796
Sir,
    Upon attending the Dean and Chapter of Westminster this

---

[2] Charles Abbot.

1211. [1] B.L. VI: 344–6. Fair copy. Docketed: '1796 Nov. 16 / Panopt. Toth. Fields / J.B. Q.S.P. to Rose Treasury / Chapter Conference.' Another fair copy (fos. 347–9) contains passages inserted as footnotes but crossed out in pencil.

day I found a disposition to treat, on some such conditions as the following—

1. That a part of Tothill Fields be allotted to the Parish or United Parishes, whereon to build a Poor House—

2. That another part be allotted to the Dean and Chapter, for a Cricket Ground for the Westminster Scholars—

3. That another part be allotted to the Dean and Chapter and Parish or Parishes, jointly or severally, to be improved for their mutual benefit by building or otherwise.

4. That the remainder only, and that as small as possible, might be leased out to the Crown, suppose for 1000 years, for the purpose of the Penitentiary House. A wish pretty generally expressed was to confine the grant to the very site of the Building itself, with no greater quantity of ground than would be contained between that and the surrounding wall (Diameter of the principal Building 180 feet—Space occupied by Building and Yard, a square of 500 foot a side—Content 6 Acres).

Whether this or any thing like this allowance can be accepted of as sufficient may appear from the following particulars.

1. The least number of convicts I can be charged with is 1000: and I stand bound to receive them, in any number. In New South Wales they have already accumulated to several thousands.

2. My Prison being at the same time a Manufactory, and one in which the goods are of the bulkiest kind, will call for room proportionable.

3. There is nothing to hinder my being called upon to receive Females: and that in a separate House.

Call, for argument sake, the greatest number of Prisoners (male and female) I can ever be called upon to make provision for . . . 2,700[2]

---

[2] At this point in the second fair copy (fo. 347 v.) there are additions to sections 2 and 3, but these are pencilled through and a copy of them in Bentham's hand in B.L. VI: 344 has a separate docket: '1796 Nov 16 / Panopt T.F. / J.B. Q.S.P. / to / Rose Treasury / Subsidy. Establishment.' This copy reads:

'Passage proposed to be omitted

2. In the Subsidiary Establishment I stand engaged to make provision for as many of the *discharged* prisoners as may choose to accept of it. These must not be crowded as in a prison: with their wives and families, they will by degrees increase to a little town. As a Prisoner, a man will not remain generally speaking, above 7 years. In the Subsidiary Establishment the succession will not be so quick: a man will have a *right* to remain there for the remainder of his days.

3. My prison being etc.

Then again after 'make provision for'	2700
2. The greatest number of persons in the Subsidiary Establishment, Wives and Families Included	2700
Total	5400

The reasons for the omission are explained in letters 1212 and 1213.

Eighty Acres (the quantity of Land at Battersea Rise) was the quantum allotted under the old system for 900 Prisoners. This was the quantity I was to have had for the 2700 persons above spoken of: being $\frac{1}{3}$ part only of the quantum of Land per head under the old system.

The Quantum proposed by the Dean and Chapter amounts, instead of the whole 80 Acres, to a part and that but a small part, $\frac{1}{6}$ or so, of a spot of 38 Acres, as the following account will show—

	Acres
Gross quantity of the Waste called Tothill Fields	$56\frac{1}{2}$
Amount of the line of Road necessary for the preserving the existing communications (breadth of the Road supposed 33 feet) according to a measurement taken from the plan—upwards of	$10\frac{1}{2}$
Proposed to be allotted for a Cricket Ground for the Westminster Scholars, being an amount equal to that of the largest existing Cricket Ground	8
Remains as above applicable to the purposes of the Establishment	38
Amount of what the Dean and Chapter are perfectly willing to give up for a pecuniary compensation	6

Consent to a sacrifice of a few acres more might not improbably be obtained: but where the whole is so far from sufficient, whether a consent, extending at any rate to no more than a part, and that probably a small part, be an object worth labouring for, is a question to be considered.

When the whole, and more than the whole is wanted, a satisfaction in the shape of a portion of the thing itself would be a species of satisfaction, adapted indeed to the purpose of a common Inclosing Act, but directly repugnant to the object of the proposed Bill.

The share that could be claimed by the Dean and Chapter as Lord, is, according to the received principle of division for Wastes, and according to what appears to be the conception of the Parish Governments, no more than $\frac{1}{15}$ or $\frac{1}{16}$ of what would be allotted to the Commoners: and accession on the part of the Dean and Chapter seems according to all appearances, more likely to obstruct than to facilitate accession on the part of those Governments, the representatives of the Commoners. An antipathy, preventive of all consent, has subsisted between the parties, time out of mind.

Instances that occurred 15 or 16 years ago have been mentioned to me: and recent occurrences have inflamed it.

The value of the actual profit made by the Dean and Chapter from the Waste for so many hundred years is admitted by them to be absolutely nothing. Projects of improvement once attempted to be realized, by the concurrence of the Parish, were by the repugnance of the Parish long ago rendered abortive: and that repugnancy is stronger now than ever.

Out of the 80 Acres requisite, whatever is not given out of their Waste, must be given, if given at all, out of cultivated lands. Whether the inconvenience to individuals be considered, or the expense to Government, the option does not seem difficult to make.

Upon the whole, the course I would take the liberty of proposing, as the clearest and shortest, is as follows—

1. Bill to explain and amend the Act of 7 July 1794, by extending the powers from Lands in severalty to Wastes and Commons.

2. Clause reciting Tothill Fields as being a Waste within the four Counties therein mentioned, but as being incumbered with a ruinous Poor House in the middle, with no more than 8 or 9 families in it—Should the Treasury pitch upon Tothill Fields, powers to pull down this Poor House.

3. Pecuniary compensation *mutatis mutandis*, as under the existing Act.—

4. Occupation immediate: compensation money in case of disagreement Lodged *pendente lite* upon the principle of the existing Act, in the hands of Trustees.

Whether the *nature* of the parties (unweildly corporate bodies) or the *temper* they are in be considered, it will appear evident enough that, although there were a certainty of their coming some time or other to an agreement, it would be impossible for an individual, circumstanced as I am, to wait the issue of it. Fourteen or fifteen years, no very immoderate duration for a Chancery Suit, especially on such a ground would be more than the value of my Life—

1212

FROM CHARLES ABBOT

18 November 1796

Frid

Upon consideration—I think *Subsidiary* etc. better omitted at present—especially as it remains in reserve producible if necessary.

Yrs C.A.

1213

TO SAMUEL AND MARY SOPHIA BENTHAM

18 November 1796 (Aet 48)

Q.S.P. 18 Nov. 1796

The Inclosed[2] /Letter to Rose contains/ is the ostensible account of the D and Chapter conference—the part relative to the Subsidy. Establishmt. has been omitted, as too alarming, at the suggestion of Skinner, confirmed by Abbot, who has been very active in his assistance, as well as intelligent in his advice. I don't know anything more about Rose's letter to the Bishop than what I told you: but from the Bishop's consenting to treat, I conclude it went, with or without a Postscript certifying the approbation of Mr. Pitt. What I believe I did not tell you, Rose said moreover he would attend the Vestry, viz. of St. John's of which he is a Member. The letter in question has pretty well committed /fixed/ the Treasury with regard to the choice: since, besides the Bishop to whom it was addressed, it passed through Wilberforce's hands as well as mine. Sooner than be thrown out altogether, I mean with your General-ship's and Puss's and Sister's approbation, to take up with the pittance their Reverences would allow me. Wyat the Architect was there as Counsel to the Chapter. Much Tittle-tattle there is neither time nor room for—Lucifer himself is humble to the Bishop. Bishop, Chapter (a very full one 8 or 9 out of 12) Wyat, all of them

1212. [1] B.L. VI: 351. Autograph. Docketed: '1796 Nov 18 / Panopt. T. Fds / C.A. Pallmall / to / J.B. Q.S.P. / Subsidy. Establ. Omitt.'
This note suggests that Bentham's letter of 16 November to Rose (1211) may not have been sent until Abbot had scrutinized it. The first sentence of letter 1213 confirms this.
1213. [1] B.L. VI: 350. Autograph. No docket or address.
[2] No doubt a copy of letter 1211 above.

ready to pull me to pieces, to take a pencil upon the spot and mark
out what part I wanted, after I had assured them over and over,
that the uses of government, not suspecting an objection, had
embraced the whole—How much for such a purpose?—how much
for such another? When the magnitude of the demand had been
display'd in a degree of force not to be resisted, they were for
driving me to the cultivated grounds. When Botany Bay had been
mentioned as an example of the numbers that might be accumulated—'So then,' cried the Bishop, 'you mean to make a Botany
Bay of it?' When they saw the establishment could not be made
out to be too little for the whole quantity, the next thing was to
make it out to be great, viz: so great as to inspire a just alarm, and
this will probably be the turn his opposition will take, if he thinks
it worth while to venture it. Wilberforce says he has need of Pitt
just now (he did not say for what) and that that is one reason for
his wanting to get an explicit declaration from Pitt about the
business, in order to make a merit of acquiescence. I paid a visit
first to Smith,[3] whom I found quite open and good humoured—I
have not seen him since. Rose was gone from office when I went but
now: but he has an appointment there for 11 tomorrow morning
and it is recommended to me to take the advantage, and be there
by $\frac{1}{2}$ after 10. It is no small advantage to have to deal with R.
rather than L.[4] C.A.[5] says the incapacity of the latter is become
notorious. C.A. has not the least apprehension from the Bps
opposition—does not think the other Bps will join him in it.

W.[6] I shall fence off with about the Jug as well as I can.

Gates with brick buttresses and stone coping finished.

Presented for acceptance today and accepted £200 from Poore—
and 2 [bills?] from Upsal—the one £50, and the other £50 I believe.

Visit from Mulford[7] during mine to the Treasury—is not to stay
long in town—no notice about calling again.

To Sister

The House quite languishing to be thrown out of [the] window by
your Sistership's fair hands. Make haste, or it will grow frantic, and
jump out of itself.

[3] Dr Samuel Smith.
[4] That is, George Rose rather than Charles Long.
[5] Charles Abbot.
[6] William Wilberforce: 'Jug' was Bentham's abbreviation for 'Juggernaut', that is
'God', or 'Providence': Wilberforce was trying to convert Jeremy to evangelical
Christianity, as he told his brother (see letter 1210, p. 301 above).
[7] Their elderly cousin, John Mulford.

On my return from the Chapter on Wednesday, who should I find coming out of Q.S.P. but the Dr and Forsyth[8]—I made them turn in again, and the Brace of Gardeners, being starving, devoured some cold leg of lamb which God's Providence had provided. They both dine with me on Monday at 5: so if your Sistership has any thing to say, now is the time to say it. Forsyth undertakes for everything—but thinks, considering the smoke, the plants will thrive better if planted in Feby or March than now. The smoke of winter in their weak state would hurt them more than the time would forward them. Your humble Servt's idea of painting the tiling and Wall invisible much applauded.

Negotiations with Treasuries, Deans and Chapters are sad enemies to gardening, and more especially to Polyanthus—Narcissus—Glass-blowing: forgive me, forgive me, dear dear Sister, this has been Gardenerishly and gibberishly speaking, an idle week: but the next is a new one.

Fullness of occupation in *irritation* and consultation about the letter herewith sent was the cause of the silence by which his Generalship was perplexed.

As to Puss,[9] it is a delicate Chapter to touch upon—to settle the etiquette, as betwixt the old idol and the new one, would puzzle the whole Corps diplomatique.

If your Naval Library happens to contain such a thing as a dictionary of maledictions, do so much as lend it me, that I may treat you with a fresh one every day you stay away.

1214

To William Wilberforce

19 November 1796 (Aet 48)

Q.S.P. – Nov. 19 1796

The inclosed,[2] my dear Friend, contains, besides a plan for future operations, the substance of the conference of Wednesday. I am to attend Mr Rose on Tuesday at ½ after 11: and, as he is

[8] William Forsyth (1737–1804), the famous gardener, who was at this time superintendent of the royal gardens at St James's and Kensington parks.
[9] The nearest Bentham gets in the correspondence to indicating a special relationship between the mysterious lady, 'Puss', and himself, or his brother.
1214. [1] B.L. VI: 352. Copy, included in Bentham's letter to his brother of same date (letter 1215).
[2] Missing.

apprised that ¼ of an hour may be requisite, I hope the matter will then be settled. I mention the time in hopes that if you happen to be back by that time, you will have the goodness to inform me: not that I know of any specific call for your assistance, but only that there *may* be a use in having, and at any rate a comfort in knowing that one has, a friend at hand.

Tittle Tattle about the conference as much as you have a curiosity for, when we meet. Lucifer humble in comparison of you know who.

1215

TO SAMUEL BENTHAM

19 November 1796 (Aet 48)

19 Novr. Mulford just been here—went with me to see the glories of the Fields—heard me read the Rosian letter etc.—said nothing about money, and went away quite satisfied. Very eager about the Haunted House on the Bank (Campbel and White's)— and put in for a nitch in it. I told him, what was true, I thought of him for the purpose when I looked at it. I Never eat so delicious a pear in my life as two of our own of the brown sort proved yesterday. Few as yet, but Forsyth will multiply them.

The communication above stairs between Babb's and [Brigstone's] I observe is made—Mulford went over it with me—I told him of your *intention* of writing to him about your marriage.

I feel quite comfortable at the thought of having Rose to myself for ¼ of an hour on Tuesday—Long never would appoint a time.

1215. [1] B.L. VI: 352. Autograph. Docketed '19 Nov. 96'.

The letter also included, on the same sheet, above the note to Samuel, a copy of a letter to Wilberforce of the same date (1214) and of an invitation to Samuel, viz. 'Lord Spencer requests the honor of General Bentham's Company to dine with the Corporation of Trinity House on Tuesday next the 22 Inst at ½ past 4 o'clock at the London Tavern—Trinity House—18 Nov—1796—The favour of an answer is desired'.

After the note to Samuel is an extract from the *Morning Herald* of 19 November 1796, beginning: 'The following is a list of the Gunboats to be employed between the Rivers and Creeks on the Coast. . .'

1216

FROM WILLIAM WILBERFORCE

21 November 1796

My dear Sir,

I am very much vexed indeed at the Conduct, tho less surprized at the Demeanor of the Bp. I really thought it possible that
he might have been susceptible of some feeling for the public Good,
when not preoccupied by private Interest: We will try what can be
made of Rose, or of the Bp thro' the influence of Govt. But I own
I fear that you would be hardly able to carry a Bill thro' both
Houses in the face of the Dn and Chrs. opposition: I say *you*; I ought
not to have it to *say*; but I doubt if it will be practicable to prevail
on Ministry to bring forward the proposal[2] themselves, as they
ought, and to support it with all their force. However we will talk
of this when we meet: I *may* probably pass thro' Town on Thursday
abt. 3 o clock which I throw out that you may know where I am
likely to be if you wish to see me and I would cheerfully come up on
Wedy. if I thought it of moment to be present at your Interview
with Rose; but I don't think that of the least consequence. I will
however give him a Line 'to quicken'. I must say, few things have
more impress'd my mind with a Sense of various bad Passions and
mischievous weaknesses which infest the human Heart, than
several Circumstances which have happened in relation to your
Undertaking. A little, ever so little, Religion would have prevented
it all, and[3] long ago have put the public in possession of the practical
Benefits of your plan. This is one amongst the many Instances I
have had occasion to observe how much a little of this only solid
principle tends to the Wellbeing of Communities. [I] ⟨n⟩eed not
repeat that it will ever give me pleasure to cooperate with you, or

---

1216. [1] B.L. VI: 353–4. Docketed: '1796 Nov 21 / Panopt. Toth. Fds / Wilberforce /
Buckden / to / J.B. Q.S.P.'

Addressed: 'Jere. Bentham Esqr / Queen Square Place / Westminster.' Franked:
'Huntingdon Novr twenty first / 1796 W free Wilberforce'. Postmark: 'HUNTINGDON
Free'.

Printed in Bowring, xi, 115–16, where, however, the date is wrongly given as
'21st April 1796'. There are also other inaccuracies.

[2] Bowring has 'proposition'.

[3] Bowring has 'I' instead of '&', which erroneously makes Wilberforce say that he
was publicising the Panopticon scheme.

desire you always to call on me for aid without Ceremony. I heartily and strongly wish I could lend you more Effectual Assistance.

In grt Haste
Yours sinly.
W.W.

Buckden
Novr. 21st 96

1217

To Samuel and Mary Sophia Bentham

22 November 1796 (Aet 48)

Q.S.P. 22d Nov.r 1796

Adjournment till tomorrow: prognostications bad and good— the good *have* it.

Bad—the following letter from Wilberforce. . .²

Now for the good—Heel-kicking from ½ after 11 till ½ after 2— Then out comes one of the Treasury Clerks from Rose with the most magnificent of apologies—Mr. Rose 'quite *shocked*' I should have been waiting there all this while—prevented from seeing me by business that *could* not be put off etc. etc. the '*shocked*' repeated 2 or 3 times—appointment for ½ after 10 tomorrow. Meantime was observed in one of my vibrations by Long, who called to me and began a chat with asking what brought me there. I told him, and producing in the course of the conversation the letter designed for Rose, he took it and desired me to go in with him into his room. Was quite of my opinion—thought it a mighty plain and simple business. Well, and as I was not to have Battersea Rise: what alteration did I expect in the terms by way of indemnity?—None at all—only that my 80 Acres here should come to more money than they would have done there. I hoped that would not be an obstacle, being much pressed for room etc.—and whatever the overplus might amount to, I would allow 8 per Cent for—nor should I want more than the 38 Acres and the meadow of communication *immediately,* but would wait for it till it was absolutely wanted, for instance 2 years. Both propositions caught at—very good—perfectly reasonable—laughing about the Cricket Ground—but admitting

---

1217. ¹ B.L. VI: 355–6. Autograph. Addressed: 'To Brigr Genl Bentham / Portsmouth Yard'.

² A copy in Bentham's hand of letter 1216 above follows at this point.

310

the necessity of it—could not suppose so small an interest as the Dean and Chapter had in the spot could prove an obstacle. Accounted to him for my being to see Rose—said perhaps he (Long) could go on with it without my troubling Rose etc. Advice from him to see Rose notwithstanding. He seemed to be making a point of making up for the ill usage with which Wilberforce had been reproaching him. Stopped before that by J. Smith[3] the Treasury Lord who had heard of Tothill Fields—and advised me to stick to it, with a good deal of questioning, and good wishes. It looks as if something were on the carpet about the interest of money. H. Thornton the Banker I told you before had made it the subject of conversation at Wilberforce's. A magnificent elogium to Trail t'other day signed S. Douglas[4] who had just borrowed it of Trail having never read it before. Questioned about it today by Long, who wanted to know the title in order to get it. I have just sent to Paynes for a copy to present him with.[5]

To Sister

Letter[6] came just in time not to be answered. Returned from Essex Street—heard of the Horses bought (so yesterday) Saw the *Hake* all but the head.

3 dozen glasses bought today at Blade's[7]—how wondrous cheap! but 6d a piece.

Well if I am to have my house cluttered up with trumpery and the matchless symmetry and good order of it disturbed, so it must be. But you tantalizing ⟨Twoad?⟩[8] when is it to be?

Saw Sister Margaret[9] who told me what a good sister I had got—gave me two Pears, and lent me two Harpsichord pieces. Plants we are to have on both sides the Paddock from Forsyth—yesterday was it not they dined here—he your Daddy and Captn Skinner.

Threw out an idea to Daddy about purchasing in the neighbourhood of Panopticon for the sake of hemming in the Establishment and securing it to his grandchildren—Took it *ad referendum*—seemed to relish it—I have no time to explain it.

---

[3] Joseph Smith.
[4] Sylvester Douglas, the future Baron Glenbervie, whose private secretary James Trail was.
[5] There follows an invoice—in a copyist's hand, dated 24 October 1796—of goods supplied to Samuel by Thomas Williams, Copper Office, London.
[6] Presumably a missing letter from Samuel and his wife.
[7] John Blades, glass manufacturer to the King, 5 Ludgate Hill.
[8] Illegible: the word looks like 'Twoad' (perhaps a facetious spelling of 'Toad').
[9] Margaret Fordyce, the younger sister of Mrs Mary Sophia Bentham.

1218

To Samuel and Mary Sophia Bentham

23 November 1796 (Aet 48)

Q.S.P. 23 Novr. 1796

Mr. Rose took my paper and read it. 'It would be extremely difficult' (he said) 'to proceed in a hostile manner /against/ with such a body as the Dean and Chapter, except they were like the Dog in the Manger, and not meaning to do anything with the ground themselves'—No want of inclination, I said, but a want of power, which came to the same thing:—I then alluded to the magnificent plan designed by the Adams's[2] so long ago, and rendered abortive by the Parishes. He answered and confirmed the allusion, by another to the plan at Dean's Yard 'poor Sam Cox's,[3] which you Mr B, as a Westminster man must remember'. From the ill success of that plan, he took it for granted that the Houses they thought of building were 'little Houses'. He then said he would 'put it into the hands of Mr Wyat, who was their Surveyor and Surveyor (or Inspector?) of the Board of Works—that he was a respectable and a reasonable man, and one with whom he could talk on the subject, whereas it would be extremely difficult to talk with such a Body as the Dean and Chapter—It would come to the same thing, as he durst to say Mr Wyat possessed their confidence. 'As he pleased,' I said—it made no difference to me, whether my 80 Acres came from the Dean and Chapter, or from anybody else—to which he made no objection. He said then, he would see Mr Wyat about it today or tomorrow, and immediately let me know. N.B. The situation in which Mr Wyat stands is that of a man who being to be employed in the capacity of Architect or Surveyor upon whatever ground can be obtained by the Dean and Chapter, has an interest in making this residue as large as possible.

Tomorrow, by way of a refresher, I shall send him a paper of Hints of a pecuniary resource, which I may perhaps inclose a copy of to your Generalship.

1218. [1] B.L. VI: 357. Autograph. No docket or address.
   [2] An untraced plan for Westminster, presumably drawn up by Robert Adam, in collaboration with his brothers, James and William, who worked with him on the Adelphi scheme.
   [3] Samuel Cox (d. 1776), a barrister, who had been concerned with the erection of houses in Deans Yard, Westminster, intended for relatives of boys at the school. According to Bentham himself 'the scheme failed; and when half-a-dozen houses were built, no new funds were forthcoming, and the houses were either pulled down or were left to decay' (Bowring, x, 28–9). Cox was godfather to Samuel Bentham.

Visit (I forgot to tell you yesterday) from Windham[4] on Monday, with his name in pencil on a scrap of paper. Enquired first for you, then for me, but John denied me, though I was then in the house. I called at his home at 12 this morning, and left my card.

To Sister—

Be a good girl, and bring back all the Heralds your thoughtless Husband is indulged with. One was kept back, containing matter I might every minute be in want of. The naval part was copied and sent to him with a Chronicle in lieu.

As you have got outlandish fish at Portsmouth, such as are not to be seen in any Christian country, you might if there happens to be an opportunity, and the fish cheap, bring with you a sample when you come: Margaret salted her Hake—a bad shift, since all salted fish are the same. The slightest difficulty, if any occurs, is not worth overcoming.

Did I tell you, there is a man reads raree-show lectures on Airs, 12 in number, on Thursday evenings at 8, to Women and children— his name Varley[5] at Cross Street Hatton Garden—Skinner and I are to enlist ourselves among the Women and children the first lecture (tomorrow) and if we like it, shall go on. If you and your Husband can find a place under either denomination, you might be of the party, when you come. But when do you come?

Whenever it is, bring with you the 2 Burkes your giddy husband stole—Great hue and cry—at last by accident I heard how they went and nothing said to nobody. A few additional pages are advertised, to a new edition but perhaps will not be given or sold to any who do not produce a copy of the old.[6]

If I send his Giddyship my Tax-Paper,[7] good your Ladyship, bring it back.

[4] Probably William Windham (1750–1810), the statesman.

[5] *The Times*, 21 November 1796, advertised that S. Varley would give at Hatton House, 16 Cross Street, Hatton Garden, 'TWELVE LECTURES ON PNEUMATIC CHEMISTRY, with Experiments and Practical Observations . . . calculated for Ladies and Gentlemen, and the younger Branches of Society, as a recreative Introduction to Chemical knowledge'. They were to be given weekly, starting on Thursday, 24 November, at 8 p.m. Tickets 2s. 6d. each.

[6] Bentham is probably referring to Edmund Burke's *Two Letters, addressed to a Member of the Present Parliament, on the Proposals for Peace with the Regicide Directory of France* (1796). The tenth edition had an additional five pages, printed on a separate sheet and could be obtained gratis by purchasers of former editions (Advertisement in *Morning Chronicle*, 12 November 1796). There is a marginal outline headed 'Burke on France', among the Bentham manuscripts (U.C. CVIII: 109).

[7] The 'Hints of a pecuniary resource' mentioned in the first part of the letter, probably the printed broadsheet, *Tax with Monopoly*, reprinted in Bowring, ii, 590–600, and discussed in W. Stark, *Economic Writings of Bentham*, i, 74–5.

1219

TO SAMUEL BENTHAM

25 November 1796 (Aet 48)

Q.S.P. Friday Novr 25 1796

Sent my Tax-Paper² yesterday morning at 8 to Mr Rose—
have heard nothing from him since. Bunce, who was here yesterday
principally to make models of Cricket Grounds, tells me that Wyat
(whose pupil he was) is notorious for being the most dilatory of all
beings. I intend therefore tomorrow to call upon Dr Smith with my
Cricket Grounds, to see whether I can get him to come into my
scheme of abandoning to them all Green's Court to do what they
please with, together with the small fragments, as also the corner by
Rochester Row, and a space in quantity between the simple /single/
triangle, and the lozenge formed by doubling it. In this space will
be placeable an 8-acre cricket ground, circular, oval with the small
end to the corner, or oval with the obtuse end to the corner, it will
come to the same thing with regard to the projection into my
domains but the latter plan will leave them more room in the
corner to play with and build upon etc.—I fancy this will meet
Smith's ideas well enough—as to the Bishop and the others, Smith
will tell me.

Surprized this morning, and pleased, to the degree you may
imagine, with a visit from Edwd Collins, announcing a fortnight's
visit tomorrow. You are not wanted therefore on *my* account, till
after the fortnight is at an end, since by every day's coincidence
I should be a loser. Your coming however will not oblige me to
send him away, since his bed may be removed to your new house
the room where Upsal slept—I forgot, he may take Jack's vacant
place.

Tolerably well pleased with Varley's lecture—well enough to go
again, and probably keep on going. His language ungrammatical,
and pronunciation vulgar beyond conception. But he seems to
understand the subject pretty well, and his apparatus seems to be
economical and well-contrived.

The broken end /pier/ at Babb's, the result of the Wall-demolition,

---

1219. ¹ B.L. VI: 358. Autograph. No docket. Addressed: 'To Brigr Genl Bentham /
Portsmouth Yard.'

² Presumably the 'Hints of a pecuniary resource' mentioned in letter 1218, p. 313
and n. 7.

was omitted to be worked up again by mistake. But I set Mr Bunce
upon them yesterday, and it is now begun upon.

1220

To Samuel Bentham

26 November 1796 (Aet 48)

Novr 26. 96

Smith could not catch Mice better if he had swallowed half
a dozen sets of fire-irons. He tells me every thing that passes in the
Conclave, as well as every where else. I was with him this morning,
made him approve my plan and he went immediately with it to the
Bp, with whom he expects to procure me an interview on Monday.
The majority rather disinclined—but the Bishop if he approve of
the plan of division, which he had no explanation of before, will
probably join and bring over the rest—especially as the advice of
the Architect (Jam. Wyat) was, what I should not have expected,
favourable. He advised them not to lose the opportunity, though
he did not know that any thing would be given up. Bunce was his
pupil—know you any mode of coming round him?—He is notorious
for dilatoriness—Gamble² the Telegraph man (Smith tells me), is
expected to be the new Prebend. Abbot, through Burton, answers
for him—Smith told me in that view—as likewise of a Proprietor
adjoining as likely to be willing to sell—In extravagant haste.

The whole negotiation committed to the Bishop. By way of
bribe, I have found ostensible reasons for the Chapter having all
the land that is given up, and the Parish none of it.

1220. ¹ B.L. VI: 359. Autograph. No docket or address.
    ² John Gamble (c. 1762–1811), who had published *Observations on Telegraphic Experiments*, 1795. He was rector of Alphamstone, Essex, and of Bradwell-juxta-Mare; he was also a chaplain to the Forces, but he did not become a prebend of Westminster.

1221

TO SAMUEL AND MARY SOPHIA BENTHAM

28 November 1796 (Aet 48)

Q.S.P. Monday Novr 28 – 96

Creatures,

The aspect of affairs is more and more favourable. Smith has been here just now, and is clear that the only thing it sticks with is the goodwill of the Bishop, who having views upon Pitt, wants to see his Ministership eat a dish of humble pye. Smith gives me anecdote and secret history about that without end. It is now late: but tomorrow I go to Wilberforce, Rose, Long etc. and get all hands aloft to set upon Pitt and make him doff his hat to the Bishop with a low bow. When Smith went to him with my sketch, two observations only were made—that no disposal was pointed out for about 20 acres of the ground: and that nothing more had been heard on the subject from Mr Pitt: This last said with a degree of meaning which shewed what stuck at heart. What is aimed at is Bribery and Corruption—a situation for a friend. I can't stay to write all the tittle-tattle details that came along with this general information: never fear, they will not be lost.

What is more, Smith has been making a spontaneous opening for me to be Keeper of the famous Cricket Ground, which is not to be less than 8 Acres, and may extend to 12, I taking on myself the expence of fencing. Hearing of 8 Acres—'What' (says the Archbp of York to Smith) 'is there to be but *one* match?'. Smith says there has been for many years more than one match at a time: but this observation may be worth to my Keepership the whole 12 Acres. Contest between Puss and Sister for the Vice-Keepership etc. etc. matters of high importance to be settled in full Council at Q.S.P.

What went to the Chapter in Pitt's name was not Rose's '*profligate* letter,' that I believe I told you of, but a still better letter in the identical hand of Mr Pitt.

The worst of it is, that no Chapter is likely to be held till a day or two after the 21st of next month. When the Bp has declared his consent, a point to labour will be the getting the Bill in without the Tothill Fields clause in the time.

The Papers may have informed you how much Pitt and Rose

1221. [1] B.L. VI: 361–2. Autograph. Docketed: '28 Nov. 96.'
Addressed: 'To / Genl Bentham / Portsmouth Yard / Novr 28.'

TO S. AND M. S. BENTHAM   28 NOVEMBER 1796

must be occupied and distressed about the Loan business[2]—this is fully sufficient to account for Rose's silence.

To S.B.

Curse the Ordnance people[3]—I hope you take care that the infamy shall fall on the heads that give birth to it, not on your's and Puss's.

To Sister

Peremptory orders are wanted about the roots: whether (frost out of the question) they are better, *without* than *with* a fire.

½ a dozen Polyanthus Narcissus's bought this day, at *Colville's*[4] for a beginning and set in water—Price 4d a piece: profit to the Agent 2d a piece 50 per Cent.

At said Colville's a thing called a Chrysanthemum, from China, full of large double poppy-like looking laciniated flowers, exactly of the colour of the Devil's wedding suit—the most artificial things ever produced by Nature.

1222

To Samuel and Mary Sophia Bentham

28 November 1796 (Aet 48)

Novr 28. 96 Q.S.P.

Letter from Margaret[2] since the packet with the plan of Cronstadt was sent off to the Admiralty 'I am commanded by my superiors, to enquire of you the proper place for Horses to stand at Livery,[3] as the General's have been at College long enough.'

Gardening commissions shall be attended to tomorrow—3 of the roots are with fire, 3 others fireless.

In haste.

---

[2] The 'Loyalty Loan', intended to meet a national deficit of 18 million pounds. It was an innovation, since Pitt appealed directly to the public, instead of through contractors. The whole sum was raised in sessions totalling less than 15½ hours, and the loan was regarded as a successful demonstration of loyalty to the government (see J. Holland Rose, *William Pitt and the Great War*, 1914 reissue, pp. 305–6).

[3] An allusion not traced.

[4] James Colville, nurseryman, King's Road, Chelsea.

1222. [1] B.L. VI: 363. Autograph. No address or docket.

[2] Apparently a missing letter from Margaret Fordyce, the younger sister of Mrs Samuel Bentham, to Jeremy Bentham, containing the message quoted.

[3] That is, to be fed and stabled.

1223

TO BISHOP HORSLEY

29 November 1796 (Aet 48)

Mr Bentham presents his respectful compliments to the Bishop of Rochester, and begs leave to submitt the inclosed Papers[2] to the consideration of his Lordship and the Chapter. Queen's Square Place Westmr.

Tuesday evening 29 Novr 1796
P.S. In obedience to what he understands to be his Lordship's commands in relation to the *void spaces*, he hopes to be able to send a copy of the graphical sketch with the requisite elucidations as far as time and the nature of the case admitt of their being given in the course of tomorrow morning.[3]

1224

TO BISHOP HORSLEY

30 November 1796 (Aet 48)

Sir

In the void spaces on each side of the proposed site of the two Penitentiary Houses, provision will require to be made, for the following purposes.
1. Reception-Houses, 2: one for each Sex.
2. Burying Ground
3. Erections in considerable number each for one person, distant from the Prison, from each other, and more especially from every spot not comprized within the establishment,—for the separate lodgment of the sick or suspected, in case of contagious disease.
4. Wood Yards (*detached* for fear of fire) *Stone* Yards, and *Warehouses*, for the finished work expected from the labour of several

1223. [1] B.L. VI: 364–5. Autograph draft. Docketed: '1796 Nov. 29 / Panopt. Toth. Fids / J.B. Q.S.P. / to / Bp of Rochester Dean's Yd / With Plan of division'.
  [2] Missing.
  [3] See letter 1224.
1224. [1] U.C. cxviii: 145. Autograph draft. Docketed: 'Observations, accompanying the Sketch of Tothill Fields—exhibiting the proposed Division—copy sent to the Bishop of Rochester 30 Nov. 1796.'
  This is a draft of the 'elucidations' Bentham promised to send the bishop with the 'graphical sketch', which is missing (see postscript to letter 1223 above.)

thousand persons, as well as for the raw materials for them to work upon. N.B. The *work* and *materials* to which the system of mechanism invented by Brig. Genl. Bentham for the purpose is adapted, are of the bulkiest kind: principally *wood* and *stone*.

5. —*Turning* and *Waiting* room, for *carriages* bringing visitors to the chapel at the time of Divine Service.

6. The great entrance at Forest [?] House (from the Horse Ferry Road) will require to be perfectly under the command of the Prison Government, for the purpose of barring the approach upon occasion, against hostile mobs, as well as cutting off the hope of clandestine escape, by the assistance of accomplices from without.

7. Distance, from all *Houses not* under the controul of the Prison Government, as well as from every spot on which *persons at large* have a *right* to set foot, distance to a degree effectually preclusive of all forbidden communication is an object uniformly regarded by all the promoters of the Penitentiary System as an indispensable requisite.

8. In the instance of some of the above articles, the demand may not present itself immediately in any very considerable magnitude yet will be continually extending itself by degrees. To specify, either in situation or magnitude, the particular spot requisite in the instance of each article, is a task for which the Undertaker con-confesses himself not as yet prepared, and which he flatters himself will not for the present purpose be thought necessary to be imposed upon him for the present purpose.

9. Mr Blackburn, the late celebrated Prison Architect, required, for a *part* only of [the] above *purposes*, and for no more than *600 prisoners* a space little if at all inferior to the space herein requested for a number which is expected to be 3 or 4 times as great in a few years. Two thousand used to be the number of *men* alone in the *Hulks only*: to say nothing of those who for want of room in the Hulks, or from other causes are consigned to *N. South Wales*, to *Newgate* and to so many other *Town* as well as *Country Prisons*. Mr Blackburn's demand was such as admitted of *reduction*: but after a reduction of 70 or 80 per cent, the remaining allowance for a number *still unlimited*, will, it is presumed, not be deemed excessive.

1225

FROM GEORGE ROSE

30 November 1796

Mr: Rose presents his Compliments to Mr Bentham, and begs he will take the Trouble of calling upon Mr Wyatt at the Office of Works on Friday between 12 and 4 o'Clock on the Subject of erecting the Penitentiary House.
Old Palace Yard

Novr. 30th.

1226

TO SAMUEL AND MARY SOPHIA BENTHAM

30 November 1796 (Aet 48)

Q.S.P. 30 Nov. 1796

Before your letter of yesterday arrived, I had already written an acceptance on the Bills in question—but luckily, not having been called for, they are still here.

To Sister

John dispatched to Essex Street about the Horses and for the Flower Roots—Not findable today—will be sent tomorrow morning, when Daddy, being at home, will give orders about the Horses.[2] The roots already in water have begun to shoot.

To S.B.

With the Cronstadt Plan was a letter from me—I hope you will have received it before this reaches you.

Beginning of Pitt's letter to the Bp according to Dr Smith's recollection of it—'Having contracted with Mr. Bentham' . . . Other words in it—'for the accommodation of the public' . . . or 'to ac-

---

1225. [1] B.L. VI: 366–7. Docketed: '1796 Nov. 30 / Panopt. Toth. Fds / Rose O. Palace Yd / to / J.B. Q.S.P. / For J.B. to call on / Wyat Surveyor of the / Board of Works and of / the Dean and Chapter.'

1226. [1] B.L. VI: 368. Autograph. No docket. Addressed: 'To / Gen Bentham / Portsmouth Yard / Novr 30th.'

[2] See letter 1222, n. 3.

commodate the public'. The Bp laid it down at the Chapter Meeting, but put it up afterwards among his own papers. This letter, could a copy of it be procured, would at least serve, upon a pinch, as ammunition against Mr Pitt.

Cronstadt Plan—John being sent to enquire about it at the Admiralty has returned with the answer—that Mr Nepean has nothing to do with franking parcels. It must therefore go by the Mail, in which case this very letter may as well go by the same conveyance.

Oisters being so cheap, would it not be good economy, should there happen to be subordinate skill and leisure enough at command, to pickle a few thousand, and bring here for winter use. The Welsh Oysters, that are sold in London out of the shells in small Barrels, are according to my unlearned taste, much better than the raw.

To S.B.

Among a multitude of sample Ports, a sort that calls itself old, and is not very new, and of which there is a large stock, appears the best or one of the best—Others go as high as 33s: this is but 31.6d and if you take ten dozen, 30s:6d: the 10 dozen would therefore come to £18. 5. 0. The printed letter having circulated this fortnight or 3 weeks, it seems doubtful whether there would be any left—I leave to your honour's indecision to decide and act accordingly.

No tidings yet of anything in the Lindegren way.

1227

TO SAMUEL BENTHAM

1 December 1796 (Aet 48)

Q.S.P. 1 Decr 1796

Lindegrens visit at last—came to Warren's Hotel[2] but yesterday. Packet this morning with a German book or two with Mrs Lindegren's Comps only on the outside. Visit in consequence by J.B. to the Hotel, and the foregoing intelligence learnt.

I hope tomorrow at last you will receive the unfortunate Cronstadt with 2 old letters ⟨J. Bian⟩ and do. newspapers. John brought the

---

1227. [1] B.L. VI: 369. Autograph. No docket or address.
    [2] Mr William Warren, hotel, 11 Charles Street, St James's Square (*Holden's Triennial Directory*, 1805).

box back from the Mail Coach place yesterday evening saying they would not take it in, being full.

Visit to Wyat at his Board of Works Office tomorrow, by Rose's desire communicated by a note. Previous visit to Rose by appointment at 11 tomorrow in consequence of a visit and note to Rose at the Treasury yesterday. This man makes appointments without difficulty—Long never would make any.

Bp out of humour because application not made to him in a *full enough* manner by Mr Pitt. Smith constantly faithful and communicative, tells me every word and paints to me every gesture. Tomorrow I hope will present something of an opening—Rose at any rate is in earnest.

Motion by Rose I observe in this day's paper for accounts of Hulk expences etc.

Horses safely lodged today in the Stable. Bill to pay for them between 2£ and 3£.

1228

To Samuel and Mary Sophia Bentham

2 December 1796 (Aet 48)

Q.S.P. Friday 2 Decr 1796

Animals,

Wyat, the formidable Wyat, is our own. It was difficult to answer for such a body, but his notion was clearly, that it 'would be for their benefit to come into the proposal'. He received me with civility, and when he had read the papers (which by the bye your animalships have not read) the civility seemed improved into respect. He is to come and see Panopticon, and to get fed, which set him a bowing and sniggering as if he liked the thoughts of it.[2] I contrived to throw the sketch of Blackburn's Battersea Rise Prison in his way. 'That's a hand not unknown to you.' O no, that's *Bunce's*. Yes—you know the sort of relation he bears to us.

No, I don't. Oh yes, I understand you. Aye, a very clever little fellow. J.B. I have often heard him speak of you in terms of great affection and respect. Who was it wrote that book about the Panopticon—You or your Brother? I—how came you to know

1228. [1] B. L. VI: 370. Autograph. Docketed: '2 Dec. 96'.
   [2] James Wyatt, the architect, was a noted *bon viveur*.

anything about it?   Ld Sheffield³ put it into my hands—I have
read it. I believe I may say the whole of it at odd times—as I could
find Leisure.   Oh yes: I remember somebody used to be saying, well
I must bring Jam Wyat here to see your Raree show—I had forgot
who it was—Ld Sheffield of Lord Somebody else. I would ask you
to come and see it—but what signifies it?—You have no time.   Oh
yes I have—I'll find time.   I'll not ask you now, what time. Your
time is not at your command—when you can make it convenient
you will let me know.   That I will.   Suppose you were to come at
a sociable hour?   With great pleasure—and so it came about.

     After all I never saw Rose. After I had vibrated from 11 till ½
after 2, a jumble of incidents brought me his Clerk, the same man
I saw before who told me that it was absolutely impossible for Mr
Rose to see me today, for that he was wholly occupied with writing
the letters about the Loan business. In the course of the conversation
the Clerk, who seems a confidential sort of a person, told me that
'*I should not lose any* point by not seeing Mr Rose before I saw Mr
Wyat'—and so it proved.

     Wyat, by his own desire kept my papers, promising to return
them in a day or two. They were Plan[s] for the Division of the land.
Your betters to take ⅔ leaving the Chapter ⅓ Cricket Ground
included 1 Sheet—Observations showing that it would be for their
interest to come into the plan, another Sheet—Sketch showing the
Division, with Observations showing the demand I should have for
the ⅔ in question. Memorandum Sister to get whipt for wanting to
fob me off with 60 Acres.

     Rencontres two with your friend Ld Spencer in the passage even
with the Treasury. The light was so that I did not see him till we
has almost crossed. How do you Mr Bentham? Something I don't
know what muttered in return. 2d Rencontre ½ hour afterwards in
the same place—had crossed again before I had well recognised
him. Cold weather Mr Bentham for you to be still at this work—by
that time we had quite passed. I hallooed out to him—Well my
Lord—you'll have no more trouble from me—I am sorry to have
had to give you so much—heartily sorry—bow from his Lordship,
who immediately after was out of sight.

     Rencontre with Wilberforce and Treasury Lord Smith. Rapid

³ John Baker Holroyd, 1st Earl of Sheffield (1735–1821), an authority on commerce
and banking, but chiefly remembered as the close friend and editor of Edward Gibbon;
M.P. 1780–4, 1790–1802; president of the Board of Agriculture, 1803; P.C. and a lord
of the Board of Trade, 1809; created Baron Sheffield in Irish peerage, 1781, and in
U.K. peerage, 1802; became Earl of Sheffield, 1816.

jaw work too long to detail, but from which I found the[y] both consider the business as in a fair train.

Young Galloway[4] has run away with the savings of the Corresponding Society so Ford[5] the Justice has just told me.

It would be a good thing enough if you happened to be here at the time Wyat got fed—he seems a pleasant man enough.

1229

To Samuel and Mary Sophia Bentham

3 December 1796 (Aet 48)

Q.S.P. Saty. 3d Decr 1796

Animalcules

Authority to get a Bill drawn—jobation from the great Lowndes for not having done it already. Message from Rose this morning at ½ after 12, that he had been waiting for me ever since 11. If any such intimation was given me by the Clerk yesterday I either did not hear it or forgot it, in my anxiety not to be too late for Wyat, under a spur given me by the said Clerk. When I got there, hurried into Rose's room—saw there not Rose he being just then gone down to Pitt, but Lowndes who on summons, had been there ever since 11 in expectance of meeting me. After explanation about the appointment Lowndes opened the conversation by saying how much Mr Rose was in a hurry to get rid of the business, by which on explanation I found he meant *dispatching* it—doing it—not leaving it undone. Rose, on coming in, told me that Wyat was not only of our way of thinking, but promised to assist on the business as much as possible—I could not this time show Rose any thing nor indeed continue the conversation, all his thoughts being engrossed by an explosion made in my hearing between him and two of the Clerks about an apprehension of there being no money in the Exchequer next week, owing to a supposed neglect among the Clerks. Resolution declared that if so and so, not a single Navy [man] could or should be paid next week—that's for you—'National

---

[4] Alexander Galloway, who, with his father, Thomas, had worked for the Benthams (see letter 1117, p. 191 above). He was an assistant-secretary of the London Corresponding Society, and employed at this time as a 'mathematical machine-maker'; later he had his own engineering business in London (see E. P. Thompson, *The Making of the English Working Class*, 2nd edn., Harmondsworth, 1968, pp. 171, 271).

[5] Richard Ford, barrister. See above, p. 140 n. 1.

1229. [1] B.L. VI: 371–2. Autograph. No docket. Addressed: 'To Genl Bentham / etc. etc. etc. / Portsmouth Yard'. Postmark: 'DE.3.96.D.'

credit would be ruined'—how they will jumble it amongst them, the Lord knows. Good opportunity had we been rich Bankers to have lent them £200,000, the sum in question, for 2 or 3 days to stop the gap.

Sent to namesake. Namesake in such tribulation incapable of doing the business.[2] Mrs B's son dying[3] as they fear—retracing in search of Lowndes—hope to have Butler[4] confirmed, being recommended by Bentham.

In haste extreme

1230

FROM PATRICK COLQUHOUN

4 December 1796

Mr Colquhoun (one of the Magistrates of Police) presents his respectful compliments to General Bentham, and begs to know on what day and at what hour he can have the honor of waiting upon him, on the Subject of his plan for Building Penitentiary Houses.

Mr Colquhoun's object as General Bentham may possibly have seen in His Treatise on the Police, is to promote the Completion of this very useful Establishment and his chief object in waiting on the General is to learn from him what obstructions are at present in the way of completing his design and whether Mr Colquhoun could be made useful in removing them?

Mr Ford accompanyed Mr Colquhoun to General Benthams about 15 months ago to Converse on the same subject but were not so happy as to meet him at home.

Charles Square Hoxton
4th December 1796

General Bentham

[2] Probably William Bentham, barrister.
[3] Perhaps a son of Mrs William Bentham by a former husband.
[4] Charles Butler, the Catholic barrister.
1230. [1] B.L. VI: 373–4. Autograph. Docketed: '1796 Dec 4 / Panopt. / Colquhoun Charles / Street Hoxton / to / J.B. Q.S.P.'
Addressed: 'General Bentham / Queen's Square Place / Westminster.' Although addressed to Samuel, the letter was clearly 'designed by description' for his brother, as Jeremy Bentham notes in his reply (letter 1232).
Patrick Colquhoun (1745–1820), a metropolitan police magistrate from 1792 to 1818, published a *Treatise on the Police of the Metropolis* in 1796 and was the author of a number of other books and pamphlets on poor relief, the liquor traffic and trade in general, including the important *Treatise on the Population, Wealth, Power and Resources of the British Empire in every Quarter of the World*, 1814.

1231

FROM WILLIAM LOWNDES

4 December 1796

Dear Sir

I am now shut up in the Waiting Room at Mr Pitts, where probably I may be left for some time. If you could come here we could talk about your Business

Downing Street

Yrs W. Lowndes

1232

TO PATRICK COLQUHOUN

6 December 1796 (Aet 48)

Sir

In the absence of the General my Brother, who in the course of his duty is at Portsmouth your note of the 4th instant, directed to him by name but designed by description for myself was opened by me.

In answer to your obliging inquiries I have the satisfaction of informing you, that the Penitentiary business is just now pushing forward with a degree of spirit, for which I make no doubt but that it has been more or less indebted to your interesting work.

The inclosed paper may seem to afford you a tolerably comprehensive view of the Penitentiary, as it stands at present modified, architecture and economy included. The Proposal it contains has been adopted with little variation in the terms of the Contract which has lain for near these two months, ready engrossed for signature.

The only remaining cause of delay is that which respects the spot, for the fixation of which a fresh Bill is in preparation.

I should have great pleasure in showing you the spot itself for which there would be still light enough so late as 3 o'clock, and the distance you come from affords me a plea for insisting on the

---

1231. [1] B.L. VI: 375–6. Autograph. Docketed: '1796 Dec 4 / Panopt / Lowndes Downg Street / to / J.B. Q.S.P. / To go to him there / Went accordingly.'
    Addressed: 'J. Bentham Esq / Queen's Square Place / Westr.'
1232. [1] B.L. VI: 377–8. Autograph draft, with signature. Docketed: '1796 Dec 6 / Panopt. / J.B. Q.S.P. to Coloquhun / Charles Square Hoxton.'

pleasure of your company afterwards, to an unceremonious dinner in a Batchelors house at 5, which will allow time enough for a glance at the models before dinner, as well as for conversation afterwards.

A course of engagements for uncertain days renders it difficult for me to propose an earlier day than Friday or Saturday in next week. I shall hope to hear that one of these two days can be made to suit your convenience.

The Penitentiary System forms the principal subject of a very diffuse work, printed these 5 years though as yet inedited, a copy of which as soon as it can be got from the Binders, should wait upon you in the meantime, if I knew of some intermediate place at which a book in 3 volumes small 8vo could be addressed to you. I have have the honour to be with much respect

Sir
Your most obedient
and obliged humble Servant
Jeremy Bentham

Mr Colquhoun.

1233

To Samuel Bentham

6 December 1796 (Aet 48)

Q.S.P. Tuesday 6 Decr 1796

The poor dear Sick Horse has been restored to health, under Puss's auspices, to a sufficient state at least for undertaking the journey, which commenced accordingly this morning, as they tell me, at 8 o'clock: and it is for this purpose, and this only, that under the same auspices, I take up the pen at present. Your John[2] reckons to be with you tomorrow between 2 and 3. I never saw him, but gave orders for his being taken care of.

Letter from Thompsons[3] for Poore at Redbridge on the subject of the 2 Bills—saying 'This is therefore to say that you *might* depend on the amount being sent to pay them before they are due and to beg you will accept them, as the returning the Bills to South[amp]ton where they were discounted will very much injure the credit of Mr Poore, for whom I am etc.' As after this letter the

1233. [1] B.L. VI: 379. Autograph. No docket or address.
[2] Evidently a servant of Samuel.
[3] Not identified.

327

infamy as well as the expense in case of the non performance of this promise would fall upon the non-performer, not on you, I shall accept the Bills if pressed to do so by any one calling on me before I have had time to receive your answer. No I shan't upon looking at your letter[4]—I shall put off the man till I can hear from you.

1234

To Samuel Bentham

9 December 1796 (Aet 48)

Q.S.P. Friday 9 Decr 1796

I can not take upon me to give the commission to Lloyd without further instructions. Your tube to be let into the Digester is I suppose to receive a thermometer tube. This indicates heat: but how is the pressure indicated—Oh, perhaps there is already a contrivance for this—I must see Lloyd about it.

Meantime what say you to using Salt in water for the Balneum to give the requisite increase of heat?

With submission might it not be an advantage if the skrew were so far extended along the outside of the tube, as to admitt of the tubes being lowered to near /close to/ the bottom of the Dissolver, or raised to near the top?—viz: for the purpose of being fixed at the most convenient height, and ascertaining whether any and what differences in point of heat result from any and what differences in point of elevation. (i.e. distance from the bottom of the vessel) in the above scale. This skrew (you may say) will add so much to the thickness of the tube, and thence diminish the accuracy of the thermometer cased in it viz: by impeding the celerity and compleatness of the communication of the temperature from /between/ the fluid to /and/ the thermometer. If this be to be apprehended, you might have two such tubes, one adapted to the one purpose, the other to the other.

Neither Edw. Collins nor I have been able as yet to meet with any thing concerning the proportions (in fluids /liquids/) between pressure and temperature.

Mr Riley[2] at the Admiralty has refused to frank any more of what he calls private letters. I did not perfectly observe the packet

[4] Missing.

1234. [1] B.L. VI: 382–3. Autograph. Docketed: '9 Dec. 96'.

[2] Edward Riley, Admiralty extra clerk, 1792–1800; junior clerk, 1800–7; senior clerk, 1807—16; first class clerk, 1816–32.

in question which Jack sent by the Post. It was at any rate better to send it thus than to run a risk of its lying at the Admiralty as Cronstadt did without any intimation till it was enquired after.

Dr Smith t'other day met Ld Grosvenor in the Street, and had some conversation with him about Panopticon. 'As far as he understood as yet,' (Ld G. said) 'he should be against it.' Per contra Skinner's friend Hale³ has had communication on the subject with Ld Salisbury: and it has been communicated to me such has been the frankness of all parties that it had been a project of Ld S: to offer his ground to Government as a site for Barracks. This will render it very pleasant treating with Estcourt (Ld S's agent at Linc. Inn) who was not at home this day when I called but is to be tomorrow at 11.

Moreover between the Willow-Walk and Campbel and White's Wharf is (I believe I told you before) a strip of land Garden Ground about 13 or 14 acres, the property of a Mr Wise⁴ whose residence and principal estate is near Warwick. I have found his Agent, Smith No. 22 Strand a China shop keeper from whom I learn that there is no likelyhood of any repugnance on the part of Mr Wise. I am to call and see maps etc. tomorrow. Mr Wise, God bless him, has been for this 4 months incapable of attending to business through /by reason of/ a family affliction and if I were to write him a letter on the subject of any of his property hereabouts he would send it and refer the business (Smith tells me) to himself, Smith. At the back of this Garden Ground of Wise's runs a meadow, which as far as I understand at present belongs to Ld Grosvenor. By letting Ld G. have an equal slice of that part of Ld Salisbury's Estate which joins upon his own the arrangement might, as it should seem be rendered a very convenient one to all parties. Moreover although Ld Grosvenor's opposition, were it determinate would be formidable, yet Ld Sy. would be a powerful co-adjutor on our side.

A pleasant circumstance attending Wise's property is that 'it is in a manner in his own hands', there being either no lease upon it or none but what is on the point of expiring.

Campbel and White's Wharf, it seems, is Wise's: but he holds a Wharf of the Dean and Chapter: and I am inclined to think it is

³ Perhaps John Hale, listed in 1781 as a Captain in the 18th Company of Royal Marines at Plymouth; put on half-pay, 1783.
⁴ Henry Christopher Wise (1738–1805), owner of part of Tothill Fields, high sheriff of Warwickshire (*Burke's Landed Gentry* and *Gentleman's Magazine*, Feb. 1805, p. 184, and Nov. 1818, p. 392).

that. The House I coveted of *White's* is not attached to the Wharf, but is his own freehold.

Edw. Collins is to be clawed away tomorrow and no determinate prospect of his coming again. His mother, whom the Devil make tobacco-stoppers of, puts her *veto*.

I don't know whether I told you that about Xmas Parlt is to adjourn to the 8th of Feby. But there is great hope of the Bill's passing before the adjournment, since the Tax Bills are to do so, and none of them are yet in.

1235

To Samuel Bentham

10 December 1796 (Aet 48)

Q.S.P. 10 Decr 96

I thought I had told you of my having seen Lindegren on Sunday—He told me he should leave town for Portsmouth on Tuesday: but that Mrs Lindegren (whom I have not seen) was to go to her friends in Kent on Monday or Tuesday for the next fortnight or three weeks. I called twice in person at the Hotel, besides once by proxy in the person of E. Collins who left a letter.[2] The second time on my return I met Lindegren just come out of Q.S.P. I shewd him the lines of your two Houses.

I have just been confabulating with Lloyd about your dissolver. He is to put in hand every thing that can be put in hand till we hear from you about it, which we expect to do on Monday. He and I agree in our ideas about it perfectly. The whole [hole?] at present made for the Valve, being in the water must be plugged up (which he says can easily be done) to make room for your *thermometer*-case which we suppose had best be in the center: and he is to think of the mode of making it moveable upon occasion for the purpose of ascertaining whether any difference in point of heat results from the thermometer-case being plunged in the water or in the steam, and in both cases nearer to or farther from the boundary of the Vessel. Supposing what Mr Varley told us in his second lecture to be true the failure of your attempt to melt pitch by steam is not to be wondered at. Explaining the difference between latent heat and sensible

1235. [1] B.L. VI: 384–6. Autograph. Docketed: 'Dec. 96.'
[2] Missing.

heat, he told us that Resin absorbed such a quantity of heat before it melted as to require almost as much heat to melt it as Iron to make it red hot. I don't know very well to think this: but if it be true, Pitch may be seen in the same or nearly the same case. It may be a bad conductor of heat while unmelted.

I have seen this morning both Mr Estcourt, Ld Salisbury's Agent, and Smith,[3] Mr Wise's Agent. Mr Estcourt had not a plan of the Estate in its present state: but shewed me a magnificent plan of it in a once projected state covered with buildings in squares and circuses, with a rental in Ground rents amounting [to] £1100 and odd or £1400 and odd a year I forget which. He acknowledged he did not look upon that plan as being *now* a feasible one. It was first stopt by a refusal on the part of Ld Grosvener to open the way for carriages by his House: and since then by a consciousness of the improbability that people would come to live there, and therefore that Builders would undertake to build Houses there. He acknowledges a willingness to treat for the whole or for a part: but that he (Mr Estcourt) expects something of a tempting price. He speaks as if great facility were to be expected on the part of his Lordship, were it only in the view of serving the public as he or an Ancestor of his had done in the instance of the Foundling Hospital who are now making thousands a year by building leases: but he conceives it to be his (Mr Estcourt's) duty to protect his Lord against his own facility. His behaviour has however been throughout extremely handsome, pleasant, flattering to a certain degree (for he knew me by reputation) and explicit. The Map of the land in its present state is in the hands of the Surveyor and Architect Payne[4] of Hammersmith who drew /projected/ the aerial Squares and Circuses —things exactly like those of the Adams for Tothill Fields as formerly mentioned.

Mr Smith was rather more upon the reserve than before: but however showed me a map of /including/ the strip in question which he opened no further, so as not to exhibit Campbell and Whites: it appears to be between about 11 and 12 acres: beyond it, on the left hand of the Willow Walk as you go from Rochester Row is a piece of about 17 Acres: but betwixt that and the 11 Acres there intervenes a piece about a third /in length/ of the length of the 11 Acres (which is but a narrow strip) belonging to Ld Grosvenor, who had before declared he would not sell.

[3] See letter 1234, p. 329 above.
[4] James Paine (1745–1829), architect; it is doubtful if he practised much after the death of his more famous father, who left him very well off.

Mr Estcourt and I settled it, that if I did not like the whole, the part the furthest from Grosvenor House viz. the Meadow of Communication and meeting[?] would be most eligible on Ld S's account as leaving free the most buildable part of the Estate.

Smith would not tell me the Rental.

The material thing is a disposition to treat in general on the part of Ld Salisbury, and no known impediment to that disposition on the part of Wise. This being established, the prices will be fixed in case of disagreement by a Jury. Wise's has no lease upon it: which happens also to be the case with ¾ or more of Ld Salisbury's, all that I had particularly coveted included.

I send you a little Sketch:[5] for you to consider what advantage there may be in having 2 necks to the Horseshoe rather than one: and whether considering the course of the river it will be material that /whether/ they be near one another or remote.

I don't know whether I shall have the Bill from Butler tonight. I called on him and found him at a stand owing to a difficulty which I enabled him to get the better of.

1236

FROM PATRICK COLQUHOUN

10 December 1796

Mr Colquhoun is much obliged to Mr Bentham for his obliging Note,[2] as well as for the very pleasing information which it Conveys, upon which he sincerely congratulates Mr Bentham to whose perseverance and public spirit the Public are much indebted.

Mr Colquhoun now anxiously hopes that nothing will occur to stand in the way of the Completion of the Panopticon which is indeed most exceedingly wanted. In case of any new difficulty it will afford him much pleasure to lend all the assistance he can for its removal.

Mr Colquhoun will with great pleasure wait on Mr Bentham on Friday next, and with a view to see the Spot he will endeavour to be

---

[5] Missing.

1236. [1] B.L. VI: 387. Docketed: '1796 Dec 10 / Panopt. / Colquhoun Charles Square Hoxton / to / J.B. Q.S.P. / 2d.'

Addressed: 'Jeremy Bentham Esq / Queen Square Place / Westminster.' Postmark: '8 o'clock / DE.12 / 96. MORN'. Stamped: 'Lombard St. / Unpaid / Penny Post'.

[2] Letter 1232.

with him at half past two or even at an earlier hour if Mr Bentham shall suggest a wish on that head.

Mr Colquhoun is much obliged to Mr Bentham for the copy he was so good as to send him of his proposals, and also for his kind intention of sending him his work on the Penitentiary System which he had the pleasure of glancing at slightly some years ago through the medium of his friend Mr Wickham.[3]

Charles Square Hoxton
10 December 1796

1237

To Edmund Estcourt

12 December 1796 (Aet 48)

Queen's Square Place Westmr 12 Dec.r 1796

Sir

Understanding it to be your intention upon Mr Payne's[2] return to instruct him to communicate with me on the subject of the proposed purchase, it has since occurred to me, that though it was in a manner settled between us that to save time I should apply to him in the mean time by letter for such communications as could be made at his present distance, yet an application of that sort from an utter stranger would stand but a very precarious chance of producing its effect without some sort of authority from you. I write this therefore to beg the favour of you if you have no objection to address a line to him for the above purpose. There seems very little chance of his being himself able to afford any very satisfactory information at his present distance from the seat of his business: but probably, with or with out the expedient of sending keys, he could give such directions to whoever at Hammersmith has charge of his affairs, as would enable such his representative to furnish the desired documents. Perhaps the purpose might be answered in a still more simple and effectual mode, were you either to give /favour/ me with a line addressed directly to somebody at his house, or to send to me the letter addressed to him, leaving it open that I might go with it to his house, and take my chance of its

[3] William Wickham.
1237. [1] B.L. VI: 390–1. Autograph draft. Docketed: '1796 Dec 12 / Panopt. Toth. Fds / J.B. Q.S.P. / to / Estcourt Stamp Office / and / Estcourt / to / Payne, Northend / Hammersmith.'
[2] James Paine.

producing the requisite effect without the circuity of passing through his hands.

> I have the honour to be,
> Sir, your most obedient
> humble Servant
> Jeremy Bentham

Ed. Estcourt Esqr.[3]

1238

TO SAMUEL BENTHAM

13 December 1796 (Aet 48)

Q.S.P. 13 Decr 1796 Tuesday

I have nothing to say worth the expense of paper: but as Lloyd is going you would conclude me dead if I did not say I was alive.

This cursed Roman Catholic fellow[2] with all his promises has not sent me my Bill yet.

With pain for company (beside Skinner) I have spent the morning in search of Payne,[3] and returned with disappointment. My companion pain was a slight tooth ache in more parts than one which I have had off and on for about these three weeks. It has like most of my pains been a poor miserable weakly sort of thing, for pain does not find stuff enough in my constitution to gain strength upon. The Payne I went in quest of is the son of a gun of an Architect that wanted to cover Ld Salisburys part of the Panopticon ground with Squares and Circus's. Estcourts letter was directed to him at Northend—he had left his residence at Northend as I found when I got there this 1½ year, and was gone to live next door to one of the Packhorses at Turnham Green beyond Hammersmith. When I came there neither was he at home, nor any Clerk of his,

---

[3] There follows a copy of a letter from Estcourt to Paine, viz. 'Dear Sir / I beg the favour of you to furnish the Bearer, Mr Bentham with any information in your power as to the quantity of land belonging to the Marquess of Salisbury situate at Westminster and that you will let him have a sight of the ground plan of his Estate in that neighbourhood according to its present circumstances / I am / Dear Sir / Your obedient Servant / Edm.ᵈ Estcourt / Lincoln's Inn / 12 Dec / 1796.

J. Payne Esq / Northend / Hammersmith / In his absence to be / opened by his Clerk.'

1238. [1] B.L. VI: 392–3. Autograph. Docketed: '13th Decr 96'.

[2] Charles Butler.

[3] James Paine.

(for I had taken the precaution to have myrmidons put into the direction) nor did he ever do there any kind of business. He has a lodging in St Martin's Lane where all his Papers etc. are. Yet Estcourt had been so particular in his supposed knowledge of him, as to know that, being gone to Hampshire, he was not to return till this day sennight. The Hampshire expedition however, though not yet begun is still in contemplation—I shall try to catch him and his Clerk tomorrow morning.

Skinner tells me that Buchan[4] is talking of going to the E. Indies. If he goes it will be, must be, with recommendations from Col. Brathwaite,[5] who is a patient of his, and being a constant invalid and a Nabob, must be a good patient.

As I was setting out in came Metcalf. He pretended it to have been his intention, when the returns moved for by Rose relative to the Convicts came before the House, to have stood up and asked Dundas what became of the Penitentiary Scheme,—of his fine speech—and the £2,000 that had been given in consequence—God forgive me—I don't think he had any such intentions—being a mute,[6] and over and above not wonderfully *serviable*—My version is, that he had heard that everything was in train, and so came with his merit-making intentions.

He had had some people dining with him, of the Navy Board cast uttering blasphemies—talking of public money thrown away in making Mast Ponds[7] /Houses/ that would have room to hold tin masts and of some ship or other that was forced to be docked or done something or [other] to at Redbridge—meaning doubtless No. 1. He himself was of course of our side. I talked to him about Administrators with the education and knowledge of Day-labourers, and wished that he might be allowed to publish the papers on both sides: adding that if this was to be the trade it must come to that. I did not ask who the people were—thinking that if *liver* was to be long'd for, better that of an *individuum vagum*, as logicians term it, than a determinate one.

Tomorrow the green cloth lays itself down in the Study, whereby

---

[4] Either Alexander Peter Buchan, a pupil of Dr George Fordyce, or his father, Dr William Buchan.

[5] Probably George Charles Braithwaite (1762–1809), who became a lieutenant-colonel in 1794; he served as aide de camp to his father, Major-general John Braithwaite (1736–1803), at Fort St. George, Madras, but went on half-pay in 1797. The baronetcy to which he succeeded in 1803 became extinct on his death.

[6] Philip Metcalfe hardly ever spoke in Parliament.

[7] One of Samuel's contrivances at this time was a 'mastpond' at Portsmouth (M. S. Bentham, *Life of Sir Samuel Bentham*, 1862, p. 134).

Sister's Visitors may tread the boards without treading up infamy. This day Buchan dines here to gratify his longing for Macaroni, item Skinner in consideration of the long and muzzling walk I have been treating him with, though I spared him part of it, leaving him at a Coffee house a mile short, to save him from a threatened rain which let me off tolerably cheap. Tomorrow Alderman Clark— Thursday Skinner to go to Varley's. Friday Colquhoun to go to Tothill Fields etc. I believe I told you I had the satisfaction of hearing from Estcourt that the Dean and Chapter have nothing to do with the *Bank*, Millbank: the trees on it are Ld Salisbury's, as well as the obligation of repairing it. So that we shall not have them to bother us when we come to cut it.

Sister! Sister! are you alive?

Here's a letter for you, made out of the same materials God Almighty made the world out of. But I got here just after 5, and betwixt that and dinner time nothing else was to be done.

Your letter of Sunday about Lloyd was of course communicated to him. He is to be the Bearer of this by the Mail.

Skinner's Map of London making man has been written to about Tothill Fields twice—and is to call on Skinner about 10 tomorrow.[8]

---

[8] William Skinner wrote to Bentham on 23 or 24 November 1796 (wrongly docketed by Bentham '1797'): 'I have enclosed your letter to Mr. Harwood, as the best and readiest way to make him understand what you wish, and have not the least doubt of his complying immediately with your request, provided the state of his map make it practicable' (B.L. VI: 507–8). Bentham's letter is missing and so are the two from Skinner to the map-maker and engraver, Richard Horwood, whose name is mis-spelt several times in the correspondence. He was preparing a large-scale *Plan of the Cities of London and Westminster, the Borough of Southwark and Parts adjoining* (issued in parts, 1792–9, 2nd edn. 1807, 4th edn. 1819).

Horwood wrote to Skinner on Saturday, 10, or Sunday, 11 December 1796 (Bentham's docket is again wrong): 'I am sorry I was not at home when your Messenger called, as I would have sent the *two Plates Engraved*, but I think they would not have been of any service as they only take in part of Tothill fields, cutting through the part/tract/wanted. In my letter [missing] I observed that the drawing of the remaining pt to the River I would complete in about a fortnight—but observing by your letter that Mr. Bentham is extremely anxious I have set about completing this part and will without fail send them to his house on Monday morning and hope that short delay will not be very material' (B.L. VI: 389).

There was, however, further delay, for on 16 December Horwood wrote to Bentham himself: 'I caught so violent a cold in getting wet in my Feet on Monday and the weather proving so exceedingly bad ever since has prevented me finishing the drg of Tothill fields—you may rely on my taking the first opportunity of completing it and calling on you' (B.L. VI: 517, wrongly dated and docketed by Bentham '1797').

A final apology came from Horwood to Bentham at the end of the year: 'I am exceedingly Sorry you have had the trouble of sending again for the Sketch of Tothill fields—I have but one excuse to make for so long neglecting you—which is I did hear from some person whom I do not at this moment recollect, that the Plan you are engaged in was either abandon'd or about to be—I have not finished engraving that

This if well done may save the expense perhaps of a survey on purpose.

I have been reading Charlotte Smiths new novel, Marchmont,[9] and much edified. There is a Mrs Bentham in it—an insolent cross-grained Governess—Young Lady's private Governess.

Wonderful elogiums everywhere of the Monk (a novel)[10]—but they say it's not fit for Ladies.

I have compounded the matter with Mr Fell Parker[11] and got 4 dozen only of his cheap wine—then in addition about $2\frac{1}{2}$ dozen of sample wine—This I hope will last me till the end of the starvation season—The rest of your generosity will help pay milk scores and keep the Devil out till you come.

1239

FROM CHARLES ABBOT

15 December 1796

I am going out after breakfast with one or more Lady or Ladies—therefore cannot come then to Q.S.P. but will contrive to call in the course of the day if released in time.

Thursd. Dec. 15.

part but I suppose the rough Sketch herewith sent will answer your present purpose, and which I believe to be tolerably correct—but there must certainly for your purpose be a particular plan taken of the ground and laid down on a larger Scale—and as I shall within 6 or 8 weeks have finished my general Plan I have no objection to do, provided it can wait so long—I wish you to understand that what I now send is only a rough working Sketch of the place and which when you have done with, I beg to have back as there are some things on it of which I have no Copy . . . ' (B.L. VI: 708–9. Docketed by Bentham '1798 Dec 24' but clearly sent two years earlier).

[9] *Marchmont, a Novel* (4 vols., 1796).

[10] The famous Gothic novel (1795), by Matthew Gregory Lewis (1775–1818); M.P. 1796–1802; his less-known *Journal of a West Indian Proprietor*, not published until 1834, showed his concern for the slaves; he had sold his plantations and supported the movement against the slave trade and slavery.

[11] Fell Parker, wine merchant, 259 Wapping.

1239. [1] B.L. VI: 394. Autograph. Docketed: '1796 Dec 15 / Panopt / C.A. Pallmall / to / J.B. Q.S.P.'
Addressed: 'Mr. Bentham.'

1240

TO SAMUEL BENTHAM

16 December 1796 (Aet 48)

Q.S.P. Friday Decr 16 1796

Search made about Horses, according to order, by the *organ* of Mr Barret[2] the Coal Merchant. No Horses or Horse ascribed either to S. or J.B.

Thanks to dear pretty Sister for her medical Advice[3]—laid up in lavender against need. No acute pain—nothing but a dull one the result or concomitant of swelling. Two stumps—one on each side and one in each jaw. Buchan dines here tomorrow—perhaps he may be charged with the extirpation of them—one or both.

Bill[4] sent by Butler to Browne[5] on Sunday night—Browne to make himself something would not send it, but kept it till 2 or 3 on Wednesday to bring it himself. J.B. in too much pain to do anything to signify to it that day. Began upon it yesterday—is now going on with it and is far advanced in it, after taking Abbot's advice about some points of prudence belonging to it yesterday. J.B. has done what related specially to Tothill Fields which is what nobody else could have done. What could have been done by others, sadly, miserably done by Butler; much cobbling necessary or it would neither answer the purpose nor pass the House. O Lord! O Lord! that there should be no option in this wicked world but between intractable noodles and tractable ones.

Great need of Sister for a Nurse: viz: to sit on t'other side the fire, in adjacency to Puss.[6]

Green Cloth laid down in as much state as if the *Board* had laid it.[7]

Work hard and rise early—bravo!

Good Boy and Girl—a sugar plum apiece.

1240. [1] B.L. VI: 395–6. Autograph. Addressed: 'To / General Bentham / Portsmouth Y⟨ard⟩.' Postmark: '⟨. . .⟩ 16.96'.
Part of the Ms. has been torn off (see n. 9 below).
[2] Barrett and Mitchell, coal merchants, Broadway, Westminster.
[3] A missing letter from Samuel and his wife is indicated.
[4] To amend the Penitentiary Act of 1794.
[5] Either their friend, William Browne, or another attorney of the same surname (there were five of them in London at the time).
[6] Either a cat, or the unknown lady friend.
[7] A humorous comparison with the Board of Green Cloth, a department of the royal household concerned with the commissariat and so called from the green cloth on the table round which the officials sat.

Shoots sent from the Garden (T. F. Garden)[8] and planted, with sticks to them in the Q.S.P. Garden. Sets of each sort at discretion of the existing Gardener. J.B. neither being Gardener, nor existing, could not meddle in it. They are said however to be, as he wished them to be, mostly in near view of the House, viz. in the Grass plot shrubbery.

[9](All well at Charlotte Street, quoth Koe.) ⟨Though⟩ts of J.B. upon the Q.S.P. Chapel—neat profits as formerly stated £6 a year: But paid 5s, observe five shillings, and no more Mr Lloyd (Island Lloyd)[10] the Landlord. No bad bargain if one could get it for 30 years purchase upon 5s or 20 times 5s, plus the value of the materials.

Collins to be advised with about it—the best way perhaps, might be to get some Reverend Divine to treat for it, as if for a project in his own line.

J.B. in a visitable condition—not a visiting one. Sleep rather a difficult operation, J.B. knows what a copious one occupying the night. Ante-jentacular[11] walk muffled with two handkerchiefs. Without this the seat of the Soul would be out of order as well as the seat of the Tooth Ache.

1241

FROM PATRICK COLQUHOUN

16 December 1796

Mr Colquhoun's respectful Compliments to Mr Bentham and is extremely concerned to hear of his illness which he sincerely hopes will be of Short duration. As there is much danger of Catching Cold at this Season of the year Mr Colquhoun hopes that Mr Bentham will not think [of] exposing himself to the Air *for a week at least* and the more especially as nothing appears to press very much at present for the proposed interview.

[8] Tothill Fields?
[9] The top portion of the second sheet, perhaps with writing on it, is torn off: about three inches are missing.
[10] The landlord of the 'island house'.
[11] A Benthamite term for 'before breakfast'.
1241. [1] B.L. VI: 397–8. Docketed: '1796 Dec 16 / Panopt. / Colquhoun / to / J.B. Q.S.P.'
    Addressed: 'J. Bentham Esqr / Queen's Square Place / Westminster.' Postmark: '7 o'clock / DE. 16./ 96. NIGHT'. Stamped: 'Lombard St. Unpaid Penny Post'.

Mr Baldwin[2] who is a most worthy and patriotic character much and justly in the Confidence of the Duke of Portland, and who has much to do in the Criminal Department was much gratified two days ago at hearing from Mr Colquhoun the progress which Mr Bentham has been able to make at the Treasury in respect to his agreement, which he is sure Mr Baldwin will be happy not only to accelerate but to assist in promoting such Legislative Regulations as may yet be necessary to carry the measure into execution, and the rather as the Duke of Portland has placed in Mr Baldwin's hands the Chief Superintendances of *Convicts Pardons* etc.

Whenever Mr Bentham's health will enable him to Call on Mr. Baldwin at the Secretary of State's office Whitehall (where he generally is every day from 12 till 3) he will be glad to see him and to learn precisely his progress, and when he expects that his Panopticon will be completed for the reception of Convicts, and whether in the meantime Mr Bentham could suggest any plan for employing a Proportion of those who at present crowd the Goals and who are not of that very depraved class who are selected for transportation to New South Wales. Upon these and other topics connected with the employment of Convicts it will afford Mr Baldwin much pleasure to Converse with Mr Bentham: and although Mr Colquhoun ventures to state this on his own authority without the knowledge of Mr Baldwin yet he is confident from the zeal of that Gentleman to improve the police of the Metropolis, and his genuine desire to do good that he will discuss the subject with great pleasure.—And Mr Colquhoun himself promises to his mind much gratification from the information which Mr Bentham is able to Convey upon all branches Connected with the subject of Penitentiary Houses: but particularly on what relates to the proper Selection of accessible *Productive Labour* applicable to the health, Strength and Situation of all the various Classes of Delinquents adjudged to be punished in this way.

Charles Square Hoxton
16 December 1796

---

[2] William Baldwin (c. 1737–1813), barrister; M.P. 1795–8 and 1802–6. He acted as Counsel in questions relating to the criminal business of the Home Office and was influential in penal policy (see L.J. Hume, 'Bentham's Panopticon: an Administrative History—I,' *Historical Studies*, xxvi (1973), 710 n. 23).

1242

FROM WILLIAM WILBERFORCE

17 [?] December 1796

My dear Sir
    How is it I have neither seen nor heard anyth'g from you this
age. Tho' swarm'd in upon by assailants on all Hands, you have
often been in my Mind. But I have not been able to get to you.
How does your Matter go on? and can I do any Service?
Where is the Genl? I have a letter to send him.
    I shall be at Home all this Evg
                                        Yours ever
                                            W.W.
Pal Yd
Saty 4 and ½ O'Clock

1243

TO WILLIAM WILBERFORCE

17 December 1796 (Aet 48)

                                    Saty. Decr 17. 97 [1796]²

    Sensible, truly sensible to your sollicitude—Unfortunately
sensible also to tooth-ach, jaw ach, and ear-ach, which have
bereft me of all active mental faculties for the present—I hope
relief from a Tooth Drawer, when I can get hold of him. Bill drawn
—but requiring alterations, such as can be made by nobody but
me. Yesterday I worked at it—today I have been fancying myself
unable. Abbot, when you happen to see him, could tell you as
much about the Bill as is worth having.
    Magnus Apollo is Latin for a Tooth-drawer—OUTIS is Greek for

1242. ¹ B.L. VI: 412–13. Autograph. Docketed: '1796 Dec 24 / Panopt. / Wilberforce
O.P. Yd / to / J.B. Q.S.P.'
    Addressed: 'Jere: Bentham Esq.'
    Bentham's docket must be wrong by a week, as this letter was evidently the one
enclosed to Samuel Bentham in letter 1245. Perhaps as a result of his toothache he
also misdated by a year letter 1243, which is clearly a reply to this letter.
1243. ¹ Bodleian Library, Oxford. Wilberforce Ms d.15/141. Autograph.
    ² As noted above (letter 1242 n. 1), this is misdated by a year: it is clearly a reply
to letter 1242, which was evidently written and received on the same Saturday, 17
December 1796.

Wilberforce as well as for Ulysses—but his sollicitude to be aliquis, is balsam to the mind.[3]

The General is at Portsmouth. I don't know when to expect him thence—certainly not for some days.

1244

To Samuel Bentham

19 December 1796 (Aet 48)

Q.S.P. 19 Decr 1796

Collins has brought a parcel of drawings about Pumps which he says will speak for themselves, but he is moreover to speak for them by tomorrow's Post: they are putting up to go by the Mail this evening.

Sadler will I suppose be in the dumps. Hornblower's Engine[2] is declared by Verdict given without hesitation (if all the papers are to be believed paragraphs being doubtless inserted by Bolton)[3] to be an infringement of Bolton's, and the objection of want of explicitness in his specification disallowed.

Johnson for Rock to [. . . ,] Spurring for S.B.[4]

'*London*' Dec. 19. 1796. The 40 Cannon Locks finished—waits for Orders where they are to be sent.

J.B. incapacitated for all business, but restored on Saty evening by a touch of Buchan's Lancet. Worked hard and well at the Bill yesterday—expect to finish it today and to get it passed by Butler tomorrow.

On the other side is the copy of a paper left by Hatchet[5] of York Street on his calling and my sending down word as was the case that I was not fit to see any body upon business.

---

[3] There are several strained classical allusions in this paragraph. The sun-God Apollo was, among other attributes, the patron of medicine, and by 'Magnus Apollo' Bentham may mean 'great doctor'. The complimentary comparison of Wilberforce to Ulysses is underlined by reference to the name of 'Outis' which the Greek hero assumed in the cave of Polyphemus (*Odyssey*). 'Aliquis' signifies 'someone or other'.

1244. [1] B.L. VI: 399–400. Autograph. No docket. Addressed: 'To / General Bentham / Portsmouth Yard.' Postmark: 'DE.19.96'.

[2] Jonathan Carter Hornblower (1753–1813), one of a family of engineers; he worked for James Watt, and his steam engine was declared an infringement of the Boulton and Watt patent in 1799.

[3] Matthew Boulton (1728–1809), engineer, in partnership with Watt at Birmingham; among his inventions was machinery for minting coins; f.r.s.

[4] The meaning of this partly illegible message has not been found.

[5] Not identified.

£50 Guineas being asked, *pounds* I suppose would be taken. Mr
Bunce whether he takes or takes not a wife, is likely to take Pupils,
some of whom by lodging or boarding or both might help fill the
House and lessen the expence. It is the house spoken of in my last—
I don't know how the business happens to be referred from neigh-
bour Hatchet to distant Hayes.[6] I shall enquire further when I can
find time. Mean time I should like to know whether Mr Bunce
desires to have the refusal of it.

'House and Premises No 26 Queen Square to be let on a running
Lease for 4 or 7 years or longer (with the usual Covenants) at 50
Guineas a Year. Mr Hayes No 332 in Oxford Street.'

Collins tells me the Navy Board people have got hold of some
project of yours relative to Store-keeping—asks me whether I know
any thing of it—being answered in the negative—expresses anxiety
at the thought of any thing of that sort getting to the Enemy before
it has been well digested.

Colquhoun talks in his book about Store keeping. There can not be
a more active Citizen. I received a 3d long note on Friday evening
I think it was offering services undertaking for assistance from
Baldwin, ci-devant Special Pleader, now M.P. Secretary ⟨of
Sta⟩te's Law Clerk, D. of Portland's right-hand man—and charged
with the Convict Department—Employment for Convicts asked
for—Answer—helping to build Panopticon.

Note of Saty[7]
Wilberforce talked on Saturday of addressing somebody or
something to you.

1245

To Samuel and Mary Sophia Bentham

20 December 1796 (Aet 48)

Thanks to Brother and Sister for the joint Letter[2]—this line
from Wilberforce,[3] who has just been pressing me into the dinner
service.[4] I have been asking him what it was he had to do with you.
He says he has not time to talk about it. He wanted to have seen

[6] An Oxford Street bookseller (see letter 1245).
[7] Note added in pencil on cover (See letter 1242, p. 341 above).
1245. [1] B.L. VI: 401. Autograph. No docket or address.
[2] Missing.
[3] Evidently letter 1242.
[4] The reading is clearly 'dinner', though 'divine' service would make better sense.

you tomorrow. Abbot not being visible today and Wilberforce interrupting me, taking the Bill back to Butler consequently stands over till tomorrow.

Hayes mentioned as receiver of Bunce's House is a Bookseller and bought the House by Auction t'other day—it is to be had from Xmas

Poor Kitty!!![5] Now for Salts and Hartshorn.

Decr 20 – 96

1246

TO SAMUEL AND MARY SOPHIA BENTHAM

22 December 1796 (Aet 48)

Q.S.P. 22 Decr 96

Puss pricks up her ears and cocks her tail at the thought of having a Sub-puss to ease her of part of the cares of Government.[2]

The bed system is a sad system. I shrug up my ears and say nothing—some people were born to obedience, and I am one of them. By order from Essex Street bed's head and tester of coarse Callico will be up on Saty. Curtains etc.—every body shrinks with horror from the responsibility of choosing. Beds head to be measured and measure sent to night to Essex Street for bed, but bed exactly according to order is supposed not to exist in the nature of things. Why it should not, I know not—Daddy, Sister, and Stewart[3] at Q.S.P. on Sunday at 6. When I spoke of a late dinner, according to order, Daddy mentioned 6, so all we can do is to take advantage of the custom and make it $\frac{1}{2}$ after 6, unless special order comes from Portsmouth for a later hour, naming the Hour.

Bill left at Lowndes's with Butler's signature. A fabric solely of J. Bian workmanship, a good half of J. Bian adamant—the remainder and no more, of Office Rubbish, for fear of the Board of Works—Butler's quill[?] sent to the Red Sea—about 5 times the length of the other with not half the matter—proportions $\frac{1}{10}$ of efficient matter $\frac{9}{10}$ Rubbish. There is a man for ⟨. . .⟩[4] amour propre —(meaning Butler) he deserves ⟨. . .⟩.[4]

[5] Bentham sometimes referred thus to Catherine II, Empress of Russia, who died from apoplexy on 17 November 1796 (cf. *Correspondence*, ii, 188 n. 4).

1246. [1] B.L. VI: 404–5. Autograph. No docket. Addressed: 'To General Bentham / etc. etc. etc. / Portsmouth Yard.' Postmark: 'DE.22.96.D'.

[2] Bentham is expecting his brother and sister-in-law to stay at Queen's Square Place.

[3] Not identified.

[4] Words illegible owing to a tear in the paper.

J.B. has had half a dozen colds of different sorts, since his last—
a slight excuse of a cough is all he at present has to boast of.

Daddy looking quite blithe and gay.

Skinner at Dinner to go to Varley's—something picked up by him
at Varley's this last night.

1247

FROM J. A. ALEXANDER

22 December 1796

Dear Sir

I have left the additional Clauses with Mr Lowndes, who is
reading over the Bill and he will be glad to see you any Morning on
the Business after toMorrow. Mr L. leaves Town next Wednesday

> I am Dear Sir
> Yr obedt Servt
> J. A. Alexander

22 Dec 1796
10 O'Clock Even.

1248

FROM CHARLES ABBOT

23 December 1796

I do assure you it is not for want of inclination—but from
absolute want of time—that I have not called upon you these two
days and this Morning I am going a few Miles out of Town.

> Yrs Ever
> C.A.

Frid. Morng.

1247. [1] B.L. VI: 406–7. Autograph. Docketed: '1796 Dec / Panopt. / Alexander /
Bedford St.'
Addressed: 'J. Bentham Esq.'

1248. [1] B.L. VI: 408–9. Autograph. Docketed: '1796 Dec 23 / Panopt. / C.A. Pallmall / to / J.B. Q.S.P.'
Addressed: 'Jer.y Bentham Esqr'.

1249
FROM CHARLES ABBOT
24 December 1796

Saty Morng
Decr 24.96.

The current week is the worst possible time for me to show my readiness to obey your requisitions.—Accounts Deeds Letters Appointments of Business and Pleasure—each in their way indispensable have prevented and must continue to prevent my calling upon you. I have hastily run over the two Drafts. All I can say is that nothing strikes me which is objectionable and I think that Mr. L.[2] must be particularly desirous of deviating into unnecessary industry if he impedes your progress for the sake of his own Additions or improvements.

1250
FROM JAMES PAINE
26 December 1796

Sir

if you will have the goodness to meet me at my apartments in St. Martin's Lane next Wednesday about 1 O Clock, I will shew you the Plan of the Ground intended to be covered with Buildings upon the Marq's of Salisbury's Estate at Mill Bank, and see how far you can be accommodated, your having pointed out the quantity wanted.

I am Sir
Your humble Servt.
J. Paine

St. Martins Lane Decr 26.96.

P.S. As I believe I shall be obliged to undertake a short Journey, in that case, I shall not be in Town any other day this Week, and if the day and hour named is not suited to your other Engagements I will either call in Queen Sqr. Place, or inform you of my return.

1249. [1] B.L. VI: 410–11. Autograph. Docketed: '1796 Dec 24 / Panopt / C.A. Pallmall to J.B. Q.S.P. / Draught approved.
[2] William Lowndes.

1250. [1] B.L. VI: 414–15. Autograph. Docketed: '1796 Dec 26 / Panopt. Toth. Fields / Payne / St Martins Lane / to / J.B. Q.S.P.'
Addressed: 'Mr. Bentham / Queen's Sqr. Place / Westmr.' Postmark illegible. Stamped: 'Covent Gdn. Unpaid Penny Post'.

1251

FROM WILLIAM LOWNDES

27 December 1796

I think this Draft does not suffly. provide for the two Cases
which may happen, either that the purchase Money may be agreed
upon, or that it may not. There sh'd be power in either case to pay
the Money into the Bank i.e. in the first Case the purchase Money,
in the 2d the reasonable price—subject to the verdict of a Jury. This
may be done by a genl Reference to the former Act.

Notice to the feoffees etc. is a separate Clause applg to the
former and the present Act.

1252

TO GEORGE ROSE

29 December 1796 (Aet 48)

Queen's Square Place Westmr. 29th Decr. 1796

Copy

Mr Bentham ⎧ To the Atty General Jany
to   ²Copies marked A sent ⎨
Mr Rose ⎩ To the Sollr General Jany

Sir

A Bill, for the purpose of the Penitentiary business, having
been settled and signed by Mr Lowndes, I take the liberty of
troubling you with it, in hopes of your having the goodness to
introduce it, if you see no objection, by the *first* convenient opportunity into the House.

The plan of the Bill, you will, I flatter myself, concur with Mr

1251. ¹ B.L. VI: 416. Docketed: '1796 Dec 27 / Panopt. / Lowndes Temple / to / J.B.
ibid. / Corrigenda in the Draft of Penitentiary Bill.'

1252. ¹ B.L. VI: 421–2. Copy, with autograph notes.
Bentham drafted a similar letter to Charles Long, beginning: 'Sir / A Bill, for the
purpose of the Penitentiary business, signed and settled by Mr Lowndes, having
been prepared by direction from Mr Rose, and Mr Rose being gone out of town, as
I understand, for a fortnight, I take the liberty of submitting it to you, in hopes of
your having the goodness to continue your assistance in relation to that business,
and accordingly to introduce it, if you see no objection, by the first convenient
opportunity into the House.' The draft is, however, docketed 'not sent' (B.L. VI:
417–18).
² Heading in red ink.

Lowndes, in thinking not only a perfectly eligible one, but in truth the only practicable one. The object of it is *general*, and *general* only—to explain and amend the existing Act, principally by extending the provision of it to '*Land in the state of Waste and Common Land*' so as that a fit spot may be composed of land in separate ownership, or of Common Land, in whatever proportions may be found most convenient.

As to *Tothill Fields* in particular, a separate string of clauses has been framed (and has received a *general* approbation from Mr. Lowndes) calculated to meet the views of the Dean and Chapter as far as those views are understood: to the end that clauses to that effect may, at a proper stage of the Bill, be moved on their part, and consented to on the part of the Treasury, shou'd the choice of that spot be persevered in on the part of the Treasury, and should the Dean and Chapter think fit to have recourse to the Treasury and to Parliament, for the *peculiar* indulgences and accommodations provided for them by those clauses.[3] All this will be matter of *grace* on the part of the Treasury: for as there is not a syllable in the Bill that bears any exclusive aspect to *Tothill Fields*, there is not a syllable of it, as to which the Dean and Chapter or anybody else, can claim to be *heard* in *Parliament*, on the ground of any *particular* interest. The Bill, if passed, will lay *that* Waste, like any *other* Waste (as land of *superior* value lies already) at the mercy of the Treasury: and it is only by coming to Parliament, and getting some such particular clauses as are above spoken of, inserted into the *General* Act, that the Dean and Chapter (unless they get a particular Act on purpose) can obtain any of those modifications and accommodations which they have appeared to wish for, or in short, either now or at any time hereafter, derive the smallest profit from the spot. I have the honor to be, with all respect.

> Sir
>
> Your most obedient and humble Servant

George Rose Esqr
    etc. etc. etc.

An Abstract of the Bill is submitted on a separate paper[4]

---

[3] Footnote in pencil: 'No use in inserting these clauses: being particular they must be paid for as such: the indulgence shewn might therefore be as well administered by a particular Act on purpose: observing only in the meantime to abstain from taking so much of the Land as it is proposed the D. and Chr and Parish shall have to themselves.'

[4] Missing: a much corrected 'Abstract of the Draught of the Penitentiary Bill . . . 1794' is in B.L. VI: 419–20. It is headed: 'B. 28 Decr 1796. Copies marked 'B' sent to the Atty and Sollr General.'

1253

FROM PATRICK COLQUHOUN

31 December 1796

Sir

Accept of my sincere thanks for your obliging present—as far as I can judge at the present moment I shall be able to wait on you on Thursday next and I will seize every spare moment I have in the interim to peruse the valuable MS you have favoured me with.[2] I will avail myself of your kind permission to Cause one of my Clerks copy your Table of Cases which to me will be an invaluable acquisition, and I will also if possible obey your wishes by Committing to paper what occurs to me, though I despair after experiencing the able manner in which you handle every subject to suggest much improvement.

On the Subject of the Poor Law however I have in my mind one momentous idea which if practicable I think would cure all those evils which every good man must deplore—I will explain it when we meet, and then I will bring with me all your MS.

> In great haste I have the honor to be with
> very much Respect
> Dear Sir
> Your very faithful and
> obliged humble Servant
> P. Colquhoun

Charles Square
31 December 1796

Jeremiah Bentham Esq.

1253. [1] B.L. VI: 423–4. Autograph. Docketed: '1796 Dec 31 / Poor / Colquhoun / Charles Squ. to J.B. Q.S.P.'
    Addressed: 'Jeremiah Bentham Esqr. / etc. etc. / Queen Square Place / Westminster.'
    [2] Bentham had evidently sent him drafts of his 'Essays on the poor laws', with a request for comments. The letter is missing.

1254

TO SIR JOHN SCOTT

3 January 1797 (Aet 48)

Queen's Square Place Westmr. 3 Jan. 1797

Sir

The Draught herewith sent waits upon you in consequence of a letter I have just received from Mr Rose,[2] in which he says—'If you will send the Draught to the Attorney General I will obtain Mr Pitts authority for its being perused and settled by the Attorney and Sollicitor General: it may thus be presented at the meeting of the House in next Month'

For the sake of elucidation, I take the liberty of adding a copy of a letter of mine marked A to which that of Mr Rose is an answer—together with 3 others marked B, C, and D,[3] and of begging that those papers together with this letter may accompany the Draught on its passing into the hands of Mr Sollicitor General: as likewise /and moreover/ that as in the instance of the *Contract* Mr Sollicitor General had the goodness to remit it to me in its amended state, previously to its official conveyance to the Treasury, the same indulgence may be extended to me in the instance of the present Draught. I have the honour to be, with all respect,

Sir,
Your most obedient
and humble Servt
Jeremy Bentham

Mr Atty. Genl.

P.S. The fair copy (containing some further corrections of Mr Lowndes's of little consequence) not having been yet sent me back by Mr Rose, I take the liberty of sending, *for the present,* a rougher copy in lieu of it. The other I hope to send tomorrow.

1254. [1] B.L. VI: 425. Autograph draft. Docketed: '1797 Jan 3 6 / Panopt / J.B. Q.S.P. / to / Atty Genl. Linc. Inn / With Penitentiary Bill / to Atty and Sollr Genl / Jan 6.'

The docket also covers letters 1255 and 1256.

[2] Missing.

[3] Letter 1252 was the one 'marked A', but no copy of it, or of that 'marked B', are with this draft; there are copies of papers marked C and D in B.L. VI: 427–9 and 430–1. C is concerned with 'Technical defects above alluded to in the Abstract of the Draught of the Penitentiary Bill Jany 1797 as existing in the Act of 7 July 1794. 34. G. 3. ch. 84. § 6.' D deals with § 4: 'Appropriation of the purchase money for the waste $\frac{1}{15}$ to the Lord: $\frac{14}{15}$ to the Parish, in case of Poor Rates.'

Since writing the above, I observe that Mr Lowndes' corrections above spoken of, are entered in the margin of the copy herewith sent.

1255

TO SIR JOHN SCOTT

6 January 1797 (Aet 48)

Q.S.P. 6 Jany 1797

Mr Bentham takes the liberty of acquainting Mr Attorney General that upon enquiry at the Treasury he has been informed that the copy signed by Mr Lowndes of the Draught of the Penitentiary Bill has been transmitted from thence to the Sollr Mr White, who it is supposed at the Treasury, either from particular directions or the supposition of its being the official course, will transmitt it in the first instance to the Sollr Genl. Should that have been the order pursued, it is Mr Bentham's humble request that the papers marked A.B.C. and D. with which he had troubled Mr Att. Genl may follow the Draught to which they belong.

1256

TO SIR JOHN FREEMAN MITFORD

6 January 1797 (Aet 48)

Q.S.P. 6 Jan 1797

Mr Bentham takes the liberty of acquainting Mr Sollr Genl. that having in conformity to directions contained in a letter from Mr Rose transmitted to the Atty Genl a duplicate Copy of the Draught of an intended Penitentiary Bill, to which were added some Papers marked A. B. C. and D. relative to the subject, he has since learnt at the Treasury that a more authentic Duplicate has been transmitted from thence to Mr White, by whom as supposed it will be laid before Mr Sollicitor Genl in the first instance.

Should this have been the case, Mr Bentham takes the liberty of apprising Mr Sollr. Genl of the existence of these Papers and of his having requested of Mr Atty Genl that in that event they may follow /be added to/ Mr Sollr Genls copy of the Draught.

1255. ¹ B.L. VI: 426. Autograph draft. Docketed with letter 1254.
1256. ¹ B.L. VI: 426. Autograph draft. Docketed with letter 1254.

1257

To William Baldwin

13 January 1797 (Aet 48)

Sir

Understanding /I understand/ myself to possess by favour of Mr Colquhoun, for a General license to /trouble/address myself to/ wait upon you on the subject of the Convict business, I look forward to a period at which that honour may be as useful as it is flattering to me. But as that period (though I hope not far distant) is not yet arrived, and as every moment I can command is occupied at present by a pursuit which will admitt of no adjournment, I mean the thorough discussion of the Poor Bill, I may not perhaps seek to avail myself of the indulgence, till some specific occasion /happens to/ presents itself on my part unless in the mean time you on your part should have any commands for me in relation to that or any other subject, in which event I should have great pleasure in attending you at your office or elsewhere at any time you will have the goodness to name.

Mean time I take the opportunity of begging the honour of your acceptance for a copy of an published work on the Penitentiary business for the present, untill a copy in a more commodious state shall have been returned from the Binders.

In regard to the construction of the building the details have in good measure been superseded by more recent amendments.

What concerns the article of management may be considered as unchanged.[2]

1258

From William Baldwin

14 January 1797

Whitehall

Sat. 14 Jan 1 o cl p.m.

Sir,

I feel myself particularly obliged to you for your Letter and

1257. [1] B.L. VI: 440–1. Autograph drafts. Docketed: '1797 Jan 13 / Panopt J.B. Q.S.P. / to / Baldwin / D. of P. Off. / Treasury Chambers.'
    [2] A crossed-out alternative draft is on fo. 441.
1258. [1] B.L. VI: 442–3. Autograph. Docketed: '1797 Jan 14 / Panopt. / Baldwin D. of Portlds Office / to / J.B. Q.S.P.'

entreat you to accept my best Thanks for the Honor you have done me in sending your Publication. I do most sincerely hope that you will be able to accomplish your great and good Plan and trust that you will rest assured of every aid which can be afforded you from this Office as far as depends upon myself.

The System of the Hulks in my opinion ought to be reprobated by every moral man, it tends to the total extinction of every hope of reformation.

If I can have your permission it is my Intention to pay you a Visit early in the next Week and as His Grace the Duke of Portland has expressed a wish to see your Model, I will take the Liberty to invite His Grace at the same time.

I hope in the mean time to have an opportunity of reading your Work by which means I may perhaps give you less trouble in explaining.

I have the Honor to be
Sir
Yr Obt Servt
W. Baldwin

1259

FROM PATRICK COLQUHOUN

20 January 1797

Charles Square Hoxton
Friday Evening 20 January 1797

Dear Sir

Although I have met with a great number of interuptions in the Course of the present week which I did not Count upon, I was resolved in some Shape or other to keep my word by Committing to writing the ideas I had formed in my mind relative to the improvement of the System of the Poor.

The inclosed Sheets[2] contain my thoughts hastily Written as they rose spontaneously in My mind for as it is the first time I ever put pen to paper on the subject of the poor, so is this the first and only Sketch I possess—I wrote it rapidly and have of Course no Copy, for it is only this moment finished. You must not therefore

1259. [1] B.L. VI: 444–5. Autograph. Docketed: '1797 Jan 26 / Poor / Colquhoun Charles Square / to / J.B. Q.S.P.'
Addressed: 'Jeremiah Bentham Esq. etc. etc.'
[2] Perhaps his 'Plan of Poor Law reform', among the Bentham Mss in U.C. CLI: 39–43.

be surprised to find in it both mistakes and inaccuracies. I trust however you will understand by it what I mean, and particularly that I do not mean *that a Joint Stock Company shall manage the poor. That was not my idea*—I mean a *Responsible Association and Agency*, as you will see explained in the MSS.

I will thank you much for your opinion upon it as soon as you can: I mean as to its *principle*, and *practicability*. I think the plan will approach as near to *Individual Management* in the way I propose to manage it as any thing *short of it* can be—but I must refer you to the MSS itself.—Had I not been so exceedingly pressed hurried and interrupted I should have treated the subject more at large. The shorter however any Subject can be compressed the better as long Papers are not read. I meant to have been with you one day this week, and even this day or tomorrow, but I find I cannot possibly accomplish it. The distance is so great and the weather is so bad, and I am moreover so inveloped in business, Official and Private, to which add the time I bestow upon the poor as you'll see from the Plan and paper now inclosed which I have drawn up and just received from the Press.[3] You will find in them some information relative to Pawn Brokers which will probably astonish you.

Let me hear from you as Soon as you can and believe me always

My Dear Sir
Yours sincerely
P. Colquhoun.

P.S. I was an hour with the Duke of Portland last monday to whom I explained Your plan as well as I was able. His Grace appeared much pleased to find you had made such good progress at the Treasury, and I have every reason to believe he will give you every assistance he can as His Grace seems anxious about the means of providing a place of labour for Convicts. I have no doubt he will be glad to see you.

Jeremiah Bentham Esqr etc.

[3] Missing.

1260

FROM WILLIAM BALDWIN

23 January 1797

Whitehall
Jan 23d 1797

Sir
    I take the Liberty to inform you that His Grace the Duke of
Portland intends himself the pleasure of attending you on Thursday
next about 12 o'clock if that time will suit your convenience. He
desires me at the same time to mention that by possibility he may
be disapointed in his Intentions, in which case he hopes you will
excuse [him] and give your permission for the Thursdy following.

I am Sir
yrs mt truly
W. Baldwin

1261

FROM ALEXANDER PETER BUCHAN

1 February 1797

Sir
    I received this morning from Mr Robertson a corrected copy of
his pamphlet² which he requested me to transmit to you.

I am Sir
yr obedt Servt
A. P. Buchan

Wednesday
Fby 1st

1260. ¹ B.L. VI: 446–7. Autograph. Docketed: '1797 Jan 23 / Panopt / Baldwin
Treasury / to / J.B. Q.S.P.'
1261. ¹ B.L. VI: 449–50. Autograph. Docketed: '1797 Feb 1 / Poor / Dr Buchan
Store St / to / J.B. Q.S.P. / Sending Robertson's pamphlet.'
    Addressed: 'Jer. Bentham Esqr.'
    ² This was the pamphlet by Herbert Robertson, advertised in the *Morning
Chronicle*, 30 Jan., 7 Feb. 1797, viz. *An Abstract of some important Parts of a Bill now
depending in Parliament intituled, 'A Bill for the better Support and Maintenance of
'the Poor'; with some Practical observations on the Effects that will probably be experienced in many Parishes, particularly those that are large and populous, if the said Bill is
passed into a Law. Prepared by a Committee of the Joint Vestry of the United Parishes
of St. Giles in the Fields, and St. George, Bloomsbury.* Printed for John Stockdale,
Piccadilly. Price 1/-. For Robertson, see letter 1263, n. 1.

1262

FROM BARON ST HELENS

6 February 1797

My Dear Sir,

Having arrived in town only last Night I have such a world of things to do this morning that it will be impossible for me to call in Qu. Squ. But I will come to you without fail tomorrow at twelve. In the mean time I send you the Accompanying Lucubrations[2] which bating a little Foppery in the style are tolerably well done and contain above all some very curious Facts which will be well worth your notice.

sincerely yrs
St H.

Monday Morng

1263

FROM WILLIAM ROBERTSON

10 February 1797

Sir

When I received your draft and the Copy yesterday between one and two o'Clock, I felt extremely anxious to compare them together myself, in the manner pointed out in your note[2]—but a very great press of urgent public business which indespensibly required my immediate and close attention, compelled me to the necessity of referring them to one of our Clerks: he being tolerably intelligent, and in general a correct copier, I hope you will find it done in such a manner as not to give you much disatisfaction. The punctuation is what I fear the most, that being a part of composition which I

1262. [1] B.L. VI: 451–2. Autograph. Docketed: '1797 Feb. 6 / Poor / Ld St H. Gt. Russel Street / to / J.B. Q.S.P.'

Addressed: 'Jeremy Bentham Esqr'.

[2] Missing.

1263. [1] B.L. VI: 456–7. Autograph. Docketed: '1797 Feb. 10 / Poor / Robertson Gr. Russ. Str. No. 95 / to / J.B. Q.S.P.'

Addressed: 'Bentham Esq. / Queen Square / Westminster.'

Herbert and William Robertson were attorneys at 95 Great Russell Street, Bloomsbury. Herbert was vestry clerk to the united parishes of St Giles in the Fields and St George, Bloomsbury, and he was the author of the pamphlet.

[2] Missing.

have always thought that every writer has, in some degree, peculiar to himself, and is to be managed in such a manner as he who expresses a sentiment is the best judge of, in order to give his argument the full force that he intends. Pardon me for making these crude and hasty observations.

I fear there is some doubt whether the *public* will ever have the benefit of your invaluable and convincing arguments on this very interesting and important subject; and though they may convince the Minister (a most desirable matter) I should very much regret the not seeing the whole thereof in print: but if you have reasons to the contrary, I can only console myself with the reflection that, as I copied the principal part of the Manuscript myself, I enjoyed the pleasure of the forcible and ingenious reasoning as I went on.

> I am with the truest respect
> Sir Your most obedt hble Servt
> Wᵐ Robertson

No. 95 Gt Russel Street Bloomsbury
10th Feb: 1797

1264

FROM ALEXANDER PETER BUCHAN

11 February 1797

Sir

I have sent you several documents from Mr Robertson (I am sorry I could not do it earlier) which I have engaged shall be returned to him this evening, as you will perceive by his enclosed note.[2] I must therefore request you to return them to him without

1264. [1] B.L. VI: 460. Autograph. Docketed: '1797 Feb. 11 / Poor / Buchan Store Str to J.B.'

[2] The note from Robertson to Buchan is dated 11 February and begins: 'I send herewith a Copy of our Vestry's Pamphlet with, wafered into it, the anonymous Letr. or Note you mention, which was sent to Bloomy. Vestry Room with a copy of last years *Heads* of the Bill—I shall want that Note again this Evening . . . I do not see any objection to Mr B's seeing Mr Ruggles's Letter, but confide in his not shewing it to any other person or mentioning it to Mr Rose etc. as I do not know that I am or am not *warranted* by the Gent, to whom it was written, to make it public.

I send also herewith the Shrewsbury Pamphlet which if Mr B. has not seen he may find worth reading. . .' (B.L. VI: 458.)

Thomas Ruggles (d. 1813) was a bencher of the Inner Temple, a magistrate and later deputy lieutenant of Suffolk and Essex. He had written *The History of the Poor, their Rights, Duties, and the Laws respecting them. In a Series of Letters*, 2 vols., 1793–4; new edn. 1797. The Shrewsbury pamphlet mentioned was Isaac Wood's (see n. 3 below).

fail, as I shall not be at home. Wood's pamphlet[3] is much the best I have seen and comes nearest yours. I have no doubt that such general reprobation will force Pitt to abandon his plan. But I do regret to think that with many well meaning people he will have the credit of having proposed a mode of relieving the poor, which he was opposed in the execution of.

yours

A. P. Buchan.

1265

FROM GEORGE ROSE

11 February 1797

Mr Rose presents his compliments to Mr Bentham and shall be very glad to see [him] at the Treasury tomorrow at Eleven o'Clock.

O. P. Yard
February

1266

TO SIR FREDERICK MORTON EDEN

13 February 1797 (Aet 48)

Queen's Square Place Westmr
13 Feby 1797

Sir

By way of homage for the instruction and entertainment I am reaping from your most valuable work,[2] permitt me to beg the honour of your acceptance for a book, which though not comprized,

---

[3] Isaac Wood, *A Letter to Sir William Pulteney, Bart. Representative in Parliament for the Borough of Shrewsbury, containing some Observations on the Bill for the better Support and Maintence of the Poor, presented to the House of Commons by the Right Hon. William Pitt.* Shrewsbury, printed by J. and W. Eddowes, 1797. Price 1/-. Wood was also author of *Some Account of the Shrewsbury House of Industry*, 1791; 4th edn., 1795.

1265. [1] B.L. VI: 459. Docketed: '1797 Feb 11 / Poor / Rose O.P. Yd / to / J.B. Q.S.P.'

1266. [1] Eden MSS. Autograph. Docketed: 'Jeremy Bentham'.

Sir Frederick Morton Eden (1766–1809) was a disciple of Adam Smith, whose principles he applied to the study of poverty, on which he wrote a great deal. See n. 2 below.

[2] Eden's important book on *The State of the Poor; or an History of the Labouring Classes in England from the Conquest to the Present Period*, 3 vols. 1797.

(as indeed it could not have been comprized) in your catalogue,[3] is not alien to the plan of it,—I am,

Sir,

Your most obedient and humble Servant

Jeremy Bentham

Sir F. M. Eden

Feb 1797

Documents not comprized in the Catalogue to Sir F. M. Eden on the Poor St Andrews and St George's Parish Rules, Orders and Accounts of the Workhouse—Printed April 1791—none printed since.

St James's Westmr. Sketch of the State of the Poor 1797—Mr B's copy just obtained from Mr. Angerstein Pall Mall—whose name is in the list of Vestrymen.[4]

1267

To WILLIAM WILBERFORCE

28 February 1797 (Aet 49)

Tuesday 28 Feb. 1797

Kind Sir

The next time you happen on Mr Attorney General, in the House or elsewhere, be pleased to take a spike, the longer and sharper the better, and applying it to the seat of honour, tell him it is by way of *memento*, that the Penitentiary Contract Bill has, for I know not what length of time, been sticking in his hands—and you will much oblige

Your humble Servant
to command—

N.B. A corking pin was applied yesterday by Mr Abbot.

[3] Eden's *State of the Poor*, iii, Appendix 18: 'A Catalogue of Publications in the English Language on Subjects relative to the Poor', listing 282 items.

[4] The first-named, untraced pamphlet is not contained in the *Catalogue* of Eden's library published in 1806, but the second one is, although not under the original title, which was: *A Sketch of the State of the Children of the Poor in the Year 1756, and of the Present State and Management of all the Poor in the Parish of Saint James, Westminster, in January, 1797.* Printed for John Stockdale, Piccadilly.

1267. [1] Bodleian Library, Oxford. Wilberforce Mss. d.13/41. Autograph, unsigned. Docketed: 'Mr. Bentham.'

The version of this letter printed in R. I. and S. Wilberforce, *Life of William Wilberforce*, 5 vols., new edn. 1888, ii, 172, omits the phrase 'to the seat of honour' and also the final short paragraph.

Bentham drafted a similar request to William Morton Pitt, but it is docketed 'not sent. Quere?' (B.L. VI: 448).

Whatever there would be any use in doing to the Bill, has been already done to it by the Sollicitor General.

1268

To William Wilberforce

6 March 1797 (Aet 49)

6 Mar. 1797

My dear Sir

I have heard it spoken of as a common practice for Atty Genls, when Draughts have been perused by Sollr. Genls in whose opinions they had confidence, to add their own signatures to those of their learned seconds, as a matter of course, and this too (I know not with what truth) with reference to present times. Would not the expedient be a proposable one? The subject-matter [is] of too little importance to occupy such high assistance etc.[2]

1269

From Arthur Young

21 March 1797

Mr Young's Compts to Mr Bentham and assures him that it will always give him pleasure to be able to assist his enquiries whenever it is in his power.

Monday Eve.

1268. [1] B.L. VI: 461. Autograph draft. Docketed: '1797 Mar 6 / Panopt / J.B. Q.S.P. / to / Wilberforce O.P. Yd / Atty Gen to sign DE confiance.'

[2] A crossed-out passage following 'high assistance' reads: 'for the benefit of which (entre nous) speaking from sad experience, I would not give two pence—but a great many two pences—a great many indeed! for the absence of it.'

1269. [1] B.L. VI: 462. Autograph. Docketed: '1797 Mar 21 / Poor / A. Young. Whitehall / to / J.B. Q.S.P.' Addressed: 'Jerey Bentham Esqr / etc. etc. etc.'

Clearly a reply to a missing written request from Bentham.

1270

To Sir John Freeman Mitford

25 March 1797 (Aet 49)

Queens Square Place Westmr 25 March 1797

Sir

Mr Attorney General whom I met yesterday by accident at Mr Wilberforce's told me that the Penitentiary Bill lies at present with you, and had the goodness to say, that whenever it came from you—*he* 'should not keep it a single moment,' unless anything came from you that should specially call upon him to consider it. Further than this I shall not trouble you than /otherwise than/ to say that, whenever the Draught goes from you to him, if you would have the goodness to direct your *Clerk* to give me advice of the transition, it would be a very material addition to your former favours. I repeat a liberty I formerly took of enclosing a letter[2] for your Brother, his present address being unknown to me.[3]

1271

To William Mitford

25 March 1797 (Aet 49)

Queen's Square Place 25 Mar. 1797

Dear Sir

A friend of mine who had been indebted to me for the pleasure of reading the only History of Greece that deserves the name was so desirous that the benefit of it should be reaped by other nations, that he addressed himself to a person who at his recommendation is translating it for the purpose of publication into French. The name either was not mentioned or has escaped me: what dwelt with me was the description: viz: the person who translated Gibbon:

1270. [1] B.L. VI: 463–4. Autograph draft. Docketed: '1797 Mar 25 / Panopt / J.B. Q.S.P. / to / Sollr Genl. Linc. Inn.'
[2] Letter 1271.
[3] There is much crossed through in this draft, including a final passage of some significance: 'In perusing the Penitentiary Contract after it had undergone your perusal, Mr Atty Genl, opposite the clause providing Superannuation Annuities for the Prisoners after discharge wrote in the margin a Query To whom payable. Of that unfortunate query the effect was a stop to the business for upwards [of] four months.'
1271. [1] New York Public Library, Manuscript Division, Miscellaneous Papers— Bentham, J. Autograph.

but whether the Histy. or the posthumous Biographical Memoirs— that too is more than I am able to say at this instant.[2] It occurred to me that possibly some ideas might present themselves to you which you might feel yourself disposed to communicate for the purpose of serving as instructions, to a person so occupied: for example the omitting or softening notes or other passages, which not being essential to the narrative might be in danger of keeping the book out of the hands of the Republican class of readers.

All this while the probability is that he is already known to you, and already in correspondence with you: but, should that happen not to be the case, I need scarcely say that I should be much flattered if you would lay your commands on me, and make use of me for the purpose—and in that way or any other enable me to contribute my mite towards the dissemination of the best antidote I know of to the raging pestilence of the times—

Believe me,
Dear Sir, with the truest respect,
Ever Yours,
Jeremy Bentham

W. Mitford Esq.

1272

FROM SIR JOHN FREEMAN MITFORD

27 March 1797

Dear Sir

My friend the Attorney General has practised a little of the Great Man upon you, tho' I believe very unwittingly. Your note[2] carried me to his chambers, where, with the assistance of the Solicitor to the Treasury, I found the Draught of an act of parliament

---

[2] None of the known translators of Gibbon's *Decline and Fall of the Roman Empire* undertook to translate Mitford into French, and this allusion cannot be traced (see Jane E. Norton, *A Bibliography of the Works of Edward Gibbon*, Oxford, 1940, pp. 140, 190 ff). The 'Memoirs of my life and writings' first appeared in March 1796 at the beginning of the *Miscellaneous Works of Edward Gibbon*, two folio volumes edited by his friend, John Holroyd, first Earl of Sheffield. They were quickly reprinted in Dublin and in Basle but not then translated (see Edward Gibbon, *Memoirs of my Life*, ed. Georges A. Bonnard, 1966, preface, p. vii).

1272. [1] B.L. VI: 465–6. Autograph. Docketed: '1797 Mar. 27 / Panopt / Sollr Gen Linc. Inn / to / J.B. Q.S.P.'

[2] Presumably the final version of letter 1270 above.

362

which you refer to, among a number of other papers, and have placed it before him. I have given him a small portion of the reproof which he has merited for his courtly conversation with you; but I must leave it to you to pile up the measure of his chastisement, by sending him an assistance to his memory, in the shape of a note, either barely monitory, or also objurgatory, as your better discretion shall suggest. For myself I shall beg leave to adopt his words; 'that I shall not keep the bill a single moment unless anything shall come from him which will specially call upon me to consider it.'

I have taken care of your note[3] to my brother, whose address is No 47, Great Marlbrough street.

> I have the honour to be
> Dear Sir,
> Your most obedt
> humble servant
> John Mitford

Jeremy Bentham Esqr.

1273

To Sir John Scott

30 March 1797 (Aet 49)

Sir

The Sollicitor-General, whom I may indulge myself in the honour of calling my friend, since it would be ingratitude in me not to consider him as such, has in a good-humoured way recommended it to me to address myself to you on the subject of a business, in which I have the misfortune to be but too deeply interested and which was sent to you three months ago, at a period of leisure, to be dispatched by a time which has elapsed these six weeks.—Were I to find myself compelled to do so, a second time, it is a matter of such serious import to me, that it would be impossible to me to treat it in any other than the most serious light.—For the chance of saving myself from a task so full of unpleasant circumstances, I shall wait yet a few days longer, in hopes that the reflections to which you can not be altogether a stranger, may in the mean time

---

[3] Letter 1271.

1273. [1] B.L. VI: 469–70. Autograph draft. Docketed: '1797 Mar 30 / Panopt. / J.B. Q.S.P. / to / Atty General / also to Sollr-General'.
Another draft is in B.L. VI: 467–8.

have operated any /some/ thing in my behalf:—I have the honour
to be, Sir,

Your most obedt and most humble
Servt
Jeremy Bentham

Mr. Attorney General.

1274

To Sir John Freeman Mitford

30 March 1797 (Aet 49)

Dear Sir

I trouble you with the inclosed,[2] in hopes that you will not
condemn me as having made an unwarrantable use, (for some use
it was absolutely necessary for me to make) of so generous a
confidence. What you know of is but a small part of what I have
suffered from the same quarter, though all from no other causes
than what you know of. Imagine and pity my situation, should
I have (what I am seriously apprehensive of) my fortune and
prospects to stake (not to speak of the service I have almost lost
the hope of rendering the public) against a character in so many
points respectable as well as amiable.

In requesting a favour of the Clerk I little thought that I was
sending the Master on a Clerk's errand, to hunt for papers so
perfectly out of date, that their very existence had become
questionable.

I have the honour to be, with the truest respect,

Dear Sir,
Your most obliged and
most obedt servant

1274. [1] B.L. VI: 470. Autograph draft. The docket to letter 1273 covers this one also.
[2] Probably a copy of his letter to the Attorney-General (1273).

1275

FROM ARTHUR YOUNG

2 April 1797

Dr Sr

For want of my papers in Town I am imperfect, but I suppose
Dyrom[2] will fill it; mine is also in Co.

1786 – 1.18. 0.
1787 – 2. 1. 2.
8 – 2. 5. 0.
9 – 2.10. 8.
1793 – 2. 8. 8.

[3] Sent in a subsequent note

1790 – 2.13. 2.
1791 – 2. 7. 0.
1792 – 2. 2. 4.

Yrs faithfully
A.Y.

1276

FROM SAMUEL ROMILLY

26 April 1797

26th April 1797

I have spoken to the Solicitor-general, and, at his recommendation, to the Attorney-general, respecting your bill; and
though the Attorney has not neglected it,—he has done what will
probably be as injurious to you. He has so fully considered it, that
he has a thousand difficulties which it will take a long time to get
over. He says it is the most unlike an Act of Parliament he ever
saw. I told him that Lowndes drew it. Was I right, or have I con-
founded it with a former bill? I begin to suspect that I have; for

---

1275. [1] B.L. VI: 471–2. Autograph. Docketed: '1797 Apr 2 / Poor Corn Price / A.
Young Whitehall / to / J.B. Q.S.P.'
  Addressed: 'Jere^y Bentham Esqr / Park.'
  Clearly a reply to a missing request from Bentham for statistical information.
  [2] Lieutenant-colonel Alexander Dyrom (d. 1830), who became a Lieutenant-
general by 1814. He wrote on military and other subjects: this probably refers to his
An Inquiry into the Corn Laws and Corn Trade of Great Britain, Edinburgh, 1796.
  [3] Inserted in Bentham's hand.
1276. [1] Bowring, xi, 116.

though Lowndes' compositions have many defects,—that of being unlike Acts of Parliament is not one of them.

Yours ever,
S. R.

1277

FROM SAMUEL ROMILLY

1 May 1797

Dear Bentham
I have attempted several times but in vain to speak to the Atty and Sollr. Genl. I will renew my Attempts tomorrow. How can I desire them to return a Draught laid before them by the Treasury to anybody but the Sollr. for the Treasury? It is as much their duty to communicate their Observns to the Treasy as to make them.

Yrs ever
S. R.
1 May 1797

1278

FROM CHARLES BUTLER

1 May 1797

Dear Sir
I saw the Attorney General today by accident, and I mentioned to him the Act of Parliament in question. He told me the Solicitor General had mentioned it to him: and had told him he did not approve of it.—That he himself had read it; and did not understand it—and seemed to insinuate the Plan of it was romantic.—

I am, Dear Sir, your most obedt h'ble Servt.
Chas Butler
Lincolns Inn
1 May 1797

1277. B.L. VI: 475–6. Autograph. Docketed: '1797 May 1 / Panopt. / Romilly Linc Inn / to / J.B. Q.S.P.'
  Bentham must have written to Romilly asking him to speak to the Attorney-General and Solicitor-General again. See letter 1279.

1278. 1 B.L. VI: 477–8. Autograph. Docketed: '1797 May 1 / Panopt. / Butler Lincs Inn / to / J.B. Q.S.P. / Ay. G. and S.G. / disapprove Draught of Bill.' Addressed: 'Jeremiah Bentham Esqr. / Park Place near Queen's Square / Westminster.' Postmark illegible. Stamped: 'Chancery Lane / Unpaid Penny Post'.

1279

F ROM S AMUEL R OMILLY

2 May 1797

2d May, 1797

Dear Bentham,
    I have done my best for you; but I am afraid you will think
I have done but little. I had a consultation this morning with the
Attorney and Solicitor General. As soon as the business of it was
over, I introduced your bill, and found that it had not been looked
at since I saw them last. However, they promised to settle it before
they parted, and I left them with the bill before them, and pens in
their hands. I pressed them to let me have the draught, or to permit
you to see it before it was returned to the Treasury, but was not
able to surmount their objections to such a proceeding. I told
them, I understood from you that they had promised, or at least
given you to understand, that they would communicate their
objections, if they had any, to you; but they had no recollection of
it, and I found I could make nothing of them. I told them, on
going away, that I should inform you that White would have the
bill to-day.

Yours ever,
S. R.

1280

F ROM S AMUEL R OMILLY

19 May 1797

Dear Bentham,
    I have not been able to get any satisfy Ansr from the S.G.
I shewed him your Letter[2] thinking it would have more weight
with him than anything I could say. He says you are very much
mistaken in supposing that a mere hint from him would have any
weight with W.[3] The fact he says is so different that he believes if

1279. [1] Bowring, xi, 116.
1280. [1] B.L. VI: 479–80. Autograph. Docketed: 'May 19 / Panopt / Romilly Linc Inn /
to / J.B. Q.S.P. / S.G. cannot ask Wh. / Wastes impracticability.'
    Addressed: 'Jeremy Bentham Esqr / Queen Square Place / Westmr.' Postmark:
'12 O'Clock / 20.MA / 97 NOON'. Stamped: 'Chancery Lane Unpaid Penny Post'.
    [2] Missing.
    [3] Joseph White.

he were to send to W to beg he would let him see the draft with the answer written by him and the A.G. W. wod refuse it. I could not press him further to expose himself to this refusal. I asked him what his objections were he said they were all objections to the bill only as a general bill and none of them would apply to a particular piece of ground. The objection was that the bill was general and that a general bill might in particular Cases be productive of great Injustice.

Yrs ever
S.R.

19 May

1281

To George Rose

22 June 1797 (Aet 49)

Q.S.P. 22 June 1797

Sir

Now that the cloud which hung over the Country when my Brother had last the honour of seeing you is in some measure cleared up,[2] I might have to accuse myself of being the author of my own destiny /delay/ if I did not sollicit the favour of your naming some day, for my attending you on the subject of the Penitentiary business.

I understood a day or two ago from Mr Baldwin that the Hulks and every other place into which a convict can be crammed are as full as they can hold: and amongst the several branches of the public service it would rather be unfortunate for the public, if this which at one time was not looked upon as among the least important, should be for ever screened from notice by the obscurity of the individual, whose interests happen to have been so unfortunately mixt with it.

The accident that has so recently taken place at Fort Cumberland[3] near Portsmouth will /may/ serve as one among but too many experimental proofs, that the existing system is as liable to fail in

1281. [1] B.L. VI: 481–2. Autograph draft. Docketed: '1797 June 22 / Panopt. Brouillon / J.B. Q.S.P. / to / G. Rose Treasury / Escapes from Fort Cumberland / Pressing about Tothill Fields.'

[2] Perhaps an allusion to the naval mutinies at Spithead (April 1797) and the Nore (May), the latter only 'in some measure' cleared up towards the end of June.

[3] A prison at the mouth of Langston harbour, three miles from Portsmouth. The frequency of 'dark, foggy weather' aided escapes (*28th Report from the Select Committee on Finance, etc., Police, including Convict Establishments, 26 June 1798*, p. 113).

so simple an article as that of safe-custody, as it always has been confessedly deficient in regard to the more arduous /points/ articles of Reformation and subsequent means of honest livelyhood.

G. Rose Esqr
    etc. etc. etc.

P.S. I have an idea to submitt, which if approved of, might expedite the business and lessen the danger, if there be any, of opposition.

1282

FROM SIR JOHN SINCLAIR

5 July 1797

Dear Sir,
    You will see from the inclosed paper, the progress made by the Board of Agriculture during our last Session, which has just concluded, and as I am applying to all the intelligent men of my acquaintance for Papers to be inserted in our transactions I cannot think of overlooking so capital a hand as Mr. Bentham.[2] The object to which I wish you would direct your attention, is the proper Management of the poor—I have not yet arranged my thoughts upon the subject, but I think the Paper might refer to the following particulars.

1. On the circumstances which occasion a number of poor in a Country, and on the obligation incumbent on the rest of a community to *assist* in their maintenance.

2. On the best means of preventing a multitude of poor, or of diminishing their number.

3. On the best means of maintaining the poor, whether by Voluntary donations, or assessment.

4. On the division of the poor, into Town and Country, into the aged, the infirm, the helpless from infancy, and the abled bodied, and of the different regulations necessary for each.

1282. [1] B.L. VI: 473–4. Autograph. Docketed: '1797 July 5 / Poor / Sinclair P.B.A. Whitehall / to / J.B. Q.S.P.'
    Sir John had become President of the Board of Agriculture in 1793.
    [2] It was in response to this invitation that Bentham prepared the series of letters on the 'Situation and Relief of the Poor', which appeared in *Annals of Agriculture*, vols. xxix, xxx, and xxxi (1797–8). They were reprinted at the time, but not published, as an *Outline of a Work entitled Pauper Management Improved*. A French translation appeared in 1802 and an English edition was published in 1812. This was reprinted in Bowring, viii, 361–439.

5. Of different Institutions for the poor, as Schools of Industry for the young, Alms Houses for the aged, Hospitals for the sick, Work Houses for the Industrious, and Panopticons or correction Houses for the Idle.

6. On friendly Societies, and the means of making them as perfect as possible.

7. On the proper Police in regard to the poor, procuring them cheap good food, as Soups etc. preventing the imposition of Shopkeepers, Pawnbrokers etc.

Conclusion—Miscellaneous Observations and the result of the whole inquiry.

These are merely hints with regard to the arrangement, which you will be able to decide on much better than I can do, but it is of great importance *to have a foundation laid*, which can be amended, and I am sure if you will dedicate your attention to this subject, that it is in your power to draw up a very valuable paper.

I remain with regard
your faithful and
Obedient servant
John Sinclair

Whitehall
5 July 1797

1283

To Sir John Sinclair

13 July 1797 (Aet 49)

Queen's Square Place, 13 July 1797

Dear Sir,

Your commands in relation to the *poor* will be fulfilled: to speak the truth, they have been anticipated. I have been thinking of nothing else but poverty for these seven or eight months. *Pauper sum—paupertatis nihil a me alienum puto.*[2] That which for inducement was not necessary, may, in the way of encouragement, be useful: and, in the way of encouragement, what can be more stimulative, than flattery from Sir John Sinclair?

1283. [1] *Correspondence of the Right Honorable Sir John Sinclair, bart.*, 2 vols., 1831, i, 483.

[2] Anglice: 'I am a poor man—I consider nothing to do with poverty indifferent to me'; an adaptation of the well-known Latin saying 'Homo sum, humani nil a me alienum puto' (Terence, *Heauton Timorumenos*, I, i, 25).

My labours, taking them altogether, will, I doubt, be too volu-
minous to look for the honour of a complete admission into the
*Fasti*³ of the Board; but extracts can be made, adapted to the
questions by which your commands to me on that subject are
conveyed. Believe me ever, with all respect, Dear Sir, your most
obedient and most humble servant.

Jeremy Bentham

Sir John Sinclair, etc.

1284

FROM ARTHUR YOUNG

July 1797

Jeremy Bentham Esqr

A Lad *full* work at 20

A Girl do. ——— at 18

Harvest ——— 6 weeks

Hay ——————— 3 weeks

average { the variations great

² From Mr A. Young in answer to Queries sent July 1797

³ Bentham is probably referring to the *Annals of Agriculture*. Arthur Young was
the secretary of the Board and his *Annals* 'provided the Board with a periodical in
which the views of its leading members could be aired at no expense' (Rosalind
Mitchison, *Agricultural Sir John*, 1962, p. 141). Bentham may, however, be alluding
to the 'Communications' to the Board, read at its meetings and published as *Communications to the Board of Agriculture*, 7 vols., 1797–1803.

1284. ¹ B.L. VI: 485. Autograph. Docketed: '1797 July / Poor / A. Young Whitehall
/ to / J.B. Q.S.P. / Earnings of Harvest time.'

² Note in Bentham's hand in red ink. In U.C. CLI: 262 is an autograph draft of
Bentham's headed 'Poor Plan. Inquirenda of Mr Arthur Young', with a marginal
note of answers to questions 1 and 2 concerning 'Capital Requisite' for hedging,
fencing or walling, and for cultivation of waste and common land, 'Per A. Young
21 Dec. 1797'.

The answers given by Young in July were to questions 3, 4 and 5, viz.
'3. What may be deemed the average duration of harvest (Grain Harvest) for the
purpose of estimating the extra earnings made during that period?
4. Do. Hay harvest?
5. Age at which the labour of a young labourer in Husbandry (taking the average in
point of growth and strength) has attained its highest value, in point of wages.'
A note by Bentham under these questions has 'Answered'.
There is a final paragraph headed 'Put these questions 21 June 1797', i.e. requests

1285

FROM SAMUEL ROMILLY

4 September 1797

Dear Bentham,

Behold a Letter from Dumont to Mr North.[2] I have twice attempted to write to Dr Parr[3] but I found it necessary to talk about you and your work and the Letter was to be sent open to you that you might inclose the Queries which were to be answered: all this was so formidable that I found it impossible to get on. I tried to write to Mr Martin[4] but I found the same difficulties tho not quite in the same degree and at last instead of sending you Letters I only send you Excuses. You certainly may send your Queries to both of them who are well known to you without any letter or if a Letter is necessary you may write any thing in my name, but really I find it impossible to write any thing myself

yrs ever

Sam¹ Romilly[5]

for 'Lists of the different operations of husbandry' . . ., 'list of stages of manufacture in each branch of manufacture', and other queries about the *Farmers Dictionary*, the report of the House of Commons Committee on the linen industry, 'Birmingham earnings', cotton manufacture—particularly at Manchester, and glass and earthenware at London.

1285. ¹ B.L. VI: 486–7. Autograph. Docketed: '1797 Sept 4 / Poor / Romilly Nowhere / to / J.B. Q.S.P.'

Addressed: 'Jeremy Bentham Esqr. / Queen Square Place / Westminster.' Postmark: '2 o'Clock / 5 SE / 97 AFTERNOON'. Stamped: 'Chancery Lane Unpaid Penny Post'.

² The Rev. John North (1746?–1818), B.A. Cantab. 1768; Fellow of Caius College, 1768–91; rector of Ashdon, Essex, 1791–1818. Dumont stayed with him in 1798 and 1800.

³ Samuel Parr (1747–1825), Latin scholar and Anglican parson; regarded as the Whig Dr Samuel Johnson, though his conversation does not appear to have been so trenchant. His political friends included Fox, the 3rd Lord Holland and Romilly; he 'exulted' in his friendship with Bentham and left him a mourning ring (see Bowring, x, 554).

⁴ Perhaps Matthew Martin (1748–1838), the naturalist and philanthropist, who was investigating mendicancy in London at this time.

⁵ There is a footnote by Bentham in pencil: 'Dumont is an honest fellow—Romilly a shabby one.' This expresses a momentary irritation; it was not his considered view of Romilly.

1286

To Caroline Fox

5 September 1797 (Aet 49)

Pauper Table Letters 5 Sept. 1797

Mr B being still in existence takes the liberty of addressing a packet to Miss Fox in the humble hope of prevailing on her to exert the favour of her interest with Lords Lansdown, Holland, Warwick and Ossory for the purpose of obtaining the communications sought for by /in/ the inclosed papers, within the sphere of their respective influences. Great management will be necessary in the instance of the most noble person first mentioned, lest he should sound the depths of the plot and discover that Count Woronzoff is at the bottom of it.[2]

P.S. 2d The luckiest opportunity in the world for three Ladies[3] to honour a certain place with a once intended visit, the owner being just beaten out of it after many a good thing by a coup de grace from the Treasurers staff now brandishing with such irresistible vigor by the Rt Hon. W. Pitt.

1287

To George Rose

7 September 1797 (Aet 49)

Pauper Population Table

J.B. Q.S.P. 7 Sept. 1797   To Geo Rose Esqr

Sir

Inclosed is a blank table which I take the liberty of troubling you with not as Secretary to the Treasury, but as a Country Gentleman, in hopes of your favouring me /if it be practicable/ with the information sought by it in as far as it may be obtainable within the circle of your Parochial influence.

1286. [1] U.C. cxxxiii: 75. Autograph draft, in pencil.
  [2] In his recollections Bentham told Bowring that 'Lord Shelburne [i.e. Lansdowne] had a certain wildness about him, and conceived groundless suspicions about nothing at all . . . About the last time I was at his house, I mentioned something about Count Woronzof, and he fancied I had been sent by Woronzof to communicate it' (Bowring, x, 117).
  [3] The long discussed visit to Queen's Square Place by the Bowood ladies: Caroline Fox and her aunts, Caroline and Elizabeth Vernon. Caroline Vernon was about to become Mrs Robert ('Bobus') Smith.
1287. [1] U.C. cxxxiii: 78. Autograph draft.

I have copies in any number it may be your pleasure to command. A paper which I have by me pointing out the specific uses of the information sought, did not appear worth troubling you with as it is not printed. You would find the information of use, I believe for any plan, be it what it may that has facts and calculation for its basis, though contrived for the purpose of a particular plan in which I have been seeking my consolation for almost this twelve-month under the distresses and disappointments with which I have been struggling for above these four years.[2]

I have etc.

1288

TO SAMUEL PARR

c. 7 September 1797 (Aet 49)

Pauper Table Letters To Dr Parr

Sir

I take the liberty of troubling you with a blank table which I am circulating, wherever I can find pretence and hope, for the purpose of getting it returned to me, with the figures /according to the instructions which it contains/. Try, I beseech you, what you can do for me—in your Parish which I suppose is like other Parishes—and to take a circle better known within the circle of your influence which is not like other /ordinary/ influences.

Copies as many more as you are /may be/ pleased to order, are at your command.[2] In proportion as you succeed you will oblige me, which is nothing—you will oblige Mr. Romilly, which is something:—you will oblige the Board of Agriculture which finds me auspices: and you will serve the /that/ public, which by the respect it testifies for you, has given itself so strong a title to your services whatever service it may be in your way to render it—I have the honour to be, Sir,

Your most obedient Servt

J.B.

[2] A reference to the frustration he had experienced concerning his Panopticon penitentiary plan.

1288. [1] U.C. cxxxiii: 80. Autograph draft.

[2] Marginal addition: 'What Mr Pitt has done /has been attempted in this way/ we all know: and the result is—*facultas non praerepta sed praedita.*' The words 'Mr Pitt has done' are crossed through; the Latin phrase means: 'the opportunity is not taken away beforehand, but provided'. The reference is to Pitt's Poor Law Bill of 1796–7, which was opposed vigorously in Parliament and outside by Bentham and others. It was finally withdrawn (see J. R. Poynter, *Society and Pauperism*, 1969, pp. 62–76).

1289

TO ARTHUR YOUNG

8 September 1797 (Aet 49)

Queen's Square Place, Westminster
8th September, 1797

Dear Sir,

It was but t'other day that I became master of a complete series of your Annals:—accept my confession, and record my

1289. [1] Partly printed in Bowring, viii, 361–2, copied from the *Annals of Agriculture*, xxix, no. 167 (1797), 393–7. Only parts of that version are printed in *The Autobiography of Arthur Young*, ed. M. Betham-Edwards, 1898, p. 308; but a final paragraph is added there, which was not included in either the *Annals* or Bowring. It has been inserted in the full version given above.

There are autograph drafts by Bentham, which include some of the material in this printed letter, in U.C. CLIV: 31–32 and 55–64. They contain additional remarks, obviously not intended for publication, but probably included in a private letter to Young, which is missing. Fo. 31 has the following passage written in red ink: 'If you print any of these Papers, especially the Table of Cases calling for Relief, do me the favour to apprise me of your determination as soon as formed, that I may apply to your Printer to print off some extra-copies for me to give away.

What you do not print pray return me. The Table of Cases etc. I am in continual want of and have no correct copy of.

The statement of the uses of the Population Table I must print if you do not, and if I knew you did not send it to press immediately, for the circulation of the Tables waits for it.'

A 'Table of Cases calling for Relief' and a 'Pauper Population Table' were printed in the *Annals of Agriculture* (see letter 1298, n. 2, p. 385 below).

Fo. 32 contains, as well as a first paragraph printed in letter 1288, passages written in red ink, with the heading 'what follows is Private and confidential' and going on 'Print this stuff in your Annals, as much or little as you please'. What comes after is crossed out, but the last two paragraphs are not crossed out and were probably included in a letter to Young, because they are mentioned in a reply from him (see letter 1295, p. 383 below). These paragraphs read: 'Will you have any scraps of my plans for your Annals? I have half a mind to send you an Outline of the whole. My fear is—lest being but an Outline without the *Defences* people should form inadequate ideas of it, and prejudice themselves against it.

In one of your Annals you have a Paper entitled Botany Bay Agriculture. If you wish it for the Annals, I could get you, I imagine, the latest present state from a professed Botanist, and the greatest and best Farmer there—Major Paterson, who before the arrival of the present Governor (Hunter) had the command of that Colony for a few months. Paterson intends publishing a Book on the subject—but he is a liberal man, and if you were to send him queries for a clew, would I dare say, give you more or less by way of answer. Write me your wishes on this head, and if they are in the affirmative I will mention it to him, and if he consents, then and then only you will have the trouble of writing your Queries.'

William Paterson (1755–1810) was a Scot who had been Lieutenant-Governor of New South Wales, 1794–5, and after revisiting Britain at this time returned to further distinctions in Australia. He is best-known as a traveller and botanist, who had written a pioneer *Narrative of four Journeys into the Country of the Hottentots and*

375

penitence. Having, on my return from my long peregrination on the Continent, lent to a friend—who had lent to another friend, whom we neither of us could recollect—the twenty-five or thirty numbers which I had taken in before that period, I postponed from time to time the completion of the series, in hopes of recovering the commencement of it. When at last shame and necessity got the better of procrastination, what a treasure of information burst upon me!—No—so long as power without—and without—shall have left an annual guinea in my pocket (blanks are better here than words) not a number of the Annals shall ever be wanting to my shelves.—Hold!—don't take me for a Jacobin, now; nor even for a croaker—What I allude to, is not any *common* burden—such as you land-owners and land-holders grunt under:—but my own ten thousand pound tax—my *privilegium*—a thing as new to English language, as it is to English practice—sole and peculiar fruit of the very particular notice with which I have been honoured by—.

This waits upon you with a proof of a blank Pauper Population Table: being a Table framed for the purpose of collecting an account of the Pauper Population in as many parishes, etc., as I may be able to obtain it from. Knowing so well your zeal for all zeal-worthy objects, and mindful of your often experienced kindness, I cannot on this occasion harbour a doubt of your assistance. But in what shape will it be most convenient and eligible for you to give it me? Will you reprint the *heads* alone, upon the plan of common letter-press, and without the form of a table? or will you accept of an impression, of the same number as that of the Annals, for the purpose of annexing a copy to each copy of your next number? This latter expedient, should it meet with your approbation, would lessen in a considerable degree the trouble to any such gentleman as may be disposed to favour me with their contributions.

Is it worth while to give the Table this indiscriminate kind of circulation? At any rate, your Editorial Majesty will I hope be pleased graciously to grant unto me your Royal Letters—*patent* or *close*, or both, addressed to *all*—and, if need be—*singular*, your loving subjects, my fellow-correspondents;—charging and exhorting them, each in his parish—and as many other parishes as may be—to fill my Tables, and send in their contributions.

Caffraria in Years 1777–8–9, London, 1789; 2nd edn. 1790; new edn. ed. V. S. Forbes and J. Rourke, Sandton, South Africa, 1980. Paterson's intended book on the botany of New South Wales did not get published, but he did write the article proposed by Bentham for the *Annals of Agriculture* (see letter 1295 and n. 3).

John Hunter (1738–1821), was Governor of New South Wales, 1795–1821. He was also a naval commander who became an Admiral in 1810.

Along with the Table you will find a MS. paper, exhibiting the importance of the information I am thus labouring to collect: you will print it in your Annals, or suppress it, as you think best. The danger is, lest there should be some, who, though they might otherwise have been disposed to furnish the information desired, may perhaps shrink back at the idea of the applications that might be made of it to the economy of the parishes in the management of which they may respectively happen to be concerned. A gentleman, who bears a principal part in the management of one of the great London parishes, had with more than ordinary alacrity consented to a general request of information. I sent him a pair of Tables, and (though this account of the *use* was not with them) he returned them with an excuse.

I also send, in MS., a *Table of Cases calling for Relief:*—a general Map of *Pauper-Land,* with all the *Roads* to it. Few, if any, of the projects I have seen, but what have appeared (the *arch-project* not excepted) to bear an exclusive—at least a *predilective*—reference to some of these cases, overlooking or slighting the rest. I send it in the state in which I propose printing it for my own book; but, in the meantime, if it be worth the honour of a place in the *Annals*, it is altogether at your service. This preparatory insertion will turn to the advantage of the work itself, if any of your Correspondents (not forgetting their Editor) would have the goodness to contribute their remarks to the emendation of it. You will not easily conceive—few heads, at least, but yours are qualified to conceive—the labour it has cost me to bring the two Tables to this state. As to the work at large, it will occupy two independent, though connected, volumes. *Pauper Systems compared:—Pauper Management improved;*—the last the Romance, the Utopia, to which I had once occasion to allude.— Romance?—how should it be anything *less?*—I mean to an Author's partial eyes. In proportion as a thing is excellent, when established, is it anything but *romance,* and *theory,* and *speculation,* till the touch of the *seal* or the *sceptre* has converted it into *practice?*—Distress, at least—distress, the very life and soul of Romance, cannot be denied to mine: for in this short and close-packed specimen, already you behold it in all its shapes.—Magnanimous President!— accomplished Secretary!—Ye, too, have your Romance.—Heaven send you a happy catastrophe, and the *fettered Lands* a '*happy deliverance!*'—Patience! patience!—Ye, too, before you are comforted, must bear to be tormented.

Apropos of Presidents—the *High Priest of Ceres*[2] having divined,

[2] Sir John Sinclair.

or not divined, my recent occupations, has been pleased to send me a mandate in form, summoning me to devote myself to this branch of his Goddess's service, that the fruits of my labours may be consecrated in her Temple at Whitehall:—so that, whatever other requisites may fail me, I shall be in no want of *auspices*. Continue yours to me.

I fear you will say to yourself that the Observations I have sent you are a sad farrago, but your miscellany, how superior soever to others in subject-matter and contents has this in common with them, that half formed ideas, so they have but matter in them, are not prohibited from presenting themselves. It is part of the character of your correspondents to have more of *substance* about them than of *form*; and of the many recommendations which join in drawing so much good company to your *conversazione*, one, nor that the least, is the convenience of being admitted to it in boots. Mine (you will say) have hobnails in them; for, somehow or other, the very idea of the person to whom I am adressing myself has insensibly betrayed me into that sort of playful confidence—that *épanchement*, as I think the French call it—which I have always felt in his company.

Believe me, with the most serious respect,

Ever yours,

Jeremy Bentham

Arthur Young, Esq., etc. etc. etc.

1290

TO ARTHUR YOUNG

[?] September 1797 (Aet 49)

To A. Young Book-keeping[2]

In Vol 2 I observe a paper of your own on Book-keeping:[3] it was with real delight I observed such a coincidence between our opinions, /in/ which is /implied/ as much as to say such a sanction to my own. From the art of Pauper Economy, studied with any attention, the transition is unavoidable to the ministering art of Book-keeping. I had already said to it myself—but said it upon

---

1290. [1] U.C. cliv: 33–5. Autograph draft.

[2] A note in Bentham's hand at the top reads 'This for a subsequent letter', but there is no evidence that it was actually sent.

[3] There is an article 'On the Accounts proper to be kept by Farmers' in the *Annals of Agriculture*, xxviii (1797), 47–64, but no article on the subject in volume ii.

paper, that Book-keeping commonly /in the confined and ordinary sense of the word/ so called, mercantile Book-keeping, is but childs play in point of difficulty in comparison of that higher species which presides or at least ought to preside over the operations of the Farmer.

Book-keeping *rationalized*—if thus I may have leave to translate your French-imported *raisonné*—Book-keeping extended in its limits as well as corrected in its language by human reason, is one of the main pillars of my system: and these two Tables you may consider as so many exercises of a tyro /the productions of a learner/ —in simple truth a learner—and that a very late one—presented /laid/ with all due awe and reverence to /fear and trembling at the feet of/ so great a master.

I had all along said to myself, that while the Penitentiary House was building, Book-keeping was one /among/ of the arts which I should have to learn for it. I had accordingly adjourned /postponed/ my schooling to that always paulo-post-futurum period, when the demands /cries/ of the Poor /burst upon/assailed my ears/ called aloud and accelerated the demand for it.[4]

Among the advantages of corresponding with you is the faculty of discarding form, and presenting ones self /making ones way/ though in/into/ good company, yet with the sanction of and after the example of the company—without ceremony and preparation. Under favour of this tacit and most convenient convention, half-formed ideas need not fear to present themselves, taking their chance for polish and completion from the hand of the Editor or some fellow correspondent. The faculty /opportunity/ shall not pass unimproved: and, since you have started Book-keeping /the subject/, accept accordingly some anticipations—mere crudities— on Book-keeping.[5]

---

[4] Marginal note: 'Mr. Pitt who knows not what dispatch is, unless it be in going to war with or without a cause'.

[5] Marginal notes in pencil, alongside this paragraph: 'Though Book-keeping is not farming ⟨. . .⟩ You have presented Book-keeping as necessary to good farming.

But under that name is included a most terrific process.

That man will have done something for agriculture who should have done anything towards stripping ⟨. . .⟩ ⟨. . .⟩ ⟨. . .⟩.' (The last words of the sentence are illegible.)

1291

To A Society

September 1797 (Aet 49)

To the Society etc.[2]

My Lords and Gentlemen

I know not whether the following /enclosed/ paper will be thought /found/ to come within the design of your benevolent institution. It is but a project: indeed but the fragment of a project: and among the papers which you have as yet published I observe nothing but facts /things done/executed/deeds done/ records of deeds done/. Yet, with submission, if the matter does not render it unworthy /exclude it from the honour/ of your adoption; the species of composition it belongs to, ought not to exclude /be considered as excluding/ it. Design is a prelude to execution: and in matters of this nature /the nature in question/a political cast/ a necessary prelude: every *aurelia* must first have been a *chrysalis*: every institution established—every deed done—must first have been a project.

Now that your Treasury is opened—and so respectable so rich a Treasury—I should be sorry /mortified I must confess/ not to be admitted to throw in my mite: and the only mite I have to bestow has the /word/ name of *project* stamped upon it. /My heart is with you—my purse should be, if I had one/. What I have to bestow— my head and my heart are /is/ with you. Silver and Gold alas! I have none[3] for you: why I have /the cause of my having/ none—a cause which I am not ashamed of—nor have need to be ashamed of—howsoever it may be with others, is not unknown to some of you—nor unlamented. Silver and Gold then I have none: but what I have—a project—that give I unto you. /Had/ Fidelity to engagements I have not been happy enough to find /been/ among the virtues of administration: if I had, I might have had something to present /to/ you with by this time besides projects. I do not mean silver and gold alone: but deeds done—deeds done for the reformation of human wickedness as well as for the relief of human

---

1291. [1] U.C. cliv: 53. Autograph draft, among 'Poor Plan' material.

[2] Bentham may have sent a letter based on this draft to the Society for the Betterment of the Condition of the Poor, founded in 1796, or to another 'benevolent institution'.

[3] The phrase 'Silver and Gold alas! I have none' is crossed out at this point, but needed to make sense.

wretchedness /misery/—deeds done such as you have had /given to yourselves/ the satisfaction of proclaiming to the world—with the implied exhortation—Go and do thou likewise.

1292

FROM MARTHA YOUNG

17 October 1797

Sir

I have the satisfaction on enquiry, to see all your papers appear to have come quite safe hither, at the time stated in the Letter I had the honor of receiving this day from you![2] I and my (now) only daughter being returned last night from a *ten weeks* Tour in order to prevent if possible the mind corroding on itself by an irreperable loss we have for ever to deplore!!! and which I fear may in some measure, have weakened Mr. Youngs efforts in a present degree, for he never sustained such deep affliction before!!! I, who am pretty nearly his age, find my memory much impaired, and hope dead! because the two children I have the blessing still to keep, are only painful witnesses of that sorrow which their dutiful behaviour does so much to alleviate; therefore I am highly culpable for dwelling so long on the past who when alive appeared to rank only as a third in affection, which all who saw her granted our plea in almost adoring her!! pardon my egotism—my mind etc. are relaxed past cure!

The bailiff who opened your parcel and acted according to the orders *therein* contained gave it to me this morning and I write this post to Mr Y. at *Stamford Post Office Lincolnshire* to mention the business of the Poor being the subject of yr papers. I am hurt the delay has so long happened—my Son[3] is at Brighton (or perhaps at Petworth) his father was on his way hither last Sunday, at Stamford,

1292. [1] B.L. VI: 488–9. Autograph. Docketed: '1797 Oct 17 / Poor / Mrs Young / Bury / to / J.B. Q.S.P.'
Addressed: 'J. Bentham Esqr / Queen Square Place / Westminster.' Postmark: 'OC.19.97.B' Stamped: 'BURY'
Martha Allen had married Arthur Young in 1765. She died in 1815. The child they had lost was Martha Anne (1783–97), their younger daughter, who died of a pulmonary consumption on 14 July 1797. 'Bobbin' was Arthur's favourite and he was deeply affected by her death.
[2] What was evidently a recent, missing, letter from Bentham inquiring what had happened to the papers he had sent to Arthur Young in mid-September.
[3] Arthur Young (1769–1827), an agriculturalist like his father, was a clergyman and curate of Cockfield, Suffolk, 1793. He compiled a *General Report on Inclosures* for the Board of Agriculture, 1807. He died in Russia, where he had purchased land.

but had a cross call back to Hull again, he writes me word yesterday. It *cannot* be the least trouble for me at all times to have the pleasure of answering the enquiry of Mr. Young's friends having only to lament my present and future inability (from heart felt grief) to do it anyway more satisfactorily

I have the honor to
remain Sir
yr Obedt etc.
M. Young

Bradfield Hall
Octr. 17th 1797

The bailiff says he forwarded your letter under cover to Mr Fydell[4] of Boston M.P. Mr. Young wrote in his last letter the following words 'I cannot now expect to be at home this fortnight', the date Octr. 15.

1293

FROM EDMUND MALONE

26 October 1797

Mr Malone presents his Compliments to Mr Bentham, and is sorry that he cannot give him any accurate information relative to the subject of his inquiry. He does not know that the Charter for the foundation of Westminster School has been printed; but there may be a chance of finding it in Rymer's *Foedera*,[2] or in his un-published Ms. Collections in the British Museum; which run from No. 4573 to 4630 in Ayscough's Catalogue of the Sloanian and other Mss.[3] If not there, he supposes it may be found in the Chapel of the Rolls, where, if the year of the foundation be known, the search will

---

[4] Thomas Fydell (1740–1812), M.P. for Boston, Lincs., 1790–1803 and 1806–12.
1293. [1] B.L. VI: 496–7. Autograph. Docketed: '1797 Oct 26 / Panopt. Toth. Fie[lds] / Malone Q. Ann St. East / to / J.B. Q.S.P. / and R.C. Bridge Str to J.B. / Hawkins.' The docket covers letter 1294 as well as 1293.
Edmund Malone (1741–1812), B.A. Trinity College, Dublin, was a barrister and author who lived in London from 1777. He was a highly-regarded scholar, who edited Shakespeare and Dryden; he also helped Boswell to revise his life of Samuel Johnson.
[2] Thomas Rymer's *Foedera*, 20 vols., 1704–35.
[3] Samuel Ayscough's *Catalogue of the Manuscripts preserved in the British Museum* ... (1782). The fifty volumes containing Sloane Mss. 4573–4630 are the collections of Rymer not printed in the *Foedera*. There is a reference to the re-founding of West-minster School in 1560 in *Foedera*, 2nd edn., 1728, xvi, 590–1.

cost but a trifle, and the officer who attends is extremely civil and intelligent.

Among the Harleian MSS No. 7025 (article 2) contains some memorandums about Westminster School

Queen Anne St East Octr 26. 1797

1294

To Richard Clark

27 October 1797 (Aet 49)

As soon as you can make it convenient, do, I pray you, try your interest with Mr Hawkins,[2] and see whether his local omniscience can supply *quoad hoc* the deficiency in Mr Malone's general intelligence. If you can obtain for me a general permission to wait on him (Mr H.) on the subject at my walking hour between 9 and 10, it may be of use.

Q.S.P. Oct. 27. 97.

Volti

Return this writ

1295

From Arthur Young

31 October 1797

Bradfield Octr. 31. 97

My Dear Sir

I have rarely been so provoked as this morn, I returned home late last night and found this morning the Lr my bailiff sent to me[2]

1294. [1] B.L. VI: 497. Autograph. Docket as for letter 1293.

Added by Bentham to the letter from Malone and returned with it, as requested, by 'R.C.' This was clearly Richard Clark, F.S.A., who lived at 10 New Bridge Street Blackfriars. He was not only an old friend of the Benthams but of the Hawkins family also. As a boy he had been introduced by Sir John Hawkins to Dr Samuel Johnson, and Letitia, Sir John's daughter, dedicated her *Anecdotes*, 1822, to Clark as 'the oldest friend of my family'. (See *Correspondence*, i passim, especially 90 n. 1.)

[2] John Sidney Hawkins (1758–1842) an antiquary, son of Sir John Hawkins, who wrote a *General History of Music* (1776).

1295. [1] B.L. VI: 498–9. Autograph. Docketed: '1797 Oct. 31 / Poor / A. Young, Bury / to / J.B. Q.S.P. Answered 1 Nov.'

Addressed: 'Jeremy Bentham Esqr / Queen Square Place, / Westminster.' Postmark: 'NO.1.97.B'.

[2] Either Bentham's letter of 8 September (1289) or the missing one mentioned in Martha Young's letter (1292).

with above 30 others that had travelled from post to post after me and at last sent home by orders to a postmaster at a Town I did not go to. I have been out 12 weeks and passed 1200 Miles. What must you think of me—and horrid for the Annals too—the last No. only half a No. for want of Ms. I find a supply here but your very valuable papers strongly seconded by me shall have precedence of all—and the proofs sent you; you will have one in a week and all in next No. —I have sent them to press.

This is all my time and harrassed mind can permit at present—a thousand thanks for yr good opinion of a Work wch you will contribute to make so much better—Send me botany bay;[3] send me the other, send all yo can.

The beginng [of] next week you will see me

yrs faithfully
A. Young

1296

FROM RICHARD CLARK

31 October 1797

R. C. to J. B.

I saw Mr. Hawkins last night within a few Hours after his return from Ramsgate; he has promised to look among his papers and to give you every assistance in his power. As you are an odd sort of Fellow he will see you at your own hour provided you apprise him of your intention two or three [days?] before that he may avoid every other engagement. I think you should not make your visit later than nine, as I know the Family hour of breakfast to be ten.

New Bridge Street
31 Octr. 1797

[3] A paper on 'the latest present state' of Botany Bay, to be written by William Paterson (see letter 1289 p. 375 above). It appeared anonymously under the title 'New South Wales and Norfolk Island Agriculture', in *Annals of Agriculture*, xxxi, no. 177 (1798), 397–417.

1296. [1] B.L. VI: 500–1. Autograph. Docketed: '1797 Oct 31 / Panopt. Toth Fd / R.C. Bridge Str. / to / J.B. Q.S.P.'
Addressed: 'Jeremy Bentham Esq. / Queen Square Place / Westminster.' Postmark: '4 o'clock / Even. OC / 31.97. Penny Post Paid.'

1297

FROM ARTHUR YOUNG

1 November 1797

Dear Sr
I wrote yesterday. I had apprehensions and so they prove. My printer cannot do the Tables, you will therefore be so good as to get 1000 of each worked off and sent to Mr J. Rackham[2] printers Bury. Am I to insert Toosey's Lr.,[3] leaving out the fees and pay? Let me know

yrs faithfully
A. Young

Wednesday

1298

FROM ARTHUR YOUNG

2 November 1797

Dear Sr.
I thought I had told you that 1000 copies of every table that demands *folding* should be sent to Mr Rackham printer Bury. If you had rather insert 2 than one you may; but a N.B. shd. be

1297. [1] B.L. VI: 502–3. Autograph. Docketed: '1797 Nov. 1 / Poor / A. Young Bury / to / J.B. Q.S.P.'
Addressed: 'Jeremy Bentham Esqr / Queen's Square Place / Westminster.' Postmark: 'NO.2.97.B'. Stamped: BURY'.
[2] John Rackham (d. 1821, aged 64). He printed the *Annals of Agriculture*, from 1786 to 1803; he was also a publisher, kept a bookshop and became a burgess of Bury St Edmunds (see John G. Gazley, *The Life of Arthur Young*, Philadelphia, 1973, p. 367 n. 25 and p. 464; C. H. Timperley, *A Dictionary of Printers and Printing*, 1839, p. 879).
[3] Philip Toosey (?1744–97), M.A. Cantab., rector of Stonham, Suffolk, 1769–97. He published in the form of a letter 'Some Observations on the Climate and Cultivation of Canada' in *Annals of Agriculture*, xxix, no. 167 (1797), pp. 493–7. The letter is dated from 'Silleri, near Quebec, 26 Oct. 1786' [a mistake for 1796?]. It is clear from it that he would shortly be moving to a farm near Detroit, which he would name Stonham Court.
1298. [1] B.L. VI: 504–5. Autograph. Docketed: '1797 Nov 2 / Poor / A. Young Bury / to / J.B. Q.S.P. / Answered 3d to Rackham.'
Addressed: 'Jeremy Bentham Esqr / Queen Square Place / Westminster.' Postmark: 'NO.3.97'.
This may be in answer to a missing letter from Bentham. The letter to Rackham of 3 November is missing.

385

added that one may be taken out for circulation, wch best on blue cover I think.[2]

Yrs
in gt haste
A. Young.

Nov. 2. 1797[3]
Reced 3d J.B.

1299

FROM WILLIAM MORTON PITT

18 November 1797

My dear Sir

    I obey your Commands[2] and forward the papers in several Covers to Mr. Arthur Young at Petworth.

yrs very sincerely
W. M. Pitt

1300

TO GEORGE ROSE

24 November 1797 (Aet 49)

Q.S.P. 24 Novr 1797
Friday

Sir

    This waits upon you with two Copies of the Tothill Fields Division Bill, one destined for the Atty Genl, the other for the Sollr Gen: both signed by Mr Butler, and each of them accompanied by an explanatory *Case*. The most effectual course for expediting

---

    [2] In U.C. CLIV: 586–8 is an autograph draft by Bentham headed 'J.B. to a journal'. It begins 'Sir, The inclosed Table, contrived by Mr Bentham for the purpose of exhibiting a compleat view of the Pauper population of this, or indeed any other country, having been handed about in a sort of print . . . I take the liberty of sending it to you, in the view of its receiving a place, if you think proper, in your interesting miscellany . . . It is intituled *Table of Cases calling for Relief*.' A table with this heading appears in Bentham's first article in the *Annals of Agriculture*, xxix, between pages 426 and 427. There is also a 'Pauper Population Table' between pages 392 and 393.

    [3] Date and following line inserted in Bentham's hand.

1299. [1] B.L. VI: 506. Autograph. Docketed: '1797 Nov. 18 / Poor / W. M. Pitt Arlington Street to J.B. Q.S.P. / Forwards Sheet I / to A. Young, Petworth'.

    Addressed: 'Jer. Bentham Esqr / Queen Square / Westmr.'

    [2] Evidently in response to a letter from Bentham, which is missing.

1300. [1] B.L. VI: 509–10. Autograph draft. Docketed: '1797 Nov. 24 / Panopt / J.B. Q.S.P. / to / Rose Treasury / sent 25th / with Tothill Fields Bill.'

the Bill would be, if you would have the goodness to convey your wishes to Mr White that the copies in question may be convey'd *instanter* to their respective destinations, without stopping in Mr White's or any other hands. The copy of the former Bill that went to the Atty and Sollr Gen., and which with their observations thereon I have by your favour been indulged with, being a fair copy taken from that which had undergone Mr Lowndes amendments, has not that gentlemans name to it, nor any other token of the Bills ever having passed through his hands: and the Sollr Genl actually asked a friend of mine [2] whose hands it had passed through. The two above-mentioned Copies of the present Bill are written exactly in the same manner as the abovementioned Copy of the other Bill, as delivered to the Atty and Sollr Genl by Mr. White, and, were they to receive a scratch or two from any other pen, other fair copies would be to be taken which would be so much more time lost. Mr Butler writes to the Atty and Sollr Genl to offer any explanations they may wish for, and to testify how thoroughly his mind has applied itself to the subject.

As for your part, Sir, I know of no reason for your consuming a single moment of your time upon the papers till they are returned to you from the gentlemen of the Long Robe. At that period, the *Case*, which, (consisting chiefly of some little historical anecdotes) will not hang heavy, together with the Heads of the Bill on ½ a sheet, will compose the whole of the task which you have the goodness to charge yourself with. [3]

Geo. Rose Esqr.
   etc. etc. etc.

---

[2] Samuel Romilly. See letter 1276, p. 365 above.

[3] Bentham's negotiation had got no further forward by the end of the year 1797. In the Treasury Board Minutes are the following entries:

'Whitehall. Treasury Chambers. 5 Dec. 1797. Present Mr Townshend, Mr. Smyth, Mr. Douglas, Mr. Pybus.

Read a Case (transmitted by Mr. Bentham) explanatory of an annexed Bill proposed to be submitted to Parliament for explaining and amending the Act of 34:Geo: 3d: Cap 84. for erecting a Penitentiary House for confining and employing Convicts by appropriating a part of Tothill Fields to the Reception of a Penitentiary House.

Transmit the Case with the Copy of the Bill to the Solicitor, and desire he will submit the same to the Consideration of His Majesty's Attorney and Solicitor-General.' (P.R.O., T.29/71, p. 405.)

There is also, in P.R.O., T.1. 794/4055.6692, a memorandum of 13 pages, in a copyist's hand, entitled:

'Case.—Stating the grounds of the annexed Bill, for appropriating a part of Tothill fields, to the reception of a Penitentiary House, intended to be erected, under the Penitentiary Contract Act of the 7th July 1794.' It is accompanied by a 'Sketch of the Waste called TOTHILL FIELDS: exhibiting the Division proposed to be made thereof, by the annexed BILL for the erection of a PENITENTIARY HOUSE. To

1301

FROM ARTHUR YOUNG

4 December 1797

Rot him—it is like his carelessness—I have written and sent it—my note went too late so in next No. it will be inserted in full

.yrs

in g. haste

A. Y.

1302

FROM SIR FREDERICK MORTON EDEN

13 December 1797

Lincolns Inn Fields
13 Dec. 1797

Sir

If you will favor me with half a dozen of your Pauper Population Tables I will send them into the Country and endeavour to procure you that information which, like myself, you found Gentlemen in Westm unwilling to communicate.

I have seen in some Copies of your most interesting book, the Panopticon, a plan of the Building. The Copy you obligingly favoured me with had not the plate; and if you have a spare one by you, I shall consider myself much obliged if you will favor me with it.

I have the honor to be Sir
Your most obt Servant
F. M. Eden

accompany the CASE, explanatory of the said BILL.' Dated '23d Novr: 1797.' Docketed: '*Mr Bentham* / No: 4055 / Rd. 4th Decr 1797 / The Lords of the Treasy. / have directd. this Case and / the Copy of the Bill to be / submitted. to the Considn. of / the Attorney and Sollr. Gen:l.'

1301. ¹ B.L. VI: 511–12. Autograph. Docketed: '1797 Dec. 4 / Poor / A. Young / to / J.B. Q.S.P.'
Addressed: 'J. Bentham Esq.'
Evidently a reply to a missing letter from Bentham complaining about an omission from his first article in the *Annals of Agriculture*: the culprit presumably was Rackham, the printer.

1302. ¹ B.L. VI: 513–14. Autograph. Docketed: '1797 Dec. 13 / Poor / Eden (Sr Fred.) Lincs Inn Fields / to / J.B. Q.S.P.'
Addressed: 'Jeremy Bentham Esqr / Queen Square Place / Westminster.'
A missing letter from Bentham is indicated.

1303

FROM SAMUEL ROMILLY

14 December 1797

Dear Bentham
    I dare say the Case was sent to the Atty Genl at the same time as the Bill for he told me that there was a great deal of Paper left with him but he had not had time to open it. If I ask him after the Case it is probable I shall have the same answer that he has not had time to open it therefore does not know what the Paper consists of. If Butler[2] will apply to him as he said he would he will do a great deal more than I can.

Yrs ever
Sam[l] Romilly

14 Dec 97

1304

TO SIR FREDERICK MORTON EDEN

c. 17 December 1797 (Aet 49)

Dear Sir
    In answer to yours of the /   /[2] the inclosed is from my Brother's wife, eldest of two daughters of Dr Fordyce.[3] Her time being to the last degree occupied, and no ready means of transcription at present at hand, I must beg your acceptance of it in the rough form in which it was put into my hands.
    The interest you appear to take in the subject being considerable, it would be gratifying to me to hear that you have found the information it conveys in any respect of use. You will observe the ulterior offer that accompanies it. Believe me ever

Dear Sir
Yours most truly
Jeremy Bentham

Sir F.M. Eden.

1303. [1] B.L. VI: 515–16. Autograph. Docketed: '1797 Dec. 14 / Panopt. / Romilly Linc. Inn / to / J.B. Q.S.P.'
    Addressed: 'Jeremy Bentham Esqr.'
    [2] Charles Butler.
1304. [1] Eden Mss. Autograph. Docketed: 'Jeremy Bentham.'
    [2] Blank in Ms. The missing date of the letter from Eden (letter 1302) is 13 December.
    [3] Mrs Samuel Bentham.

1305

FROM SIR FREDERICK MORTON EDEN

18 December 1797

Sir Frederick Eden is much obliged to Mr Bentham for his Sketches on the Poor: he will immediately send the Tables into the Country and hopes they will be returned with some useful information. Sir Frederick will be happy if Mr Bentham will do him the favor of dining with him tomorrow or Wednesday, or Thursday, as is most agreable, at 5 o'clock precisely. Tomorrow, however, and Wednesday, Sir Fredk is obliged to go out in the Evening at 8 o'clock.

Lincolns Inn Fields
18th Dec. 1797.   [2] Memo to dine with him
                                               Thursday 20th

1305. [1] B.L. VI: 518–19. Autograph. Docketed: '1797 Dec 18 / Poor / Sir F. Eden Linc Inn Fds. / to J.B. Q.S.P. / Called with it and I saw him.'
 Addressed: 'Jeremy Bentham Esqr.'
 [2] Note in Bentham's hand; but 20 December 1797 was a Wednesday.

INDEX

Note. This is an index of names of persons occurring in the text and notes. References throughout are to page numbers, except in the case of Bentham's correspondents, where the figures in italic type after the sub-headings 'Letters to' and 'Letters from' refer to the serial number of the letters. The abbreviation 'biog.' indicates a biographical note on the person indexed.

In the case of Bentham himself (J.B.), only references to his works are indexed. His brother, Samuel, to whom constant reference is made throughout the letters, is indexed only as a correspondent.

An analytical index to the correspondence as a whole will be provided in the final volume of this part of the edition.

INDEX

GREVILLE, George (*cont.*)
Letter to: *967*
Letter from: *972*
GROSVENOR, Richard, 1st Earl Grosvenor: 48n., 260, biog. 260n., 300 & n., 329, 331
GROSVENOR, Richard, Viscount Belgrave (later 2nd Marquis of Westminister): 48n., 260, biog. 260n., 300 & n.
GUYOT DE PITAVEL, F.: 73n.

HALE, John (Captain, R. M.): 329 & n.
HAMILTON, Emma, Lady (née LYON): 156 & n., 157
HAMILTON, Sir William: 155n., 156, biog. 156n.
HANKS, Richard: 215n.
HARDING (HARDEN): 225n., 226, 235, 236, 239
HARRIES (HERRIES?): 244
HARRIS, James, Baron Malmesbury (later Earl of Malmesbury): 6 & n., 269n.
HARRISON, John: 214–15, 214n.
Letter from: *1140*
HARRISON, Thomas (land agent): 48, 214 & n., 215–18, 219–21, 222, 228, 229, 246
Letter to: *1141*
Letter from: *1142*
HARROWBY, Lord: See RYDER
HASTINGS, Warren: 35 & n.
HATCHET, Mr: 342, 343
HAUTEVILLE, Comte de: 256, 266
HAWKESBURY, Lord: See JENKINSON
HAWKINS, Sir John: 383n.
HAWKINS, John Sidney: 383 & n., 384
HAWKINS, Letitia: 383n.
HAYES, Mr (bookseller): 343, 344
HOBART, Robert (later 4th Earl of Buckingham): 1n., 44 & n.
HOLROYD, John Baker, 1st Earl of Sheffield: 323, biog. 323n., 362n.
HOOPER, Mr: 206 & n.
HORNBLOWER, Jonathan Carter: 342 & n.
HORSLEY, Samuel (bishop): 285 &

n., 287, 289–93, 296, 297, 298, 300, 301, 305, 306, 309, 315, 316, 318–319, 320, 321
Letters to: *1199, 1223, 1224*
HORT, Sir John: 52
HORWOOD, Richard (map-maker): 336 & n.
HOWARD, John (prison reformer): 60n., 61, 66
HOWE, Richard, Earl Howe: 39n., 45
HOWLETT, John: 86, biog. 86n.
HUNTER, John (colonial governor) 375 & n.
HUSKISSON, William: 17 & n.
HUTCHINSON, Mr: 17

JACKSON, Francis James: 269 & n.
JAY, John: 53, biog. 53n., 76, 128–9, 129n.
Letter to: *1053*
JAY, Peter Augustus: 76, 128 & n., 129
JEFFERSON, Thomas: 3 & n.
JENKINSON, Robert Banks, 2nd Earl of Liverpool: 98, biog. 98n., 253 & n.
JERVIS, John (later Earl of St Vincent): 163 & n.
JOHN (Jeremy Bentham's servant): 171, 172, 173, 177, 313, 320, 321–2
JOHN (Samuel Bentham's servant): 327
JOHNSON, Mr: 342
JOHNSON, Dr Samuel: 372n., 383n.
JOHNSTONE, Sir George, bart.: 53n.
JOHNSTONE, William: See PULTENEY
JONES, Mr (plumber): 298n., 299
JONES, Thomas: 178n.

KALCKREUTH, Friedrich Adolf von, Count: 9 & n.
KING, John: 17 & n., 142, biog. 142n.
KLUCH (maidservant): 287
KOE, John Heide: 164, biog. 164n., 295, 339
KOE, John Herbert: biog. 164n., 244n.

L., Mrs: 39n., 49 & n.
LACLOS, Pierre C. de: 225n.
LANSDOWNE, Lord: See PETTY

396

INDEX

LA ROCHEFOUCAULD, François Frédéric de, duc de La Rochefoucauld-Liancourt: 145 & n., 159–62
Letter to: *1085*
Letter from: *1075*
LA ROCHEFOUCAULD D'ENVILLE, Louis Alexandre, duc de: 254
LAUDERDALE, Lord: See MAITLAND
LAW, Thomas: 1
LAWRENCE, Sir Soulden: 95, biog. 95n.
LENNOX, Charles (Lieutenant-colonel): 102 & n., 103
LEOPOLD II, Emperor of Austria: 7 & n.
LEWIS, Matthew Gregory: 337 & n.
LIANCOURT, Duc de: See LA ROCHEFOUCAULD
LILFORD, Lord: See POWYS
LINDIGREN (LINDEGREN), Andrew: 70–1, 105, 117, 321, 330
LINDIGREN, Mrs. Andrew (née Hanbury): 127 & n., 213, 321, 330
LIVERPOOL, Lord: See JENKINSON
LLOYD, Mr ('Island'): 339 & n.
LLOYD, John L.: 101, 141n., 172 & n., 176, 178, 186, 187, 209, 212, 267, 277, 328, 330, 336
LONG, Charles (later Baron Farnborough): 27, biog. 27n., 29–30, 32–3, 34, 35, 41, 44, 52n., 54–6, 58, 62, 64–5, 71n., 77 & n., 78–9, 80, 81, 82, 83–4, 85, 88–9, 92–3, 96, 97–8, 99, 103, 106n., 114, 116n., 117, 118–21, 133, 133–4, 135n., 136, 137, 138, 139, 140, 144, 145–6, 145n., 146–7, 147–51, 162n., 169–70, 181–182, 193, 194, 197, 210, 211, 230–232, 237–9, 243–4, 245, 259–61, 264, 269, 270, 274, 282, 286, 306 & n., 308, 310, 311, 316, 322, 347n.
Letters to: *958, 1003, 1008, 1014, 1035, 1038, 1039, 1059, 1076, 1077, 1078, 1096, 1106, 1152, 1157, 1163, 1165, 1174*
Letters from: *962, 999*
LORD, Thomas: 291 & n.

LOUGHBOROUGH, Lord: See WEDDERBURN
LOUIS XVI, King of France: 7n.
LOWNDES, William: 27 & n., 30–1, 31n., 91 & n., 116, 134, 135, 138, 139, 274, 289, 324, 325, 326, 344, 345, 346, 347 & n., 348, 350, 351, 365, 366, 387
Letters from: *1231, 1251*

MACARTNEY, George, Baron Macartney (later Earl): 75n., 268n.
MACDONALD, Sir Archibald, bart.: 239, biog. 239n., 240
MACDONALD, Lady Louisa (née Leveson-Gower): 239–40, 239n.
Letter from: *1158*
MACINTOSH, William (captain): 268 & n.
MACKENZIE, Henry (author): 100n.
MACPHERSON, Sir John, 1st bart.: 53, biog. 53n.
MAITLAND, James, 8th Earl of Lauderdale: 254 & n.
MALMESBURY, Lord: See HARRIS
MALONE, Edmund: 382–3, 382n., 383n.
Letter from: *1293*
MANN, Mr (linen-draper): 298n., 299
MARKHAM, William, Archbishop of York: 4, 34–5, 46, 47–8, 48n., 58, 316
Letters to: *941, 965*
Letter from: *979*
MARTIN, James: 268 & n., 295
MARTIN, Matthew: 372 & n.
MARTIN and Company, bankers: 14 & n., 84, 276, 277, 295
MASERES, Francis: 90 & n.
MAURICE, Frédéric Guillaume: 200n.
MEARES, John (explorer): 185 & n.
MELVILLE, Lord: See DUNDAS
MESSANT, Mr: 51
METCALFE, family, 145n., 159–60, 160n.
METCALFE, Philip: 74, 74–6, 159–60, 160n., 274, 335 & n.
Letter to: *997*
Letter from: *996*

397

INDEX

399

INDEX

WHITE, Joseph: 31 & n., 135, 137, 139, 151, 157–8, 162 & n., 169, 170, 193, 210, 211, 234 & n., 240, 245, 282, 351, 367, 368, 387
Letters to: *1079, 1159*

WICKHAM, Eleanora Madeleine (née BERTRAND): 19

WICKHAM, William: 18–19, biog. 18n., 333
Letter from: *952*

WILBERFORCE, William: 45 & n., 112 & n., 126, 132, 134, 134–5, 165, 179n., 187n., 190, 193 & n., 194, 210–12, 252–8, 259, 261–2, 264, 265, 266, 269, 277, 279, 280, 281, 282, 285, 286–7, 293, 296, 297, 298–9, 298n., 300n., 301, 305–306, 306n., 307–8, 308n., 309–10, 311, 316, 323, 341 & n., 341–2, 343–4, 359–60, 360, 361
Letters to: *1118, 1119, 1136, 1171, 1175, 1189, 1191, 1192, 1207, 1214, 1243, 1267, 1268*
Letters from: *1033, 1057, 1060, 1061, 1113, 1173, 1190, 1195, 1203, 1205, 1216, 1242*

WILKES, John: 161

WILKINSON, Mrs (Bentham's cook): 172, 173, 174, 177, 280

WILLIAM GEORGE FREDERICK, Prince of Orange: 163 & n.

WILLIAMS, Thomas (copper-smith): 206 & n., 209, 280, 311n.

WILSON, Edward (upholsterer): 204 & n., 205 & n., 206

WILSON, George: 44, 50n., 96, 135, 177, 199
Letter from: *1062*

WILSON, Jane (née BADGER-WELLER), Lady: 235n., 237, 238–239, 248–51, 258

WILSON, Sir Thomas Maryon, 7th bart.: 235n.

WILSON, Sir Thomas Spencer, 6th bart.: 225n., 226, 230, 235–7, biog. 235n., 241, 242
Letter to: *1156*

WINDHAM, William: 76 & n., 108, 313

WISE, Henry Christopher: 329 & n., 331, 332

WOOD, Isaac: 358 & n.

WOODLEY, William: 272n.

WRIGHT, Charles: 164 & n.

WURMSER, Count Dagobert Siegmund von: 6n., 9

WYATT, Charles: 218 & n.

WYATT, James (architect): 176n., 305–6, 312, 314, 315, 320, 322, 323, 324

WYCOMBE, Lord: See PETTY

YORK, Duke of, See FREDERICK AUGUSTUS

YOUNG, Arthur: 85–7, 86n., 88, 89–90, 92, 187n., 360, 365, 371 & n., 375–8, 375n., 378–9, 378n., 381, 382, 383–4, 385–6, 386n., 388
Letters to: *1005, 1007, 1289, 1290*
Letters from: *1010, 1013, 1269, 1275, 1284, 1295, 1297, 1298, 1301*

YOUNG, Rev. Arthur: 381 & n.

YOUNG, Martha (née ALLEN): 381–2, biog. 381n.
Letter from: *1292*

YOUNG, Martha Anne: 381 & n.

YOUNGER, Thomas: 219 & n.

ZABIELLO, General: 10 & n.

402

CORRIGENDA
(Volume 3)

p. 42, last line	*For* loan *read* load
p. 122, lines 4 and 8	*Transpose* and
p. 251, line 8	*For* Quand *read* Quant
p. 350, line 2	*Read* antipodagrical
p. 362, middle	*For* 35d.6d. *read* 35s.6d.
p. 372, line 3	*For* plain *read* plainly
p. 594, n. 4, line 2	*After* 14–15 *delete* /25–26
lines 3–4	*For* beyond the mouth of *read* in
p. 628, n. 2, line 6	*For* on the same day, 9 July *read* three days later, 12 July
p. 636	*After* EATON, William *insert alias* ETON
p. 636	*For* FREDERICK I *read* FREDERICK II
p. 646	*After* YOUNG, Arthur: *for* 524 *read* 324

403